Jeffrey Gunn
Outsourcing African Labor

Africa in Global History

Edited by
Joël Glasman, Omar Gueye, Alexander Keese,
and Christine Whyte

Advisory Board:
Joe Alie, Felicitas Becker, William Gervase Clarence-Smith, Lynda Day,
Scholastique Diazinga, Andreas Eckert, Babacar Fall, Toyin Falola, Matt Graham,
Emma Hunter, Erin Jessee, Isabella Kentridge, Colleen Kriger, Kristin Mann,
Patrick Manning, Conceição Neto, Vanessa S. Oliveira, Lorelle Semley, Ibrahim
Sundiata

Volume 4

Jeffrey Gunn

Outsourcing African Labor

Kru Migratory Workers in Global Ports, Estates and Battlefields until the End of the 19th Century

DE GRUYTER
OLDENBOURG

ISBN 978-3-11-125898-0
e-ISBN (PDF) 978-3-11-068033-1
e-ISBN (EPUB) 978-3-11-068041-6
ISSN 2628-1767

Library of Congress Control Number: 2021936032

Bibliographic information published by the Deutsche Nationalbibliothek
The Deutsche Nationalbibliothek lists this publication in the Deutsche Nationalbibliografie; detailed bibliographic data are available on the Internet at http://dnb.dnb.de.

© 2023 Walter de Gruyter GmbH, Berlin/Boston
This volume is text- and page-identical with the hardback published in 2021.
Cover image: "Kroomen launching a boat", Sketch by Captain's Clerk Charles F. Sands, reproduced from his journal kept on board the U.S. Brig Porpoise during her anti-slavery cruise off West Africa, 1848. Courtesy of Mr. W. F. Sands, 1939.
Printing and binding: CPI books GmbH, Leck

www.degruyter.com

I dedicate this book to my Kru brothers and sisters and my family: Saowakhon Pansri, Sandra and David Gunn, Julie, Frank, Logan, Blake, and Hailey Rozsas.

Acknowledgements

No great undertaking can be completed alone. In this spirit, I would like to thank my wife, Saowakhon Pansri, my parents, Sandra and David Gunn, my sister and her family, Julie, Frank, Blake, Logan, and Hailey Rozsas, my cousins, Terrence Jon and Jay Craig, and my lifelong friends Jon Brohman, Jeff Vanderby, Josh Mills, Matt Lindsay, Michael Morris, Julie Quinn, Julie Tamaki, Kristian Shepherd, and Bill Merritt for their encouragement, love, and support throughout the completion of this book.

I am extremely grateful to my mentor and friend Paul Lovejoy for always driving me to perform at my best and for the incredible opportunity to travel the world for research and conferences. I give special mention to George Brooks at Indiana University for generously providing me with many boxes of unpublished sources from the 1970s, and Suzanne Schwarz and Stephen Rockel for enthusiastically sharing information on the Kru when they came upon it in their own research. And, I thank Mark Williamson for his sketches.

The completion of this book has been a monumental journey, which has led me to conduct research in Sierra Leone, Liberia, Ghana, the United Kingdom, Trinidad and Tobago, Guyana, and the United States. None of these research trips would have been possible without the support of several scholarship programs and funding from key institutions. I would like to gratefully acknowledge the support I received to finance my doctoral studies, which inform this book, from the Social Sciences and Humanities Research Council of Canada (SSHRC), the Ontario Graduate Scholarship Program (OGS), The Harriet Tubman Institute, and the Department of History at York University.

I extend a deep sense of gratitude to members of the Kru communities I visited in Sierra Leone including Chief Tuleh Davis, Rev. Joseph Kamara, and Doe Smith; in Liberia, Kru Governor Alice Weah, Deputy Governor S. Tugbe Worjloh, Rev. Nyanford Gibson, Anthony Teah, Jacob P. Myers, Moses Baryor, Edwin Wiah, and L. Slewion Kontons; and in Ghana, Okyeeme Gikafo and Allwei Bonso III. It is an honor to share your stories and memories of Kru workers in your communities.

I would like to give thanks to those friends whose efforts made for successful research trips including Aiah Yendeh, Taziff Koroma, and Abdullai Brima, for their guidance and lodgings in Freetown, and to Charles for motorcycle transport from Sierra Leone to Liberia; Kae Sun for arranging lodgings in Accra, Rev. Kwaku Darko-Mensah for his hospitality, and Sidney Palupa for his guidance, transportation, and translations; Connie Abbe and Silvastone for providing lodgings in London while I worked at the British Library, The National Archives and

SOAS; Nigel Baptiste and his family for providing lodgings while researching at the National Archives and the University of the West Indies in Trinidad and Tobago; Eon and Marilyn Sinclair for providing contacts in Guyana, and Osric Best for his time and generosity; George and Elaine Brooks for their hospitality in Bloomington, Indiana; and Bruno Véras, Leidy Alpízar, Vanessa Oliveira, and Dina Issakova for assistance with logistics. Sections of this book were written in various locations including Toronto, Rice Lake, Thailand, and the Hollywood Hills. I would like to thank the Pansri family in Nakhon Ratchasima for their hospitality, as well as Donald Colhour and Terrence Jon for their generosity and the opportunity to write at the Luftschloss in the Hollywood Hills.

It is a great privilege to share the story of the Kru. It has been a grand adventure.

Contents

List of Tables —— XI

List of Figures —— XIII

Foreword —— XV

Introduction: A Free Wage Labor African Diaspora —— 1
    Diaspora —— 10
    Identifying the Kru —— 15
    Significance of Hiring the Kru —— 24
    Tracing Surfboats —— 29

Chapter 1: Surfboats —— 34
    European Contact —— 34
    Social Organization —— 38
    Transformations on the Coast —— 43
    Slave Trade —— 48

Chapter 2: Freetown – A Catalyst for Diaspora —— 72
    Founding of Freetown —— 72
    Freetown and British Anti-Slavery Patrols —— 79
    Krutown —— 93
    Relationship with the Homeland —— 99

Chapter 3: The Expansion of Kru Labor in the Royal Navy —— 103
    Atlantic Ocean Network —— 104
    Freetown —— 104
    Cape Coast —— 105
    Ascension Island —— 107
    Fernando Po —— 109
    Simon's Town —— 115
    Indian Ocean Network —— 121
    Zanzibar —— 126

Chapter 4: Kru Labor in Expeditions and Military Campaigns —— 129
    Expeditions —— 130
    Clapperton's Second Expedition, 1825–27 —— 130
    Lander Brothers' Expedition, 1830 —— 132
    Laird Expedition, 1832–33 —— 132

Niger Expedition, 1841–42 — 133
Baikie Expedition, 1854 — 136
Bonny and Calabar — 138
Zambezi Expedition, 1858–1864 — 140
Military Campaigns and Naval Brigades — 143
First Opium War, 1839–42 — 143
Occupation of Lagos, 1851–52 — 146
Asante Campaign, 1873–74 — 150
Anglo-Zulu War, 1879 — 152
Sudan Campaign, 1884–85 — 155

Chapter 5: Kru Labor in the British Caribbean — 158
Policy and Immigration — 159
Nature of Employment — 166
Settlement Patterns — 172

Chapter 6: Growth in Diaspora and Decline in the Homeland — 179
Colony of Liberia — 180
Transformations on the Kru Coast — 191
Borders — 201

Conclusion: Kru Free Wage Laborers in Global History — 209

Appendix A: Muster Lists, 1819–20 — 219
HMS Whistle — 219
HMS Myrmidan — 220
HMS Myrmidan — 220
HMS Tartar — 221

Appendix B: Interviews — 222
I. Freetown, Sierra Leone — 222
II. Monrovia, Liberia — 223
III. Accra, Ghana — 223

Glossary of Kru Language Terms — 224

Bibliography — 226
Primary Sources — 226
Secondary Sources — 238

Index — 255

List of Tables

1.1 Annual slave exports on the Windward Coast (1760s)
1.2 Kru service on slave ships
2.1 Population of Freetown
2.2 Pay list for Kru, HMS Snapper, September 5 – December 31, 1819
2.3 Pay list for Kru, HMS Morgiana, June 1 – October 1, 1819
3.1 Kru population in Ascension Island
3.2 Kru population in Fernando Po
3.3 Kru gravestones in Simon's Town, South Africa
3.4 Kru on Royal Navy Ships in the Indian Ocean, 1862 – 1869
3.5 Kru gravestones in Grave Island Cemetery, Zanzibar
4.1 Kru wages in the Bight of Biafra
4.2 Kru serving on HMS Ships in the assault on Lagos
5.1 Kru working sea transport in Demerara, 1842

List of Figures

1.1 Kru surfboat, c. 1732 (via c. 1688)
1.2 Kru surfboats, c. 1890
1.3 Kru currency, ring
1.4 Kru Coast
1.5 Kru mark, c. 1830
1.6 Three Kroomen of Sierra Leone, c. 1775
2.1 Kru headman in Freetown, c. 1890
2.2 Kru with oars, c. 1892
2.3 Krootown Bay, c. 1910
2.4 Krootown Road, Freetown, c. 1910
2.5 Krootown, c. 1910
3.1 Kru stationed in Simon's Town, c. 1889
4.1 The Zulu War – the naval brigade landed from the HMS Active, c. 1879
6.1 Krootown, Monrovia, c. 1886
6.2 Krootown, Monrovia c. 1903
6.3 Map of the Commonwealth of Liberia, 1839
6.4 Kru Coast, 1885

Foreword

The Kru occupy a special place in African history. Inhabitants of coastal West Africa from eastern Liberia to western Côte d'Ivoire, their men found employment on ships that crossed the Atlantic and in the ports that dotted its coast. They migrated as workers to the Caribbean and fought along British imperialists crafting an empire in Africa. Unusual in their labor history, the Kru weathered the period of trans-Atlantic slavery and the inception of colonial rule of Africa not by building a centralized state or becoming victims of enslavement but by filling a niche in the Atlantic economy that was unique in their participation and essential in the implementation of exploitative regimes that shaped the Americas and Africa. Despite this important role, they have largely gone unnoticed in the reconstruction of trans-Atlantic slavery and the European, especially British, domination of the emergent global world of the eighteenth and nineteenth centuries. This study by Jeffrey Gunn highlights the history of migrant Kru labor in a detailed exploration of where the Kru worked, why they sought employment far beyond their coastal villages, and the willing role they performed in risky occupations that had little protection from abuse or exploitation.

Conceptually, Gunn builds on the work of Paul Gilroy on the Black Atlantic, John Thornton's study of trans-Atlantic impact, and my own work on transformations resulting from slavery in Africa. He offers a fresh perspective and analysis for uncovering meanings of race, ethnicity, enslavement, labor, and gender in the Black Atlantic and beyond in the eighteenth and nineteenth centuries. The multi-disciplinary nature of Gunn's research on Kru labor intersects African history, African diaspora history, wage labor history, British history, Atlantic history, maritime history, Indian Ocean history, colonial history and more. His meticulous analysis of a plethora of sources as diverse as wage lists, oil paintings, gravestones, court cases, work songs, estate records, and postcards reveals the scope of the Kru labor experience is much larger than previously recognized within any single work.

The homeland of coastal West Africa from where the Kru men came and where they usually returned once they fulfilled their labor contracts is in itself an anomaly. It might be expected that the strip of coast where their fishing villages were located would have been identified as the Kru coast, but such has not been the case. Instead, Europeans referred to this part of the Guinea coast as the ivory or grain or pepper coast, made famous as a source of ivory tusks from the interior when elephants were still plentiful there and from which the modern country gets its name, or as a source of foodstuffs, most often rice rather than grain but nonetheless essential to feed the ships that passed along its shores.

Ironically, the settlement of former slaves and the descendants of slaves from the United States in what became an informal American colony in Africa that came to be known as Liberia would take precedent. The conquest that extended Liberia to encompass its present boundaries subjugated the Kru as well as many others in the interior who spoke the same or a related language. An indigenous name did not prevail.

Despite the importance of the Kru in manning slave ships and then British naval vessels charged with suppressing the slave trade, the Kru have been overlooked in yet another strange way. Atlantic shipping inevitably needed sailors and members of crews because until midway through the nineteenth century tropical disease laid waste the Europeans who manned the ships. For the slave trade, it was always necessary to have enough sailors on board to prevent or suppress any resistance among the imprisoned enslaved Africans on board, and the necessity of replacing sick and dying sailors continued during the period of suppression. Small gangs, often numbering no more than half dozen or so of Kru men, provided the necessary labor. They were recruited on a regular basis and enabled trade and military action that otherwise would have been impossible. But the recognition that seems obvious was not to be extended. Their homeland was designated the "Windward Coast" because from the perspective of European ships, the stretch of coast was to the windward of the Gold Coast and the Bights of Benin and Biafra. The people who actually lived there and found gainful employment in the occupation of the Atlantic were relegated to a namelessness that was not even assigned to the enslaved and those taken off slave ships whose ethnicity was recognized. In modern scholarship "Windward Coast" predominates in the analysis of the slave trade and its suppression, most notably in the website, database, and academic analysis that derive from "Voyages: The Trans-Atlantic Slave Trade" (www.voyages.org) that has transformed the study of trans-Atlantic slavery but has continued to silence the history of the Kru.

Gunn's book addresses the fascinating question of how it was that Africans from coastal West Africa from where so many of the enslaved deportees came somehow virtually avoided their own enslavement. He raises the interesting question of how it was that an American colony of former slaves could migrate from the United States to found Liberia and subsequently confiscate the land and sovereignty of people who had successfully resisted being enslaved themselves but rather had become essential to the operation of the slave trade and then its suppression. These contradictions stand out even more starkly because their ethnic name and the language they spoke were coincidentally identical to the occupations that they performed: the Kru were members of ship crews. Yet the term Kru has nothing to do with the English term for sailors, crew. Gunn's study helps to correct a number of misconceptions about the slave trade and suppression and rescues the Kru from an obscurity that is certainly not warranted.

There is earlier scholarship on the Kru and their history, but Gunn has superseded that work through his careful search for where the Kru actually migrated, both temporarily and permanently. Within Kru Studies, Gunn's study provides a fresh examination of Kru labor and builds on works by George Brooks, Ronald Davis, Andreas Massing, Merran Fraenkel, Elizabeth Tonkin, Jane Martin, Monica Schuler, and Diane Frost. While previous studies tended to analyze Kru in their homeland or were limited to a single labor community such as Freetown, Gunn analyzes multiple facets of Kru labor on the West African coast, on estates in the Caribbean, in the Royal Navy, and on battlefields throughout the African continent. In short, his research illuminates the truly global scale of their labor experience. Thereby he provides historical perspective to their unusual role in a world that was dominated by the Atlantic slave trade and its suppression.

Paul E. Lovejoy

Introduction
A Free Wage Labor African Diaspora

African laborers known simply as "Kru" or "Kroomen" from the west coast of Africa played a significant role in the history of global trade in the nineteenth century. Navigating ships through adverse surf, currents and sub-sea terrain, transporting cargoes, hiring out their labor on European and American commercial and military ships sailing the West African coast, Kru mariners and shoreside laborers worked for wages in-kind and eventually monetary wages. They labored in ports in West Africa before expanding their services throughout the Atlantic, Indian, and Pacific Oceans. Beginning as early as perhaps the fifteenth century, Kru-speaking peoples traded with passing ships until the 1790s when the British offered free wage labor contracts to Kru seafarers who made the journey from their homeland on the Kru Coast (modern Liberia and Côte d'Ivoire) to work in Freetown in the Sierra Leone Peninsula. Almost immediately, they established a labor community in Freetown that gradually grew to nearly half of the port's population in the first decade of the nineteenth century and ensured their regular employment on British ships sailing the West African coast.[1] This period saw the expansion of Kru labor beyond ships in shoreside infrastructural projects, porterage, and domestic work.

The establishment of Freetown proved to be a catalyst affecting Kru labor as it became institutionalized through free wage labor contracts and had a deep impact on Kru social, political, and economic norms in their diaspora community and homeland. While Kru continued to trade with passing ships on the coast, the traditional age-set system that governed intergenerational power structures in their communities gradually shifted towards supplying a steady flow of migratory laborers for contracts abroad based on ever-growing demand. Competition between the Liberian state (founded in 1847) and European powers to harness the economic benefits of Kru labor fostered increased growth in Kru diaspora communities as Kru workers sought economic opportunities beyond the reach of Liberian policy. By the close of the nineteenth century, Kru workers had established diaspora communities throughout the Atlantic and Caribbean and forged shipboard communities while contributing to abolition and military campaigns in the Indian and Pacific Oceans and on the African continent.

---

[1] Thomas Ludlam, "An Account of the Kroomen on the Coast of Africa," *The African Repository and Colonial Journal* 1, no. 2 (1825): 45; Christopher Fyfe, *A Short History of Sierra Leone* (London: Longmans, 1962), 44.

This book is about the Kru free wage labor force that worked with the British on ships and shoreside in ports and on estates, used their expert mariner skills in navigation, delivered and received cargoes, carried weapons, and engaged in battles at the front in such theatres as Hong Kong and southern Africa. Kru oral traditions, ship captain and traveller accounts, British Royal Navy muster lists, official policy in Britain and its colonies, gravestones, paintings, sketches, music, and postcards illuminate the global nature of the Kru diaspora. Although Kru worked on contract with other Europeans and Americans, particular attention is focused on their service with the British who offered the bulk of their contractual employment and whose relationship had a much more profound socio-economic impact in their homeland and diaspora communities.

The deep roots of their diaspora can be traced to fishing villages that grew into trading towns along the West African coastline known interchangeably as the Malaguetta Coast, Grain Coast, Pepper Coast, Windward Coast, and by the nineteenth century, based on the mass export of Kru laborers, the Kru Coast.[2] The identity of its Kru-speaking inhabitants became associated with surfboats and the practice of paddling and fishing far out to sea as observed by de Sintra in 1461 and Duarte Pacheco Pereira in 1508.[3] Kru oral traditions suggest the Portuguese were their first European trading partners following their migration from the interior to the coast.[4] Within several decades of Pereira, in 1555, Captain William Towerson recognized what appeared to be a shared language among the inhabitants of the Malaguetta Coast.[5] His observations are supported by Kru oral traditions and twentieth century linguists, Dietrich Westermann and M.A. Bryan,

---

[2] Ronald W. Davis, *Ethnohistorical Studies on the Kru Coast* (Newark: Liberian Studies Monograph Series 5, 1976), 5.

[3] Pedro de Sintra, *Voyages of Cadamosto*, Second Series, 80, trans. Gerald Crone (London: Hakluyt Society, 1927), 83–84; Duarte Pacheco Pereira, *Esmeraldo de Situ Orbis*, Second Series, 80, trans. and ed. George H.T. Kimble (London: Hakluyt Society, 1936), 110.

[4] Kru belonging to the Proper Kru, Gbeta and Kabor *dakwe* are thought to have migrated down the St. John River before dispersing eastward on the coast. Interviews with Deputy Governor S. Tugbe Worjloh in New Krutown, Monrovia on December 11, 2012 and Doe Smith (retired labor lawyer and son of Kru headman) in Krutown, Freetown on December 13, 2012 suggest the interior migration to the coast occurred at an unknown date before contact with the Portuguese who became their first European trading partners (see Appendix B for a full list of interviewees). Also see Jo Mary Sullivan, "The Kru of Liberia," review of *Ethnohistorical Studies on the Kru Coast* by Ronald W. Davis, *The Journal of African History* 19, no. 2 (1978): 282; Christine Behrens, *Les Kroumen de la Côte Occidentale d'Afrique* (Bordeaux: Center d'études de Géographie Tropicale, 1974), 7.

[5] William Towerson, "Voyage to Guinea in 1555," 241, accessed on June 14, 2018, https://www.e-reading.club/chapter.php/80243/53/Kerr_-_A_General_History_and_Collection_of_Voyages_and_Travels%2C_Vol.VII.html.

who subdivided the region between Cape Mount (modern Liberia) and the Bandama River (Côte d'Ivoire) into two Kru dialect clusters. Belonging to the family of Niger-Congo languages (according to Joseph Greenberg), Kru speakers in the west between the Bassa region and Sassandra River constituted the Bakwé cluster, while those in the east between the Sassandra River and the Bandama River formed the Bété cluster.[6] The fundamental role of the surfboat in subsistence and trade and shared language became the lasting hallmarks of Kru identity along the coast. Beyond the vantage of European ship captains and merchants, Kru-speaking peoples had many layers of identity that distinguished one community from another including dialect, *dako* (territorial unit based on collective historical tradition), village, trade items, and in some cases, secret society affiliation and ceremonial masks.

Maps remain a testament to the presence of Kru-speaking traders in the region as early as the sixteenth century. The earliest historical mention directly associated with the Kru dates to 1588, when a location named "Crua" on the southeastern coast of the Malaguetta Coast appeared on a map in James Welsh's *A Voyage to Benin beyond the Country of Guinea made by Master James Welsh, who set forth in the Yeere 1588*.[7] Nearly a century later, Olfert Dapper mentioned a town called "Crouw" or "Krau" in the same vicinity in 1686.[8] According to Kru oral traditions, the name "Krao" (also pronounced "Klao" or "Claho") was the original name of the people in the region before it morphed to "Kru" or "Kroo."[9] Around 1600, Pieter de Marees located a village named "Crou" in the same region that was described by Levinus Hulsius several years later in 1606.[10] Between the seventeenth and nineteenth centuries, Crou became a

---

[6] Interviews with Kru Chief Davis in Krutown, Freetown, on December 4 and 5, 2012, Smith and Deputy Governor S. Tugbe Worjloh reveal that the Kru language was a binding factor between coastal peoples even while recognizing their internal differences. Dietrich Westermann and M.A. Bryan, *Languages of West Africa* (London: Oxford University Press for International African Institute, 1952), 48–54; Joseph H. Greenberg, *The Languages of Africa, International Journal of American Linguistics* 29, no. 1 (Part 2) (Publication of the Indiana University Research Center in Anthropology, Folklore and Linguistics, 25) (Bloomington: Indiana University, 1963), 8, 39, 167.
[7] James Welsh, "A Voyage to Benin beyond the Countrey of Guinea made by Master James Welch, who set forth in the Yeere 1588," in *The Principle Navigations, Voyages, Traffiques and Discoveries of the English Nation*, ed. Richard Hakluyt, vol. 6 (London: J. MacLehose and Sons, 1904), 451.
[8] Harry Johnston, *Liberia* 2 vols. (London: Hutchinson & Co., 1906), 1: 88.
[9] Interviews with Deputy Governor Worjloh and Smith suggest that Kru oral tradition recognizes the name Kru having evolved from "Krao" or "Klao". Ronald Davis also suggests that the word "Krao" is the most plausible origin of the word Kru. See Davis, *Ethnohistorical*, 2.
[10] Pieter de Marees, *Description and Historical Account of the Gold Kingdom of Guinea*, 1602, eds. A Van Dantzig and Adam Jones (London: British Academy, 1987), 7, 14.

major trading town and watering station that was frequently included on maps of the region and played a role in the naming of local inhabitants on the coast.

Early trade between Europeans and Kru-speaking peoples suggests that ship captains formed a dependency on Kru surfboats in order to conduct trade on their coast. As early as the seventeenth century, Kru were observed as essential to European landings through the challenging surf and rocky seabed that characterized their coastal waters as they transported Europeans from ship to shore and back in their surfboats for the purpose of trading, watering, and replenishing supplies.[11] Furthermore, the design and number of occupants in the boats, which ranged from single-manned craft to three or more paddlers, are reminiscent of Pereira's description of local boats nearly two centuries earlier and reveal the deep roots of mariner tradition in Kru-speaking communities in the region.[12]

With trade firmly established on the coast by the seventeenth century, Kru-speaking peoples entered the next phase of labor by working on European ships sailing the coast as one Spanish ship manifest in Elmina Castle dated to 1645 indicates.[13] In order to ensure that Kru seafarers were not enslaved but free to labor on ships, early nineteenth century accounts and Kru oral traditions first recorded in the 1850s tell of a form of scarification applied by the Kru that dated to at least the early seventeenth century known as the "Kru mark".[14] The mark was made

---

11 Jean Barbot, *A Description of the Coasts of North and South Guinea, and of the Ethiopia Inferior, Vulgarly Angola… And a New Relation of the Province of Guiana, and of the Great Rivers of Amazons and Oronoque in South-America* (London: A. & J. Churchill, 1732), 128–141. Barbot's account was published in English in 1732, 20 years after his death in 1712. The publication was based on observations he made during his 1678–79 and 1681–82 voyages, which was originally published in French in the 1688. It is most probable that the 1732 publication was enhanced by his brother James Barbot who may have added details based on his voyage to West Africa in 1699. See P.E.H. Hair, Adam Jones and Robin Law, eds., *Barbot on Guinea: The Writings of Jean Barbot on West Africa: 1678–1712* (London: Hakluyt Society, 1992).
12 Pereira, *Esmeraldo*, 110.
13 The "Journal of Sao Jorge da Mina" is in K. Ratelband, ed., *Vijf Dagregisters van Het Kasteel Sao Jorge da Mina (Elmina) aar de Goudkust, 1647–1945* (Gravenhage: Martinus Nijhoff, 1953), 11. See George E. Brooks, *The Kru Mariner in the 19th Century: A Historical Compendium* (Newark, Delaware: Liberian Studies Monologue Series no. 1, 1972), 2; Reverend John Leighton Wilson, *Western Africa: Its History, Conditions and Prospects: With Numerous Engravings* (New York: Harper and Brothers, 1856), 103. Wilson does not mention the exact date but suggests that the Proper Kru were the first to work on European vessels before all other Kru-speaking peoples.
14 Parliamentary Papers, "Reports from Commodore Sir George Collier concerning the Settlements on the Gold and Windward Coasts of Africa," vol. 12 (1820), 15; Esu Biyi, "The Kru and Related Peoples, West Africa, Part I," *Journal of the African Society* 29, no. 113 (1929): 72; Reverend Connelly, "Report of the Kroo People," *American Colonization Thirty-Ninth Annual Report* (1856): 38. Interviews with Reverend Joseph Kamara in Freetown on December 12, 2012, Chief Davis, and

by an incision down the forehead with a needlepoint and charcoal (in some cases dyed blue), often accompanied by three incisions on the cheeks, which became widely recognized amongst European slave traders and African merchants as a signifier of Kru identity, independence, and immunity from enslavement.[15] It seems that scarification may well have been a cultural development within Kru communities as a direct response to trading with Europeans, which in theory ensured that the Kru were not enslaved. It may also be that Kru scarification practices preceded European contacts and were adapted to a new system of trade with Europeans, yet this remains speculative.[16] While it is not clear whether all Kru-speaking peoples bore the mark from its inception, it became what one nineteenth century observer called a "passport" that was supposed to guarantee Kru laborers return passage to their villages following the completion of shipboard work.[17] The Kru mark continues to be remembered in Kru oral traditions and it was frequently mentioned in nineteenth century ship captain, missionary, and traveller accounts throughout West Africa and became a marker of Kru identity in their diaspora in locations as varied as British Guiana and Zanzibar.[18]

The founding of Freetown in 1792 opened a new era of Kru employment with the British as they established a permanent diaspora community that supplied

---

Worjloh revealed that Kru oral tradition remembers tattooing as having been practiced since trading with Europeans was inaugurated. Worjloh revealed that the mark could be blue or black and was created using a needlepoint and charcoal, which left a permanent mark. For a discussion on tattooing and scarification in West Africa, see Katrina Keefer, "Scarification and Identity in the Liberated Africans Department Register, 1814–1815," *Canadian Journal of African Studies* 47, no. 3 (2013): 537–553; Katrina Keefer, "Group Identity, Scarification, and Poro Among Liberated Africans in Sierra Leone, 1808–1819," *Journal of West African History* 3, no.1 (2017): 1–26.

15 Parliamentary Papers, "Reports from Commodore Sir George Collier concerning the Settlements on the Gold and Windward Coasts of Africa," vol. 12 (1820), 15; J.W. Lugenbeel, "Native Africans in Liberia – Their Customs and Superstitions," *African Repository* 28, no. 6 (1852): 173; George Thompson, *The Palm-Land; Or West Africa, Illustrated: Being a History of Missionary Labors and Travels with Descriptions of Men and Things in Western Africa*, 2nd ed. (Cincinnati: Moore, Wilstach, Keys & Co., 1859), 189; Robert Clarke, "Sketches of the Colony of Sierra Leone and Its Inhabitants," *Transactions of the Ethnological Society of London* 2 (1863): 354; Adolphe Burdo, *The Niger and the Benueh; Travels in Central Africa*, trans. Mrs. George Sturge (London: Richard Bentley and Son, 1880), 83; Agnes McAllister, *Lone Woman in Africa: Six Years on the Kroo Coast* (New York: Eaton and Mains, 1896), 142–143.

16 Connelly, "Report," 38.

17 Journal of the House of Commons, vol. 76, Appendix, No. 6 *Aprilis*, 1821, p. 787.

18 Henry Kirke, *Twenty-Five Years in British Guiana* (London: S. Low, Marsten, 1898), 171–172; Reverend J.J. Halcombe, *Mission Life: A Magazine of Information about Church Missions and the Countries in which They are Being Carried On* (London: Lothian and Co, 1866), 58–59.

the British with a readily available labor pool for work on ships and shoreside. Whereas they had previously only been hired as transient workers between their trading towns, ships, and worksites, they now remained for longer contractual work periods as an institutionalized system of migratory labor based on 18-month to three-year contracts developed between Kru villages and Freetown. Their quarter gradually became known as "Krootown", and later, Krutown.[19] Perhaps the most visible marker of the Kru diaspora, Krutown provided a space where the Kru spoke their language and dialects, sang their music, practiced secret society rituals, and maintained direct links with their homeland, as evident in the street names that were named after specific Kru villages.[20]

Following the British decree to abolish the trans-Atlantic slave trade in 1807, Kru were increasingly employed in the British Royal Navy and tasked with intercepting slave ships throughout the Atlantic Ocean, and from the 1860s, the Indian Ocean. Increased work opportunities on commercial and military vessels coupled with the Kru's ability to find employment in Freetown for other destinations throughout the Atlantic enabled a broad network of labor communities to emerge. Krutowns modelled after the one in Freetown and smaller quarters soon developed in Cape Coast, Ascension Island, Fernando Po, Simon's Town (South Africa), Monrovia, and Lagos as a result of their service in the Royal Navy.[21] Other diaspora communities such as those in Calabar and Bonny in the Niger Delta and across the Atlantic in Trinidad and British Guiana were the result of commercial contracts in agriculture, marine transportation, timber, and mining.

As job opportunities increased in the nineteenth century, the Kru's reputation and cultural influence grew exponentially affecting language, literature, art, and music throughout the Atlantic world. The Kru maintained their hard-

---

19 *Proceedings of the Royal Colonial Institute*, vol. 13 (London: Sampson Low, Marston, Searle and Rivington, 1882), 65; *Missionary Register for 1817*, vol. 5 (London: Seeley, 1817), 251; *The Christian Observer* 15, no. 11 (1816): 756.
20 See Chapter 2.
21 All of the Krutowns and quarters mentioned were founded as a result of their employment with the British with the exception of Monrovia. Kru traded in Cape Mesurado for centuries and they are thought to have formed a permanent diaspora community in the first decade of the nineteenth century. Their community in Monrovia provided the same services to British ships as they did in their homeland, loading and unloading cargoes and bringing crew from ship to shore and back. Kru hired in Monrovia also had the opportunity to work on British ships and circulate between the network of Krutowns throughout the Atlantic. Their employment became more complicated with the founding of the colony of Liberia in 1822 as American Colonization Society agents sought to control their labor through taxation as discussed in Chapter 6. See Merran Fraenkel, *Tribe and Class in Monrovia* (Oxford: Oxford University Press, 1964), 71.

working reputation as the "Irishmen of Western Africa" compelling Captain John Whitford to boldly proclaim that the Kru were the "only African race on the West Coast that can be depended upon to work for merchants or on board ships."[22] Across the Atlantic, in January 1862, *The New York Times* ran a piece that described Kru mariners as an "invaluable adjunct to a cruiser on the coast."[23] Sailing between their homeland villages and diaspora communities, Kru were instrumental in the spread of a creolised version of English as the lingua franca of trade along the West African coast.[24] They were observed by ship captains and missionaries as speaking creolized versions of English, French, Dutch, and Portuguese.[25] Kru were routinely referenced in Victorian literature, most notably by Rudyard Kipling and Charles Dickens, who illuminated the connection between Kru seafarers and the British public, both bound by the production and transportation of commodities such as palm oil.[26] Their cultural influence extended into the twentieth century, as artist Pablo Picasso took inspiration from Grebo (Kru-speaking peoples) masks during his blue period in order to produce one of his most famous pieces, *The Guitarist*.[27] The rhythms and call-and-response singing style informing Kru work songs on ships sailing between their villages and diaspora communities (which occasionally included guitar accompaniment) is recognized in oral traditions and scholarly literature as having influenced the

---

[22] John Whitford, *Trading Life in Western and Central Africa* (Liverpool: The "Porcupine" Office, 1877), 27.
[23] January 4, 1862, *The New York Times*, 2.
[24] For an informative discussion on the spread of so-called "Pidgin English" as a lingua franca in West Africa, see David Dalby, *Black through White: Patterns of Communication* (Bloomington: Indiana University of African Studies Program, 1970), 1–40.
[25] Wilson Armistead, *A Tribute for the Negro: Being a Vindication of the Moral, Intellectual and Religious Capabilities of the Coloured Portion of Mankind* (Manchester: William Irwin, 1848), 252; Edward Manning, "Six Months on a Slaver," in *Slave Ships and Slaving with an Introduction by Capt. Ernest H. Pentecost, R.N.R.* (1879), ed. George Francis Dow (1927; repr., Cambridge, MD: Cornell Maritime Press, 1968), 326; William Bosman, *New and Accurate Description* (London: J. Knapton, 1705), 484.
[26] Charles Dickens, "Our Phantom Ship," in A Collection of British Authors, vol. CCXII: *Household Words* V (Leipzig: Tauchnitz, 1852): 363–378; Charles Dickens, "Cheerily, Cheerily!" *HouseHold Words: A Weekly Journal*, no. 131 (Saturday September 25, 1852): 25–31; Maragret Mendelawitz, *Charles Dickens Australia: Selected Essays from Household Words 1850–1859 Book Two* (Sydney: Sydney University Press, 2011), 125–126; Rudyard Kipling, *From Sea to Sea* in *The Writings in Prose and Verse of Rudyard Kipling*, vol. 16, Part 2 (London: Charles Scribner's Sons Publications, 1899), 75.
[27] Jonathan Hay, "Primitivism Reconsidered (Part 2): Picasso and the Krumen," *Res: Anthropology and Aesthetics* 69–70 (Spring-Autumn 2018): 227–250; Christine Poggi, "Picasso's First Constructed Sculpture: A Tale of Two Guitars," *The Art Bulletin* 94, no. 2 (June 2012): 274–298.

growth and popularity of palm wine guitar styles throughout West Africa in the 1920s.[28]

The Kru case exemplifies Frederick Cooper's call to "remember how much Africa has been shaped by its connections to the rest of the world and how much the world as we know it has been shaped by the labor of Africans."[29] Yet, until recently, as important as they were, the Kru largely remained a silent partner in the canon of British maritime history. British-Kru working relations were informed by race but in a way that was unique from the institution of slavery, which sought to dehumanize the enslaved. While the British hired the Kru, they were never perceived as equals but were frequently assigned the derogatory term "Kroo Boys."[30] Regardless of their intention and any sentiment the British felt towards the Kru, the application of the term "boys" to Kru of all ages and rank meant that they were not considered real men in the European sense simply because of their black race and their perceived lower position of societal development in stadial theory.[31] They were often romanticized by the British as an "exotic" "other." Assigned almost animalistic properties in some written accounts and newspaper images, they were perceived as perfect for meeting the arduous physical demands required on contracts in tropical climates, while British

---

28 Cynthia Schmidt, "Kru Mariners and Migrants of the West African Coast," in *Garland Encyclopedia of Music*, ed. Ruth Stone (New York: Routledge, 1997), 386–398; Horatio Bridge, *Journal of an African Cruiser*, ed. Nathanial Hawthorne (London: Wiley and Putnam, 1845), 16–17; John Smith, *Trade and Travels in the Gulph of Guinea* (London: Simkin, Marshall, 1851), 105; May 12, 1849, *The Athenaeum Journal of Literature, Science and Fine Arts*, no. 1124 (London, J. Francis, 1849), 482. I was able to record a traditional Kru work song as sung by Chief Davis during an interview in Freetown on December 4, 2012. He revealed that work songs functioned to uplift the morale of Kru laborers.
29 Frederick Cooper, "African Labor History," in *Global Labour History: A State of the Art*, ed. Jan Lucassen (Bern: Peter Lang, 2006), 91–116.
30 They are referred to as "Krooboys" in Henry Buckler, *Central Criminal Court. Minutes of Evidence, Taken in Short-Hand*, no. 618 (London: George Herbert, 1836), 510; Thomas Stevens, "Punjabee Well-Jumpers and Krooboy Divers," *Harper's Round Table* VIII (September 27, 1887), 7.
31 A product of the Scottish Enlightenment, stadial theory refers to the four stages theory of human societies, which proposes that human societies evolve from a primitive society characterized by hunting and pastoralism and agriculture before they reach the commercial stage, which was the fourth stage and regarded as the most civilized. Europeans understood themselves to inhabit the fourth stage, while African societies were assigned a place in the lower three stages. For further discussion of the four stages of stadial theory see Nathaniel Wolloch, "The Civilizing Process, Nature, and Stadial Theory," *Eighteenth-Century Studies* 44, no. 2 (2011): 245–259; Ronald Meek, *Social Science and The Ignoble Savage* (Cambridge: Cambridge University Press, 1976), 5.

sailors were deemed "unfit" for such labor.[32] Kru oral traditions show that they were well aware of uneven socio-economic relations in their workplaces, yet wages and the opportunity to rise in social status back in their homeland outweighed any animosity they felt towards the British.[33] After all, Kru had largely rejected two of the most important symbols of British culture in the period: Christianity and literacy.

However, the character and actions of Kru laborers were shrouded in ambiguity having worked towards the abolition of the trans-Atlantic slave trades on British, French, and American ships, and Royal Navy vessels tasked with intercepting slave *dhows* (slave ships circulating between the Middle East and East Africa) in the Indian Ocean, while also transporting enslaved Africans on slave ships along the West African coast bound for the Americas.[34] In some cases, Kru served on slave ship voyages from West Africa to the Caribbean, most notably to Cuba between the 1830s and 1850s.[35] As a result of these overlapping labor trajectories, the Kru free wage labor diaspora and labor networks that developed may point to the entrepreneurial nature of the Kru as a mechanism of survival in the face of encroaching capitalist and colonial forces in their homeland.

---

32 Edward Bold, *The Merchant's and Mariner's African Guide* (Salem: Cushing and Appleton, 1823), 122; Charles Rockwell, *Sketches of Foreign Travel: And Life at Sea! Including a Cruise on Board a Man-of-War, as Also a Visit to Spain, Portugal, the South of France, Italy, Sicily, Malta, The Ionian Islands, Continental Greece, Liberia and Brazil; And a Treatise of the Navy of the United States* (Boston: Tappan and Dennet, 1842), 258. The romanticization or exoticization of the African was an important part of constructing the colonial subject or "other" from the vantage of the imperial gaze of the European. For a discussion on nineteenth-century European racism that regarded Africans as uncivilized, savage or "other" see V.Y. Mudimbe, *The Invention of Africa: Gnosis, Philosophy, and the Order of Knowledge* (London: James Currey, 1988), 1–23; V.Y. Mudimbe, *The Idea of Africa* (London: James Currey, 1994), 1–70; Meek, *Social Science*, 5; Edward Said, *Orientalism* (New York: Vintage, 1978), 1–30.
33 Interviews with Chief Davis, Smith, and Deputy Governor Worjloh suggest that the Kru remember contractual labor with the British with a sense of pride.
34 See Abdul Sheriff, *Dhow Cultures and the Indian Ocean: Cosmopolitanism, Commerce and Islam* (Oxford: Oxford University Press, 2010); Abdul Sheriff, *Slaves, Spices and Ivory in Zanzibar: Integration of an East African Commercial Empire into the World Economy, 1770–1873* (Athens, OH: Ohio University Press, 1986); Erik Gilbert, *Dhows and the Colonial Economy of Zanzibar, 1860–1970* (Athens, OH: Ohio University Press, 2004).
35 "M.L. Melville and James Hook to the Earl of Aberdeen, Sierra Leone, August 14, 1844," no. 69, in General Report of the Emigration Commissioners vol. 2, *Correspondence with the British Commissioners at Sierra Leone, Havana, Rio De Janeiro, Surinam, Cape of Good Hope, Jamaica, Loanda, and Boa Vista Relating to the Slave Trade* (London: William Clowes and Sons, 1845), 84.

Diaspora

The Kru free wage labor diaspora is framed within the concept of an "African diaspora." Alusine Jalloh proposes the following model:

> The African diaspora was born out of the voluntary and involuntary movement of Africans to various areas of the world since ancient times, but involuntary migration through the trans-Saharan, trans-Atlantic, and Indian Ocean slave trades accounts for most of the black presence outside of Africa today. The concept of the African diaspora has also come to include the psychological and physical return of people of African descent to their homeland, Africa.[36]

Jalloh's emphasis on the "voluntary" movement of Africans and both the "physical" and "psychological" return to a homeland resonates with the Kru who routinely circulated between diaspora communities and their homeland on the Kru Coast in timeframes dictated by the terms of their contracts. Their diaspora was unique from the larger enslaved populations in the Americas, which derived its number from an estimated 12.8 million Africans who were sent from Africa.[37]

The Kru diaspora can be qualified as a free wage labor diaspora based on several factors. These include that the Kru were paid for their labor (whether in-kind or cash), they served on limited-term contracts, they had the power and choice to continue to labor or terminate a contract, and they carried reference letters known as "books" that ensured future employment as they circulated between labor communities and their homeland. Wage labor historians Peter Scholliers and Leonard Schwarz have defined wage labor as "(legally) free labor done by a person for another person or an institution."[38] The editorial board of the *International Review of Social History*, despite their critical stance towards the shortcomings of free labor, suggests that a primary feature of free wage labor in the Marxist sense is that the worker is "free of non-economic compulsions to

---

36 Alusine Jalloh, "Introduction," in *The African Diaspora*, eds. Alusine Jalloh and Stephen E Maizlish (College Station: Texas A&M University Press, 1996), 3.

37 Trans-Atlantic Slave Trade Database www.slavevoyages.org. The estimated figure of 12.8 million refers to the number of Africans who left Africa. The third edition of Paul Lovejoy's *Transformations in Slavery* (2011) shows that the number of enslaved Africans who left has risen from 12.5 million to 12.8 million, according to Lovejoy's calculations. See Paul Lovejoy, *Transformations in Slavery: A History of Slavery in Africa*, 3rd ed. (Cambridge: Cambridge University Press, 2011), 18.

38 Peter Scholliers and Leonard Schwarz, "The Wage in Europe Since the Sixteenth Century," in *Experiencing Wages: Social and Cultural Aspects of Wage Forms in Europe since 1500*, eds. Peter Scholliers and Leonard Schwarz (New York: Berghahn Books, 2004), 7.

work."[39] While some Kru were most certainly sold into the trans-Atlantic slave trades over the course of four centuries, Kru oral traditions, British official papers, and wage lists reveal that the great majority of Kru were engaged in a voluntary diaspora both during and after the trans-Atlantic slave trade era in which they worked for wages and were not enslaved.

In the nineteenth century, regardless of where Kru worked, official accounts reveal that the British considered them as "free labourers" or "free agents" and they thus had a large degree of self-determination.[40] Royal Navy and commercial ships created a fluid diasporic space that could not contain the Kru within a rigid racial system based on a zero-sum outcome that was the order informing white-black racial relations throughout much of the world in the nineteenth century in the form of slavery.[41] Kru did however run the risk of enslavement when sailing on slave ships to the Caribbean where they could be arbitrarily sold into slavery.[42] While serving on Royal Navy vessels tasked with intercepting slave ships, Kru risked capture should the impounded vessel be overthrown en route to the disembarkment port before continuing their voyage to the Americas.[43] Kru frequently led the charge, boarded slave ships, and served on battlefields in naval brigades, putting their lives at risk for which some were awarded

---

39 Editorial Committee, "Free and Unfree Labour," *International Review of Social History* 35, no. 1 (1990): 1.

40 H. Barkly, "Minutes of Evidence Taken Before the Select Committee on Sugar and Coffee Planting," Fifth Report from the Select Committee on Sugar and Coffee Planting Together with Minutes of Evidence, And Appendix, March 18 1848 (1848), 24; Despatches from the Right Honorable Earl Grey to Governor Barkly, Enclosure in no. 19, July 5, 1850, Accounts and Papers, Sugar Growing Colonies, vol. 9, Session February 4-August 8 1851 (1851), 402; Robert Gordon Latham, *The Ethnology of British Colonies and Dependencies* (London: J. Van Voorst, 1851), 38.; J.G. Cruickshank, "African Immigrants After Freedom," *Timehri: The Journal of the Royal Agricultural and Commercial Society of British Guiana* 6, Third Series (1919): 81.

41 Zero-sum is a concept rooted in game theory that proposes that one party can only benefit at the expense of another party. In the case of British-Kru relations, both parties were able to benefit economically from contractual labor despite racial hierarchies underscoring their relationship. See Alan D. Taylor, *Mathematics in Politics: Strategy, Voting, Power and Proof* (New York: Springer, 1995), 1–2, 21–25; Robert Harms, *Games Against Nature: A Cultural History of the Nunu of Equatorial Africa* (Cambridge: Cambridge University Press, 1988), 1–10.

42 Manning, "Six Months," 326, 349. Manning reveals that the Kru were paid in tobacco and clothes for their service of managing the enslaved on the trans-Atlantic voyage. Yet, he also implies that some Kru may have been sold upon arrival in the Caribbean, which is at odds with nearly all other nineteenth century accounts; see Chapter 1.

43 Eighteenth and nineteenth-century accounts mention the enslavement of free laboring African crewmen who were detained and sold in the Americas; see British and Foreign State Papers, 1822–1823, "Inclosure – Evidence of Quashie Sam" (London: James Ridgway and Sons, 1850), 522.

medals.⁴⁴ Their normal role as stevedores, porters, and boatmen could be augmented at a moment's notice to heroic status.

However, their mobility was not uniform amongst the nineteenth century workforce. On ships, Kru worked alongside British sailors and other Africans such as the Fante, Yoruba, Liberated Africans, "Seedies", and Asian "Lascars."⁴⁵ Peter Linebaugh and Marcus Rediker illuminated the diverse nature of ship crews in the period, who formed a "multi-racial, multi-ethnic, international working class."⁴⁶ Unlike enslaved black seamen who worked on British ships in the Caribbean in the eighteenth and nineteenth centuries and who had a degree of mobility, contracted Kru were not operating under the same socio-economic structure of slavery and were therefore not obliged to remain on the ship if they were not satisfied that the terms of their contractual employment were not being met.⁴⁷ Enslaved seafarers and bondsmen were usually identifiable in wage books of the period with a line indicating the wages due to their master.⁴⁸ In stark contrast, wage lists and the migratory nature of their employment signal that Kru were not enslaved on British vessels in the nineteenth century.

---

44 Roy Dutton, *Forgotten Heroes: Zulu and Basuto Wars including Medal Roll 1877–8–9* (Prenton: Infodial, 2010), 374; ADM 127/40, "Acting Lieutenant Henn to Commander Colomb, 6 May 1869, and Admiralty to Commodore Heath," no. P270, September 21, 1869; Raymond C. Howell, *The Royal Navy and the Slave Trade* (London: Croom Helm Ltd, 1987), 71.
45 "Seedies" was the name assigned to Liberated Africans who served on ships along the east coast of Africa. The term "seedies" derives from the word *sayyids*, which was the term applied to Africans in India. The British term evolved to refer to sailors from Zanzibar and the Swahili coast in the nineteenth century. See Alessandro Stanziani, *Sailors, Slaves and Immigrants: Bondage in the Indian Ocean World, 1750–1914* (New York City: Springer: 2014), 63. "Lascars" was the term assigned to Arab and Southeast Asian sailors who engaged in labor with the British. For information on the origins of the word "Lascar" and their labor with the British see Michael H. Fisher, Shompa Lahiri, and Shinder S. Thandi, *A South-Asian History of Britain: Four Centuries of Peoples from the Indian Sub-Continent* (Westport, CT: Greenwood World Publishers, 2007), 6–9.
46 Peter Linebaugh and Marcus Rediker, "The Many-Headed Hydra: Sailors, Slaves and the Atlantic Working Class in the Eighteenth Century," *Journal of Historical Sociology* 3, no.2 (1990): 225–252. Although focusing on the eighteenth century, their findings on the diverse nature of crews continued to inform crews on nineteenth-century British ships.
47 For further discussion on enslaved seamen serving on British ships see Heather Cateau, "Itinerant Slaves: On the Plantation's Margins-Hired Slaves and Seamen," paper presented at the Association of Caribbean Historians 35th Annual Conference, Universidad Interamericana de Puerto Rico, San Juan, Puerto Rico, April 28-May 2, 2003.
48 An example is found in Captain John Small's wage book for the *Hawk* in 1781. He hired six Fante seamen and one enslaved black seaman as he sailed from West Africa to Liverpool. John William, the enslaved black seaman, held bondsman status and was forced to give his earnings to his master. See Ray Costello, *Black Salt: Seafarers of African Descent on British Ships* (Oxford: Oxford University Press, 2012), 33. For information on West Indian seamen working on serving

Beyond ships and ports in the Atlantic, Indian and Pacific Oceans, Kru also formed an important component of a mixed labor force in ports and on estates in the Caribbean.[49] In the post-slavery period after 1838, the British government provided economic initiatives for West Africans to work in the Caribbean plantation setting. British planters understood hiring migrant workers as a strategic maneuver to compete with slave-produced crops in French, Spanish, and Dutch domains and ultimately realize their 1815 goal at the Congress of Vienna by abolishing all illegal trans-Atlantic slave trading and slavery. The consensus amongst planters in the British Caribbean was that they needed an immediate new source of labor as a result of the shortage caused by Emancipation.[50] Kru were part of an economic "experiment" in the region and were hired along with Indians, Chinese, emancipated African descendants as well as African laborers including Yoruba, Ibo, and Congos.[51] However, unlike the emancipated Africans who in many cases remained on their former master's grounds and indentured workers from Asia who were tied to estates in the Caribbean with the threat of punishment for breaking contractual obligations, Kru laborers had mobility and the choice of working on contracts or seeking out new opportunities.[52]

In Trinidad and British Guiana, they were frequently recorded as moving between jobs and were "unindentured", meaning not tied to any single estate or

---

on ships see Alan Cobley, "Black West Indian Seamen in the British Merchant Marine in the Mid Nineteenth Century," *History Workshop Journal*, no. 58 (Autumn, 2004): 259–274.

49 For further discussion on the mixed labor force on ships see Costello, *Black Salt*, 68. For mixed labor force on plantations and estates in the Caribbean see Rebecca Scott, *Slave Emancipation in Cuba: The Transition to Free Labor, 1860–1899* (Pittsburgh: University of Pittsburgh Press, 2001).

50 "Topic: Labour Problem and African Immigrants," West Indies Committee Papers 1833–1843 Box 4, Folder 1, Minutes July 1833-June 1843, Resolutions of the Standing Committee of West India Planters: On Immigration, February 18, 1842, 109. West Indiana Special Collections Library, The University of the West Indies, Trinidad and Tobago.

51 Newspapers and magazines of the period frequently referred to African labor in the British Caribbean as an "experiment." See *The Economist*, January 15, 1848, in *The Economist Weekly Commercial Times, Bankers Gazette*, and *Railway Monitor*, vol. 6 (London: Economist Office, 1848), 60.

52 For a discussion on the differences between free wage labor and indentured labor in the British Caribbean see Tayyab Mahmud, "Cheaper than a Slave: Indentured Labor, Colonialism and Capitalism," Seattle University School of Law Paper Series, *Whittier Law Review* 34, no. 215 (2013): 215–243. For indentured labor in the West Indies and the Indian Ocean world see Stanziani, *Sailors*, 89–91, 114. See also David Northrup, *Indentured Labor in the Age of Imperialism, 1834–1922* (Cambridge: Cambridge University Press, 1985), 4–9, 16–50, 80, 144.

port for a prescribed period.[53] Law professor Tayyub Muhmud and labor historian Alessandro Stanziani have distinguished free labor from indentured labor, a form of unfree labor, in terms of consequences and the connections between laborer and specific estate or ship, the free laborer being exempt from the rules informing indentureship.[54] Therefore, the power dynamics governing Kru labor differed from both slavery and indentured servitude that characterized nineteenth-century labor in the British Caribbean.

In the context of the Caribbean, the Kru diaspora showed signs of continuity and change. "Krooman's Village" in Trinidad was reminiscent of the Krutowns in West Africa, albeit on a smaller scale. Although they were employed in agricultural production, many returned to their traditional role in marine transportation between estate and ships. By comparison, one of their most populous communities in British Guiana known as Canal No.1 adjacent to the Demerara River was inhabited by Kru along with many other Africans, most notably Yoruba. The Kru became members of multi-ethnic communities that Stuart Hall has characterized as being structured by cultural "hybridity."[55] Kamau Braithwaite and Édouard Glissant have emphasized the significance of the unique social and cultural influences affecting identity in the Caribbean as being as much if not more of a factor in the "creolization" process as European and African influences.[56] While some Kru maintained a unique identity with the application of the Kru mark and continued to work in marine labor using surfboats and flotillas, new opportunities to own land independently and obtain contracts without the need of a headman or foreman led some Kru to permanently remain in British Guiana, thereby ending the migratory labor cycle between their homeland and diaspora communities that had characterized and sustained their work in West Africa and elsewhere. Intermarriage with Creoles and Yoruba workers resulted in a new generation of Kru with multiple African ancestry and their amalgamation into the wider Creole community, as reflected in the lack of Kru categories in official documents by the early twentieth century. The Kru's work

---

53 Accounts and Papers, Emigration, Session 3 February to 12 August 1842, vol. 21, Correspondence Relative to Emigration, 1842, Extract Minute from the Proceedings of the Immigration Committee, Tuesday the 25th May 1841, James Hackett, Agent-General (London: William Clowes and Sons, 1842), 368.
54 Mahmud, "Cheaper than a Slave," 215–243; Stanziani, *Sailors*, 63, 89–91, 114.
55 Stuart Hall, "Cultural Identity and Diaspora," in *Identity: Community, Culture, Difference*, ed. Jonathan Rutherford (London: Lawrence & Wishart, 1990), 235.
56 Kamau Brathwaite, *The Development of Creole Society in Jamaica, 1770–1820* (Oxford: Clarendon, 1971), 1–30; Éduoard Glissant, *Poetics of Relation*, trans. Betsy Wing (Ann Arbor The University of Michigan Press, 1997), xi-xx, 5–37; Édouard Glissant, "Creolization in the Making of the Americas," *Caribbean Quarterly* 54, no. 1–2 (2008): 81–89.

experience in the British Caribbean differed from West African ports where they have maintained a distinct Kru identity in their diaspora communities well into the twenty-first century.

Regardless of where the Kru labored, the headman or foreman became the most significant enabler in the Kru free wage labor diaspora. A position which most probably developed from the lead trader and paddler who directed surf-boats to European ships and conducted trade first observed in the sixteenth century, the headman was the intermediary between Kru laborers and British employers.[57] They were tasked with selecting a labor gang, distributing food and wages, maintaining discipline, and negotiating contractual terms.[58] Laborers were drawn from the age-set system that traditionally spawned a warrior class and was largely redirected towards migratory labor. Adolescent laborers completed contracts as a right-of-passage into adulthood with the goal of becoming headmen one day themselves. Headmen were necessary in the organization of labor on commercial and military contracts and the higher wages they received compared with regular laborers reveals the hierarchal structure governing their contracts. The labor gang was expected to hand over an agreed upon percentage of their wages to both their headman and village leader, the *krogba*, following the completion of a contract. An entirely new socio-economic system based on contractual wage labor developed from periodic trade on the coast to a system of outsourcing based on timeframes, monetary value, and British demand – all of which was dependent on the headman.

Identifying the Kru

One of the most contentious issues facing historians regarding Kru labor lies in the pursuit of a simple answer to the complex question: who were the Kru? What is known about the Kru prior to the nineteenth century is that Kru-speaking peoples made a living in fishing, rice, salt, ivory, and agricultural trade, with a specialization in boating and transporting commodities, Europeans, and enslaved Africans in the era of the trans-Atlantic slave trades along the West African

---

[57] In 1555, Towerson noted that all transactions were to be completed through one individual. See Richard Hakluyt, ed., *The First Voyage Made by Master W. Towerson to the Coast of Guinea in the Yere 1555* (London: J. MacLehose and Sons, 1904), 184–85.

[58] Thomas Ludlam, "An Account of a Tribe of People called Kroomen, inhabiting a small District of the Grain Coast of Africa, between Cape Mount and Cape Palmas," *The Sixth Report of the Directors of the African Institution The Sixth Report of the Directors of the African Institution Read at the General Annual Meeting* (London: African Institute, 1812), 95–96.

coast. They inhabited the region between the southeastern coast of modern-day Liberia and southwestern extremity of Côte d'Ivoire from perhaps as early as the fifteenth century. Oral traditions tell of an inland migration to the coast by the *Claho* people (or Krao/Klao), which most likely took place prior to the mid-fifteenth century, however, the exact date remains unknown.[59]

From the perspective of the Proper Kru, the Kru homeland, which became known as the Kru Coast in the nineteenth century, refers to the region between the Cestos River and Grand Cess River in the southeastern coast of Liberia.[60] According to primary published documents and Kru oral tradition first recorded in the nineteenth century, the five main trading settlements within the region included Nana Kru, Little Kru, Krobah, Settra Kru, and King William's Town (King Weah's Town) on the Kru Coast.[61] As early as 1812, former Governor of Sierra Leone Thomas Ludlam recognized these towns as the heart of the Kru homeland from which migratory laborers cycled back and forth to Freetown. This position was upheld by Kru oral traditions recorded in the 1850s by Reverend Connelly in his *American Colonization 39th Annual Report*, Reverend John Leighton Wilson, and Sigismund Wilhelm Koelle in his linguistic milestone *Polyglotta Africa*, published in 1854.[62] These remained some of the most significant trading towns in the nineteenth century with populations numbering 600 or more each and a regional population estimated to be upwards of 40,000.[63] Although the people residing in the towns recognized themselves as Proper Kru, they functioned autonomously, traded independently with Europeans and amongst themselves, and could as easily find themselves celebrating intermarriage between members of the towns as entering into conflict with one another.

However, the concept of a Kru homeland is more complex than limiting it to the five settlements inhabited by the Proper Kru and has been a topic probed by scholars for decades. The Kru Coast was not static, but evolved over time as evi-

---

59 Connelly suggests the Kru migrated from the interior to the coast around the year 1600; see Connelly, "Report," 38–40. However, some scholars suggest it was upwards to 400 years earlier than Connelly's account in 1856; see Behrens, *Les Kroumen*, 7.
60 Dan Webster, *Report of the Secretary of State* (September 14, 1850), 75.
61 Ludlam, "Account," 88; Connelly, "Report," 38–40; Sigismund Wilhelm Koelle, *Polyglotta Africana* (London: Church Missionary Society House, 1854; republished 1963), 4; Wilson, *Western Africa*, 101.
62 Ludlam, "Account," *Sixth Report*, 88; Connelly, "Report," 38–40; Koelle, *Polyglotta*, 4; Wilson, *Western Africa*, 101.
63 This figure includes the Proper Kru region between the Cestos River and Grand Cess River and Cape Palmas. See Mr. Pinney, Canfield and Alward, "Report of Messrs Pinney, Canfield and Alward," *The Missionary Chronicle* 8 (1840): 213; *The Missionary Chronicle* 11 (1843): 6; "Miscellany," *The Missionary Magazine* 46 (1866): 120.

dent with the application of the term "Kru" to peoples living beyond the geographical boundaries of the Proper Kru villages. Even within the boundaries of the Proper Kru, there were other trading towns in the vicinity, which included Crou, Crou Settra, Sinoe, Sanguin, Wappo, Nifo, Rock Cess, River Cess, Sasstown, and Picaninny Cess, some of which maintained a long-standing tradition of trade.[64] Adjacent to these trading centers, a significant number of smaller fishing villages dotted the coast containing inhabitants who were frequently identified as "Fishmen", "Fishermen" or "Fishes" who belonged to the Kabor and Gbeta *dakwe*.[65] They were often represented as being in competition with the Proper Kru in many ship captain accounts of the period.[66] Moreover, there were Kru-speaking communities in the hinterland who belonged to the Matro, Bolo, Nanke, and Bwa *dakwe*.[67]

Several factors seem to be at play when conceptualizing who identified as Kru and who was categorized as Kru both within and outside of their communities. Linguistics have been a crucial factor informing analyses of Kru identity. Although the Proper Kru towns and others in the vicinity formed the hub of Kru exchange with Europeans in the region, all of the communities on the coast, between the Mesurado River (Monrovia) and the Bandama River (west of Abidjan), were inhabited by people who could be categorized as Kru speakers.[68] Guenter Schroeder and Andreas Massing propose that as early as the sixteenth century dialects of a common language were recognized between villages

---

64 For an overview of the many trading towns see the map "Guinea Itself, as Well as the Greatest Portion of Nigritia or the Land of the Blacks, the One Called Ethiopia Inferior by Modern Geographers, the Other Southern Ethiopia", published by German firm Homännische Erben, 1743. For more discussion on the difference between Proper Kru and "Fishmen" see Wilson, *Western Africa*, 103–104; Davis, *Ethnohistorical*, 21; Ibrahim K. Sundiata, "The Rise and Decline of Kru Power: Fernando Po in the Nineteenth Century," *Liberian Studies* 6, no. 1 (1975): 27.
65 Elizabeth Tonkin, "Sasstown's Transformation: The Jlao Kru 1888–1918," *Liberian Studies Journal* 8, no. 1 (1978–1979): 3; Jo Mary Sullivan, "Mississippi in Africa: Settlers Among the Kru, 1835–1847," *Liberian Studies Journal* 8, no. 2 (1978–1979): 83, 86–88. Dakwe is the plural form of *dako*.
66 Ludlam, "Account," 44.
67 Merran Fraenkel, "Social Change on the Kru Coast of Liberia," *Africa* 36, no. 2 (1966): 154–155; Diane Frost, *Work and Community Among West African Migrant Workers Since the Nineteenth Century* (Liverpool: Liverpool University Press, 1999), 7.
68 Guenter Schroeder and Andreas Massing, "A General Outline of Historical Developments within the Kru Cultural Province" (paper presented at the Second Annual Conference on Social Research in Liberia, Bloomington, Indiana, April 30-May 2, 1970), 5. See also Jeanne Hein, "Portuguese Communication with Africans on the Searoute to India," in *The Globe Encircled and the World Revealed*, ed. Ursula Lamb (London: Routledge, 2016), 6.

along the Malaguetta Coast.[69] Kru speakers including the Proper Kru, Bassa, Grebo (Glebo), Krahn, Sapo, Neyo, Wane, Godié, Bété, and Dida inhabited this vast coastal region.[70] All of these peoples were frequently categorized and hired as "Kru" laborers and seafarers by European and American ship captains and merchants based on a shared language.

Maps played a significant role in the European perception of Kru identity. Between the sixteenth and nineteenth centuries, the region was named after the commodities that dominated trade such as the Malaguetta Coast, Pepper Coast, Grain Coast, Ivory Coast, Tooth Coast, and, later, nautical terminology, the Windward Coast.[71] Setracrou (Settra Kru), Crou, Sanguin, Wappo, Tabou, and Bereby were frequently marked as trading towns on maps dating to the mid-seventeenth century.[72] John Ogilby's 1670 map included towns between the Cestos River and Cape Palmas within the Greya Cust (Grain Coast) and towns to the east of the Cavalla River in the Tand Cust (Tooth or Ivory Coast).[73] In contrast to most maps of the period, Herman Moll's 1704 map placed Sino, Sanguin, and Setra Kru (Settra Kru – a Proper Kru town) in the Ivory Coast rather than belonging to the Grain Coast.[74] In 1837, American Colonization Society (ACS) agent Jehudi Ashum published a map with a special note on the Kru in the region between the Cestos and Grand Cess Rivers which read: "Kroos are the waterman and laborers of the coast."[75] Ashmun's note not only revealed the unique persona the Kru had formed based on their long history of trade and sea-

---

69 Ibid., 5.
70 Louis Henrique, *Les Colonies Françaises*, vol. 5 (Paris: Maison Quantin, 1890), 203; Élisée Reclus, *The Universal Geography: Earth and Its Inhabitants*, ed. A.H. Keane (London: J.S. Virtue & Co., 1885), 233; Ronald W. Davis, "The Liberian Struggle for Authority on the Kru Coast," *International Journal of African Historical Studies* 8, no. 2 (1975): 227; Frost, *Work*, 7–8.
71 Writing in the 1960s, Merran Fraenkel has suggested the Kru ancestral migration to the coast occurred some 400 years ago; see Fraenkel, "Social Change," 154. This date is confirmed by Kru oral traditions as revealed during an interview with Deputy Governor Worjloh.
72 Nicolas Sanson, *Afrique* (Paris, 1650); John Ogilby and Jacob van Meurs (engraver), "Africae Accurata Tabula" (London, 1670); William Berry, *Africa Divided According to the Extent of Its Principall Parts in Which Are Distinguished One from the Other the Empires, Monarchies, Kingdoms, States, and Peoples...* (London, 1680); Hermann Moll, "New and Exact Map of Guinea," in Bosman, *New and Accurate*, n.p; Barbot, *Description*, 136; Jacques Nicholas Bellin, *Carte de la Coste Occidentale D'Afrique* (Paris, 1739). A settlement containing a variant of the name Kru appears in the map of the Windward Coast in Bernard Martin and Mark Spurrell, eds., *The Journal of a Slave Trader (John Newton) 1750–1754* (London: Epworth, 1962), 117.
73 Ogilby and van Meurs, "Africae".
74 Moll, "New," n.p.
75 Jehudi Ashmun, "Map of the West Coast of Africa from Sierra Leone to Cape Palmas, Including the Colony of Liberia," 1830.

faring, but also implied the important economic role the Kru could play in the newly-established Liberian Commonwealth.

A combination of shared language and maps that showed the close geographical proximity of their trading towns served as variables informing Kru identity from the perspective of European traders and Kru-speaking peoples alike. While the five trading towns came to define the region known as the Kru Coast in the nineteenth century, earlier maps show that only some of the Proper Kru trading towns had formed in previous centuries or were relevant enough to garner mention. Yet, the inhabitants in the region between Cape Mesurado and the Bandama River were recognized as Kru people from the European perspective. From the vantage of Kru-speaking peoples, they would have easily identified the differences amongst themselves based on their *dako*, dialect, secret society affiliation (if any), and geographic location of their towns, and continued to trade with Europeans regardless of their external label.

Scholars have influenced the perception of Kru identity and their homeland based on analytical parameters. Kru have mostly been studied within the national boundaries of Liberia or Côte d'Ivoire in isolation from one another, resulting in a fragmented image of the Kru homeland. This separation is not limited to political boundaries, but has been influenced by both the language used by the scholar in his/her writing and their sources primarily in English, French, German, Dutch, Spanish, and Portuguese. Writing in English and relying mostly on British and American sources, George Brooks and Ronald Davis limited their discussion of the Kru within the boundaries of Liberian state (although the map on Davis' book cover includes one town to the east of the Cavalla River).[76] Christine Behrens, writing in French and relying mostly on French sources, concentrated her study on Bakwé and Bété Kru-speaking groups who are identified as Kroumen or Croumaines between the Cavalla and Sassandra Rivers within the boundaries of Côte d'Ivoire.[77] Jelmer Vos, writing in English while relying on Dutch sources, limited the greater part of his study of the region within Côte d'Ivoire with minimal connection to the Proper Kru region. He noted that many Kru were sold into the trans-Atlantic slave trade for enslavement in Dutch Guiana, which seems to be at odds with practices in the Proper Kru region.[78] Relying on French sources, Jonas Ibo's contention that Kru-speaking Neyo laborers fabricated Kru identities for the purpose of obtaining work contracts near the Sassandra River may apply to his period of study in the twentieth

---

76 Brooks, *Kru Mariner*, 50; Davis, *Ethnohistorical*, 31–35.
77 Behrens, *Les Kroumen*, 27–28.
78 Jelmer Vos, "The Slave Trade from The Windward Coast: The Case of the Dutch, 1740–1805," *African Economic History* vol. 38 (2010): 29–51.

century, but is not so readily acceptable in earlier centuries when notions of Kru identity were emerging.[79]

Thus far, the problem has been extrapolating a segment of Kru-speaking peoples and projecting that group as representing the total experience of Kru traders, seafarers, and laborers on the coast. Although Andreas Massing sought to resolve this issue by examining what he termed the "Kru Cultural Area", which included the region between the Cestos River in Liberia and the Sassandra River in Côte d'Ivoire, he was criticized by Elizabeth Tonkin, a pioneer of Kru studies in the early 1960s, for a lack of recognizing the unique specificities between Kru-speaking peoples in the region, while generalizing diverse groups under a single "Kru" conceptual category.[80] Thus, the most productive approach towards analyzing the activities of Kru-speaking peoples has been to read Behren's work on Kroumen communities in Côte d'Ivoire in collaboration with works focused on Kru communities in Liberia while using a range of multilingual primary sources in English, French, German, Dutch, Portuguese, and Spanish and oral traditions offered by Kru-speaking peoples.

Official records provide another avenue of inquiry into the nature of Kru identity. The designation of "Kroomen" in official documents including muster lists, shipping records, ordinances, estate registers, the Navy List, and ship captain accounts points towards a unique identity that differentiated Kru from other categories such as "Africans", which included Yoruba, Ibo, Congo or Liberated Africans.[81] Indeed, Frederick McEvoy attributed the creation of Kru ethnicity to external factors where their group identity emerged in contrast with other African labor groups serving on ships and in British ports in West Africa.[82] Based

---

79 Jonas Ibo, "Le phénomène "Krouman" à Sassandra: la marque d'une institution séculaire," *Canadian Journal of African Studies* 32, Issue I (1998): 65–94.
80 Andreas Massing, *The Economic Anthropology of the Kru* (Wisbaden: Steiner, 1980), 10–21. For information on various Kru-speaking peoples within the region see Elizabeth Tonkin, *Narrating Our Pasts: The Social Construction of Oral History* (Cambridge: Cambridge University Press, 1995), 22; Elizabeth Tonkin, review of *The Economic Anthropology of the Kru (West Africa)* by Andreas Massing, *The International Journal of African Historical Studies* 16, no. 1 (1983): 101–103.
81 Liberated Africans (frequently referred to as receptives) were Africans whose slave ships were intercepted and who were delivered to Freetown or Monrovia. See John Rankin, "Nineteenth- Century Royal Navy Sailors from Africa and the African Diaspora, Research Methodology," *African Diaspora* 6 (2013): 183–184.
82 Frederick D. McEvoy, "Understanding Ethnic Realities among the Grebo and Kru Peoples of West Africa," *Africa* 47, no. 1 (1977): 62–80. For a similar process that informed Hausa traders in West Africa, see Abner Cohen, *Custom and Politics in Urban Africa: A Study of Hausa Migrants in Yoruba Towns* (London: Routledge, 1969).

on their close geographical proximity, the Grebo (Glébo as they were sometimes known to the east of the Cavalla River), Bassa, Sapo, and Krahn, among others, were amalgamated under the ethnic category of Kru. Lawrence Breitborde went further and suggested that their identity was equally influenced in their homeland by the Liberian state based on Port of Entry and land acquisition laws that were aimed at controlling Kru manpower and the profitability of the Kru Coast.[83] By considering what McEvoy determined to be the three most important identity markers in the region including *dako*, *dea* (village), and patrilineage, as well as the age-set system and secret society affiliations which transcend *dako*, Kru identity becomes increasingly complex in its analysis.[84]

Another layer informing Kru identity is the link between ethnicity and occupation. The importance of Kru as crew is indisputable. In 1856, Rev. Connelly reported on the correlation between the Kru and their reputation for serving on ships dating back to the seventeenth century with the Portuguese.[85] However, it has sometimes been thought that the term "Kru" and the English term "crew" are purely related because the Kru worked as crew on British ships. Lynell Marchese has argued that the term "Kru" resulted from their employment on ships stating: "the homonymy with crew is obvious, and is at least one source of the confusion among Europeans that there was a Kru/crew tribe."[86] Similarly, Diane Frost has proposed that the Kru formed an "ethnic-occupational" identity that was a response to trade with Europeans. She suggests that the morphing of their identity from *Claho* (their original name in oral tradition) to Krao/ Klao to Kru was based on their role in the "crew" associated with ships.[87] While her position holds true in the nineteenth century following their labor in Freetown after which their identity crystallized and came to encompass a wider group of communities under the Kru label, it must be emphasized that a distinct Kru ethnic group can trace its roots to a much earlier period before its dispersal.

Furthermore, it is possible to argue the connection between the words "Kru" and "crew" is a coincidence in the English language and is not reflected in other

---

[83] Lawrence Breitborde, "Structural Continuity in the Development of an Urban Kru Community," *Urban Anthropology* (1979): 111–130.
[84] McEvoy, "Understanding," 62–80.
[85] Connelly, "Report," 39.
[86] Lynell Marchese, "City Countryside and Kru Ethnicity," *Africa* 61, no. 2 (1991): 186–201; Lynell Marchese, "Kru," in *The Niger-Congo Languages*, ed. Bender Samuel (Lanham: University Press of America, 1989), 113–119.
[87] Frost, *Work*, 10.

European languages.[88] For example, Portuguese, Spanish, Dutch, and French ship captains referred to a community in the region as "Crou" in the early seventeenth century before they were hired en masse on board ships sailing the coast, which confirms the identification of the Kru is not related to the English word "crew."[89] Similarly, English merchant James Welsh identified a community named "Crua" in 1588, before they worked on British vessels, which also demonstrates that there is no association between "Kru" and "crew."[90] A closer look at the work of vernacular connections proposed by P.E.H. Hair may shed some light on how the name "Kru" pre-dated their work on ships and how the correlation between Kru and crew may only be arbitrary.[91] As Behrens has shown, the Kru were known interchangeably as "Krou, Kru, Krew, Krow, Crew, Carow, Courou, Crou, Kroo, Croo, Kroe... Krewmen/Krewmens, Croumane/Croumanes, Kroemens... Kruboy, Kruman, Krumani, Krooman, etc." between the sixteenth and nineteenth centuries.[92] Hence, many of the inhabitants residing between the Cestos and Grand Cess Rivers identified as Kru long before they were routinely hired for work on ships sailing down the West African coast.[93] Moreover, the inhabitants of the region continue to self-identify as Proper Kru or simply Kru in the twenty-first century and they are listed as Kru in Liberian government censuses.[94] A testament to the spread of the Kru label, the inhabitants to the east of the Cavalla River including a mixture of Grebo, Bété, and Godié peoples continue to be identified as Krou or Kroumen in government census records in Côte d'Ivoire.[95] The Kru language is the force that binds all Kru-speaking peoples along the coast in Liberia and Côte d'Ivoire. Yet, while they may have accepted the label Kru while engaging in trade and employment abroad, they maintained

---

88 The word "crew" shows no similarity to Kru in Portuguese (*tripulação*); French (*équipage*); Spanish (*tripulación*); or Dutch (*bemmaning*).
89 Behrens, *Les Kroumen*, 23.
90 Welsh, "Voyage," 451.
91 P.E.H. Hair, "Ethnolinguistic Continuity on the Guinea Coast," *The Journal of African History* 8, no. 2 (1967): 247–268; P.E.H. Hair, "An Ethnolinguistic Inventory of the Upper Guinea Coast before 1700," *African Language Review* 6 (1967): 32–70.
92 Behrens, *Les Kroumen*, 13.
93 Johnston, *Liberia*, 1: 88.
94 Kru-speaking peoples who inhabit Grand Kru County, Sinoe County, River Cess County, Maryland County, Grand Bassa County, and Montserrado County form a great proportion of the total population, as shown in a national demographic survey conducted in 2008. See Government of the Republic of Liberia 2008 Population and Housing Census, Preliminary Results. Accessed on May 1, 2017, https://www.emansion.gov.lr/doc/census_2008provisionalresults.pdf.
95 Kroumen formed 8.5 percent of the total population in a demographic survey conducted in Côte d'Ivoire 2018. Accessed on May 1, 2017, https://www.indexmundi.com/cote_d_ivoire/demographics_profile.html.

a clear understanding of the internal differences between their communities and the multi-tiered nature of their identities.

One of the most valuable avenues for understanding Kru identity arises from oral traditions. Conversations with Kru leaders in their villages and diaspora communities provides rare information that is simply inaccessible through written sources. Although subjective, in many cases, they confirm known traditions and practices that were recorded in primary and secondary sources, while adding nuances and fresh information on Kru labor. Kru studies by Ronald Davis, Elizabeth Tonkin, and Diane Frost included interviews with Kru community members, which proved valuable for understanding their labor experiences.[96] This study includes interviews with Kru community members who in some cases worked on ships or had immediate family members who worked in the nineteenth century as headmen.[97] Understanding how the Kru remember their own histories provides an invaluable layer to the meaning of Kru identity.

Given all of these variables informing Kru identity and its dissemination, I argue that a more precise way of analyzing the trajectories of Kru laborers and making meaningful connections between diaspora community and homeland village is to be very specific about the segment of Kru under analysis based on the geographic location of their villages or places of embarkation, if known. This allows for analysis to move between the general label Kru and more specific hybrid identities, which trace labor itineraries between specific region or village and workplace and identifies the different experiences of Kru to the west of the Cavalla River who mostly worked with British compared with those to the east whose greatest employer was the French. As such, for the purposes of analysis, Kru laborers are more accurately identified as Bassa-Kru, Proper Kru, Grebo-Kru, Bété-Kru, Bakwé-Kru, Neyo-Kru, Godié-Kru, Dida-Kru, and so forth. Hyphenated identities provide an analytical template for understanding the specificities of the inhabitants residing in key sub-regions within the Kru Coast.

Once the region or place of hiring is known, a second level of identity analysis becomes possible and an understanding of *dako* affiliation is necessary. For instance, in the case of the region between the Cestos and Grand Cess Rivers, *dakwe* include: Jloh, Kabor, Gbeta, Sasstown (or Pahn), Grand Cess (or Siklio),

---

96 Davis, *Ethnohistorical*, 197–202; Elizabeth Tonkin, "The Boundaries of History in Oral Performance," *History in Africa* 9 (1982), 273–284; Elizabeth Tonkin, "Jealousy Names, Civilized Names: Anthroponomy of Jlao Kru of Liberia, *Man* New Series 15, no. 4 (1980), 653–664; Frost, *Work*, 44, 175, 221, 227.
97 Doe Smith's father was a headman. Smith was 90 at the time of the interview in 2012 and his father was working on ships at the close of the nineteenth century.

and the "Five Tribes" or Proper Kru.⁹⁸ In the case of the Grebo residing between the Grand Cess and the Cavalla Rivers, there are Garaway-Grebo, Palmas-Grebo, and Half-Cavalla Grebo, among others, whom identify with *dakwe* and specific villages.⁹⁹ The same level of complexity informs all regions of the Kru Coast and understanding the inhabitants' hybrid identities provides a starting point for a deeper exploration of the peoples involved in Atlantic trade in each region. Perhaps most significantly, it is important to recognize that their work experience in Freetown crystallized a sense of "Kru" or "Kroomen" identity from the perspective of the British, other Europeans, and amongst Kru-speaking peoples.¹⁰⁰ Although the Kru had engaged in trade with Europeans for centuries, it was not until the 1790s that the Kru or Kroomen label became commonplace amongst the peoples between Cape Mesurado and the Bandama River, as evident in historical records, increased employment, and the recognition of their homeland as the Kru Coast thereafter.

Significance of Hiring the Kru

The story of the Kru contributes a vital chapter in the history of precolonial wage labor in Africa and offers insights towards the evolution of outsourcing wage labor practices on a global scale. Kru seafarers were routinely recorded on British Royal Navy wage lists as early as 1819, receiving rank-based wages in an era when Atlantic slavery was prevalent and nearly a century before the implementation of cash-crop wages in the colonial era in Africa.¹⁰¹ While the transformative socio-economic effects of precolonial wage labor have been investigated by Paul Lovejoy and Catherine Coquery-Vidrovitch in the period of transition from slavery to free labor in West Africa, Peter Gutkind in his exploration of Fante seafarers on the Gold Coast, and Stephen Rockel in his study on Nyamwezi caravans in East Africa, the temporal, geographic, and socio-economic scale of the Kru

---

98 Fraenkel, "Social Change," 155.
99 *British and Foreign State Papers, 1856–1857*, vol. 48 (London: William Ridgeway, 1866), 586.
100 For further discussion on the crystallization process affecting Kru identity see Jeffrey Gunn, "Krutown: A Catalyst for the Kru Diaspora," in *Sierra Leone: Past and Present*, eds. Paul Lovejoy and Suzanne Schwarz (Trenton, NJ: Africa World Press, 2021), in press.
101 ADM 30/26 "Muster Lists, Pay List for African Krou employed on board His Majesty's Brig Snapper between the 5th day of September and 31st December 1819," The National Archives, Kew, United Kingdom; source: ADM 30/26. June 1, 1819 to October 1, 1819. "Muster Lists, Pay List for African Krou employed on board His Majesty's HMS *Morgiana*, between 1 June 1819 to 1 October 1819," The National Archives, London, United Kingdom; ADM 30/26, "Muster list of Kroomen Serving on Various Ships," The National Archives, Kew, United Kingdom.

free wage labor diaspora renders it truly unique from all other African diasporas.[102]

Although other African laborers worked on European vessels, in ports and agriculture, what distinguished the Kru from their competitors, including Cabinda seafarers in Angola, Fante canoemen on the Gold Coast, Sereer and Wolof boatmen in Dakar, and Vai workers in the Gallinas, to name a few, was the longevity of their service with the British (between the sixteenth century and twentieth century having served in WWI and WWII and beyond), the geographical breadth of their laboring activities in the Atlantic, Indian and Pacific Oceans, the diversity of their roles which ranged from pilots, interpreters, divers, porters, gunners and stevedores serving on Royal Navy and commercial ships, their service in naval brigades engaged in British military campaigns, the volume of Kru who were awarded medals for their naval and military service, their establishment of diaspora communities named "Krutowns", the appearance of the category "Kroomen" on muster lists and official records compared with other workers from the continent who were collectively grouped under the label "Africans" despite distinctions between them, and the long-term infrastructural impact of their laboring contributions in the construction of such engineering marvels as the Panama Canal, Suez Canal, and Congo-Railway.

Questions arise as to how the Kru were able to garner a generally favorable reputation in the face of eighteenth century pseudo-scientific theories and nineteenth-century Victorian views that ordered the world according to European supremacy and subjected Africans to the lower echelons of humanity and, in some cases, a sub-human species.[103] The humanity of the African was an element in eighteenth-century religious debates between monogenetic theory and polygenetic theory, which had been born out of Columbus' arrival in the Americas.[104]

---

[102] Peter C.W. Gutkind, "Trade and Labor in Early Precolonial African History: The Canoemen of Southern Ghana," in *The Workers of African Trade*, eds. Catherine Coquery-Vidrovitch and Paul E. Lovejoy (Beverly Hills: Sage Publications, 1985), 25–49; Peter C.W. Gutkind, R. Cohen, and Jean Copans, eds., *African Labor History* (Beverly Hills: Sage Publications, 1978), 1–10; Catherine Coquery-Vidrovitch and Paul E. Lovejoy, eds., *The Workers in the African Trade* (Beverly Hills: Sage Publications, 1985); Stephen Rockel, *Carriers of Culture: Labor on the Road in Nineteenth-Century East Africa* (Portsmouth, NH: Heinemann: 2006), 4–5.
[103] David Hume, *Essays: Moral, Political and Literary*, vol. 21 (London: n.p. 1741), 1–35; Edward Long, *The History of Jamaica. Reflections on Its Situation, Settlements, Inhabitants, Climate, Products, Commerce, Laws and Government*, vol. 2 (London: n.p., 1774), 363.
[104] The arrival of Columbus in the Americas caused a crisis for Europeans because the Amerindians challenged traditional notions of the Biblical origins of humankind and they needed to be accounted for. See Colin Kidd, *British Identities Before Nationalism: Ethnicity and Nationhood in the Atlantic World, 1600–1800* (Cambridge: Cambridge University Press, 1999), 9–33.

While monogenetic theory proposed the common origin of all humanity as explained in the Bible, polygenetic theory suggested that there were plural origins of humankind and other subhuman species that were arranged in a hierarchal fashion.[105] Even for those who accepted the African's place in Mosaic theology, their blackness was often associated with the biblical curse of Ham's descendants, the Canaanites, or the mark of Cain.[106] Africans were assigned a subhuman status by prominent Scottish philosopher David Hume whose pseudo-scientific arguments regarded Africans as a separate species, more animal than human.[107] Stadial theory proposed four stages in which Europeans represented the culmination of civilization and African societies the lower stages in evolution.[108]

Given the European inclination to enslave Africans en masse rather than hire them, hiring the Kru was not only a way of obtaining a cheap labor force, but a means of combating the trans-Atlantic slave trades as their example revealed that it could be more profitable and moral to hire Africans for the benefit of the British empire rather than enslave them.[109] For abolitionists like Olaudah Equiano (Gustavus Vassa) and Ottobah Cugoano (John Stuart) (themselves formerly enslaved), to hire the Kru was to humanize the African within an evolving

---

105 Kidd, *British Identities*, 15.

106 Mosaic theology was concerned with tracing the ancestry of the various ethnic groups of humanity in order to secure their position in a biblical framework. Since the publication of Benjamin of Tudela's *The Itinerary of Benjamin of Tudela* in the twelfth century, it was commonly believed that the black skin color of the African was the mark of a curse from God like that which had been given to Cain or Ham's descendants, the Canaanites, in the Bible, thereby permitting their enslavement by the descendants of Shem and Japheth from whom Europeans and Asians supposedly traced their origins. Apologists for the slave trade used this concept to justify enslaving Africans. See Kidd, *British Identities*, 9; David M. Goldenberg, *The Curse of Ham: Race and Slavery in Early Judaism, Christianity, and Islam* (Princeton: Princeton University Press, 2003), 156, 183; M.N. Adler, ed., *The Itinerary of Benjamin of Tudela* (New York: Philipp Feldheim Inc., 1907), 62, 68. For the original story of Ham in the Bible see *Genesis 9:25*.

107 Hume, *Essays*, 1–35.

108 Wolloch, "Civilizing Process," 245–259; Meek, *Social Science*, 5.

109 The reasons for the abolition of the British trans-Atlantic slave trade continue to be debated in scholarship; see Eric Williams, *Capitalism and Slavery* (Chapel Hill: The University of North Carolina Press, 1944), 126–177; Christopher Leslie Brown, *Moral Capital: Foundations of British Abolitionism* (Chapel Hill: North Carolina Press, 2006), 1–28; Sir Reginald Coupland, *The British Anti-Slavery Movement*, 2nd ed. (London: Frank Cass & Co. Ltd, 1964), 36–56; Selwyn H.H. Carrington, *The Sugar Industry and the Abolition of the slave trade, 1775–1810* (Gainsville: University of Florida, 2002), 7, 10, 217; Roger Anstey, *The Atlantic Slave Trade and British Abolition, 1760–1810* (London: MacMillan Press Ltd, 1975), 127, 140–141; 190–193, 234–235; Seymour Drescher, *Econocide: British Slavery in the Era of Abolition*, 2nd edition (Chapel Hill: University of North Carolina Press, 2010), 165, 184–185.

Atlantic capitalist system that continued to make large profits in the trans-Atlantic slave trades.[110]

Therefore, it is very significant that the Kru were hired for their labor, and represent an anomaly when compared to the 12.8 million enslaved Africans in the trans-Atlantic world.[111] After all, Africans were sold into the trans-Atlantic slave trade along the same coast, and yet the Kru were able to avoid mass enslavement. One probable reason arose in the late-eighteenth century, when the ever-increasing British need for local labor in West Africa based on malarial, climatic, and manpower concerns led to a willingness of the British and the Kru to experiment with free wage labor contracts.[112] The high mortality rate of European sailors in West Africa played a significant role in the decision to hire Kru mariners on the Kru Coast.[113] West Africa had been widely known as the "white man's grave" until the mid-nineteenth century because of the high mortality rate of European sailors due to a lack of immunity to malaria and yellow fever.[114] Stephen Behrendt estimated that 17.8 percent of British crews died on voyages between West Africa and Liverpool between 1780 and 1807.[115] Over 1,203 sailors in the British West Africa Squadron died as a result of fever between 1825 and 1845.[116] In the face of high mortality rates, it was common for Kru and other African seafarers hired on the coast to continue with the ship on its voyage across the Atlantic to the West Indies to spare British crew.[117] It was not until the advent of quinine and its increasing availability in the second half of the nine-

---

[110] Ottobah Cugoano, *Thoughts and Sentiments on the Evil and Wicked Traffic of The Slavery and Commerce of the Human Species, Humbly Submitted to The Inhabitants of Great-Britain, By Ottobah Cugoano, A Native of Africa* (London: n.p., 1787), Eighteenth Century Online, accessed July 7, 2014, 135; Olaudah Equiano, *The Interesting Narrative and Other Writings*, 1789, ed. Vincent Carretta, 2nd ed. (London: Penguin Books Ltd, 2003), 144.

[111] Trans-Atlantic Slave Trade Database, www.slavevoyages.org; Lovejoy, *Transformations*, 18.

[112] Newspapers and magazines of the period frequently referred to African labor in the British Caribbean as an "experiment." See *The Economist*, January 15, 1848, in *The Economist Weekly Commercial Times, Bankers Gazette, and Railway Monitor*, vol. 6 (London: Economist Office, 1848), 60.

[113] Philip Curtin, "'The White Man's Grave': Image and Reality, 1780–1850." *Journal of British Studies* 1, no. 1 (1961): 94–110.

[114] Ibid., 94–110.

[115] Stephen D. Behrendt, "Crew Mortality in the Transatlantic Slave Trade in the Eighteenth Century," *Slavery & Abolition* 18, no. 1 (1997): 49–71.

[116] Alexander Bryson, *Report on the Climate and Principle of Diseases of the African Station* (London: William Clowes and Sons, 1847), 177.

[117] Alexander Falconbridge, *An Account of the Slave Trade on the Coast of Africa*, 2nd ed. (London: James Phillips, 1788), 63.

teenth century that Europeans could serve on ships in West Africa more efficiently.[118]

Further support can be found by looking at trans-Atlantic shipping figures, which reveal that the Windward Coast (which included the region known as the Kru Coast) was the second lowest region exporting enslaved Africans with approximately 230,000 between 1500 and 1880 in the British legal and illegal eras of trans-Atlantic slave trading.[119] Low figures may point to the lack of natural harbors, perilous surf, and rocky sub-sea terrain that made for difficult ship landings and anchorage in the region. Because Europeans could not easily transport commodities from ship to shore nor bring goods and enslaved captives to the ships, they came to rely on the Kru as their workers in trade.[120] Hence, the Kru Coast was a region where Europeans could buy provisions as well as hire workers for their voyages along the West African coast. For their part, the Kru could take advantage of the opportunity to work on ships for wages. These trans-Atlantic statistics, which are numerically low when compared with other slaving regions in West Africa and West Central Africa in the same period, suggest that the natural environment played a crucial role in positioning the Kru as workers and traders with the British in the early stages of their trading relationship.

Analyzing the Kru calls for a rethinking of diaspora and notions of race in the Atlantic world. The Kru engaged in a different kind of diaspora built on free wage labor contracts and circulated between British ports maintaining and evolving their culture through the establishment of Krutowns and community settlements. A crucial component of Paul Gilroy's argument in *Black Atlantic* is that diaspora communities originated in slavery, which, in turn, shaped transnational black identity. As such, Gilroy suggests that African diaspora communities collectively created "a counterculture of modernity."[121] Gilroy's focus on the impact of slavery raises interesting questions as to whether the migration of the

---

118 For a full discussion on European mortality rates due to disease in West Africa see Curtin, "White Man's Grave," 94–110; Philip Curtin, *Death by Migration: Europe's Encounter with the Tropical World in the Nineteenth Century* (Cambridge: Cambridge University Press, 1989); Philip Curtin, "The End of the 'White Man's Grave'? Nineteenth Century Mortality," *Journal of Interdisciplinary History* 21, no. 1 (Summer 1990): 63–88.
119 See Trans-Atlantic Slave Trade Database at http://www.slavevoyages.org.
120 Francis Bacon, "Cape Palmas and the Mena, or Kroomen," *The Journal of the Royal Geographical Society of London* 12 (1842): 199. The role of the natural environment informing socio-economic activity has been explored by Gutkind, "Trade and Labor," 25–49; Gutkind, Cohen, and Copans, *African Labor*, 1–10; Harms, *Games*, 1–10.
121 Paul Gilroy, *The Black Atlantic: Modernity and Double Consciousness* (New York: Verso, 1993), 25–26, 218.

Kru, as free laborers in an era of both slavery and emancipation, can inform Gilroy's insights on modernity, "double consciousness", and the meaning of blackness in the nineteenth century Atlantic world.[122] The complex nature of the Kru case reveals the limitations of Paul Gilroy's "Black Atlantic" framework, which needs to be expanded in order to contemplate the social, economic, and political dimensions of other black experiences in the Atlantic. In short, both systems of slavery and free labor must be considered in the project of constructing black identity in the Atlantic world.

By the close of the nineteenth century, the Kru economy in Liberia was in a state of decline. Walter Rodney's position that Europeans undermined African societies economically and politically through the creation of colonies, while having merit, is incomplete.[123] The Kru story adds a complex layer demonstrated through the case of Americo-Liberian settlers who played a major role in the colonization process in Liberia. As indigenous Africans, Kru were perceived by Americo-Liberians as uncivilized savages who were not included in Liberian settler society unless they converted to Christianity and thus became "civilized."[124] While it is important to recognize that the ACS inaugurated the colonization process and funded the settlers, it is equally as important to understand the ways the Liberian state continued to marginalize the Kru through regulation, taxation, and the acquisition of land, all of which led to a series of military conflicts by the mid-nineteenth century. The wider processes of European colonization and global capitalism framed the Kru's socio-economic experience on British contracts. Yet, the Kru experienced a unique form of settler colonization distinct from any other region of Africa in the nineteenth century.

Tracing Surfboats

Tracing the Kru free wage labor diaspora means following the water trails of their surfboats through time. Thus, the chapters in this book follow the evolution of their diaspora with a chronology that bears the markers of continuity and transformation emblematic of each stage. In Chapter 1, the role of the surfboat in Kru communities is analyzed as the enabler of the Kru free wage labor dia-

---

122 Ibid., 25–26, 218.
123 Walter Rodney, *How Europe Underdeveloped Africa* (Washington: Howard University Press, 1972), 115–142, 231–319.
124 Yekutiel Gershoni, *Black Colonialism. Americo-Liberian Scramble for the Hinterland* (Boulder: Westview Press, 1985), 1–10; Charles Henry Huberich, *The Political and Legislative History of Liberia*, 2 vols. (New York: Central Books, 1947), 2: 724; Fraenkel, *Tribe*, 13.

spora. Surfboats, shared language, the Kru mark, headmen, gender roles, shipboard labor, and naming practices provide the framework for studying their diaspora as it emerged from their villages. Two of the earliest known images of the Kru reveal that they crafted a unique identity as traders, boatmen, and laborers in their villages, on European ships and in workplaces along the West African coast prior to the nineteenth century. The chapter establishes their villages as the homeland in their free wage labor diaspora that followed.

Chapter 2 investigates the presence of Kru in Freetown, Sierra Leone after 1792. Krutown effectively became their first diaspora community and created a space for new meanings in the role of headmen, the Kru mark, age-set system, and the role of women to emerge. Royal Navy wage lists published in 1819 – 1820 allow for an assessment of the number of Kru serving on Royal Navy ships and their pay rates. By the late 1820s, at least, Freetown became the main hub of Kru employment on British vessels and provided the opportunity for their diaspora to rapidly expand throughout the Atlantic. Most significantly, employment in Freetown resulted in the crystallization of Kru identity and their homeland, known thereafter as the Kru Coast, from the perspective of British employers and Kru-speaking peoples alike. While most Kru laborers were contracted from the Proper Kru region between the Cestos and Grand Cess Rivers, Grebo and Bassa laborers, both Kru-speaking peoples, migrated from the adjacent regions and were simply categorized as Kru upon arrival in Freetown by British officials. While Proper Kru self-identified as Kru, an unprecedented hybrid Grebo-Kru and Bassa-Kru identity emerged in the context of Freetown based on common language, similar occupations, and place of residence in Krutown. While all Kru-speaking communities in the homeland maintained their distinct identities, Freetown served as a melting pot where Grebo and Bassa workers accepted the label "Kru" out of convenience, which carried a positive reputation in the nineteenth century and ensured access to contracts. While it is important to recognize that the label "Kru" or "Kroomen" was not in regular use by the British or other Europeans until the 1790s after they engaged in contractual labor in Freetown, the roots of Kru identity for one segment of Kru-speaking peoples in the region between the Cestos and Grand Cess Rivers can be traced to at least the sixteenth century.

Chapter 3 investigates the Kru diaspora communities that developed in Cape Coast, Ascension Island, Fernando Po, and Simon's Town, South Africa, as a result of their service in the Royal Navy. While some Kru continued to work on slave ships in the Cuban slave trade in the nineteenth century, increasingly, Kru labor was instrumental in the suppression of the trans-Atlantic slave trades in pursuit of Cuban, French, and Brazilian slave ships. Population figures are examined in order to reveal the size of Kru communities in Ascension Island and

Fernando Po. Kru gravestones enable an analysis of the demographics of their community in Simon's Town. As in the Atlantic, Kru were hired on Royal Navy ships in the Indian Ocean to assist in the suppression of the slave trade, particularly between 1862 and 1881, by intercepting slave *dhows*. Kru operated out of Simon's Town in South Africa, Zanzibar, the Seychelles, Aden, Basra, Bombay, and Trincomalee. In the Indian Ocean, their diaspora network was founded on the decks of Royal Navy ships as no diaspora communities were established shoreside. Rather, Royal Navy ships became cultural spaces where Kru were able to evolve their seaborne practices first developed in their homeland on the Kru Coast. However, gravestones provide physical evidence of their lasting presence in Zanzibar, a major depot for resupplying ships and delivering recaptives. The chapter closes by reflecting on the socio-economic relationship between diaspora communities, ships, and homeland on the Kru Coast as traditional power structures between *krogba*, headmen, and women increasingly adjusted in response to migratory labor.

Chapter 4 examines Kru labor in the context of the British Navy, Army, and Merchant Marine. Between the 1820s through the 1880s, Kru served in British expeditions of exploration and diplomatic and military campaigns in several parts of Africa and Asia. The British depended on the Kru as boatmen, pilots, porters, and collectors of water and wood. Kru service in various expeditions is analyzed including Hugh Clapperton's second expedition to the Sokoto Caliphate (1825–1827), the series of Niger River expeditions led by Richard and John Lander (1830), Macgregor Laird, Richard Lander, and R.A.K. Oldfield (1832–1833), William Allen, Henry Dundas Trotter, and Bird Allen (1841–1842), and William Balfour Baikie (1854), and David Livingstone's Zambezi Expedition (1858–1864). The expeditions paved the way for Britain's increased involvement in the Niger Delta as palm oil production soared from the 1850s. As a result of their service in these expeditions and the palm oil industry in the Niger Delta, Kru established diaspora communities in Bonny and Calabar. During the same period, Kru were involved in military campaigns in Asia and Africa, including the First Opium War (1839–1842), the occupation of Lagos (1851–1852), the campaign against Asante (1873–1874), the Anglo-Zulu War (1879), and the Sudan Campaign (1884–1885). Rather than forming permanent labor communities through their involvement in these military campaigns, Kru expanded their labor network as they sailed between ports and enlisted for specific campaigns without further establishing settlements. The exception was Lagos, where a sizeable Kru diaspora community developed in tandem with an increase in harbor work and infrastructural projects following British occupation. Kru participation in exploratory and military campaigns not only points to the diverse nature of their labor experience but also raises questions about the nature of empire and race in the nineteenth century.

Chapter 5 analyzes the Kru diaspora in the British Caribbean from the early 1840s through the 1890s. The nature of Kru contracts and their laboring activities on estates, wharves, and canals in Jamaica, Trinidad, and British Guiana are examined. Estate records listing Kru workers' lodgings, occupation, wages, and names are analyzed. The socio-economic impact of purchasing land, the decline of headmen and traditional channels of gift-giving, the establishment of Krooman's Village in Trinidad and the Kru community in Canal No. 1 in British Guiana, and intermarriage with Creoles illuminate some of the greatest transformations in their communities. These factors prevented their regular return to the Kru Coast and limited the development of diaspora communities in the Caribbean between 1841 and 1900, thereby altering the pattern of Kru diaspora formation.

Chapter 6 examines the social, economic, and political relationship between the Kru and the colony of Liberia between 1822 and 1846, and the Republic of Liberia between 1847 and 1900. The relationship between the Kru and Liberia was a determining factor in the pattern of Kru migration from the middle of the nineteenth century onward. Analysis of the laws affecting the Kru diaspora community in Monrovia reveal the extent of Liberian attempts to control and profit from Kru labor. Following statehood, Port of Entry Laws were legislated, which imposed a tax on Kru labor. In attempting to evade taxation, Kru migration to their diaspora communities in West Africa increased. The chapter investigates Liberian state measures that fostered competition between the British and French in their attempt to assert greater social, economic, and political control in the region. As a result, some Kru were inclined to remain in Freetown or accept French contracts in Libreville beyond Liberian authority. Kru who remained in their communities on the Kru Coast were subjected to state-sanctioned land acquisition. Legislation impeded the authority of the *krogba* and headmen and, by the 1870s, led to a shift in the Kru economy away from shipping contracts towards increased palm oil production. Equally disruptive was the state strategy to support Christian missions on the Kru Coast, which resulted in increased conversion to Christianity amongst the Kru. The chapter closes by suggesting Liberian policies created a labor drain on the Kru Coast while increasing economic opportunities in Kru diaspora communities in the later decades of the nineteenth century.

What has emerged thus far is a fragmented history of the Kru. This book offers a comprehensive diaspora framework for the analysis of the migration of Kru workers in the Atlantic, Indian, and Pacific Oceans. Their service in commercial and military contexts which represents a movement of free wage labor transformed the Kru Coast into a homeland that nurtured a diaspora and staffed a vast network of workplaces. As the Kru formed permanent and transient working communities, they underwent several phases of social, political, and economic innovation, which ultimately overcame a decline in employment in their homeland on the Kru Coast by the end of the nineteenth century by increasing employment in their diaspora

Chapter 1
Surfboats

The heart of the Kru free wage labor diaspora was the surfboat. It provided the means for fishing, subsistence, trade, and travel between communities on the West African coast. The Kru's specialized ability to maneuver surfboats through heavy coastal surf enabled Kru-speaking peoples to trade with Europeans, work on their vessels, and became emblematic of Kru identity at home and abroad. Thomas Ludlam, Governor of Sierra Leone, claimed that when he arrived in Freetown in 1797 it was "a gross absurdity to imagine that a Krooman would do any kind of work unconnected with boats and shipping."[125] From the earliest known image of the Kru first drawn in the seventeenth century to the travel sketches, newspaper drawings, photographs, and postcards in the centuries that followed, the Kru were shown to be intimately connected with their surfboats. Kru oral traditions continue to remember their command of surfboats as the single most important cultural marker that enabled trade and transportation, whether on calm rivers or traversing adverse surf out to sea.[126]

European Contact

The Portuguese were the first Europeans to make contact with the inhabitants of the Malaguetta or Grain Coast between Cape Mount and Cape Palmas, trading in malagueta pepper by the 1460s.[127] A decade later, the Portuguese coasted the shores of what gradually became known as the Ivory Coast trading for ivory before constructing a permanent settlement, São Jorge de Mina, on the Gold Coast in 1482.[128] Based on his voyage, Dutch trader Pieter De Marees published an account in 1602 that included copper plate images of Fante canoemen transporting people, commodities and livestock at El Mina.[129] As Peter Gutkind has shown, Portuguese sources from the period describe the canoemen as a mixture of

---

125 Ludlam, "Account," 48.
126 Chief Davis and Deputy Governor Worjloh spoke of the essential role of surfboats in commerce and social life in Kru communities on the Kru Coast and abroad.
127 Gutkind, "Trade and Labor," 340.
128 Ibid., 340.
129 Pieter De Marees, *Beschryvinghe Ende Histoische Verhael Van Het Gout Koninckrijck Van Gunea Anders de Gout-Custe de Mina Genaemt Liggende In Het Deel Van Africa* (S-Gravenhage: Martinus Nijhoff, 1912), 121, 124–125.

free and unfree laborers and provide insight into the hierarchal social order informing relations between headmen or foremen and regular workers that structured their services.¹³⁰ The canoemen were so vital to operations at El Mina that Portuguese King Manuel I issued the *Ordenações Manuelinas* in 1514, ordinances that regulated labor relations between the canoemen and ship captains through protocol and remuneration.¹³¹

As valuable as the malagueta trade was on the Grain Coast, there is no evidence that the ordinances were applied to boatmen in the Kru region. Unfortunately, no images like those produced by de Marees are known to exist that show the similar function Kru mariners played in transporting people and commodities on their surfboats for the period. Rather, only fragmentary Portuguese and later British, Dutch, German, and French accounts attest to their presence. However, the references are telling as to the nature of their surfboats, crews, mariner activities and items of trade, which offer a glimpse of Kru-speaking communities on the Grain Coast.

Some of the earliest European accounts of the region by fifteenth-century explorer Pedro de Sintra and sixteenth-century cartographer Duarte Pacheco Pereira suggest that the Kru's ancestors were fishermen when the Portuguese began trading in the region.¹³² Their descriptions of the construction of local surfboats, the inhabitants' masterful navigation of challenging surf, fishing several leagues out at sea, and a trading process, which included transporting commodities by paddling surfboats between shore and ship, closely resemble Kru practice in the centuries that followed.¹³³ In 1508, Duarte Pacheco Pereira commented on the adept skills of local African fisherman at Rock Cess and the distinct shape of their surfboats: "The negroes of this coast… are great fishermen and go two or three leagues out to sea to fish, in canoes which, in shape, are like weavers' shuttles."¹³⁴

---

130 Peter C.W. Gutkind, "The Canoemen of the Gold Coast (Ghana): A Survey and an Exploration in Precolonial African Labour History (Les piroguiers de la Côte de l' Or (Ghana): enquête et recherche d' histoire du travail en Afrique précoloniale)," *Cahiers d' Études Africaines* 29, no. 115–116 (1989), 345.
131 Gutkind, "Canoemen," 344. While Gutkind refers to the laborers as canoemen, I refer to Kru watercraft as surfboats, which according to the Dictionary of Nautical Words and Terms were designed specifically with the purpose of traversing ocean surf. In order to access ocean waters for fishing, trade, and travel, the Kru designed boats specifically for the purpose of mastering challenging surf that otherwise prohibited voyages. See C.W.T. Layton, *Dictionary of Nautical Words and Terms*, rev. Reverend G.W. Miller, 4th ed. (Glasgow: Brown, Son & Ferguson, 1994), 343.
132 de Sintra, *Voyages*, 83–84; Pereira, *Esmeraldo*, 110.
133 Ibid., 83–84; Ibid., 110.
134 Ibid., 110.

Later in the sixteenth century, English captain James Welsh described seafarers from the region south of the Cestos River approaching his vessel in groups of three paddlers: "at afternoone there came a boate frome the shoare with 3. Negroes from a place (as they say) called Tabanoo."[135] Although surfboats containing three paddlers were most frequently observed in the centuries preceding the nineteenth century, there were also single-manned boats, which may have lent themselves to calmer river waters or may have been used strictly for the purpose of fishing rather than carrying large quantities of trading goods between ship and shore and vice versa. Kru oral traditions support a range of sizes of surfboats for fishing and trading with a varying number of occupants depending on the circumstance.[136]

Based on his voyages to the Cestos River in the seventeenth century, Jean Barbot published a drawing of what is most probably Kru-speaking peoples in their surfboats, which is their first known depiction.[137] The Cestos River marks the traditional boundary of the Proper Kru to the east and Bassa peoples to the west, both of whom spoke Kru and used their watercraft to trade with Europeans. Moreover, Kru oral traditions and European accounts suggest that Kru were firmly established traders in the region prior to the late-seventeenth century.[138] Although Barbot's sketch was most probably created in 1688 and published in 1732 (Figure 1.1[139]), more than two centuries after Pereira's account, the design of the craft maintained its "weavers' shuttle" appearance.[140] The image depicts three paddlers in a single vessel and the accompanying oar used for paddling. Although the Kru often paddled their vessels individually, the number of paddlers in this image is significant because it reveals that paddling could be a team activity that required more than one paddler in order to traverse heavy surf when going out to sea with heavy cargo or to trade with Europeans. The high-lifting ends of the craft were necessary for progressing through coastal surf and the slightly broader mid-section of the craft used to transport people,

---

135 Welsh, "Voyage," 451.
136 Interview with Deputy Governor Worjloh revealed the varied sizes and purposes of surfboats.
137 Barbot, *Description*, 128–141. Given Kru-speaking peoples had migrated to the region and were already engaged in trade with Europeans for more than a century it seems most accurate to label the individuals as Kru-speaking peoples rather than strictly Kru because they may not have self-identified as Kru.
138 Interviews with Deputy Governor S. Tugbe Worjloh in New Krutown, Monrovia on December 11, 2012 and Doe Smith in Krutown, Freetown on December 13, 2012; Sullivan, "The Kru," 282; Behrens, *Les Kroumen*, 7.
139 The image of the three individuals in the surfboat appears in Barbot's 1688 publication.
140 Ibid., 128–141.

Figure 1.1: Kru surfboat, c. 1732 (via c. 1688).
Source: Barbot, *Description,* Plate F, accompanying p. 128.

commodities, and fish bore the hallmarks of surfboat design.¹⁴¹ The sketch also implicitly suggests that there was a lead paddler who sat at the back, directed the others, kept time and steered, a role which most probably evolved into the Kru headmen on European contracts in the centuries that followed.¹⁴²

Nineteenth-century descriptions and images reveal continuity in Kru surfboat manning and design. In 1859, George Thompson described Kru surfboats: "the canoes are made very thin and light so that two men can pick one up that is sufficiently large to carry them."¹⁴³ The Kru's ability to maneuver the craft individually and in teams would have characterized earlier periods. Paddling through turbulent surf meant that the Kru sat on the bottom of the boats with the exception of the lead paddler, as Thompson noted: "indeed it is very difficult to sit in any other position, in a common Kroo canoe, without turning over. While in them they wear but little clothing."¹⁴⁴ Because of the risk of capsizing and for improved maneuverability, the Kru wore very little clothing while paddling, which could simply be a loincloth. The light weight of the surfboats enabled the Kru to transit between ships and shore with ease and to portage between rivers inland when necessary.¹⁴⁵

---

141 Layton, *Dictionary,* 343.
142 The evolution of the lead paddler to headman is discussed at length below.
143 Thompson, *Palm-Land,* 190.
144 Ibid., 190.
145 For more discussion on Kru surfboat and paddling techniques see William Barry Lord and Thomas Baines, *Shifts and Expedients of Camp Life, Travel and Exploration* (London: Horace Cox, 1871), 134.

Kru constructed their surfboats for fishing and the transport of goods using Bombax wood, which was like teak in terms of firmness and weight. William Allen and Thomas Thomson described the useful nature of Bombax wood in the construction of marine craft on the Niger Expedition of 1841:

> The *Bombacea* [Bombax] are the largest [trees] in Africa, some of them being one hundred and fifty feet from the base of the first branch, while the buttresses by which these immense trees are supported often occupy a circumference of fifty or sixty feet. They are truly the giants of African forests; the wood being very soft and buoyant, is suitable for canoes, but scarcely for any other purpose.[146]

The Bombax tree was essential for the construction of Kru surfboats. Kru dug out single trunks, which Bacon claimed could "carry more bulk than a common ship's long-boat, and can take in two large puncheons side by side."[147] By the nineteenth century, each surfboat typically held between one and 12 paddlers, which meant that commodities and people could be carried from shore to ship speedily.[148] The light wait of smaller craft meant that the Kru frequently brought their mid-sized surfboats aboard European ships for quick transport to shore when needed and for a means of returning to their village following the completion their job.

A sketch in H. Grattan Guinness' 1890 account depicts Kru paddling out in single-manned craft to trade with Europeans (Figure 1.2). Indeed, Kru surfboats provided the foundation for trade with Europeans at all stages of their interaction over the centuries.

Social Organization

Fishing and boating lay at the heart of Kru socio-economic activity in communities, which were patrilineal.[149] Each patrilineage was known as a *panton*.[150] The

---

[146] William Allen and Thomas Richard Heywood Thomson, *Narrative of the Expedition to the River Niger, in 1841*, vol. 2 (London: R. Bentley, 1848), 218.
[147] Bacon, "Cape Palmas," 201.
[148] Rockwell, *Sketches*, 258. See Charles F. Sands, "West African kroomen in surf, 1848." US Brig Porpoise on Anti-slavery cruise. 1848. Naval Historical Center. Photo# NH63104.
[149] All power structures had a male authority figure. See Ludlam, "Account," 45. For scholarship on Kru patrilineal power structures see Fraenkel, "Social Change," 154–172; Tonkin, *Narrating*, 34; Davis, *Ethnohistorical*, 23, 109, 142; Brooks, *Kru Mariner*, 74, 88, 110; Thomas E. Hayden, "Kru Religious Concepts," *Liberian Studies Journal* 7 no. 1 (1976–1977): 13–22; Ibrahim Sundiata, *Brothers and Strangers: Black Zion, Black Slavery, 1914–1940* (Durham: Duke University Press, 2004), 69.

NATIVES OF THE KROO COAST GOING OUT TO MEET A STEAMER FREIGHTED WITH THE WHITE MAN'S "FIRE-WATER."

Figure 1.2: Kru surfboats, c. 1890.
Source: H. Grattan Guinness, *The New World of Central Africa: With a History of the First Christian in the Congo* (London: Hodder and Stoughton, 1890), 148.

eldest member deemed physically and mentally fit known as a *panton nyefue* headed the *panton*.[151] Settlements were generally composed of a number of *panton* each serving as a residential unit. As such, *panton* in various settlements

---

150 The Kru terms presented in this section are based on the research conducted by scholars between the 1950s and 1970s. See Fraenkel, "Social Change," 154–155; Davis, *Ethnohistorical*, 22–26; Brooks, *Kru Mariner*, 74–75.
151 Davis, *Ethnohistorical*, 23.

could also share the same name. Collectively, *panton* sharing political officers based on a collective historical tradition formed a territorial unit known as a *dako*.[152] The highest officer in a *dako* was known as the *krogba* or "father of the town" and he was democratically selected by a group of *panton nyefue*. The process of selecting the *krogba* differed from settlement to settlement. The power of the *krogba* rested on the influence of the *panton nyefue*.[153] The *krogba* was accountable to the body of *panton nyefue* who had selected him, held offices, and tempered his authority.

In 1825, Hugh Clapperton commented on the relationship between the *krogba* and the *panton nyefue:*

> The Government is Monarchial but the advice of the Elders has to be taken before any thing of important can be under taken ~ this authority descends by inherit. if the son is too young the deceesed kings brother is elected ~ if he behaeves ill they depose him – the Elders of the people are the electors – his authority is limited by the elders of the people who form a council.[154]

Clapperton observed that Kru succession was based on a system of inheritance. Despite the monarchical comparison, the *panton nyefue* held the authority to elect whom they saw fit for office should the *krogba* not meet expectations. Werner Korte, Andreas Massing, and Ronald Davis have suggested that Kru agriculturalist settlements generally rotated the *krogba* among various *panton*, in contrast to Kru fishing settlements, which tended to select the *krogba* from a single *panton*.[155] Regardless of the selection process, Kru oral traditions stress the responsibility of the *krogba* to ensure his actions worked for the benefit of the community, which could otherwise lead to his removal.[156]

The *krogba* lived in a compound, located in an isolated area within the vicinity of the *krogba's panton*. The *panton nyefue* had their own building known as a *tugbejia* where town business was conducted and disputes were resolved.[157] The office of the *gbaubi* or *gbo bi* known as the "father of the army" held nearly equal authority as the *krogba* and although the *gbaubi* was a political position formed

---

152 Ibid., 23.
153 Ludlam, "Account," 45.
154 Jamie Bruce Lockhart and Paul E. Lovejoy, eds., *Hugh Clapperton into the Interior of Africa: Records of the Second Expedition, 1825–1827* (Leiden: Brill, 2005), 84.
155 Werner Korte and Andreas Massing, "Institutional Change among the Kru, Liberia- Transformative Response to Change," in *Africana Collecta*, vol. 2, ed. Dieter Oberndorfer (Dusseldorf: Bertelsmann University, 1971): 119–121; Davis, *Ethnohistorical*, 23.
156 Interview with Chief Davis and Deputy Governor Worjloh.
157 Davis, *Ethnohistorical*, 26.

to counterbalance the authority of the *krogba*, it was the younger men who led the soldiers.

Age-sets formed a crucial component that structured Kru societies. Age-sets transcended *panton* lines and consisted of three male groups including children, young adults, and elders. Each age-set required responsibilities and afforded privileges. Initiation into adulthood from *kofa* (young adult) to *gbo* (adult warrior) was accompanied by circumcision and ceremony. The initiation process was called *gbau* or *gbo* and sometimes culminated with the new members of the adult group attacking a nearby village with the purpose of displaying their strength. Behrens suggests the initiation ceremony took one week to complete: "Une initiation d' une semaine, simple entraînement militaire, marquait pour les jeunes gens de 16 à 24 ans le passage à l' âge adulte."[158] The age of initiation varied because the transition to adulthood was based on the physical and mental readiness of each candidate. Males were not recognized as adults until they had completed the ceremony. They were placed under the mentorship of a warrior and expected to fulfil all required duties of protocol, which included working his agricultural land.[159]

The goal of most young Kru was to become prominent warriors, marry wives, and expand their kinship group. One avenue to prominence was in fishing, which earned a living and organized young men bound by age-grade regulations in groups. They worked under a lead paddler who was responsible for the surfboats and their navigation. According to the anthropological research of Guenter Schroeder in the early 1970s,

> ...the majority of the Kroomen were drawn from the age-group of the young men – often called *kofa* – who in traditional society had economic as well as military functions. The age-group of the young men had to work on the farms of the warriors, they exercised certain policing functions within the community, and in war they were auxiliary corps to the *gbo*, the age of the warriors. Most of these young men were directed by a man who belonged to the oldest group within the age group itself or now even to the next higher age-group. He was responsible for the conduct of the group within the town and during the work on the farms but on the other hand he spoke up for their interests.[160]

---

158 Behrens, *Les Kroumen*, 52; see also Fraenkel, "Social Change," 154.
159 Thomas E. Hayden, "A Description of the 1970 Grand Cess Gbo" (unpublished paper, 1972), n.p.; Davis, *Ethnohistorical*, 25.
160 Guenter Schroeder, "Letter to George Brooks," March 31, 1971, 2–3. See Guenter and Dieter Seibel Schroeder, *Ethnographic Survey of Southeastern Liberia: The Liberian Kran and the Sapo* (Newark, Delaware: Liberian Studies Association, 1974). Also see Schroeder and Andreas Massing, "A General Outline of Historical Developments within the Kru Cultural Province" (paper presented at the Second Annual Conference on Social Research in Liberia, Indiana University, April 30-May 2, 1970).

Whether laboring in agriculture or fishing, these units of work and social organization formed the basis for their future employment on European ships.

Membership in secret societies played an important role in some Kru communities. The most commonly documented society on the Kru Coast was *Bo, Boviowah, Sedibo* (a subsect of Bo) or *Gbo*.[161] Neil Carey has suggested that Bo is a sub-group of the Poro secret society, which dominated the interior of this part of West Africa. The supreme Poro bush spirit was honored by wearing a mask and was generally known as *Kwi* and more significantly as *Nyaswa*.[162] In 1856, Wilson observed that there were four classes in the Kru secret society known as *Bo* including the *Gnekbade* (elders), *Sedibo* (soldiers), *Kedibo* (youngest men), and *Deyâbo* (doctors).[163] The *gnekbade* represent the elders who held the most power and from which the *panton nyefue* were the most prominent members tasked with selecting the *krogba*. They served as a senate during the meetings and had two officers including the *bodio* and the *worabanh*. The *bodio* kept fetishes and was a high priest, and the *worabanh* served as the military leader in times of war.[164] The *sedibo* required a payment for membership comprising of a cow.[165] The *ibadio* and *tibawah* were officer roles in this class. The youngest men had little influence and belonged to the *kedibo* class. A fourth class known as the *deyâbo* or doctors formed a separate group.[166] The distinction between the Kru political organization and Bo organization resided in the payment of a cow for membership, which was not required for transition into the warrior status known as *gbau*.[167]

Kru women played a significant role in subsistence, local trade, and enabling trade with Europeans. While Kru fishermen exchanged their fish locally, and in the interior, Kru women grew many types of crops that were used for both subsistence and commerce. Sweet potatoes and plantains formed their subsistence diet while rice and malagueta pepper served the dual function of subsistence for their family units and trading with Europeans. As wives, their duties were to raise children and manage the domestic duties of the household. In 1812,

---

161 Davis, *Ethnohistorical*, 24.
162 Neil Carey, "Comparative Native Terminology of Poro Groups," *Secrecy: The Journal of the Poro Studies Association* 1, no. 1 (2014): 2.
163 Wilson, *Western Africa*, 130. Although John Leighton Wilson described what he perceived to be Kru political structure in the 1856, Ronald Davis has shown that he was in fact observing the organization of Bo; see Davis, *Ethnohistorical*, 24.
164 Wilson, *Western Africa*, 130
165 Ibid., 130.
166 J. Wilson, "Letter from Africa, No.1," *African Repository* 15, no. 16 (1839): 265.
167 Wilson, *Western Africa*, 130.

Ludlam observed "agricultural labour is conducted chiefly by women."[168] Similarly, in 1834, Holman noted that Kru women "perform all the field-work, as well as necessary domestic duties."[169] In 1854, Reverend Connelly observed the role of elderly women:

> The Kroo women–especially those who are old and incapable of other labor–are constantly and industriously engaged in making salt by boiling down sea water; and this is a principal article of trade with the interior tribes.[170]

Although these sources were published in the nineteenth century, it seems probable that Kru women had performed these duties in previous centuries. Written accounts and Kru oral traditions recognize that women's laboring efforts were of paramount importance on the Kru Coast as they produced the agricultural commodities that were traded in local and Atlantic economies with Europeans.[171] Over the course of several centuries, all of the social, economic, and political institutions in Kru societies would be greatly impacted through trade with Europeans.

Transformations on the Coast

Several markers of the Kru diaspora in the nineteenth century trace their origins to trade in previous centuries. The English began trading in the region in the 1550s and they did not establish a lasting presence in West Africa until the seventeenth century in such places as Sierra Leone, the Gambia, and the Gold Coast.[172] The trading process was initiated by Europeans using gunfire, smoke signals, raising a flag on their ship or setting anchor within visible range of a town.[173] The Kru then proceeded to approach the European vessel in a large

---

168 Ludlam, "Account," 43–44.
169 James Holman, "Mr. Holman's Travels," *The Asiatic Journal and Monthly Register for British and Foreign India, China and Australasia* 14 (1834): 64.
170 Connelly, "Report," 40.
171 Interview with Deputy Governor Worjloh revealed that women played a fundamental social and economic role in Kru communities.
172 P.E.H. Hair, "Attitudes to Africans in English Primary Sources on Guinea up to 1650," *History in Africa* 26 (1999), 51.
173 William Durrant, "The Kru Coast, Cape Palmas and the Niger," in *Vacation Tourists and Notes of Travel in 1861*, ed. Francis Galton (London: MacMillan and Company, 1862), 293–294; Paul Barret, *L'Afrique Occidentale: La Nature et l'homme Noir*, vol. 1 (Paris: Chalamel, 1888), 78; Bosman, *New and Accurate*, 486.

fleet of surfboats.[174] In 1555, English Captain William Towerson observed that all trade and transactions were conducted through one lead trader or a lead paddler who guided the surfboat fleet to the European vessel.[175] Europeans indicated the items they wished to trade by reading aloud a list and through visual signals.[176] All business with Europeans was performed by Kru males and the lead trader alone would decide the terms of exchange on the vessels.[177] During his voyage in 1698, William Bosman observed a Kru boatman who boarded his ship near the town of Baffoe with the purpose of trading who supposedly held the rank of "captain", meaning most likely that he was a lead trader or chief.[178] Brooks' exploration of Kru socio-political structures in their homeland and headmen structures in their workplaces led him to conclude that the origins of headmen required further investigation.[179] It seems probable that the origins of the headman (foreman) may be found in the lead trader/lead paddler whose negotiating skills in the sixteenth century mirrored the headman's role in negotiating the terms of wage labor contracts in the nineteenth century.

Trade was not limited to the decks of European vessels. Kru transported European traders and crew to their villages so that trading could commence with the *krogba* of the village. Perhaps, agricultural trade was done on the ships because it was easier to transport commodities through the surf in sizeable quantities with less risk of loss whereas trade in enslaved Africans took place shoreside under the authority of the *krogba* due to higher value and higher risk of financial loss. In any case, the relationship between the lead trader on ships and the *krogba* in the village between the sixteenth and eighteenth centuries resonates with the relationship between the headman and the *krogba* in the nineteenth century. The lead trader and headman alike were responsible for organizing the terms of trade and later contracts, while the *krogba* remained the ultimate

---

174 Hakluyt, *First Voyage*, 184–85; Johann von Lübelfling, "Johann von Lübelfling's Voyage of 1599–1600," in *German Sources for West African History 1599–1669*, ed. Adam Jones (Wiesbaden: Steiner, 1983), 28; Nicolas Villault, *Relation des costes d'Afrique, appellées Guinée: avec la description du pays, moeurs & façons de vivre des habitans, des productions de la terre, & des marchandises qu'on en apporte, avec les remarques historiques sur ces costes* (Paris: Chez Denys Thierry, 1669), 148–149; Ludlam, "Account," 44–45.
175 In 1555, Towerson noted that all transactions were to be completed through one individual. See Hakluyt, *First Voyage*, 184–85.
176 Ibid., 184–185.
177 Ivana Elbl, "The Portuguese Trade with West Africa, 1440–1521" (Ph.D. thesis, University of Toronto, 1986), 599–600.
178 Bosman, *New and Accurate*, 484.
179 Brooks, *Kru Mariner*, 9.

beneficiary governing the whole system as he received a share of all trading revenue, and in the nineteenth century, a cut of all migratory laborer wages.

Kru trade with Europeans was based on an assessment of the value of commodities and labor, which involved payment in-kind with goods.[180] In 1554, English Captain John Lok anchored off the coast seeking to obtain grains and water for his crewmen.[181] A century later, John Ogilby observed that the Kru trading town, Krow (Crou), was a well-known watering spot, where cotton seeds and beads where exchanged for pots of fresh water.[182] Kru traded rice, ivory, palm oil, malagueta pepper and provided ships with plantains, wood, and cassava. In exchange for these items, they received cotton cloth made from East India fabric, tobacco, hats, leather trunks, cowries, English shawls and handkerchiefs, firearms, and bar iron.[183] During his 1693 voyage to the region, Captain Thomas Phillips noted the cost of malagueta pepper: "I bought 1000 weight of it at one iron bar (value in England three shillings and six pence) and a dashy of a knife or two to the broker."[184] Some of the malagueta pepper he purchased was used to feed the enslaved Africans on his ship Hannibal, which was thought to remedy their sick condition and painful stomachs.[185] In 1825, Clapperton noted that "They [Kru] trade in Ivory, Palm oil and Rice in exchange for cotton cloth."[186] Rice, water, and food supplies provided by the Kru proved valuable for European crews on board merchant ships sailing the coast.[187] Kru were recorded as wearing cowrie shells on necklaces, as well as on their arms and ankles, which the lead trader bartered for tobacco, hats, and shirts.[188] Over the centuries, Kru developed a taste for European and American fashions for which they were willing

---

180 Ludlam, "Account," *Sixth Report*, 88–89.
181 John Lok, *The second voyage to Guinea set out by Sir George Barne, Sir John Yorke, Thomas Lok, Anthonie Hickman and Edward Castelin, in the yere 1554. The Captaine whereof was M. John Lok* (London, 1554), 522.
182 John Ogilby, *Africa: being an accurate description of the regions of Egypt, Barbary, Lybia, and Billedulgerid, the land of the Negroes, Guinee, Ethiopia, and the Abyssines, with all the adjacent islands... Collected and translated from most authentick authors... by John Ogilby* (London: T. Johnson, 1670), 470.
183 Ludlam, "Account," 44–45.
184 Thomas Phillips, "Journal," in *Churchill's Collection of Voyages*, vol. 6 (London: n.p., 1746), in *Slave Ships and Slaving with an Introduction by Capt. Ernest H. Pentecost, R.N.R.*, ed. George Francis Dow (1927; repr., Cambridge, MD: Cornell Maritime Press, 1968), 54.
185 Ibid., 54.
186 Bruce Lockhart and Lovejoy, *Hugh Clapperton*, 85.
187 Ludlam, "Account," 43.
188 Manning, "Six Months," 315.

Figure 1.3: Kru currency, ring.
Source: Sketch of a Kru ring by artist Mark Williamson.

to trade one of their most valued forms of currency, cowrie shells, in order to acquire clothing that was perceived as foreign and may have represented status.

A major innovation in Kru communities towards a wage economy was the development of a local currency in the form of circular brass bars known as *tien*, or *dwin* (Figure 1.3).[189] These bars not only held monetary value but also spiritual significance. Kru oral traditions reveal that these items known as *tien* were living objects or water spirits found in lagoons, rivers, and creeks that could be tamed and serve as a protector or guardian.[190] The value of their currency known as "Manilly" was mentioned by Horatio Bridge:

> I have procured some of the country-money. It is more curious than convenient... The "Manilly," worth a dollar and a half, would be a fearful currency to make large payments in, being composed of old brass-kettles melted up and cast in a sand-mould. The weight being from two to four pounds.[191]

Throughout the nineteenth century, the Kru engaged in a multi-currency economy. Depending on the employer, they were paid in manilly or in-kind, meaning

---

[189] William C. Siegmann and Cynthia E. Schmidt, *Rock of the Ancestors: Namoa Koni* (Suakoko: Cuttington University College, 1977), 82.
[190] Siegmann and Schmidt, *Rock*, 82.
[191] Bridge, *Journal*, 106.

in goods valued at a wage rate determined in Pound-sterling, US dollars, and other currencies.

Manilly also known as "manillas" remained a form of currency in the 1890s. Mary Kingsley described the value of the manilla in Kru trade as follows:

> They [the Kru] get paid in manillas, which they can, when they wish, get changed again into merchandise either at the factory or on the trading ship. The manilla is, therefore, a kind of bank for the black trader, a something he can put his wealth into when he wants to store it for a time.[192]

Kru accumulated manillas through trade and the completion of contracts before cashing them out in the form of merchandise. The value of the manilla was maintained by the value of Kru labor on European vessels and in factories.

Before the nineteenth century, bartering and payment in-kind were the basis of trade and seaborne labor between Kru and Europeans on the West African coast. Thereafter, pay lists show that a combination of payment in-kind and monetary wages became the norm for Kru working on British ships.[193] The manilly's heavy weight most certainly made payment in-kind and eventually coins and paper money more desirable and may explain its gradual disappearance as a form of currency. The transition from bartering and payment in-kind to monetary wages had a profound impact on all aspects of Kru society as traditional hierarchal power structures evolved through European trade.

Trade with Europeans led to another significant innovation in naming practices that affected Kru identity. In the eighteenth century, it was common for British merchants to give the *krogbas*' sons English names.[194] The practice of an African trader or leader adopting an English name had been the norm since at least the seventeenth century. In 1698, William Bosman recognized that "the Great or Principal Men hereabouts, assumes an European Name."[195] Based on his 1721 voyage to West Africa, Royal Navy surgeon John Atkins observed that "Tom Freeman" and "Bottle of Beer" were the names given to the sons of the *krogba* on the Grain Coast.[196] While "Tom Freeman" sounded like a typical British name, "Bot-

---

192 Mary Kingsley, *West African Studies*, 3rd ed. (London: Routledge, 2011), 70.
193 See Royal Navy Pay Lists in Chapter 2.
194 During his voyage to West Africa in 1698, William Bosman mentioned African traders named James and Peter. James, presumably the lead trader, boarded his vessel. See Bosman, *New and Accurate*, 484.
195 Bosman, *New and Accurate*, 480.
196 John Atkins, *A Voyage to Guinea, Brasil, and the West-Indies: In His Majesty's Ships, the Swallow and Weymouth. Describing the Several Islands and Settlements, Viz, Madeira, the Canaries, Cape de Verd, Sierraleon, Sesthos, Cape Apollonia, Cabo Corso, and Others on the Guinea*

tle of Beer" was humorous and Africans were often given fanciful names after alcoholic beverages, seafaring terminology or English royalty. Pay lists show that the name "Tom Freeman" became a standardized name that was frequently recorded for Kru serving in the Royal Navy a century later.[197] Hence, some Kru adopted a dual identity whereby they maintained their Kru names and embraced English names when engaged in trade with the British. Whether it was meant to be a playful gesture or condescending from the perspective of British merchants, according to Atkins, the inhabitants took a sense of pride in adopting an English name.[198] Besides creating a favorable rapport between the trading parties, it may also have been understood as a sign of status reinforcing traditional power structures, as only the *krogba* and his sons seem to have been named during the period.[199] Although it remains unknown when the practice of naming began in the region, it was in full swing by the early eighteenth century and would be commonplace by the nineteenth century amongst all Kru serving on British Royal Navy ships.

Slave Trade

The Kru economy became connected with European slave trading, perhaps as early as the late fifteenth century.[200] In the early sixteenth century, Pereira noted that slaves could be obtained from a town southeast of the Cestos River.[201] English involvement in the slave trade on the Grain Coast was minimal in the sixteenth century. P.E.H. Hair has suggested that the majority of the trade between the English and African traders up to 1640 was largely in non-slaving commodities and only thereafter the slave trade gained momentum.[202] The Grain Coast region differed from other slaving regions on the West African

---

Coast; Barbadoes, Jamaica, & c. in the West-Indies. The Colour, Diet, Languages, Habits, Manners, Customs, and Religions of the Respective Natives and Inhabitants. With Remarks on the Gold, Ivory, and Slave-trade; and on the Winds, Tides and Currents of the Several Coasts (London: C. Ward and R. Chandler, 1735), 63–69.
197 See Royal Navy Pay Lists in Chapter 2.
198 Atkins, *Voyage*, 63–69.
199 Ibid., 63–69.
200 Elbl, "Portuguese Trade," 467, 471, 475–476; Toby Green, *The Rise of the Trans-Atlantic Slave Trade in Western Africa, 1300–1589* (Cambridge: Cambridge University Press, 2011), 5.
201 Duarte Pacheco Pereira, *Esmeraldo de Situ Orbis: côte occidentale d'Afrique du sud marocain au Gabon*, trans. and ed. Raymond Mauny (Bissau: Centro de Estudos da Guiné Portuguesa, 1956), 104.
202 Hair, "Attitudes," 53.

coast in terms of the number of enslaved Africans that were traded and the features of the natural environment. In some cases, surfboats carried only three or four enslaved Africans to European vessels and captains used the method of collecting the enslaved at various towns on the coast in order to augment their numbers. Overall, the slave voyages database shows that the region never produced the numbers that were comparable with the Gold Coast, Bight of Benin, Bight of Biafra or Angola. The Kru Coast, which was a part of the region notated as the Windward Coast, was in fact the second lowest slave exporting region in Africa.[203]

The natural environment or what Gutkind deemed the "physiographic features" of the coast played a major role in the limited number of enslaved Africans traded and transported to the Americas from the region and served to position the Kru as trading partners and laborers with Europeans.[204] The role of the natural coast, currents, high surf, winds, and sub-sea terrain all combined to make it difficult for Europeans to anchor and tender to shore. Dr. Francis Bacon's description of the seacoast revealed the navigational challenges:

> The outline of the sea-shore is very irregular, the sandy beach being at intervals of about 5 or 6 miles broken by the sharp rocky points, prolonged occasionally into long reefs, partially visible above the water, which constitute the most formidable among the peculiar perils which the navigator encounters along this fatal coast. Notwithstanding this general conformation of points and bights, there is not one bay or harbour, or even roadstead, offering the least shelter to vessels. This remark may also be extended to the whole coast of Western Guinea, from Cape St. Ann to Cape Formoso. Vessels always anchor in the open sea, at from 1 to 5 miles distance from the land, after carefully ascertaining the quality of the bottom by repeated soundings, generally in from 5 to 25 fathoms. The surf on the beach is everywhere formidable, like that on the river-bars, but the danger to life is comparatively trifling, for though a "*capsize*" is an every-day occurrence, it is seldom difficult to scramble out upon the beach with no worse injury than a complete immersion in sea-water of the comfortable warmth of 86 degrees Fahrenheit. The landing is almost always effected in the light and ingeniously constructed canoes of the natives, as there are few places where a boat would not be stove by the surf. Gales of wind are almost unknown on this coast, though short furious tornadoes are frequent throughout the year, most common, however, in the spring and autumn.[205]

Despite these adverse conditions, which hampered Europeans from tendering ashore, the Kru took advantage of the opportunity to work for Europeans by

---

203 See Trans-Atlantic Slave Trade Database at http://www.slavevoyages.org.
204 Gutkind, "Trade," 25. The role of the natural environment in making landings difficult was recognized by Pietr de Marees in 1602; see de Marees, *Description*, 14.
205 Bacon, "Cape Palmas," 199.

transporting commodities and slaves on surfboats between the ships and shoreside.[206] Their surfboats provided the means to trade with Europeans rather than face mass enslavement and reflect John Thornton's position that trade between Europeans and Africans was built on parity relations prior to the nineteenth century.[207]

Portuguese, Dutch, French, and English maps, traveller accounts, dictionaries, and commerce booklets between the sixteenth and eighteenth century mention Kru communities including Sestre Crou (Settra Kru), Crou, Petit Crou (Little Kru), Grand Crou (Grand Cess), Wapo (Wappo), and Sanguin between the Cestos River and Grand Cess River, Gerowae (Garroway) and Cape Palmas between the Grand Cess River and Cavalla River, and Cavally, Bereby, Tabou, Drouin (Drewin), San Pedro, and Lahou between the Cavalla River and Bandama River as the main slave trading centers on the coast and attest to ongoing interaction.[208] However, not every town appears together on every map. Nicolas Sanson's 1650 map contained the names Sangwin (Sanguin) and Vappa (Wappo). John Ogilby's 1670 production contained a number of Kru trading centers including Sanguin, Crou, and Tabou.[209] He divided the region at the Cavalla River between the Greya Cust (Grain Coast) in the west and the Tand Cust (Tooth or Ivory Coast) in the east. Despite the demarcation, local seafarers in both regions came to be recognized by ship captains and merchants as Kru even while they most certainly self-identified according to their local village and *dako*.[210] A decade later,

---

206 For more discussion on the indigenous economies of Kru sub-groups see Jo Mary Sullivan, "Fishers, Traders and Rebels: The role of the Kabor/Gbeta in the 1915 Kru Coast (Liberia) Revolt" (paper presented to the University of Aberdeen Symposium in Aberdeen, Scotland 1985), 51; Tonkin, "Sasstown's Transformation," 3; Fraenkel, *Tribe*, 77; Monica Schuler, "Kru Emigration to British and French Guiana, 1841–1857," in *Africans in Bondage: Studies in Slavery and the Slave Trade*, ed. Paul E. Lovejoy (Madison: University of Wisconsin Press, 1986), 157.
207 John Thornton, *Africa and Africans in the Making of the Atlantic World, 1400–1800* (Cambridge: Cambridge University Press, 1998), 1–10, 13–42, 43–71.
208 See Towerson, "Voyage," 194; Villault, *Relation*, 146; Ogilby, *Africa*, 414; Bosman, *New and Accurate*, 485; Timothy Childe, *A System of Geography: Or, A New and Accurate Description of the Earth, In All of its Empires, Kingdoms, and States, Part of the Second, Containing the Description of Asia, Africa, and America* (London: Printed for Timothy Childe, 1701), 124; Manoel Pimentel, *Arte de Navegar: Em que se Ensinam as Regras Praticas, E os Modos de Cartear, e de Graduar a Baleftilha por via de Numeros, e Muitos Problemas uteis á Navegaçaõ* (Lisboa: Francisco da Silva, 1746), 249–251; Jacques Savary Des Bruslons, *Dictionnaire Universel de Commerce* (Paris: Jacques Estienne, 1723), 1059; Antoine Augustin Bruzen de La Martinière, *Le Grand Dictionnaire Géographique et Critique* 5 (Paris: Gosse, 1735), 72. See also excerpts from William Towerson's 1555 voyage to the Grain Coast in Johnston, *Liberia*, 1: 64–65.
209 Ogilby and van Meurs, *Africae*.
210 McEvoy, "Understanding," 62–80.

William Berry's 1680 map omitted Sanguin but kept Crou, Taboo (Tabou), and added Grand Setters (Grand Cess).[211] Cartographers who included Grand Cess, Cape Palmas, Tabou, Berbi (Bereby), and Lahou are of particular interest because these were not Proper Kru trading towns, but were inhabited by Grebo (or Glebo) and Bété peoples, all of whom spoke Kru languages.

Within Proper Kru boundaries, Settra Kru and Little Kru remained centers of trade for centuries while towns including Nana Kru, Krobah, and King William's Town (King Weah's Town) do not commonly appear on maps in the region until the nineteenth century.[212] However, these trading towns may have been present but were known by a different name or existed as smaller villages that grew in size, garnering the title of Proper Kru, the perceived heartland of Kru trade in the nineteenth century. The name that consistently appears on maps and in accounts of the region dating to the 1580s is "Crua", more accurately pronounced "Crou".[213] The label was gradually applied to all peoples in the vicinity beyond the original town, thereby expanding the conceptual boundaries of Kru peoples from a European perspective and adding new layers of meaning to Kru-speaking peoples in the region.

Figure 1.4 shows many of the main Kru trading towns that were present in the nineteenth century. Although the region regarded as the Kru homeland is traditionally located between the Cestos and Grand Cess Rivers, the Proper Kru towns are more accurately located between the Sino and Dubo Rivers on the map (Figure 1.4).[214]

Commerce booklets, narratives, and maps demonstrate that the Kru were impacted by European contact. The Kru expanded their traditional economy in fishing, salt, rice, and other agricultural commodities to include the Atlantic economy, which presented a new demand for enslaved Africans. The procurement of enslaved Africans for trade on the coast suggests that some of them came from the interior in Proper Kru region, albeit in small numbers. According to Ludlam, the Kru themselves occasionally kidnapped so-called "Bushmen" from the interior and offered them for sale on the coast, although how common and old

---

211 Berry, *Africa Divided*. His map of Africa was based on Alex-Hubert's 1674 map, which in turn was based on Nicolas Sanson's 1650 map. The name Grand Sesters and its variants not only reference the river, but are frequently accompanied by a circle adjacent to its mouth indicating the town Grand Cess that was a major trading center.
212 Ludlam, "Account," *Sixth Report*, 88; Connelly, "Report," 38–40; Koelle, *Polyglotta*, 4; Wilson, *Western Africa*, 101.
213 Welsh, "Voyage," 451.
214 The map does not include all Proper Kru towns.

52 — Chapter 1: Surfboats

Figure 1.4: Kru Coast.
Source: Sketch of the Kru Coast by artist Mark Williamson.

this practice was remains unclear.[215] It is probable that the Kru developed their own small-scale interior slave trade network in the forests in the hinterland and beyond. They were cut off from the large-scale Juula and Malinke network in the savannah to the north by an impenetrable forest belt, which limited trade.[216] This meant that the enslaved were most likely Krahn, Sapo, Sikon, and possibly other Kru-speaking peoples. The enslaved were acquired in the interior in exchange for gold, firearms, and, later, cowries and East Indian fabrics offered by Kru traders who had frequent contact with Europeans.[217] However, Vos has suggested that the practice of Kru kidnapping other Kru-speaking peoples in the Proper Kru region by way of raiding villages or selling criminals was more common than previously believed by scholarship. He referred to the sizeable presence of Kru-

---

215 Ludlam, "Account," 47.
216 Vos, "Slave Trade," 46.
217 Elbl, "Portuguese Trade," 367, 516; Ludlam, "Account," 43.

speaking enslaved Africans in Dutch Guiana in the later eighteenth century and the fact women and children, who may have been more vulnerable to capture, dominated the market. This may signal that Kru were willing to sell other Kru-speaking peoples beyond their own villages and *dako*.[218] Vos' claim seems probable when considering the competition between villages to attract European trade as well as the tensions that existed between Kru *dako* given the periodic attacks between their autonomous communities that could result in the accumulation of prisoners of war. However, Vos' claim is at odds with Kru oral traditions, which hold that very few Kru were enslaved, signalling the importance of differentiating the Kru community in question.[219]

By comparison, access to the Bandama River at Lahou in the eastern extremity of the Kru Coast ensured that Mandingo peoples were acquired through Sudanese trade networks in the north by way of Guro and Asante polities by river and overland.[220] Baule and Guro warfare may have also augmented the supply as prisoners who were sold.[221] It is important to examine the social, economic, and political dynamics of each section of the Kru Coast when analyzing trade and determining the origins of the enslaved.

Adam Jones published a list of estimates regarding annual enslaved African exports for European ships from various Kru-speaking communities that most probably dates to the 1760s (Table 1.1).[222] The list provides the opportunity to analyze each section of the Kru Coast and identify the degree of engagement with the slave trade. The Bassa region between Cape Mesurado and the Cestos River exported 1,800 enslaved Africans; the Proper Kru between Cestos River and Grand Cess River, 2,150; the Grebo between Grand Cess River and Cavalla River, 800; the Grebo, Bété, Wané, and Neyo between the Cavalla River and Sassandra River, 1,150; and Dida residing between Sassandra River and the Bandama River, 500. The estimates reveal the Proper Kru region produced the most annual exports of all Kru speaking regions. The main hubs were Cape Mesurado in Bassa territory, Cestos River and Krou Sestre in Proper Kru territory, the Cavalla River (which supplied Grebo territory on both sides of the river), Drewin and Rivière S André in Grebo, Bété, Wane and Neyo territory, and Dida territory between

---

218 Vos, "Slave Trade," 46.
219 Interviews with Deputy Governor Worjloh revealed that the Kru considered themselves exempt from enslavement and very few were ever sent to the Americas. It may be that this only applied to Kru-speaking peoples on the coast who traded with Europeans whereas those Kru-speaking peoples in the interior remained enslaveable.
220 Ibid., 45, 51.
221 Ibid., 45.
222 Jones suggests the undated list from the eighteenth century could be from the 1760s.

Table 1.1: Annual slave exports on the Windward Coast (1760s).

Location	Number of Enslaved Exports
Cape de Mounte	300
Petit Cap de Monte	100
Petit Mesurade	100
Rivière S. Paul	200
Cap Mesurade	500
Rio Junko	100
Gran Junko	100
Petit Barsay	100
Grand Barsay	200
Tapequenin	200
Petit Sestre	200
Petit Coulou	200
Grand Coulou	200
Rio de Sestos	500
Petit Sestre	200
Isle Palma	100
Sanguin	200
Bassa	200
Rivière Sino	50
Sestre Krou	200
Krou Sestre	400
Droma	200
Badrou	50
Petit Sestre	200
Gojava	150
Grand Sestre	200
Cap de Palmas	200
Riviere Cavallos	400
Pequenin Drouin	500
Tabo	50
Taho	200
Rivière S André	400
Cassaret	200
Cap Laho	300
Jacques Laho	400
Jacen Jacko	300
Issini	500
Total	8,450

Source: 2 Paris, Arch. Nat., C6i8, "Remarques. Etat en appersu des Esclaves que peuvent retirer les Nations de l' Europe de la Côte Occidentale d' Afrique," in Adam Jones and Marion Johnson, "Slaves from the Windward Coast," *The Journal of African History* 21, no. 1 (1980): 28.

the Sassandra and Bandama Rivers. Based on Esu Biyi's division of the region into Upper Kru between Cape Mesurado and the Cavalla River and the Lower Kru peoples between the Cavalla River and Bandama River, comparative analysis shows that the Upper Kru exported 4,950 and the Lower Kru 2,050 enslaved Africans annually.[223] Hence, the Kru-speaking peoples residing between Cape Mesurado and Cavalla River exported more than double the number in the region between the Cavalla and Bandama Rivers. The larger number of trading towns in the former region may explain the sizeable difference. Besides the turbulent surf on the coast, the forests which limited the number of enslaved Africans that were obtained for sale could explain the low number of exports for the entire region compared with other slaving regions in Africa. The relationship between the Kru and the slave trade, whether it was formal or tacit, seems to have characterized a considerable part of the socio-economic dynamics of the Kru Coast.

In order to ensure that the Kru themselves were not enslaved, Kru oral traditions and written accounts detail a form of scarification known as the Kru mark which was applied to distinguish Kru from other Africans and preserve their freedom. While the earliest known written account referencing the mark dates to 1819, Kru oral traditions tell of the mark emerging in tandem with Portuguese trade.[224] Esu Biyi suggests that the Kru mark developed at least as early as the sixteenth century and became standard practice in the centuries that followed.[225]

The emergence of the "Kru mark," a form of scarification on the face, became an important identifying feature of trade between Kru and Europeans. The Kru mark consisted of a single vertical line in the middle of the forehead or a collection of three to five incisions on the forehead. Charcoal or some other substance was rubbed into each cut so that when it healed it produced a blue or black mark, although the difference in colour seems to have been insignificant.[226] Commodore George R. Collier provided a clear description of the Kru mark in 1819:

---

[223] Biyi, "Kru," 73–74. Note that non-Kru speaking regions have been omitted when analyzing the numbers.
[224] Parliamentary Papers, "Reports from Commodore Sir George Collier concerning the Settlements on the Gold and Windward Coasts of Africa," vol. 12 (1820), 15; interviews with Chief Davis, Smith, and Deputy Governor Worjloh revealed that Kru oral tradition remembers tattooing and scarification as having been practiced since trading with Europeans had been inaugurated and that the purpose of the Kru mark was for protection from enslavement.
[225] Biyi, "Kru," 72.
[226] McAllister, Lone Woman, 142–143. See also Lugenbeel, "Native Africans," 173.

> The face of the Krew man is however always disfigured with a broad black line from the forehead down to the nose, and the barb of an arrow, as thus (→), on each side of the temple. This is so decidedly the Krew mark, that instances have occurred of these men being claimed and redeemed from slavery, only from bearing this characteristic mark of independence…[The Kru mark] is formed by a number of small punctures in the skin, and fixed irremoveably by being rubbed, when newly punctured, with a composition of bruised gunpowder and palm oil.[227]

The Kru mark reinforced kinship relationships and identification. The function of the mark was its importance in recognition. Collier recognized the Kru mark as a form of disfigurement, but he understood that for the Kru, the mark was associated with independence and implied that they were immune from enslavement. Those who had the scarification were able to engage in trading and laboring activities with Europeans without fear of enslavement as the mark served to distinguish the Kru from people of the interior, who were readily enslavable from both Kru and European perspectives.

Ship captain Adolphe Burdo understood the importance of the mark as late as 1880, claiming that the Kru mark was "a sign of their independence," although by then the risk of enslavement had virtually disappeared.[228] As mentioned above, it seems that scarification may well have been a cultural development within Kru society as a direct response to trading with Europeans. It may also be that Kru scarification practices preceded European contact and were adapted to a new system of trade with Europeans.[229] Regardless, the crucial role of the Kru as agents transporting enslaved Africans and commodities in the slave trading era nonetheless ensured that the Kru mark was generally respected by British and other European traders.

T. W. Ramsay provides the earliest known sketch of a Kru mark in 1830 (Figure 1.5). Ramsay's illustration shows a blue line running downwards on the Kruman's forehead onto the bridge of the nose, which extends down to the chin. Another set of blue line incisions run laterally across the temple. His chest also appears to have blue marks around the nipples, although the significance of scarification in this region of the body remains unknown. His hat and umbrella became a symbol of Kru employment with the British as they adopted some European fashion. The fish in his hand reveal the Kru's deep connection with the sea in their homeland and diaspora communities.

---

227 Parliamentary Papers, "Reports from Commodore Sir George Collier concerning the Settlements on the Gold and Windward Coasts of Africa," vol. 12 (1820), 15; see also Brooks, *Kru Mariner*, 34.
228 Burdo, *Niger*, 83.
229 Connelly, "Report," 38.

Figure 1.5: Kru mark, c. 1830.
Source: T. W. Ramsay, *Costumes on the Western Coast of Africa* (np, 1830), 19.

Subsequent sketches reveal the prevalence of the Kru mark. In 1859, George Thompson provides a sketch of a man with a Kru mark alongside illustrations of Kru canoes and rafts. Although the image is grainy in the original, Thompson's illustration shows continuity with Ramsay's sketch, which includes a line running downwards from the Kruman's forehead onto the bridge of the nose and other incisions running laterally across the forehead. Another incision appears on the right cheek.[230]

Similarly, in 1863, Robert Clarke' sketch shows a line running downwards on the forehead towards the nose. Clarke's sketch shows that the Kru mark could be a black line down the forehead. Clarke described the mark as "a black stripe, extending from the forehead along the ridge of the nose."[231] He also referred to incisions "at the outer angle of each eye are similar short horizontal lines."[232] In addition to the Kru mark, some Kru also "tattooed [their bodies] with figures of stars."[233] The significance of the stars is unknown. However, Clapperton suggested that besides the Kru mark on the forehead, Kru were "marked on the tem-

---

230 Thompson, *Palm-Land*, 189.
231 Clarke, "Sketches," 355.
232 Ibid., 355.
233 Ibid., 355.

ples, breasts and arms – but the latter are only ornament [sic]."[234] The mark served to protect the Kru trading on the coast and for those who worked on ships from the seventeenth century and throughout the globe in the nineteenth century it became a marker of the Kru diaspora for those who bore the mark.

It is important, however, to recognize that as the geographical boundaries of the Kru Coast expanded beyond the region associated with the Proper Kru not all of those who spoke or identified as Kru wore the mark. Rather, the practice seems to have only been limited to the Proper Kru and Kru-speaking peoples residing between the Cestos and Grand Cess Rivers. Nineteenth-century accounts and images do not indicate that Bassa, Grebo, Bété, and Dida laborers applied the mark. Therefore, the mark serves to limit the links between Kru laborers in their diaspora and place of origin to specific regions of the Kru Coast with a degree of certainty.

While the Kru continued to trade with European traders along their coast into the nineteenth century, they entered the next phase of their commercial relationship with Europeans by working on ships sailing the West African coast in the seventeenth century, and perhaps earlier. An entry in the "Journal of Sao Jorge da Mina" (Elmina Castle) dated February 6, 1645, mentions the word "Krao" with reference to a crew member on board a docked Spanish ship.[235] Brooks has suggested that this date represents the earliest available example of Kru on board a ship sailing the West African coast.[236] The name suggests connections with the Krao people, the original name of the Kru, or the town known as Crua, which was referenced by Captain James Welsh in 1588.[237]

Kru were not the only Africans serving on European ships sailing the West African coast, but were part of a mixed labor force composed of free laborers, bondsmen, and the enslaved. Ray Costello's study has shown that as early as 1547, Africans served on European ships, as was the case for Jacques Francis, an enslaved African, tasked as a diver in the attempt to salvage King Henry VIII's warship *Mary Rose* off the coast of Mauretania.[238] Kevin Dawson's recent

---

[234] Bruce Lockhart and Lovejoy, *Hugh Clapperton*, 86.
[235] Ratelband, *Vijf Dagregisters*, 11; see Brooks, *Kru Mariner*, 2; Wilson, *Western Africa*, 103. Wilson does not mention the exact date, but suggests that it was the Proper Kru who first worked on European vessels before all other Kru-speaking peoples.
[236] Brooks, *Kru Mariner*, 2.
[237] Welsh, "Voyage," 451.
[238] Costello, *Black Salt*, xx, 3; see also Gustav Ungerer, "Recovering a black African's voice in an English lawsuit: Jacques Francis and the salvage operations of the Mary Rose and the Sancta Maria and Sanctus Edwardus, 1545-ca 1550," *Medieval and Renaissance Drama in England* 17 (2005): 255–271.

study has revealed that many enslaved Africans served as salvage divers whose labor was sought based on their perceived prowess in aquatic environments.[239] During his 1595 voyage, Sir Walter Raleigh kept a personal slave of African-descent aboard his ship while sailing the Caribbean. Although his duties remain unknown, it reveals that enslaved Africans were serving on British ships from at least the sixteenth century.[240] In 1702, the Royal African Company sought two enslaved Africans between the ages of 16 and 20 per ship. They were referred to as "privilege negroes", which meant the captain and upper ranked crewmembers were permitted to own and use the enslaved for duties aboard their ships with the option of selling them during or after the completion of the voyage or keeping them in their private households in England.[241] Abolitionist Olaudah Equiano (Gustavus Vassa) provides some insights into the nature of enslavement on British Navy vessels in the eighteenth century, having served on HMS Roebuck, HMS Savage, HMS Preston, HMS Royal George, and HMS Namur, where he was denied prize money, but was eventually able to save enough funds through private trade to purchase his manumission.[242]

In West Africa, "Grumettas" were frequently mentioned serving on ships and at slave factories. The word "grumetta" derives from the Portuguese word *grumete*, which was rooted in the creolized version of Portuguese spoken in the region of Bissau.[243] *Grumete* was the term applied to an African apprentice seaman serving on Portuguese ships who sometimes appeared to have been free and other times enslaved.[244] In his examination of slave trader Philip Beaver, Billy Smith noted that "most grummettas were Africans, although some were mixed-race Creoles."[245] Smith refers to them as "hired workers" who were employed in groups of several hundred workers under slave traders on the island of Bolama. He later added that "most grumettas" were "working people, hired

---

239 Kevin Dawson, *Undercurrents of Power: Aquatic Culture in the African Diaspora* (Philadelphia: University of Pennsylvania Press, 2018), 61, 89.
240 Sir Walter Raleigh, *The Discovery of Guiana* (1595; repr., London: Cassell, 1887), 77.
241 Costello, *Black Salt*, xx; John Latimer, *The Annals of Bristol in the Eighteenth Century* (London: Butler & Tanner, 1893), 144, 146; Alexander Peter Kup, "Instructions to the Royal African Company's factor at Bunce, 1702," *Sierra Leone Studies*, no. 5 (December 1955), 52.
242 See Paul Lovejoy's website dedicated to Equiano, https://equianosworld.org, accessed June 1, 2020. Also note the author composed "Equiano's Journey" in honor of Equiano for use on the website.
243 Billy G. Smith, *Ship of Death: A Voyage that Changed the Atlantic World* (New Haven: Yale University Press, 2013), xiv, 267, 132 ff.
244 Costello, *Black Salt*, 15.
245 Smith, *Ship*, 132.

temporarily, not unlike many of the colonists who had migrated to Bolama."[246] He used the term "most" because in other instances, references indicate that *grumettas* were often slaves and hence stand in stark contrast to the Kru who were rarely enslaved.

James Searing describes *grumettas* as slaves who were employed on Bunce Island. The slave trading firm owned by Alexander and John Anderson in the 1780s employed them for the purpose of "navigating out craft along the Coast, and in supplying our out-factories with goods, and bringing back the returns to Bance Island."[247] Bruce Mouser has shown that *grumettas* worked at slave factories on Iles de Los and that when they went to Sierra Leone they received "protection."[248] In 1815, Robert Thorpe wrote on the "redemption of the grumettas" in Sierra Leone, where they were liberated from slavery as "indented servant[s]."[249] The words "protection" and "redemption" suggest that *grumettas* were enslaved. Similarly, in 1824, James Stephen identified them as "life-servants" under the heading "Sources of Private Slavery."[250] Stephen suggested that *grumettas* were enslaved to specific individuals. Mouser has shown that it was common for British slave traders to have between 400 and 500 *grumettas* in their service on the Iles de Los.[251]

In contrast, in 1794, Carl Wadstrom referred to them as "free native labourers" in Sierra Leone who were employed on British ships. He described *grumettas* as being paid for their labor while employed on vessels sailing on the coast.[252] He identified them as Bullom when in fact they were more likely Bija-

---

[246] Ibid., 267.
[247] James Searing, *West African Slavery and Atlantic Commerce: The Senegal River Valley, 1700 – 1860* (Cambridge: Cambridge University Press, 1993), 95. See also House of Commons Sessional Papers, vol. 68, 262.
[248] Bruce Mouser, "Shifting the Littoral Frontiers of EurAfrican and African Trade in the Northern Rivers of Sierra Leone, 1794: Opportunities and Challenges from Changing Conditions" (paper presented at Sierra Leone Studies and Liberian Studies Associations Joint Meeting Charleston, South Carolina April 1994), 12.
[249] Robert Thorpe, *A Letter to William Wilberforce, ESq M.P., Vice President of the African Institution* (London: F.C. and J. Rivington, 1815), 7.
[250] James Stephen, *The Slavery of the British West India Colonies Delineated, As it Exists in Both Law and Practice and Compared with the Slavery of Other Countries* (London: Joseph Butterworth and Son, 1824), 362.
[251] Bruce Mouser, "Iles de Los as Bulking Center in the Slave Trade, 1750 – 1800," *Outre-Mers Revue d'histoire* 313 (1996), 86.
[252] Joseph Corry, *Observations Upon the Windward Coast of Africa* (London: G. and W. Nichol, 1807), 9. For a study of the *grumettas* see Searing, *West African Slavery*, 95 and references in note 8; Claude George, *The Rise of British West Africa* (London: Houlston and Sons, 1903); Smith, *Ship*, 132; Bruce Mouser, "Shifting the Littoral Frontiers," 12; David Hancock, *Citizens of the World:*

go.²⁵³ While *grumettas* have been identified as servants, slaves, and free laborers in various regions on the Upper Guinea Coast, they differed from the Kru who were paid for their labor in-kind and in monetary wages by the nineteenth century and most certainly before.²⁵⁴ Moreover, based on their trading relationship on the coast where the British formed a dependency on Kru surfboats in order to trade, working on British ships positioned the Kru as free laborers as compared with the various forms of labor experienced by *grumettas*. The distinction between *grumettas* and Kru was based on where they came from on the African coast, which was a great distance apart and informed by the very different environmental conditions affecting trade between Europeans and their villages.

Despite their differences, there is evidence that in the eighteenth century, Kru may have been categorized as *grumettas* by some merchants regardless of differences in ethnicity, state of freedom, and geographical origins. Those *grumettas* sailing southwards on round trips in the "sloop trade" from Bunce Island to the Windward Coast were most probably Kru based on the fact that Kru villages were engaged in slave trading and they were already serving on European ships sailing the coast during the period.²⁵⁵ Moreover, Kru were shown to be present in the Sierra Leone peninsula as early as 1775 before the founding of Freetown in 1792. Gabriel Bray's 1775 painting (Figure 1.6) is very significant not only because it is most probably the second known image of the Kru, but the first to name them directly in the title using the word "Kroomen".²⁵⁶ The title of the painting, "Three Kroomen of Sierra Leone", reveals that they had carved out a unique persona beyond their homeland shores by the eighteenth century and that they were making trips on British ships between their villages and Sierra Leone by the 1770s.²⁵⁷ However, even though Bray recognized a distinct Kru iden-

---

London Merchants and the Integration of the British Atlantic Community, 1735–1785 (Cambridge: Cambridge University Press, 1995); Brooks, *Kru Mariner*, 3.

253 Carl Bernhard Wadstrom, *An Essay on Colonization, Particularly Applied to the Western Coast of Africa, with some Free Thoughts on Cultivation and Commerce* (London: Wadstrom, 1794), 58, 304.

254 Fante canoemen had been remunerated since the early sixteenth century and there is no reason to believe that this was not the case for Kru seafarers. See Gutkind, "Canoemen," 345.

255 Joseph Opala, "Bunce Island: A British Slave Castle in Sierra Leone, Historical Summary," Appendix in Christopher DeCorse, "Bunce Island Cultural Resource Assessment and Management Plan," Report prepared for the U.S. Embassy in Sierra Leone and Sierra Leone Monuments and Relics Commission (November 2007), 5.

256 Gabriel Bray, "Three Kroomen of Sierra Leone," c. 1775, Bray album, PAJ2038. National Maritime Museum, Greenwich, London, United Kingdom, accessed on April 21, 2017, http://collections.rmg.co.uk/collections/objects/201002.html.

257 Opala, "Bunce Island," 5.

Figure 1.6: Three Kroomen of Sierra Leone, c. 1775.
Source: Gabriel Bray, "Three Kroomen of Sierra Leone," c. 1775, Bray album, PAJ2038, National Maritime Museum, Greenwich, London, United Kingdom. Courtesy of the National Maritime Museum.

tity, it is highly probable that most Bunce Island officials simply never bothered to distinguish Kru from *grumetta* laborers in their accounts.

Once working on European ships, Kru served as interpreters known as "talkmen." They played a crucial role in the bartering and trading process between Europeans and Africans along the coast.[258] Their role as interpreters was to win the confidence of village traders and attract them on board coasting vessels for trading. Captain J.A. Carnes recognized the Kru as valuable traders and claimed "without these people the traffic must be carried on by signs."[259] Since the Kru language was spoken from Cape Mesurado to the Bandama River, the Kru were able to communicate with people in many villages.[260] They frequently brought their own small surfboats on board European vessels for the purpose of carrying messages between vessels, trading posts, and villages. They served

---

258 Brooks, *Kru Mariner*, 13–22.
259 J.A Carnes, *Journal of a Voyage from Boston to the West Coast of Africa; with a full Description of the Manner of Trading with the Natives on the Coast* (Boston: J.P. Jewett and Co., 1852), 86.
260 Ibid., 277–280. Also see George Howland, "Captain George Howland's Voyage to West Africa, 1822–1823," in *New England Merchants in Africa: A History Through Documents, 1802–1865*, eds. Norman Bennett and George E. Brooks (Boston: Boston University Press, 1965), 110.

other functions such as moving cargoes between shoreside and ship and could terminate their services at their leisure before returning home.[261] Their surfboats also provided a means of transportation home following their service.[262] Hiring Kru was economical from the British perspective because they could provide their own means home should the ship not make a return voyage to their village and they were able to fish and eat rice for subsistence at little if any cost to the British beyond their labor.

Sailing between towns on the coast, Kru were instrumental in the spread of a creolized version of English as the lingua franca of trade along the West African coast.[263] Kru were recorded as being able to communicate, even if in a limited manner, in a variety of languages including French, Dutch, and Portuguese.[264] Creolized versions of European languages became the language of commerce in the region and positioned the Kru for increased labor opportunities with the British, other Europeans, and Americans.

Serving on European ships had a direct impact on the evolution of the most significant figure in the Kru free wage labor diaspora: the headman. Shipboard labor necessitated the position of a Kru foreman known as headman, which as shown above was a natural extension of the lead trader or lead paddler who for centuries had conducted shipside trade back on their coast.[265] While approaching a ship for hire, the headman was identifiable by sometimes holding a red rag, which he waived from side to side in order to keep his paddlers' oar strokes in time with one another.[266] The headman negotiated trade, labor terms, recruited and managed the team of workers that was hired for the voyage. Working in a group served the purpose of completing tasks with greater efficiency and provided protection for Kru from enslavement while trading with European ships.

By the nineteenth century, the means of securing employment on European and American vessels on the Kru Coast mirrored the trading process that had characterized earlier periods. Upon arrival of a vessel, a body of surfboats ap-

---

261 Brooks, *Kru Mariner*, 19.
262 Carnes, *Journal*, 141.
263 For an informative discussion of the spread of Pidgin English as a lingua franca in West Africa, see Dalby, *Black*, 1–40.
264 Manning, "Six Months," 326; Bosman, *New and Accurate*, 484.
265 For a discussion on the evolution of lead paddlers and canoemen in the creation of labor class hierarchies see James Hornell, "Kru Canoes of Sierra Leone," *The Mariner's Mirror* 15, issue 3 (1929): 233–237; James Hornell, "String Figures from Sierra Leone, Liberia and Zanzibar," *The Journal of the Royal Anthropological Institute of Great Britain and Ireland* 60 (1930): 81–114; Dawson, *Undercurrents*, 110; Gutkind, "Canoemen," 339–376; Gutkind, "Trade and Labor," 38.
266 Manning, "Six Months," 314.

proached and boarded the ship anchored at sea before the headman negotiated the terms of service.[267] Captain J. Carnes described trade on the Kru Coast as follows, although he used the term "canoe" to refer to the surfboats:

> Having arrived opposite the town, we anchored within three quarters of a mile of the shore, glad of having some prospect of a trade with the natives. Our anchor had hardly reached the bottom before the surface of the water betwixt us and the shore was dotted with canoes in every direction. In a few moments we were nearly surrounded with them, and the native Africans came on board in great numbers fearlessly and as confidingly as children rushing into their mother's arms.[268]

As Carnes verifies, the Kru had clearly established a close relationship with merchant vessels. The diverse roles performed by Kru as traders and interpreters for European and American merchants shows how the Kru were important in commerce. Despite the large volume of Kru boarding the ship, a hierarchal order led by a headman ultimately ensured employment.

The most significant revelation Carnes offers is the practice of Kru headmen presenting what he called a "book" in order to secure employment for his gang of laborers. The "book" was essentially a letter of recommendation that was placed in wooden or tin containers and leather pouches. Carnes detailed the hiring process as follows:

> ...as soon as they [Kroomen] stept upon the deck, presented to our captain their "books," (as they call them) or letters of recommendation which they had received from masters of vessels, in which was specified their qualifications for trading, their good conduct, etc. These men are necessary and absolutely indispensable, on some parts of the coast, as they are generally acquainted with the English language so as to be understood, and therefore valuable as "traders," as through them communications can be easily made and interpreted to the other natives, whereas without these useful people the traffic must be carried on by signs, a much more difficult and tedious business for all concerned. After perusing their "books," or credentials of character, our captain engaged two or three of these kroomen to assist us in our traffic with their sable brethen along these shores. As soon as everything on board was arranged for the transaction of business, a brisk trade was immediately opened....[269]

---

267 A.C.G. Hastings, *The Voyage of the 'Dayspring'* (London: John Lane – The Bodley Head, 1926), 52–54; Frost, *Work*, 39.
268 Carnes, *Journal*, 85–86; Brooks, *Kru Mariner*, 19; see also Barret, *L'Afrique Occidentale*, 69.
269 Carnes, *Journal*, 85–86.

In 1811, Captain Samuel Swan described the book as "a recommendation – any paper with writing on it is called by them a Book."[270] The fact that Kru headmen carried a "book" or letter of recommendation from a previous captain shows that they had experience working with Europeans and Americans on their vessels and that they required a written certificate and some ability to speak English for future employment. Since the headman was responsible for selecting a labor gang, he would have had the first opportunity of employment in this episode. Despite the fact the captain selected only three laborers, they most certainly would have been headmen in rank rather than regular laborers who were on a lower tier of employment opportunities and followed hierarchal protocol.

The practice of presenting books or reference letters continued and eventually all Kru seafarers were required to present their books in order to ensure employment. In 1842, while referring to a headman, Captain Midgley noted: "Each man, on going on board a ship takes a 'book,' or character, and produces it to the captain."[271] While Midgley mentions that every man carried the book by the 1840s, Kru oral traditions suggest that employment was based on a hierarchy of experience with the headman deciding who would accompany him on the voyage prior to presenting the book, a practice maintained into the twentieth century.[272] Yet, for the most part Kru did not learn to read and write in English. The letters were needed simply as proof of previous employment.

While the Kru served on merchant ships since at least the seventeenth century, only sporadic documentation exists prior to the nineteenth century. However, the Kru expanded their service on slave ships well into the nineteenth century, and by the 1830s the Cuban slave trade offered an abundance of employment opportunities. Kru were hired on slave ships that traded to the Rio Pongo, Rio Nunez, and the Gallinas near Cape Mount.[273] The multitude of waterways and rugged terrain in these locations were ideal conditions for loading slave ships,

---

270 Samuel Swan, "Memoranda on the African Trade (1810–1811)," in *Yankee Traders, Old Coasters and African Middlemen: A History of American Legitimate Trade with West Africa in the Nineteenth Century*, Appendix J, ed. George E. Brooks (Boston: Boston University Press, 1970), 318–320.

271 Thomas Midgley, "Report on the Select Committee on the West Coast of Africa Together with Minutes of Evidence Appendix and Index, Part 2," in *Irish University Press Series of British Parliamentary Papers* (Shannon: Irish University Press, 1968), 592. See also Johann Büttikofer, *Travel Sketches from Liberia: Johann Büttikofer's 19th Century*, eds. Henk Dop and Phillip Robinson (Leiden: Brill, 2012), 574.

272 Interviews with Chief Davis and Smith suggest that the headman selected his labor gang or crew well into the twentieth century.

273 Hilary Teage, "The Slave Trade," *African Repository* 12, no. 5 (1836): 158–160; Anonymous, "Slave Trade," *African Repository* 13, no.7 (1837): 224–225.

which sought to avoid detection by British Royal Navy ships tasked with their interception. Kru served as pilots, waterers, and interpreters sailing between slave factories along the coast.[274] Their familiarity with creolized Portuguese and Spanish proved to be a valuable asset for employment in the Cuban and Brazilian slave trades as well as English on American slavers.[275] Some Kru continued to be identified by their Kru mark and were often given fanciful English names associated with seafaring by slavers such as "Main-stay," Cat-head", "Bulls-eye", and "Rope-yarn."[276]

Nineteenth-century slaver narratives reveal the Kru's role in slave factories that were erected on the West African coast. In one case in 1808, the Coralline set sail from Rio to Cape Palmas and hired 40 "Kroomen" (most probably Grebo who spoke Kru) with their surfboats, which they brought aboard the ship before sailing up the coast.[277] The Kru assisted in building makeshift settlements, which included sheds with coverings surrounded by picket fences.[278] One trading center they helped to establish was Rio Basso, which became the staging point for attaining enslaved Africans between Cape Palmas and Rio Gambia.[279] Kru also served as lookouts or spies on the beaches and islands leading to slave trading depots, as was the case when they were employed by Pedro Blanco, an infamous slave trader in the Gallinas, who is believed to have shipped more than 5,000 enslaved Africans annually between 1822 and 1839.[280] They relayed messages of approaching Royal Navy vessels to the lagoon where Blanco's slave factory reside in order avoid detection and interception.[281] However, in

---

274 James Holman, *Travels in Madeira, Sierra Leone, Teneriffe, St Jago, Cape Coast, Fernando Po, Princess Island, Etc., Etc.*, 2nd edition (London: Routledge, 1840), 178–179; Frost, *Work*, 32; FO 84/197, no. 72–73, "Havana: Commissioners Schenley and Madden. Dispatches," July-December 1836, The National Archives, Kew, United Kingdom; Parliamentary Papers; House of Commons and Command, "Havana" vol. 50, (1896), 88; Manning, "Six Months," 326.
275 Manning, "Six Months," 326.
276 Ibid., 326; George Howe, "The Last Slave Ship," 1890, in *Slave Ships and Slaving with an Introduction by Capt. Ernest H. Pentecost, R.N.R.*, ed. George Francis Dow (1927; repr., Cambridge, MD: Cornell Maritime Press, 1968, 352–382: 359).
277 Richard Drake, "Revelations of a Slave Smuggler: being an Autobiography of Capt. Richard Drake, an African Trader for Fifty Years – from 1807 to 1857 [New York, 1860]", in *Slave Ships and Slaving with an Introduction by Capt. Ernest H. Pentecost, R.N.R.*, ed. George Francis Dow (1927; repr., Cambridge, MD: Cornell Maritime Press, 1968), 229.
278 Ibid., 229.
279 Ibid., 229.
280 George Francis Dow, ed., *Slave Ships and Slaving with an Introduction by Capt. Ernest H. Pentecost, R.N.R.* ([1927] The Marine Research Society; Cambridge, MD: Cornell Maritime Press, 1968), 19.
281 Ibid., 19.

1837, Kru were reported by an informant to have simultaneously worked for Cuban slave traders and the Royal Navy in its suppression activities. According to the report, a Kru seafarer alerted the British of the departure of a Cuban slave ship, which enabled Royal Navy ships to intercept it.[282] The Kru seemed to have no moral qualms about being simultaneously employed in the slave trade and its suppression on Royal Navy ships. In 1845, Horatio Bridge reported that the Kru remained "active agents" both in slave factories and on board slave ships.[283] In 1848, Bouët-Willaumez described the Kru's role in transporting the enslaved from factory to ship:

> Les esclaves, une fois vendus aux traitants négriers, sont enfermes par ces derniers dans de vastes cases de paille et de bamboo nommées "barracons", ou les malheureux sont enchaînés et surveillés avec soin; s ices barracons sont des succursales de traite établies dans l'intérieur, ils n'y séjournent pas longtemps; des que leur nombre est suffisant pour former une caravane, ils sont dirigés vers le foyer de traite principal, établi non loin du bord de la mer. Ils partent ainsi sous la garde et la conduit de quelques "barraconners" ou nègres geoliers; ces barraconniers sont le plus souvent des Kroumanes our noirs de la côte de Krou.[284]

Slave factories became the laboring sites where the Kru worked and lived. However, there is no evidence that they established a formal quarter in association with slave factories. The slave trade depended upon quick boarding times for the enslaved at secret locations especially after the British, Americans, and French increased their suppression of the slave trade in the 1840s.[285]

In 1836, the *African Repository* reported that there were approximately 100 slave vessels in operation on the Kru Coast and in the vicinity of Rio Pongo and the Gallinas.[286] Ten of the captured vessels were Cuban slave ships with many more operating in the region.[287] Infamous slave trader Theophilus Canot

---

282 Drake, "Revelations," 229.
283 Bridge, *Journal*, 53; Brooks, *Kru Mariner*, 81, 90; Frost, *Work*, 32.
284 Édouard Bouët-Willaumez, *Commerce et Traite des Noirs aux Côtes Occidentales D'Afrique* (Paris: Imprimerie Nationale, 1848), 194. See also Behrens, *Les Kroumen*, 32.
285 The Anglo-French Agreement in 1845 between the British and French and the Webster-Ashburton Treaty in 1842 ensured that each party would provide a minimum of 25 ships in the Atlantic region off the coast of West Africa in pursuit of intercepting slave ships and delivering the enslaved to such ports as Freetown, Monrovia, and Libreville. See Jean Allain, "The Nineteenth Century Law of the Sea and the British Abolition of the Slave Trade," *British Yearbook of International Law* 78, issue 1 (2007), 375.
286 Teage, "Slave Trade," 158–160; "Auxiliary Societies," *African Repository* 12, no. 8 (1836): 247.
287 Anonymous, "Slave Trade," *African Repository* 13, no. 7 (1837): 224–225.

suggested that Kru were hired for transporting slaves on Cuban ships (he used the term Spanish) in the Rio Pongo.[288] He described the Kru as "amphibious" as a salute to their ability to transport cargoes of human beings from shore to ship in adverse surf conditions.[289]

Kru service was not limited to transporting enslaved Africans on slave ships, as they also served on the trans-Atlantic voyages. Routinely, Cuban ships took in goods in New York before sailing for Havana and having their ships refitted for the purpose of transporting enslaved Africans. In the 1830s, some Kru were observed serving on Cuban slave ships, including the Preciosa. The Royal Navy intercepted the Preciosa and its crew was captured. After the Liberated Africans aboard were disembarked in Belize, Kru sailed on HMS Pincher to Havana. They were asked by British authorities to testify against slave ship Captain Jousiffe in the Admiralty Court in Havana and the Court of Mixed Commission in Freetown, Sierra Leone.[290] The Kru were not punished by the British for their service on slave ships but seem to have been routinely asked to testify against slave ship captains, as was the case with Captain Jousiffe. Perhaps the Kru were not held responsible for the activities of the ship captain. The British clearly adopted a policy that did not disrupt the contractual labor they had developed with the Kru. Even so, the Kru apparently did not provide evidence against Jousiffe. As a result, the Kru were held in Freetown awaiting the judge for the trial, but their fate remains unknown.[291]

The relationship between the Kru and Cuban slave traders was important enough for one *krogba* to send five Kru to work in Havana in 1835.[292] Their goal was to learn "Spanish fashion," meaning Spanish trading practices, mannerisms, and language. The five Kru, who were in fact Bassa who spoke Kru from the region immediately to the northwest of the Cestos River, reportedly served as domestic servants in Don Joaquim Gomez's household.[293] This is the

---

[288] For information on Canot's slave trading operations in the region see Bruce Mouser, "Théophilus Conneau: The Saga of a Tale," *History in Africa* 6 (1979): 97–107.

[289] Theophilus Canot, *Revelations of a Slave Trader; or Twenty Years' Adventures of Captain Canot* (London: Richard Bentley, 1854), 187–189.

[290] FO 84/197, no. 72–73, "Havana: Commissioners Schenley and Madden. Dispatches," July-December 1836, The National Archives, Kew, United Kingdom; Parliamentary Papers; House of Commons and Command, "Havana" vol. 50 (1896), 88.

[291] Parliamentary Papers, Correspondence with the British Commissioners, "Her Majesty's Commissioners to Viscount, 23 September 1837," vol. 50, no. 9 (1838), 5–6.

[292] Naval Database, Cygnet, accessed March 11, 2017, http://www.pbenyon.plus.com/18-1900/C/01243.html.

[293] "M.L. Melville and James Hook to the Earl of Aberdeen, Sierra Leone, August 14, 1844," no. 69, in General Report of the Emigration Commissioners vol. 2, *Correspondence with the British*

only known source that mentions Kru-speaking peoples working on shore in Havana. It seems that any plans for a labor scheme never advanced beyond the Kru serving on ships between the Kru Coast and Havana.

Kru were observed working aboard the Thomas Watson in 1860, a slaver that had sailed from Sandy Hook, United States, to West Africa in order to purchase enslaved Africans before proceeding to Cuba. Kru were tasked with maintaining order amongst enslaved Africans as they were transported from barracoon (factory or building holding the slaves prior to departure) to surfboat before being paddled to the awaiting slave ship for boarding.[294] Once on board, they were often responsible for leading and arranging the enslaved below deck.[295] Kru were divided into gangs and given their own section "to clean and a number of negroes to attend to."[296] Other Kru were stationed on deck to perform manual seaborne labor or "whatever was required of them."[297] During the trans-Atlantic voyage, their duties included feeding the enslaved, maintaining order, especially at night when the risk of mutiny may have been more prevalent, and carrying out physical discipline towards the enslaved as directed by Cuban captains.[298]

Documentation exists that shows Kru served on slave ships between 1808 and 1860, as shown in Table 1.2. The evidence is probably incomplete because only British officials and slavers who decided to allot special mention to the Kru in reports, narratives, and muster lists have survived. Records are limited to those Cuban, British, and American. It is likely that Kru worked on other slave ships as well. With the exceptions of the Coralline in 1808 and Thomas Watson in 1860, the low number of Kru working on the ships may show that they were more frequently engaged shoreside loading enslaved Africans rather than in great numbers on ships. This was most probably because of the illegal nature of the slave trade and the lack of institutionalized contractual labor that characterized their relationship with the British during the same period.

Whether engaged in so-called "legitimate commerce" or the slave trade, the Kru continued to be admired for their prowess as seamen and provided a valuable service as a disciplined workforce. While Kru expanded their slave trading network beyond the Kru Coast to include Rio Pongo, Rio Nunez, the Gallinas,

---

Commissioners at Sierra Leone, Havana, Rio De Janeiro, Surinam, Cape of Good Hope, Jamaica, Loanda, and Boa Vista Relating to the Slave Trade (London: William Clowes and Sons, 1845), 84.
294 Manning, "Six Months," 321.
295 Ibid., 330.
296 Ibid., 327.
297 Ibid., 327. For more information on slave ship crews see Emma Christopher, *Slave Ship Sailors and Their Captive Cargoes, 1730–1807* (2006), 52.
298 Ibid., 326, 330, 332, 339.

Table 1.2: Kru service on slave ships.

Year	Name of Ship	Number of Kru Serving
1808	Coralline	40
1808	Florida	Unknown
1832	Planeta	Unknown
1834	Preciosa	5
1841	L'Antonio	Unknown
1844	Constancia[a]	5
1845	Lady Sale	4
1853	Cameons	Several
1860	Thomas Watson	20

Source: Drake, "Revelations," 229; FO 84/197, no. 72–73, "Havana: Commissioners Schenley and Madden. Dispatches," July-December 1836; House of Commons and Command, "Havana," vol. 50 (1896), 88; Accounts and Papers of the House of Commons, "Minutes of Evidence taken Before the Duke de Broglie," Enclosure 1 in no. 149, vol. 6 (1847), 249; Dow, *Slave Ships*, chapter 16; Abel Stevens and James Floy, eds., *The National Magazine* 3 (1853): 451; Parliamentary Papers, Correspondence with the British Commissioners, "Her Majesty's Commissioners to Viscount, 23 September 1837," vol. 50, no. 9 (1838), 5–6.

[a] *Constancia* was believed to be a slave ship disguised as a commercial ship that was intercepted off the Sherbro River in 1844. There were five Kroomen among her crew. Several Spanish crewmen had previously been penalized for slave trading; see "M.L. Melville and James Hook to the Earl of Aberdeen, Sierra Leone, August 14, 1844," no. 69, in General Report of the Emigration Commissioners vol. 2, *Correspondence with the British Commissioners at Sierra Leone, Havana, Rio De Janeiro, Surinam, Cape of Good Hope, Jamaica, Loanda, and Boa Vista Relating to the Slave Trade* (London: William Clowes and Sons, 1845), 84.

and across the Atlantic to Cuba, they never established lasting diaspora communities in these locations as they did elsewhere in the Atlantic. Kru oral traditions remember their role in slave trading as an unsavory facet of their employment with Europeans and Americans, and reflect more favorably upon their service on Royal Navy ships tasked with abolishing the trans-Atlantic slave trades.[299]

---

[299] Interview with Deputy Governor Worjloh revealed that the Kru acknowledge their role in both legitimate trade and the slave trade.

A distinct Kru identity grew over time in the region between Cape Mesurado and the Bandama River between the fifteenth and nineteenth centuries. Trade with Europeans led to a socio-economic shift in Kru communities towards a wage economy. Kru embraced their roles as tradesmen and interpreters. English naming practices created a dual identity for Kru and reinforced traditional power structures between the *krogba*, his family, and community members. The Kru mark may have surfaced as a response to trade with Europeans as some Kru sought to distinguish themselves from other people who were enslavable. The role of headmen evolved from the organization of the traditional surfboat to facilitate work on European ships. The advantages of hiring the Kru were that they provided cheap labor, they were self-sufficient and capable of procuring their own food including fish and rice, and provided their own transportation back to their villages. Their knowledge of coastal waters meant that they were able to go to villages further along the coast in their surfboats to establish trade ahead of European vessels. Kru played a major role in the spread of creolized English and other European languages as the lingua franca of the coast. The seeds of their diaspora began to grow as the Kru moved from coastal trade to shipborne labor on European vessels sailing the West African coast and beyond. The Kru would soon enter a new phase of employment once the British established a permanent settlement at Freetown in 1792, which initiated the formation of a sizeable diaspora community beyond their homeland.

Chapter 2
Freetown – A Catalyst for Diaspora

The establishment of Freetown in 1792 on the peninsula at the mouth of the Sierra Leone River offered new opportunities for Kru labor, impacted Kru identity and stimulated the growth of their diaspora.[175] While Kru were already working in the Sierra Leone peninsula and were employed on European ships sailing the coast, they were now encouraged to extend their employment in so-called "legitimate" trade with the British to include contracts in Freetown. Surfboats remained at the heart of Kru labor activity in the port as they moved people, commodities, and supplies shipside and shoreside. The opportunity to earn steady wages resulted in the creation of a labor cycle based on migration and homecomings that would structure Kru contracts with the British thereafter.

Founding of Freetown

Inspired by a number of factors including the abolition movement in Britain, abolitionists pushed for the creation of a free society for repatriated Black Loyalists and free black peoples from London in the Sierra Leone peninsula in West Africa.[176] The timing of this initiative was significant as the British slave trade was at its height in the later decades of the eighteenth century. Britain was the premier force driving the Industrial Revolution, whose machinery and markets required raw materials and since the West Indian monopoly over sugar prohibited its importation from all sources other than its plantations, abolishing the slave trade became the target that would liberate other markets and producers of raw materials.

The Abolition Society, whose members and affiliates included William Wilberforce, Granville Sharp, Thomas Clarkson, Olaudah Equiano (Gustavus Vassa), and Ottobah Cugoano (John Stuart) among others, lobbied members of government against the British slave trade based on moral and economic arguments.[177] Influenced by their efforts, in April 1787, London's Black Poor (as many free blacks were labelled) along with British settlers set sail for Sierra

---

175 Ludlam, "Account," 43–55.
176 Black Loyalists fought with the British in the American Revolution and were guaranteed land settlement in Nova Scotia before being relocated to Sierra Leone in 1792.
177 Robin Blackburn, *The Overthrow of Colonial Slavery, 1776–1848* (London: Verso, 1988), 138.

Leone in order to establish Granville Town in the "Province of Freedom."[178] However, the settlement was short-lived as disease, adverse weather conditions, and an attack by local ruler King Jimmy in 1789 led to its destruction.[179]

In 1791, the Sierra Leone Company was established with the role of administering the land in the Sierra Leone peninsula, which had originally been purchased by officials on behalf of the Committee for the Relief of the Black Poor between 1787 and 1788. Prominent abolitionists including William Wilberforce, Granville Sharp, Thomas Clarkson, and John Clarkson were the directors of the Sierra Leone Company. The Colony of Sierra Leone was founded on the ideology that slave trading was prohibited, Africans would be treated as equals with Europeans, and missionaries would educate Africans.[180] Beyond philanthropic concerns, 1,833 shareholders raised £235,000 worth of capital in support of its founding and there was the expectation that the colony would generate income and markets.[181]

Perhaps even more influential for Kru workers was the abolitionist goal of creating an African labor force and market for British commodities. Olaudah Equiano (Gustavus Vassa) and Ottobah Cugoano (John Stuart), two formerly enslaved Africans who became prominent abolitionists in London, offered financial solutions in order to combat economic arguments that were made by apologists regarding the vital importance of the trans-Atlantic slave trade to Britain's economy. Equiano proposed a solution that dealt with the economic void and the demand for an alternative source of revenue that would result from abolition:

> As the inhuman traffic of slavery is now taken into the consideration of the British legislature, I doubt not, if a system of commerce was established in Africa, the demand for manufactures would most rapidly augment, as the native inhabitants would insensibly adopt the British fashions, manners, customs, &c. In proportion to the civilization, so will be the consumption of British manufactures... The wear and tear of a continent, nearly twice as large as Europe, and rich in vegetable and mineral productions, is much easier conceived than calculated... It is trading upon safe grounds. A commercial intercourse with Africa opens an inexhaustible source of wealth to the manufacturing interests of

---

178 Stephen J. Braidwood, *Black Poor and White Philanthropists: London's Blacks and the Foundation of the Sierra Leone Settlement 1786–1791* (Liverpool: University of Liverpool, 1994), 5–128.
179 For a detailed history of the origins of Sierra Leone see Fyfe, *Short History*, 28.
180 For a study on missions and education in Sierra Leone see Katrina Keefer, "Mission Education in Early Sierra Leone, 1793–1820," (Ph.D. dissertation, York University, 2015).
181 Suzanne Schwarz, "'A Just and Honourable Commerce': Abolitionist Experimentation in Sierra Leone in the Late Eighteenth and Early Nineteenth Centuries," (paper presented at The Hakluyt Society Annual Lecture 2013), 8, 16. Magbaily Fyle, *A Nationalist History of Sierra Leone* (Freetown: self-published, 2011), 46.

Great Britain... [therefore]... The abolition of slavery, so diabolical, will give a most rapid extension of manufactures... The manufacturers of this country must and will, in the nature and reason of things, have a full and constant employ, by supplying the African markets.[182]

Sierra Leone was perceived by abolitionists as the perfect location in Africa for the British to experiment with African labor. The British already had a presence in the region through seaborne trade, which included a working relationship with transient seafarers including the Kru. Abolitionists believed Africa had the potential to provide British manufacturers with a massive labor force and a new market double in size compared with Europe, which could produce profits that exceeded the African slave trade.[183] Equiano proposed moral terms with which to conduct business with Africans. By starting a new kind of commercial relationship with Africa based on wage labor contracts, profits had the potential to soar based on low labor costs. Moreover, Equiano proposed that Africans would adopt the fashions of Europe and their demand for products would supply a steady stream of income for the British manufacturers. They would also provide the workforce based on mutually beneficial labor relations similar to those proposed by Ottobah Cugoano.[184] Whether Equiano or Cugoano were aware of Kru laborers or not, based on centuries of trade and service on European ships, the Kru seemed to be the ideal African workers abolitionists had envisioned.

Following its inception in 1792, Kru seafarers entered a diverse laboring port governed by Sierra Leone Company administrators, composed of Nova Scotians (Black Loyalists), the Black Poor (those who had survived the 1789 destruction of Granville Town), and later, Jamaican Maroons (1800).[185] Kru interacted with local Africans including the Temne, Loko, Sherbro, Kissi, Bulom, Mande, and Susu as well as Fulani traders who formed their own trading diaspora, which extended from Freetown to Futa Jalon in the West African interior. Freetown was perhaps the most multicultural and vibrant laboring port in West Africa in the 1790s and first decade of the nineteenth century.

---

182 Equiano, *Interesting Narrative*, 233–234.
183 Ibid., 234.
184 Cugoano, *Thoughts*, 133.
185 For an in-depth discussion of these groups see Christopher Fyfe, *A History of Sierra Leone* (Oxford: Oxford University Press, 1962), 1–80; Magbaily Fyle, *The History of Sierra Leone* (Freetown: Sierra Leone Adult Education Association, 1988), 69.

As discussed above, Kru were present on the Sierra Leone peninsula serving on European ships from at least the 1770s.[186] However, the founding of Freetown offered unprecedented steady employment. On October 1, 1793, soon to be governor of the colony Zachary Macaulay observed the Kru, whom he called "crewmen", arriving from their villages on the Windward Coast on the James and William vessel, which delivered ivory, pepper, and rice.[187] He distinguished the Kru from other Africans whom he considered "indolent", as being "active, athletic and tractable" and noted that 15 of them were to remain in Freetown to potentially be "employed in different craft."[188] Similarly, Dr. Thomas Winterbottom, an English physician, who practiced in Freetown during his stay between 1792 and 1796, described an employment cycle whereby Kru were hired on ships for periods of several months in the capacity of sailors and stevedores who loaded and unloaded cargo in such places as Freetown before returning to their villages.[189] Winterbottom's narrative demonstrates that by the early 1790s, the Kru had established a reputation as sailors and traders with an "industrious" nature.[190] The main differences from their previous employment with the British included that their seafarers were to remain in Freetown on a semi-permanent basis for marine work in the bay. They embarked on round-trip voyages from Freetown in addition to their villages on the Kru Coast. For the first time, they engaged in migratory free labor that was not directly connected with the slave trade.

Kru laborers became crucial to operations in Freetown Bay from the 1790s. Governor Ludlam observed that they dominated marine activities.[191] Similarly, in 1802, William Cobbet recognized their role as seamen tasked with manning

---

186 Christopher Fyfe has suggested that 1793 marks the arrival of Kru laborers in Freetown. See Fyfe, *History*, 78. This date has been widely accepted by scholars as the beginning of Kru employment in Freetown despite the fact Fyfe presented no documented evidence. The earliest known direct references to the Kru in Freetown are by Zachary Macaulay in 1793 and Thomas Winterbottom who described the period between 1792 and 1796. When Winterbottom's description and Macaulay's journal are read in collaboration with John Clarkson's diary entry on 6 November, 1792 in which he provided a description of "free labourers", and the fact that the Kru were present in Sierra Leone since the 1770s as evidenced by Gabriel Bray's 1775 painting, it becomes highly plausible that the Kru began to work for merchants in Freetown from its inception in 1792. See John Clarkson, Governor Clarkson's Diary, "November 6 1792," in *Sierra Leone After A Hundred Years*, ed. Ernest Graham Ingham (London: Seeley, 1894), 146.
187 Suzanne Schwarz, "Zachary Macaulay and the Development of the Sierra Leone Company, 1793–4, Part I: Journal, June-October 1793," *History and Culture* 4 (2000): 67.
188 Ibid., 67.
189 Winterbottom, *Account*, 8–9.
190 Ibid., 9.
191 Ludlam, "Account," 48.

small craft in the bay.[192] Much like they did in their villages, Kru were at the heart of marine operations in the harbor moving commercial goods on their surfboats between ship and shore and vice versa. The Kru also served as woodcutters and gatherers and were heavily involved in the timber trade, which required them to use their surfboats in order to float African teak to awaiting ships for export to Europe.[193]

An increase in the duration of contracts offered by the British between the eighteenth and nineteenth century played a significant role in the development of the Kru free wage labor diaspora in Freetown. Ludlam provided a description on the length of Kru labor contracts in the 1790s:

> When hired by the month, their wages depending on the time they are at work, not upon the work performed… they are fond of task work, or working by the piece; and exert themselves exceedingly when the reward is proportioned to the labour.[194]

Ludlam's description reveals that the Kru worked on a monthly basis, the succession of which usually lasted between six months and 18 months before the Kru returned to their villages.[195] This timeframe represented a longer period than the typical one to three months on merchant ships sailing the West African coast. The Kru community in Freetown was growing and they were more inclined to remain for longer periods that promised steady wages.

Ludlam also reveals that besides receiving a monthly salary, Kru were interested in task work where they could hire themselves for a second job while in Freetown. In 1811, Thomas Coke observed that Kru were employed by settlers as "hewers of wood and drawers of water," that is as common laborers.[196] Their inclination towards a combination of regular wages and task-based labor became the norm as they expanded their diaspora communities to British Gui-

---

192 William Cobbett, "Evidence in Support of the Statement, January to June 1802," in *Cobbett's Annual Register (Political Register)* vol. 1 (London: Cox and Baylis, 1802), 883.
193 For further discussion on the Kru's duties see J.B. Webster, A.A. Boahen, and H.O. Idowu, *The Growth of African Civilisation: The Revolutionary Years. West Africa Since 1800* (London: Longman, 1973), 167; Elizabeth Tonkin, "Creating Kroomen: Ethnic Diversity, Economic Specialism and Changing Demand," in *Africa and the Sea*, edited by J. Stone, 27–47 (Aberdeen: Aberdeen University African Studies Group, 1985), 41.
194 Ludlam, "Account," 48.
195 Ludlam, "Account," *Sixth Report*, 94; Holman, "Mr. Holman's Travels," 64.
196 Thomas Coke, *An Interesting Narrative of a Mission, Sent to Sierra Leone, in Africa: By Methodists, in 1811: to Which is Prefixed, An Account of the Rise, Progress, Disasters, and Present State of that Colony: The Whole Interspersed with a Variety of Remarkable Particulars* (London: Paris & Son, 1812), 44.

ana and Trinidad in the 1840s.[197] The Kru seem to have understood the value of their labor and would only work proportional to their economic reward. John Peterson has suggested that the presence of the Kru workforce in Sierra Leone enabled the Nova Scotians and other early settlers to form a merchant class above the Kru and other African working class.[198] Regardless, Kru were eager to earn wages in Sierra Leone in order to send income back home to their families in Kru settlements.

Kru formed a very small labor force in Freetown before the early nineteenth century. They were estimated at only 15 in 1793, which was insignificant when compared to the number of Nova Scotian settlers, which was 1,190. Within a decade their numbers had only increased to several dozen. William Cobbett's report suggested there were 60 Kru working in Freetown in 1802, although the Colonial Office's "List of Inhabitants of Freetown, 1802" claimed there were 90 Kru. As seen in Table 2.1, the figures show that the Kru population in Freetown gradually grew from a small number in the eighteenth century to a significant number in the early nineteenth century with fluctuating numbers but a steady presence thereafter.[199]

Table 2.1: Population of Freetown.

Year	Total Population	Kru Population
1793	1,125–1,200	15
1800	1,200–1,500	40–50
1801	1,200–1,500	60
1802	1,615	60–90
1809	2,000	800
1811	2,518	601
1816	2,518	700
1817	2,833	650
1818	4,430	505
1819	4,450	749
1820	4,785	615
1822	5,643	947
1826	7,483	1,100
1831	15,210	504
1846	15,000	730
1848	18,190	743

---

197 See Chapter 5.
198 John Peterson, *Province of Freedom: A History of Sierra Leone 1787–1870* (London: Faber and Faber, 1969), 85.
199 Figures between 1812 and 1815 are currently unknown.

Table 2.1: Population of Freetown. *(Continued)*

Year	Total Population	Kru Population
1850	16,679	560
1859	18,035	560
1891	30, 033	1,234
1901	34, 463	1,903
1921	44,142	4,744

Source: William Cobbett, "Evidence in Support," 883; CO 270/8, January 22 – September 6 1802, "List of Inhabitants of Freetown, 1802,"; Barbara Harrell-Bond, *Community Leadership and the Transformation of Freetown, (1801–1976)* (Berlin: De Gruyter Mouton, 1978), 31, 71; Missionary Register for MDCCC XIX Containing the Principal Transactions of the Various Institutions Propagating the Gospel: With Proceedings, at Large, of the Church Missionary Society (London: L.B. Seeley, 1819), 399; Walter Scott, *The Edinburgh Annual Register, For 1825*, 18 (Edinburgh: John Ballantyne and Company, 1826), 47; Kenneth Macaulay, *The Colony of Sierra Leone Vindicated from the Misrepresentations of Mr. Macqueen of Glasgow* (London: Cass, 1826), 17; Farah J. Griffith and Cheryl J. Fish, *Stranger in the Village: Two Centuries of Travel Writing* (Boston: Beacon Press, 1999), 102; Accounts and Paper, Session 1 February-1 August 1849, vol. 34 (1849), 304–305; Michael Banton, *West African City: A Study of Tribal Life in Freetown* (Oxford: Oxford University Press, 1957), 225; David Brewster, *The Edinburgh Encyclopedia* 17 (1832): 274–275; "Census for 1820," *Royal Gazette and Sierra Leone Advertiser* (Saturday July 8, 1820), n.p.; Walter Chapin and David Watson, *The Missionary Gazetteer* (Woodstock: David Watson, 1825), 132; *The Missionary Register for 1817* (London: L.B. Seeley, 1817), 355; James Cleland, *Enumeration of the Inhabitants of the City of Glasgow and County of Lanark. For the Government Census with Population Statistical Tables relative to England and Scotland*, 2nd ed. (Glasgow: John Smith & Son, 1832), 220; Robert Kuczynski, *Demographic Survey of the British Colonial Empire*, vol. 3 (London: Oxford University Press, 1953), 80; Ludlam, "Account," 45; Macaulay, *The Christian Observer*, 756; Samuel Charles Wilks, ed., *The Christian Observer: Conducted by Members of the Established Church, Given by Disciples Divinity House* 18, no. 11 (1819): 859; *A Gazeteer of the World, or Dictionary of Geographical Knowledge, Compiled for the Most Recent Authorities, And Forming a Complete Body of Modern Geography*, vol. 3 (Edinburgh: A. Fullarton & Co., 1859), 465; Reclus, *Universal Geography*, 210; William Fox, *A Brief History of the Wesleyan Missions on the West Coast of Africa* (London: Aylott and Jones, 1851), 193; John MacGregor, *Commercial Statistics: A Digest of the Productive Resources, Commercial Legislation, Custom Tarriffs, of All Nations. Including All British Commercial Treaties with Foreign States*, vol. 5 (London: Whittaker and Company, 1850), 124; Arthur Thomas Porter, "The Development of the Creole Society of Freetown, Sierra Leone" (Ph.D. dissertation, Boston University, 1960), 37

When Cobbett's conservative estimates are compared with Ludlam's figure, then the number of Kru rose from approximately 60 workers in 1802 to 800 workers in 1809. Magbaily Fyle and Christopher Fyfe have suggested that in 1808 the population of the entire Colony of Sierra Leone was 2,000, which would mean that Kru workers played a pivotal role in the colony's economic activities by providing perhaps 40 percent of its total population.[200] By the 1820s, Captain James Holman suggested that the Kru had earned a "decided preference" in Freetown in the role of servants and laborers over their African competitors.[201] This may have stemmed from their willingness to live in Freetown and engage in longer commercial and Royal Navy contracts for periods of between 18 months and three years by the 1820s.[202] Most revealing, the figures show that the Kru population in Freetown experienced significant growth from 1809.[203] The increase was most certainly a result of the opportunity to serve in the British Royal Navy based in Freetown beginning in 1808.

Freetown and British Anti-Slavery Patrols

The transfer of governance from the Sierra Leone Company to the British Crown on January 1, 1808 played a significant role in the growth of the Kru population in Freetown. A combination of delays and irregularities in charter status, the inability to raise sufficient funds, and famine rendered the Company in financial ruin by 1807.[204] Overall, the British government spent £96,516 on the Company and nearly twice as much on expenditures in Freetown.[205]

1808 also marked the year that the Royal Navy began patrolling the Atlantic off the coast of West Africa with the goal of intercepting slave ships following the 1807 decree to abolish British participation in the trans-Atlantic slave trade. Freetown became the central port assigned with British anti-slave trade operations in the Atlantic. Until 1819, it housed the Vice Admiralty Court tasked with adjudicating the fate of slave ship captains and the resettlement of recaptives and, after 1819, the Court of Mixed Commission that fulfilled the same function.

Africans were employed as free laborers on British ships in the 1770s in West Africa, although they had served in various capacities as free and unfree laborers

---

200 Magbaily Fyle, *Historical Dictionary of Sierra Leone* (Lanham: Scarecrow Press, 2006), xviii; Fyfe, *Short History*, 44.
201 Holman, *Travels*, 190–191.
202 Anonymous, *The Monthly Magazine; Or, British Register* 56, no. 390 (1824): 493.
203 Figures between 1812 and 1815 are currently unknown.
204 Alexander Peter Kup, "John Clarkson and the Sierra Leone Company," *The International Journal of African Historical Studies* 5, no. 2 (1972): 212; James W. St. G. Walker, *The Black Loyalists: The Search for a Promised Land in Nova Scotia and Sierra Leone, 1783–1870* (Toronto: University of Toronto Press, 1992), 245–247; Joseph Corry, *Observations*, 6–7.
205 Walker, *Black Loyalists*, 186, 246; Michael J. Turner, "The Limits of Abolition: Government, Saints and the 'African Question', c. 1780–1820," *The English Historical Review* 112, no. 446 (1997): 320–321.

aboard naval and commercial vessels since at least the sixteenth century.²⁰⁶ The Navigation Act of 1651 required that all British ships contain three-fourths British subjects, which kept an open door, even if limited, for the official employment of foreigners.²⁰⁷ In the Caribbean, the impressment of slaves of African descent on Royal Navy ships had been an unofficial practice at the discretion of captains since the early eighteenth century until measures were taken in 1746 to limit the number of impressed seamen.²⁰⁸ In contrast, Costello has suggested that British Royal Navy ships offered free black sailors a sense of protection from enslavement, especially following the Somerset case in 1772 when slavery was effectively outlawed in England.²⁰⁹ Charles Foy has captured the precarious nature of black employment on Royal Navy ships in the eighteenth century by showing that enslaved sailors could obtain their freedom at the captain's discretion, and yet, even free laborers continued to face the constant threat of re-enslavement during voyages.²¹⁰

Shortages in manpower in wartime served as a significant factor in the decision to hire African sailors and affected the rise and fall in the overall number of seamen serving in the Royal Navy.²¹¹ The size of the Royal Navy had risen from 36,000 in 1740 to 140,000 in 1815 before returning to 90,000 in 1817 following the Napoleonic wars.²¹² The need to expand the navy in wartime was reflected in the British practice of gang impressment via the Quota Acts of 1795 and 1796 in which English ports and towns were purged of men taken on board ships to serve in order to meet increased manpower needs in the face of the Revolution-

---

206 Costello, *Black Salt*, 40. Costello analyzed the wage list for the Hawk in 1781 which revealed wages received by Fante seamen from the Gold Coast sailing to Liverpool.
207 Henry Fry, *The History of North Atlantic Steam Navigation: With Some Account of Early Ships and Shipowners* (London: S.L. Martson, 1896), 18.
208 Denver Brunsman, *The Evil Necessity: British Naval Impressment in the Eighteenth-Century Atlantic World* (University of Virginia Press, 2013).
209 Costello, *Black Salt*, 73. For information on the Somerset Case which resulted in the Mansfield Decision see James Walvin, *Black Ivory: A History of Slavery in the British Empire*, 2nd ed. (Oxford: Blackwell Publishers Ltd., 2001), 12, 13 and chronology unpaginated.
210 Charles R. Foy, "The Royal Navy's Employment of Black Mariners and Maritime Workers, 1754–1783," *The International Journal of Maritime History* 28 no.1 (2016): 31; Charles R. Foy, "Britain's Black Tars," in *Britain's Black Past*, ed. Gretchen H. Gerzina (Oxford: Oxford University Press, 2020), 70.
211 Christopher Lloyd, *The Nation and the Navy: A History of Naval Life and Policy* (London: The Cresset Press, 1954), 130.
212 Ibid., 130.

ary Wars with the French.[213] It is highly probable that Kru sailors working in Freetown, possibly Liverpool, and aboard British merchant ships on the coast of West Africa were sought for service on British Royal Navy ships in the eighteenth century, yet records remain scarce. One challenge is that Royal Navy pursers did not begin to officially record the origins of the sailors until 1764, and tended to use general labels such as "African" regardless of their ethnicity, which makes it more challenging to decipher Kru sailors for that period.[214]

However, in the early nineteenth century, Kru were frequently recorded in Royal Navy pay lists, muster lists, and captains' logs. Beginning January 15, 1808, HMS Derwent arrived in Freetown and began its anti-slave trade patrols before being joined by HMS Solebay several months later. By 1811, the count had risen to four ships including HMS Ganymede, Trinculo, Kangaroo, and Amelia. Thereafter, Kru sailors served on Royal Navy ships engaged in intercepting slave ships in the Atlantic. Four Kru sailors named Ben Freeman, Jack Savey, Prince Will, and Ben Coffee are listed as boarding HMS Thais for a four-month voyage as supernumeraries in Sierra Leone on November 19, 1812 before sailing to Ambriz in Angola and disembarking back in Freetown on March 16, 1813.[215] This remains one of the earliest known records of Kru serving in the Royal Navy. Moreover, Freeman's reference letter or "book" has been preserved in the National Maritime Museum in Greenwich. It is actually a powder horn with text carved in ivory, which reads: "BEN FREEMAN, BORN AT, KREW CETRA IS A Sober Honest Man. has SAILED in HM SHIP THAIS from SIERRA LEONE TO AMBRIZ to the SATISFACTION of the OFFICERS."[216] The information contained his place of birth being Krew Cetra on the Kru Coast, his character, destination, and appraisal. His "letter" shows that the Kru were circulating the Atlantic in anti-slaving activities on voyages of at least four months within several years of British suppression. These "books" or letters of reference continued to be used throughout the nineteenth century in order to secure future employment.

Based in Freetown, Kru were highly valued by the Royal Navy for similar reasons they were valued by British commercial merchants, namely for their ability to man and land boats in order to conduct operations smoothly. Kru seamen had an advantage over shoreside workers because of the specialized surfboat skills

---

213 Niklas Frykman, "Seamen on Late Eighteenth-Century European Warships," *International Review of Social History* 54, no. 1 (2009): 69–70; Lloyd, *Nation*, 132; Mark Philip, ed., *The French Revolution and British Popular Politics* (Cambridge: Cambridge University Press, 2004), 107.
214 Vincent Carretta, "Black Seamen and Soldiers," review of *Black Salt: Seafarers of African Descent on British Ships*, by Ray Costello, *Eighteenth-Century Life* 38, no. 3 (Fall, 2014): 150–153.
215 NMM, ZBA 2465.
216 NMM, ZBA 2465.

required to work on Royal Navy contracts.[217] As Schwarz has demonstrated, British anti-slave ship patrols landed between 11,909 and 12,178 individuals between 1808 and 1819.[218] In 1819, the Preventative Squadron, more commonly known as the West Africa Squadron, was created with the specific task of intercepting slave ships along a 2000-mile stretch of the West African coastline.[219] In the same year, a Court of Mixed Commission replaced the Vice Admiralty Court in Freetown, the first in an international system of anti-slave trade courts.[220] Initially, seven Royal Navy ships were sent from England to Freetown to serve in the Preventative Squadron and patrol the Atlantic. Thereafter, the size of the patrol varied from five ships in 1822 to 30 ships on patrol in 1847. Based at the West Coast of Africa Station in Freetown, they sailed between a network of ports from Ascension Island and Fernando Po to St. Helena and the Cape of Good Hope. The squadron operated until 1870 and it is estimated that between 1808 and the 1860s, the squadron captured 1,600 slave ships and delivered more than 213,000 recaptives for resettlement.[221]

Wage rates in the Royal Navy were governed by rank and experience. Table 2.2 shows the variation in pay between Kru headmen and regular crewmembers on HMS Snapper between September 5, and December 31, 1819. There were 12 Kru on board. Their rates of pay were usually £4 8s. 6d. for the total voyage, although several received more, as high as £5 4s. 2d., plus an additional payment in tobac-

---

217 Surgeon Peter Leonard, *Records of a Voyage to the Western Coast of Africa in His Majesty's Ship "Dryad," And of the Service on that Station for the Suppression of the Slave Trade, in the Years 1830, 1831, and 1832* (Edinburgh: William Tait, 1833), 56.
218 Suzanne Schwarz, "Reconstructing the Life Histories of Liberated Africans: Sierra Leone in the Early Nineteenth Century," *History in Africa* 39 (2012): 182.
219 Junius P. Rodriguez, ed., *The Historical Encyclopedia of World Slavery*, vol.1 (Santa Barbara: ABC-Clio), 20–21; David Northrup, "African Mortality in the Suppression of the Slave Trade: The Case of the Bight of Biafra," *Journal of Interdisciplinary History* 9 (1978): 47–64; *The Westminster Review*, vol. 51 (New York: Leonard Scott and Company, 1849), 273.
220 For scholarship on Mixed Commission Courts see Farida Shaikh, "Judicial Diplomacy: British Officials and the Mixed Commission Courts" in *Slavery, Diplomacy and Empire: Britain and the Suppression of the Slave Trade, 1807–1975*, eds., Keith Hamilton and Patrick Salmon (Eastbourne: Sussex Academic Press, 2009), 42–64; Tara Helfman, "The Court of the Vice Admiralty at Sierra Leone and the Abolition of the West African Slave Trade," *The Yale Law Journal* 115, no. 5 (2006): 1132–1134.
221 Stuart A. Notholt, "Sailing Against Slavers," *Soldiers of the Queen* issue 134 (Sept, 2008): 29; Andrew Pearson, "Waterwitch: A Warship, Its Voyage and its Crew in the Era of Anti-Slavery," *Atlantic Studies* 13, no. 1 (2016): 114; David Eltis, "The Volume and Structures of the Transatlantic Slave Trade: A Reassessment," *William and Mary Quarterly* (2001), 58.

Table 2.2: Pay list for Kru, HMS Snapper, September 5 – December 31, 1819.

African Names	Rank	Tobacco	Full Wages	Net Wages
Jack Savage (1)	Ord	3s 8d	£5 4s 2d	£4 8s 2d
Tom Freeman (1)	Sm		£4 8s 6d	£3 18s 8d
Jumbo	Ord		£5 1s 2d	£4 11s 4d
Bottle Beer	Sm	3s 8d	£4 8s 6d	£3 15s 6d
Jack Savage (2)	Ord	3s 2d	£5 1s 2d	£4 8s 2d
Ben Freeman	Sm		£4 8s 6d	£3 18s 8d
Ben Roberts	Sm		£4 8s 6d	£3 18s 8d
Jack Brown	Sm	3s 2d	£4 8s 6d	£3 15s 6d
Ben Coffee	Sm		£4 8s 6d	£3 18s 8d
Tom Freeman (2)	Sm		£4 8s 6d	£3 18s 8d
Big William	Sm	3s 2d	£4 8s 6d	£3 15s 6d
John Freeman	Sm	3s 2d	£4 8s 6d	£3 15s 6d

Source: ADM 30/26 "Muster Lists, Pay List for African Krou employed on board His Majesty's Brig Snapper between the 5th day of September and 31st December 1819," The National Archives, Kew, United Kingdom. "Or" signified Ordinary Seaman, while "Sm" signified Seaman.

co valued as 3s. 8d. in most cases. It seems that their service in the West Africa Squadron paid higher rates than their previous service on HMS Thais in 1812.[222]

On HMS Snapper, a Kru seaman classified as an ordinary seaman (meaning that he had achieved the rank of headman in Kru society and was a headman on the current voyage) named Jack Savage received £5 4s. 2d. (5 pounds, 4 shilling, 2 pence) full wages, while Jumbo, also ranked an ordinary seaman, received £5 1s. 2d. The slight difference in wage rates may suggest that Jack was the second headman on the voyage. Different pay for those Krumen with the same rank suggests that those with more sea experience were paid more than those who had accumulated less sea time. Full wages refers to the total wages earned for the duration of the contract over a three-month period. "Nett Wages" refers to deductions that were made for any expenses the Kru incurred using tobacco or other consumables. Not all consumables are listed in the muster list for every crewmember, yet they would have incurred some expenses as evidenced by the difference in full and net wages.

When compared with the previous table, Table 2.3 illustrates that wage rates could differ from ship to ship. In 1819, Kru headman Tom Freeman on HMS Morgiana received a rate of £5 5s. 6d., while regular Kru seamen received £4

---

222 NMM, ZBA 2465.

12s. 3d. However, John Peter, also a headman, received a salary of £5 10s. 6d., which may indicate that he had more experience at sea than Freeman. HMS Morgiana had a crew of 24 Krumen, more than double the number of Kru on board HMS Snapper. The ability to work on a variety of Royal Navy ships over a three-year contractual period represented a new model of employment for Kru seamen who had typically served between six and 18-month contracts on commercial ships and ashore in Freetown (see Appendix A for a list of Kru seamen serving on Royal Navy Ships in 1819 and 1820).[223] The longer term at sea may be attributed to the considerable distances of voyages and the irregular frequency of intercepting slave ships.

Naming practices first developed through trade in Kru villages evolved on Royal Navy ships. While headmen, the *krogba*, and his family members were initially distinguished from other inhabitants by virtue of their English names in their villages as discussed above, the use of English names on ships became standard practice for all Kru seamen in the nineteenth century. It appears that the names of Kru sailors were initially assigned to them by Royal Navy captains. In 1833, a list of English names and corresponding Kru names was compiled and featured in *The Monthly Review*. The recommended English name was listed next to the Kru name as follows: Jack Ropeyarn/Namboe, Jack Fryingpan/Tabooa, Great Tom/Yiepam, Peas Soup/Woorawa, Will Centipede/Blattoo, Jack Neverfear/Nieca, Jack Toggle/ Niepa, Tom Seedy/ Ba Sidi, Government Packet/Niaie.[224] Presumably their Kru names were the actual names of workers at the time. The function of their English names was to enable smooth communication between British and Kru seamen. Kru oral traditions recall that as the Kru economy became increasingly dependent on British contracts, Kru social status came to be defined by service with the British.[225] The practice of adopting an English name became widespread for all Kru seamen and especially for those Kru who served in the Royal Navy. As English names became common, rank came to distinguish headmen from regular workers in terms of higher pay.

Kru enlisted on Royal Navy ships continued to earn wages that were higher than on commercial contracts. Initially, the captain and crew of Squadron vessels were entitled to prize bounties for every slave ship that was captured. Prize earn-

---

[223] Jane Martin, "Krumen 'Down the Coast'": Liberian Migrants on the West Africa Coast in the 19th and early 20th century," *The International Journal of Historical Studies* 18, no. 3 (1985): 407–408.

[224] See Ralph Griffiths and George Edward Griffiths, eds., "Exposure of the Slave Trade," *The Monthly Review* 1, no.1 (London: G. Henderson, 1833), 26.

[225] Interviews with Chief Davis and Smith indicated that service in the Royal Navy increased status within Kru communities.

Table 2.3: Pay list for Kru, HMS Morgiana, June 1 – October 1, 1819.

African Names	Rank	Full Wages	Net Wages
Tom Freeman (1)	Ord	£5 5s 6d	£5 5s 6d
John Purser	Sm	£4 12s 3d	£4 12s 3d
Half Dollar	Sm	£4 12s 3d	£4 12s 3d
Bottle of Beer	Sm	£4 12s 3d	£4 12s 3d
Jack Wise	Sm	£4 12s 3d	£4 12s 3d
Joe Harris	Sm	£4 12s 3d	£4 12s 3d
Tom Freeman (2)	Sm	£4 12s 3d	£4 12s 3d
Tom Toby	Sm	£4 12s 3d	£4 12s 3d
Jim Freeman	Sm	£4 12s 3d	£4 12s 3d
Tom Freeman (3)	Sm	£4 12s 3d	£4 12s 3d
Tom Peter	Sm	£4 12s 3d	£4 12s 3d
Jack Freeman	Ord	£5 5s 6d	£5 5s 6d
Billy Williams	Sm	£4 12s 3d	£4 12s 3d
Joe Andrews	Sm	£4 12s 3d	£4 12s 3d
Jack Purser	Sm	£4 12s 3d	£4 12s 3d
Jim Rufus	Sm	£4 12s 3d	£4 12s 3d
John Grey	Sm	£4 12s 3d	£4 12s 3d
Hugo Williams	Sm	£4 12s 3d	£4 12s 3d
Jack Boo	Sm	£4 12s 3d	£4 12s 3d
Jack Freeman	Sm	£4 12s 3d	£4 12s 3d
Jack Jim	Sm	£4 12s 3d	£4 12s 3d
Tom Will	Sm	£4 12s 3d	£4 12s 3d
Tom Harris	Sm	£4 12s 3d	£4 12s 3d
John Peter	Ord	£5 10s 6d	£5 10s 6d
Total		£112 18s 9d	£112 18s 9d

ings had been a Royal Navy wartime practice stretching as far back as at least the Seven Years War.[226] The Abolition Act explicitly stated prize values of £40 for a male, £30 for a female, and £10 for a child.[227] The hierarchal and gendered nature of the prizes reflected the value of males, females, and children in the trans-Atlantic slave trades in the first half of the nineteenth century. The practice of receiving prize money was discontinued during the 1840s due to the high rate of slave ship seizure. Had the practice of prize money continued, the amount associated with children might have risen dramatically as children became highly

---

[226] See Equiano, *Interesting Narrative*, 47.
[227] John Raithby, *The Statutes Relating to the Admiralty, Navy, Shipping and Navigation in the United Kingdom from 9 Hen. III. to 3 Geo IV., inclusive with Notes* (London: George Eyre and Andrew Strahan, 1823), 742.

valued in the trans-Atlantic slave trades in the last decades of slave trading between the 1850s and 1870s.[228]

Kru received their share of the prize money based on naval rank. Kru headmen, second Kru headmen, and regular Krumen along with their British counterparts were classed by the Royal Navy as follows: a Kru headman was considered eighth class and he was entitled to two shares of the prize earnings; ninth class second head Kroomen received one and a half shares; eleventh class regular Kroomen received three-fourths of a share.[229] Rank in the Royal Navy was determined by *Regulations and Instructions relating to H.M. service at Sea* first published in 1731.[230] The rank of Ordinary Seamen was applied to those British sailors who had served one year at sea, Able Seamen to those with three years' experience. Comparing the Kru salary with British seamen of similar rank reveals that the difference was not very significant for headmen during their first year of service. In 1807, British Ordinary Seamen were paid £1 5s 6d. per month, which was comparable with Kru headmen who held the rank of Ordinary Seamen.[231] However, regular Kru sailors continued to receive less pay than British sailors of the lowest rank.

Over the course of the nineteenth century, Kru headmen rose in rank to become petty working officers. The Navy List in 1878 indicates that Headmen held the rank of First Class Working Petty Officer and Second Headmen that of Second Class Working Petty Officer.[232] The second Kru headman became more common after the advent of steamships, which led to increased employment on ships engaged in trans-Atlantic voyages between Africa and Europe and the Caribbean based on the belief that the Kru were better suited to labor in the hot conditions in the engine room as firestokers and coal trimmers compared with British seamen.[233]

---

228 For information on changing prices of the enslaved in the eighteenth and nineteenth century see Paul Lovejoy and David Richardson, "Competing Markets for Male and Female Slaves: Prices in the Interior of West Africa, 1780–1850," *The International Journal of African Historical Studies* 28, no. 2 (1995): 261–293; David Geggus, "Sex Ratio, Age and Ethnicity in the Atlantic Slave Trade: Data from French Shipping and Plantation Records," *The Journal of African History* 30, no. 1 (1989): 23–44.
229 Admiralty, *The Navy List* (London: John Murray, 1850), 196–197.
230 Lloyd, *Nation*, 135.
231 Ibid., 138.
232 C.E. Warren, *The Royal Navy List* (London: Witherby & Co., 1878), 256.
233 Diane Frost, "Ethnic Identity, Transience and Settlement: The Kru in Liverpool Since the Late Nineteenth Century," in *Africans in Britain*, ed. D. Killingray (London: Frank Cass & Co., 1994), 88–106.

Kru were paid wages in-kind, meaning that they received goods that were valued based on a British wage rate for the Royal Navy, merchant ships, and commercial labor in Freetown. While contracts stipulated wage rates, both the British and Kru agreed upon their corresponding value in goods. As the nineteenth century progressed, Kru workers routinely received a 10s advance.[234] The advance was used to secure their labor for the period of the contract in Freetown or on ships. The advance was a significant development in the context of Freetown because it showed that the Kru were beginning to understand the market value of their labor, which was a service. While Eric Hobsbawn has commented on the long period it took for English workers in the Industrial Revolution to appreciate the value of their labor based on the principle of market demand versus use-value, it seems the Kru were well aware of the great value placed on their services by the mid-nineteenth century and came to expect an advance before accepting contracts.[235]

Following the completion of the contract, items were carried home to the Kru Coast and traded for iron bars, cattle, and other items of value in Kru society.[236] Other times, the Kru sold their items for cash in Freetown. In 1845, R.G. Butts suggested the Kru received cloth for their labor at a value of £1 4s. per piece, which they then cut into smaller pieces and sold at a price of between 6s. 8d. and 8s. 4d. for cash.[237] However, even by the 1880s and 1890s, it was still more common to convert a cash wage into "marketable items."[238]

One significant distinction affecting working conditions in Freetown and on Royal Navy ships as compared to their villages was that Kru headmen received standardized monthly wages and earned a higher salary from the British based on their managerial skills as shown in Tables 2.2 and 2.3. They also received a portion of pay from each member of their gang.[239] This entrenched the hierarchy first established in Kru villages between headman and workers to an even greater degree and provided an incentive for laborers to aspire to become headmen.

---

234 Smith, *Trade*, 100–103; Anonymous, "Negro Civilization," *Journal of Health and Disease* 2, no. 3 (1847): 259; Frost, *Work*, 26.
235 Eric Hobsbawm, *Labouring Men: Studies in the History of Labour* (London: Weidenfeld and Nicholson, 1964).
236 Smith, *Trade*, 103.
237 Accounts and Papers, "Report of R.G. Butts to the Governor of British Guiana, 13, March 1845," Session 18 November 1847–5 September 1848, vol. 44 (1848), 28.
238 Hugo Zöller, *Das Togoland und die Sklavenküste* (Berlin: Verlag von W. Spemann, 1885), 56; Ernest Graham Ingham, *Sierra Leone After A Hundred Years* (London: Seeley, 1894), 274.
239 Mary Kingsley, *Travels in West Africa* (New York: Macmillan, 1897), 644–655; Raymond Leslie Buell, *The Native Problem in Africa*, vol. 2 (New York: The Macmillan Company, 1928), 774–781; Fyfe, *History*, 135.

By the 1890s, the headman's salary in some cases doubled that of regular workers. In 1890, H. Guinness observed that a gang of 25 Kru were hired in Freetown on what she termed "usual terms," as follows:

> For a year's service, the hirer to pay travelling expenses both ways. These men are so much in demand as labourers that they get pretty good pay, and always expect a month's wages in advance. The headmen have two shillings each day, and the others one shilling. They have to be fed and lodged, and sent home if ill, so that they are pretty expensive helpers.[240]

While all of the workers expected advanced wages, their contracts had expanded to cover food, housing, travel and sickness expenses.

One of the most important duties the headman performed was to ensure the discipline of his labor gang. Captain Napier Hewett described the headman's role as follows:

> [Regular Krumen and apprentices were to] pay implicit obedience to the chief of the gang; obey his instructions, and are amenable only to his rules and punishments. The captain of the vessel, when desirous to punish a Krooman, complains to the head-man, who inflicts summary justice, and as his orders are never disobeyed, or his judgment impeached, it would appear as though he exercised some powerful and mysterious influence over his people; and as he himself is equally attentive to the orders of the captain, the links in the chain of responsibility and discipline are complete.[241]

The Kru were very particular that the Kru headman was the individual to deal out punishment for insubordinate behaviour amongst the Kru. Punishment by proxy worked very well for the British who left it to the Kru to carry out their disciplinary orders, which could include floggings.[242] While there were some cases in which the British captain intervened and carried out the discipline, this was considered taboo amongst the Kru and could result in their refusal to work, abandonment of their complement of the crew or the boycotting of captains known to mistreat Kru seamen.[243] Moreover, if Kru workers were undisciplined it

---

240 Guinness, *New World*, 213.
241 J.F. Napier Hewett, *European Settlements on the West Coast of Africa: With Remarks on the Slave Trade and the Supply of Cotton* (London: Chapman and Hall, 1862), 113.
242 Reverend J. Clarke, "The West African Company," *Anti-Slavery Reporter* 2, no. 16 (Wednesday, August 11, 1841): 170.
243 *The Church Missionary Review* 32, no. 12 (1881): 725; Frost, *Work*, 72.

could cost them a payment, as was the case for one drunken Kru in 1884, who had to pay a penalty of 15s.[244]

The selection of headmen on Royal Navy ships and commercial vessels docked in Freetown could take two forms. The earliest known source addressing the issue is Captain Thomas Midgley's 1842 report that suggested the progression towards becoming a headman was based on merit.[245] According to Midgley, headmen were appointed by the British based on their previous service and the nature of the notes in their books, which described their experience and character.[246] A second way was for a headman to pass on his book to another Kruman whom he in effect recommended by doing so.[247] Essentially, the headman was a foreman, a term that was adopted nearly a century later in the British Attorney General's Office.[248]

Figure 2.1 shows a Kru headman dressed in a blue-striped robe. As early as 1811, Thomas Coke observed Kru laborers in Freetown who wore "no clothing, excepting a handkerchief, or a piece of blue cloth tied about their middle, and sometimes a hat."[249] Coke did not distinguish the headman's attire from regular workers. However, he did mention that the blue cloth was highly valued by the Kru.[250] By 1890, the robe may have been directly associated with the authority of headmen as indicated by the sketch's original title "A Kroo-Boy Headman," which included the word "Dressed" in brackets. The fact the headman was dressed seems to suggest that this was his official attire. Wearing the robe distinguished headmen from regular Kru workers who were frequently pictured as shirtless with a white cloth covering around their loins (see Figure 2.2). Although the quality of the image is not good, it seems that there is no Kru mark on the forehead, which may indicate that the practice of scarification declined because of the diminished threat of enslavement following the abolition of the trans-Atlantic slave trades. The term "Kroo-Boy" which accompanied the image in the text was derogatory and part and parcel of the European racist perception that

---

244 John Langdon, "Three Voyages to the West Coast of Africa, 1881–1884," in *Travel, Trade and Power in the Atlantic, 1765–1884*, eds. Betty Wood and Martin Lynn (Cambridge: Cambridge, 2002), 268.
245 "Report on the Select Committee on the West Coast of Africa Together with Minutes of Evidence Appendix and Index, Part 2," in *Irish University Press Series of British Parliamentary Papers* (Shannon: Irish University Press, 1968), 592.
246 Ibid., 592.
247 Ibid., 592.
248 Cited in Frost, *Work*, 38. Frost used the following source: Colonial Secretary's Office, Lab 83, Attorney General, 1937 The National Archives, Kew, United Kingdom.
249 Coke, *Interesting Narrative*, 45.
250 Ibid., 46.

Figure 2.1: Kru headman in Freetown, c. 1890.
Source: Guinness, *New World*, 214.

often regarded Africans as uncivilized and child-like.[251] Yet, the British depended on the Kru for their labor and they remained a valuable resource for British enterprise in West Africa. In contrast with the Kru headman, the Kru seamen pictured above in Figure 2.2 in 1892 by Louis Gustave Binger are not wearing a robe and were most probably regular laborers. Most nineteenth century sketches of the Kru show them wearing loincloths, while images of the robe are rare and lend credence to its association with headmen.[252]

---

[251] For a discussion on nineteenth century European racism that regarded Africans as uncivilized, savage or "other", see Mudimbe, *Invention*, 1–23; Mudimbe, *Idea*, 1–70; Meek, *Social Science*, 5; Said, *Orientalism*, 1–30.

[252] Images of Kru wearing a loincloth can be found in the following sources: *The Illustrated London News*, May 8, 1853, 461; "Kroomen Disembarking From the 'Michalla' at Wady Halfa," *The Graphic* 30, December 6, 1884, 597; "The Nile Expedition For The Relief General Gordon – Towing The Armed Steamer 'Nasaf-El-Khair' Over The Second Cataract, Beyond Wady Halfa," *The Graphic* 28, October 11, 1884, 276; Sands, "West African kroomen"; Captain's Clerk Charles F. Sands, "West African kroomen launching a boat, 1848." US Brig Porpoise on Anti-slavery cruise. 1848. Naval Historical Center. Photo# NH63103; *Voyage au Congo*, directed by Herr Marc Allégret (Paris: Independent, 1927).

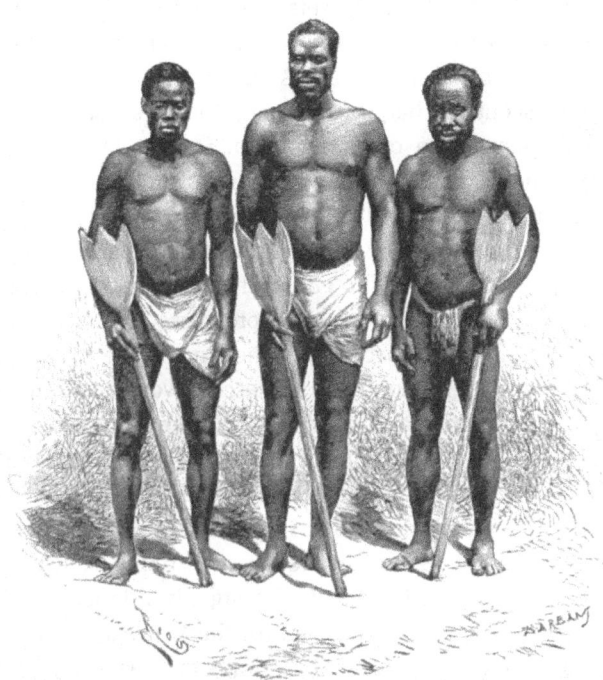

Figure 2.2: Kru with oars, c. 1892.
Source: "Piroguiers kroumen," photograph by Ch. Alluaud, in Louis Gustave Binger, *Du Niger au Golfe de Guinée, par le pays de Kong et le Mossi*, vol. 2 (Paris: Hachette et Cie, 1892), 311.

Employment with the British in Freetown depended on headmen as much as it had in prior times on board European ships. Moreover, headmen organized recruitment to ensure that future generations of Kru would remain employed under British contracts. Young men formed the pool of laborers who followed their headman to Freetown.[253] They could be drawn from a Kru headman's *dako* and belonged to an age-set, which had traditionally formed the next generation of warriors as discussed in Chapter 1. As the number of Kru workers in Freetown increased in the early nineteenth century, the expectation that young men would serve as workers on ships and shoreside projects grew exponentially.

---

253 F. Harrison Rankin, *The White Man's Grave: A Visit to Sierra Leone, in 1834*, vol. 1 (London: Richard Bentley, 1834), 149.

In the context of Freetown, traditional age-sets were adapted to meet labor demands. The progression from adolescent to adult was marked by the transition from young laborer to regular worker. Behrens has shown that many laborers began their service as adolescents: "chaque Krooman... part de chez lui vers 13 and 14 ans, sous la responsabilité d'un Headman."[254] A complement of eight or ten Kru workers formed the labor gang, which could be upwards to 25 and 100 depending on the type of work.[255] After serving on several contracts over a period of three or four years, they would return as independent laborers.[256] Similar to the transition from *kofa* to *gbo* in their homeland communities, after three or four years of service, an adolescent progressed to the status of a regular worker with the possibility of becoming a headman. The Kru would have appreciated the three-step progression from adolescent worker to adult laborer to headman based on their understanding of the right-of-passage from *kofa* to *gbo* to *krogba* in Kru society. Indeed, the units of work and social organization rooted in age-grade regulations which informed mariner trade in their villages formed the basis for their employment on British ships and, by extension, diaspora communities such as their settlement in Freetown.[257] Young men would have shown due protocol towards their headman who organized labor on their behalf for the same reasons they held great respect for the *krogbas* of their respective *dakwe* who were selected based on merit (and in some cases *panton* affiliation) and were accountable to their communities on the Kru Coast.

Laborers were expected to hand a portion of their earnings over to their headman.[258] The power dynamic between the headman and his workers was based on apprenticeship. The young men learned their craft from their headman and the adult laborers who formed the labor pool. In 1840, James Holman suggested Kru workers first had to learn the "White man's fashion", meaning they had to acquire a familiarity with working on British contracts and working

---

254 Behrens, *Les Kroumen*, 56.
255 Ibid., 56.
256 Parliamentary Papers, "Report of a Commission of Inquiry into the State of Sierra Leone, part 1," vol. 7 (1827), 312. See also William Davies, *Extracts from the Journal of the Rev. William Davies, 1st, when a Missionary at Sierra Leone, Western Africa; Containing some Account of the Countrey* (New York: Wesleyan Printing Office, 1835), 26.
257 Guenter Schroeder, "Letter to George Brooks," March 31, 1971, 2–3. Schroeder was involved in *Ethnographic Survey of Southeastern Liberia: The Liberian Kran and the Sapo* (Newark, Delaware: Liberian Studies Association, 1974). Also see Schroeder and Andreas Massing, "A General Outline of Historical Developments within the Kru Cultural Province" (paper presented at the Second Annual Conference on Social Research in Liberia, Indiana University, April 30-May 2, 1970).
258 Holman, *Travels*, 186.

with white British sailors and administrators.[259] Adolescent workers could not advance to adult laborers until they had some experience working in an environment that was directed by British operations. The adaptation of the age-set system towards supplying a steady labor force on British contract marks a major shift in the nature of the socio-economic structures informing Kru communities.

Krutown

The greatest marker of the emerging Kru diaspora in Freetown was the establishment of Krutown. Since their arrival in Freetown around 1792, Kru resided on the shores of what became known as Kroo Bay. Many of the Kru lived in the "Kru Reservation" which after its formal establishment in 1816 was known as Kroo Town (or Krutown).[260] British authorities purchased the land from Eli Ackim adjacent to Kroo Bay for the purpose of providing a specific quarter for the Kru.[261] The convenient location on the ocean allowed the Kru to fish for subsistence and pull their surfboats ashore following work. Following the establishment of Krutown, the Kru population fluctuated between a few hundred to over a thousand over the course of the nineteenth century. In 1816, a report indicated that there were 700 Kru living in "Krooman's Town" alone.[262]

The establishment of an officially designated area in Freetown for Kru workers provided the British with a readily available labor pool. For Kru migrants, Krutown gave them a semi-permanent, and even a permanent home, depending on how long they remained in Freetown. Most significantly, Krutown provided the Kru with a cultural space that was their own in which they could speak their native Kru language, carry out rituals associated with their Bo secret society, and for those few who brought their wives and children a place to raise their families, which became steadily more important by the later nineteenth century.

The close connection between homeland on the Kru Coast and the diaspora community in Freetown was evident in the street names that were assigned in Krutown, which included "Nana Kroo," "Little Kroo," "Settra Kroo," "King Wil-

---

259 Ibid., 186.
260 *Proceedings of the Royal Colonial Institute* 13 (London: Sampson Low, Marston, Searle and Rivington, 1882): 65; *Missionary Register for 1817*, vol. 5 (London: Seeley, 1817), 251; *The Christian Observer* 15, no. 11 (1816): 756.
261 *Proceedings of the Royal Colonial Institute* 13 (London: Sampson Low, Marston, Searle and Rivington, 1882): 65.
262 Zachary Macaulay, ed., *The Christian Observer: Conducted by Members of the Established Church, Given by Disciples Divinity House* 15, no.11 (1816): 756.

Figure 2.3: Krootown Bay, c. 1910.
Source: Lisk-Carew Brothers Postcard, Gary Schulze Collection, accessed May 15, 2017, http://www.sierra-leone.org/Gspostcards.

Figure 2.4: Krootown Road, Freetown, c. 1910.
Source: Lisk-Carew Brothers Postcard, Gary Schulze Collection, accessed May 15, 2017, http://www.sierra-leone.org/Gspostcards.

liam," and "Grand Cess," all of which radiated outward from Krootown Road towards Krootown Bay (Figure 2.3, Figure 2.4, and Figure 2.5).[263] The streets were named after several of the Kru's main trading towns in Proper Kru settlements

---

263 See Brooks, *Kru Mariner*, 79.

Figure 2.5: Krootown, c. 1910.
Source: Lisk-Carew Brothers Postcard, Gary Schulze Collection, accessed May 3, 2017, http://www.sierra-leone.org/Gspostcards.

on the Kru Coast. The only exception was Grand Cess, which was a village composed of Siklio Kru established adjacent to the Grand Cess River from at least the seventeenth century. Possibly, members from each community were housed on the appropriate street linked to their specific village and *dako*.

While the postcards date to the first decade of the twentieth century, the layout of the town remained the same since the early nineteenth century and hence later images accurately reflect what Krutown looked like throughout the century. As the Lisk-Carew postcards reveal, Krutown was the center of the Kru diaspora in Freetown.[264]

Even though their community was largely populated by the Proper Kru, Krutown gradually also became home to more and more Grebo and Bassa laborers, all of whom spoke Kru. While census records amalgamated these groups under the general heading of "Kru" in Freetown, they would have been able to distinguish between who was Proper Kru and who were Grebo and Bassa, not least because their autonomous communities competed for trade and were sometimes in conflict back in their homeland.[265] Despite their differences, they accepted the general label of "Kru" in the context of Freetown as evidenced by the name of

---

[264] Between 1910 and 1925, Alphonso and Sylvester Lisk-Carew, known in published photographs as the Lisk-Carew Brothers, took photos in Freetown and throughout the Colony of Sierra Leone. Their images were used on postcards. Some of their works are available at: http://www.sierra-leone.org/Gspostcards.
[265] Ludlam, "Account," 46; Fraenkel, "Social Change," 154–155.

their quarter – Krutown. After all, no Grebo Town or Bassa Town was ever created within the boundaries of Freetown during the period.[266] As work increased in Sierra Leone, so too did those Kru speakers beyond the Proper Kru towns who wanted to obtain employment. However, there is little evidence that any Grebo, Bété, Neyo, Wane or Dida laborers to the east of the Cavalla River in Côte d'Ivoire ever made their way on contract to Freetown. Although some did work with the British, they appear more frequently on French ships and itineraries working in such locations as Libreville.[267] Perhaps, the closer proximity of Proper Kru villages made them the prime candidates for contracts in Freetown.

The Kru mark continued to have special significance in Krutown. While the Kru did not have to secure protection from enslavement in Freetown after 1807 as they did while serving on European and American vessels on the coast, the mark served to distinguish them from other laboring African groups such as the Yoruba and Vai.[268] Each African community had its own quarter in Freetown including Congo Town and Maroon Town. Beyond these quarters, other communities were founded including Cossoo Town, Bambara Town, Cabenda Town, Bassa Town, and Jolify Town.[269] The main distinction was that these towns were composed of recaptives, or formerly enslaved Africans, who were delivered to Freetown. The Kru mark ensured that they were readily identified by the British, other African peoples, and amongst themselves. It may have even given the Kru an advantage over competing laborers because of the hardworking reputation they had garnered. For instance, in 1823, Edward Bold "strongly recommended" the Kru to all ship captains on the West African coast based on their "hard-working" nature.[270] The Kru mark in Freetown made them that much easier to single out and hire.

In addition to the Kru mark, it seems that regular employment in the British Royal Navy also led to the tattooing of an anchor on the arm, which seems to have been an innovation in Freetown. Robert Clarke observed the practice in

---

266 Eventually, Bassa Town was founded outside of the boundaries of Freetown and it was inhabited by recaptives along with the neighboring towns.
267 Service with the French is discussed in Chapter 6.
268 The Yoruba, Fante, and Vai had their own facial marks on the cheeks and forehead. For information on Yoruba, Fante, and Vai facial markings see Keefer, "Scarification," 537–553; Keefer, "Group Identity," 1–26; Toyin Falola and Fallou Ngom, *Facts, Fiction and African Creative Imaginations* (London: Routledge, 2009), 86; Olanike Orie, "The Structure and Function of Yoruba Facial Scarification," *Anthropological Linguistics* 53, no. 1 (2011): 15–33; James Obunbaku, "The Use of Tribal Marks in Archaeological and Historical Reconstruction," *Research on Humanities and Social Sciences* 2, no. 6 (2012): 251–260.
269 Population Return for Sierra Leone, May 1, 1813, CMS/CA1/E3/76.
270 Bold, *Merchant's and Mariner's*, 45.

Freetown: "the figure of an anchor is sometimes traced upon their arms, in imitation of the English seamen with whom they associate."[271] The traditional Kru mark and the tattoo on the arm thereby became distinct items in identification. As contracts with the British became an increasingly important source of revenue for the Kru economy, a tattoo on the arm may also have symbolized prestige amongst the Kru.

The establishment of Krutown necessitated the creation of a new position called the Krutown Headman (later the Kru Tribal Headman).[272] While its origins can be traced to the early nineteenth century when a "principal chief" maintained authority over the Kru community, the position was eventually formalized.[273] British authorities in Sierra Leone began appointing Krutown Headmen for the purpose of keeping order amongst the Kru working in that colony. In 1849, Lieutenant Frederick Forbes described the position:

> Krutown is under superintendence of a headman, who receives a shilling a day, and he is held responsible for the good behaviour of his tribe. Besides this he has large emoluments, receiving a fee for all returning and from new members: the superintendent of each street is under him.[274]

The growth in the communities that made up Freetown, many of which were designated as "towns," led the British to appoint officials in order to ensure law and order and the "good behaviour" of its inhabitants. At various times in the nineteenth century, Kru were noted as being quarrelsome.[275] The Krutown Headman was expected to deal with any difficulties within the Kru community.

The Krutown Headman differed from the headmen on ships who were tasked with administering their workers. Rather, he was responsible for the administration of Krutown and sat at the top of the hierarchal order in the Kru community. Superintendents were responsible for maintaining order on their street and reporting to him. In some ways, this mirrored the organizational layout of Kru villages back home in which each street was frequently managed by a leader or member of

---

271 Clarke, "Sketches," 355.
272 The term Krutown Headman, later renamed Kru Tribal Headman, continues to be used in the twenty-first century. See http://slconcordtimes.com/as-protest-against-kroo-tribal-head-continues/. For information on the acquisition of land for the Kru see *Proceedings of the Royal Colonial Institute*, vol. 13, 1881–1882 (London: Sampson, Low, Marston, Searle and Rivington, 1882), 65.
273 Coke, *Interesting Narrative*, 45.
274 Lieutenant Frederick Forbes, *Six Months' Service in the African Blockade*, 1849 (London: Dawsons, 1969), 19.
275 See Holman, *Travels*, 65, 69; CO 267/56, "MacCarthy to Bathurst, 23 September 1822"; Frost, *Work*, 127.

the *panton nyefue* who answered to the *krogba*.[276] All Kru laborers were expected to pay their headman in their labor pool as well as the Krutown Headman, who was described as "a king or headman in Sierra Leone who settles their own disputes."[277] His authority and responsibilities mirrored the role of the *krogba* in the Kru homeland, who also collected money from Kru laborers and held administrative responsibility for their community. Similar to the ship headman and shoreside headman, he was the intermediary between the Kru and the British ensuring the overall discipline and well-being of the entire Kru community in Freetown.

By the 1860s, the Krutown Headman played a central role in the hiring process as merchant ship captains sought Kru seamen. Those merchants seeking Kru labor applied to the Krutown Headman who then called upon a ship headman to obtain the required number of laborers.[278] Whereas the Kru had once been hired from their surfboats directly on the Kru Coast, in Freetown, the Krutown Headman was responsible for supplying British captains with a ship headman who in turn provided a labor gang from whom he extracted a fee from each Kru laborer. He also charged a fee to the British authorities for providing labor.[279]

Kru women did not begin to immigrate to Krutown to any extent until the later nineteenth century. Krutown guaranteed a place for the Kru and their families to reside without the worry of searching for land for their lodgings.[280] Although Krutown was part of an urban setting, it seems Kru women were initially limited to the household and prevented from trading in the markets by their husbands.[281] However, by the close of the nineteenth century the opening of the City Market on Kroo Town Road meant that some Kru women eventually had the opportunity to sell fish and produce in the market.[282] Their role signifies a change from their villages where males engaged in trade with Europeans. Women could now trade directly with fellow Kru, Temne women, and other Africans.[283]

Kru oral traditions remember one of the most significant transformations that impacted Kru women in Freetown was their role as overseer of communal households. The oldest wife of a Kru headman was assigned the authoritative role of

---

276 "Miscellany," *The Missionary Magazine* 46 (1866): 120.
277 *The Church Missionary Intelligencer and Record* 6 (1881): 725.
278 Hewett, *European Settlements*, 113.
279 For further discussion on the Kru Tribal Headman see Frost, *Work*, 39; Harrell-Bond, *Community Leadership*, 97.
280 Harrell-Bond, *Community Leadership*, 7; Frost, *Work*, 120.
281 Frost, *Work*, 102; Lynn Schler, *Nation on Board: Becoming Nigerian at Sea* (Athens: Ohio University Press, 2016), 96.
282 Joseph Bangura, *The Temne of Sierra Leone: African Agency in the Making of a British Colony* (Cambridge: Cambridge University Press, 2017), 172; Frost, *Work*, 208.
283 Bangura, *Temne*, 171–172.

being responsible for the management of Kru sailors who lodged at the headman's house while awaiting their next contract. She was tasked with feeding and ensuring the discipline of sailors who remained in Freetown between contracts. The workers were expected to give the headman's eldest wife a portion of their earnings and became like "extended family members" of the headman.[284] Although official responsibility for maintaining the "good behaviour" of the community in Krutown was assigned to the Krutown Headman, the wives of headmen became crucial background players who made it happen on the ground.

Relationship with the Homeland

The Kru's homecoming experience was an essential component that maintained their diaspora in Freetown. British contracts in Freetown based on standardized timeframes that could range from six months to 18 months and even three years created a regular cycle of homecoming protocol that influenced Kru culture in their homeland. Following the completion of a contract, the great majority of Kru would disembark in Freetown and remain in Krutown before accepting their next contract, but many also returned to their villages whether or not they intended to return to Freetown for further employment.

Through employment in Freetown, the British offered the Kru an alternative means for raising their bride-price obligations, wealth, and prestige. Kru laborers hoped to acquire as many wives as possible for elevating their social status and expanding their kinship group. Using their payments in iron bars, cattle, brass kettles, and blue baft, the Kru built houses and purchased wives.[285] In 1825, Captain Robert Pearce of HMS Brazen observed that upon the Kru's homecoming, the following process unfolded:

> [Kru] lay out in merchandize such as cloths, hats, muskets, Powder, Iron Bars, tobacco in stone jars, Large Brass pans, beads, knives & c &c with fruits of their labour on their return they purchase as many wives as they can maintain – their rank there afterwards estimated according to the proportion of that scale of establishment.[286]

---

284 Smith, personal interview, December 13, 2012.
285 Holman, *Travels*, 186–187; Lugenbeel, "Native Africans," 15; Holman, "Mr. Holman's Travels," *The Asiatic Journal*, 64; *Sixth Report of the African Institution* (1812): 68–70; *The Analectic Magazine* 1 (1813): 12–13; Smith, *Trade*, 100.
286 Bruce Lockhart and Lovejoy, *Hugh Clapperton*, 418.

Pearce showed that the Kru exchanged the items they had earned in Freetown for wives in their villages. Similarly, Hugh Clapperton claimed that a Kruman was "esteemed according to the No of his wives."[287]

The cost of purchasing wives was expressed in 1840 by Holman who observed: "For the first wife, they pay two bullocks, two brass kettles, one piece of blue baft, and one iron bar."[288] He did not mention how much each subsequent wife cost but seemed to suggest that the first wife was the most expensive. This may have been because the first wife had authority over the other wives the Kruman acquired following contracts. During interviews with the Kru in 1860, Reverend Thomas Charles learned about the cost of purchasing a wife. A Kruman named Tom Pepper explained: "S'pose he people be poor, he sell for twenty dollar; s'pose he no want sell much, he be price fiftee dollar."[289] Pepper indicated that the price was determined by the bride's father and could range between $20.00 and $50.00.[290] The price differential depended on whether the bride came from a poor or wealthy family – the wealthier the family the higher the cost of their daughter. The cost of a wife was paid for in goods at a pre-determined monetary value.

The socio-economic impact of the Kru free wage labor diaspora in Freetown was thereby felt at home in their settlements. Whereas the headman was once solely responsible for organizing labor on vessels visiting the coast, the institutionalization of their position through higher wages enabled the headman to become a pillar of authority both in their workplace and in their homeland on the Kru Coast. Their role in securing future employment was so important that regular Kru laborers were gradually expected to give their advance to their headman following the negotiation of a contract.[291]

The protocol of gift-giving and the incentive for pursuing contracts became intimately ingrained in Kru society. Contracts created social prestige and enabled social mobility. Value was measured by gift-giving and the accumulation of wives. Kru provided for their family bringing back gifts, which could be used to accumulate social value or be traded with Europeans on the Kru Coast.

---

[287] Ibid., 86.
[288] Holman, *Travels*, 187.
[289] Reverend Charles W. Thomas, *Adventures and Observations on the West Coast of Africa, and Its Islands* (New York: Derby and Jackson, 1860), 107.
[290] Ibid., 107.
[291] Smith, *Trade*, 100–103; Thomas Joseph Hutchinson, *Impressions of Western Africa* (London: Longman, 1858), 47–54, 137, 282; Thomas Joseph Hutchinson, *Ten Year's Wandering among the Ethiopians; with sketches of the Manners and Customs of the Civilized and Uncivilized Tribes, From Senegal to Gaboon* (London: Hurst and Blackett Publishers, 1861), 96, 209.

Gifts given to the *krogba* played a role in maintaining traditional power dynamics in Kru villages. The *krogba* continued to hold his position of authority over the community and in the process was able to increase his wealth. Because of these demands, many Kru would only remain in their homeland for several months before they returned to Krutown for further employment.[292]

As discussed with reference to the slave trade, the Kru were already making voyages from their villages to the Sierra Leone Peninsula prior to the establishment of Freetown in 1792. However, the cyclical nature of their migration between their homeland and their community in Freetown became standardized through contractual labor in the nineteenth century. In 1840, Captain James Holman described the Kru work cycle:

> The following trait in the history of the Kroomen, or natives of the Kroo country, upon that part of the coast called the Grain Coast, is curious… The Kroomen… are almost the only people on the coast who voluntarily emigrate, to seek for labour out of their own country. They come to Sierra Leone, to work in any capacity in which they can obtain employment, until they are possessed of sufficient property to enable them to purchase several wives… Before they are able to accomplish this object, they are obliged to make several visits to Sierra Leone, as they do not like to be absent more than two or three years at a time from their own country. The average duration of this voluntary banishment is perhaps about eighteen months. A sketch of the progress of the Kroomen, from their first visit to Sierra Leone to the final consummation of their wishes, in the attainment of their paradise… one of whose usuages is that of seeking abroad, during the vigorous years of life, the means of dwelling with ease and comfort in old age at home.[293]

Holman's description dates to 1840, but it reveals several significant features that informed the Kru free wage labor diaspora that clearly date back to the late eighteenth century.[294] These include: the Kru voluntarily immigrated to Sierra Leone for work; they completed at least several contracts that on average lasted 18 months; they continually circulated between homeland and workplace; they were compensated for their labor; their objective was to purchase wives and thereby expand their kin group; they eventually returned to the Kru Coast following retirement. Kru would not permanently return to the Kru Coast until they had accumulated enough wages that would effectively elevate their status

---

[292] Coke, *Interesting Narrative*, 45–46; Ludlam, "Account," *Sixth Report*, 68–70; *The Analectic Magazine* 1 (1813): 12–13; Lugenbeel, "Native Africans," 15.
[293] Holman, "Mr. Holman's Travels," 64.
[294] Migratory labor cycles informing Kru labor developed in the 1790s and were firmly established by the early nineteenth century in Freetown. See Winterbottom, *Account*, 8–9; Coke, *Interesting Narrative*, 45–46.

in Kru society. Holman's account is corroborated by Kru oral traditions and numerous sources that discuss the cyclical nature of Kru labor in Freetown.[295]

The opportunity to earn wages in-kind and later monetary wages created a fundamental shift in notions of power and authority within Kru communities as they began to labor in Freetown. Although the gradual process had begun in their communities since they first traded with Europeans on the coast, the process was accelerated in Freetown. Because of the regular timeframes of the British contracts, greater amounts of capital accumulation could be had versus the ununiform nature of trade on the coast. Suddenly, there was great incentive to obtain contracts in Freetown and ascend the social hierarchy at home. Kru sought to gain capital accumulation through the commerce of selling their labor for the purposes of climbing the social ladder from regular laborer to headmen to Krutown Headman and in some cases to *krogba*.[296]

Perhaps most significantly, employment in Freetown resulted in the crystallization of Kru identity and their homeland, known as the Kru Coast, from the perspective of British employers and the Kru alike. As discussed above, while most Kru were contracted from the Proper Kru region between the Cestos and Grand Cess Rivers, other Kru-speaking peoples migrated from the adjacent regions and were simply categorized as Kru upon arrival in Freetown by British officials. While Proper Kru self-identified as Kru, an unprecedented twofold Grebo-Kru and Bassa-Kru identity emerged in the context of Freetown based on common language, similar occupations, and place of residence in Krutown. As a result, the conceptual parameters of the Kru homeland gradually expanded. It is important to remember that the label Krumen or Kroomen was not regularly applied by Europeans until the 1790s. Labor in Freetown and trade on the coast reverberated and resulted in new meanings of Kru identity and the renaming of their homeland as the Kru Coast as it was known thereafter in the nineteenth century. The Kru would gradually expand the geographical breadth of their free wage labor diaspora to other British ports in West Africa and beyond while serving on Royal Navy and commercial ships.

---

295 An interview with Chief Davis revealed that the goal of Kru laborers was to complete as many contracts as possible before retiring in their village or in their diaspora community in Freetown. Sources that support the idea that the Kru were engaged in a free wage labor diaspora in Freetown by circulating between their homeland and Krutown include Lugenbeel, "Native Africans," 15; Ludlam, "Account," *Sixth Report*, 68–70; *The Analectic Magazine* 1 (1813): 12–13; Parliamentary Papers, "Report of a Commission of Inquiry into the State of Sierra Leone, part 1," vol. 7 (1827), 312; Davies, *Extracts*, 26.
296 Coquery-Vidrovitch and Lovejoy, *Workers*, 17.

Chapter 3
The Expansion of Kru Labor in the Royal Navy

British expansion in the Atlantic and Indian Oceans in the nineteenth century led to an increase in Kru employment. Kru continued to be hired in their homeland on the Kru Coast and diaspora community in Freetown. During the 1820s, increased service in the Royal Navy's West Africa Squadron led them on itineraries throughout West Africa, the Atlantic islands, and as far afield as southern Africa as part of the British initiative to repress the trans-Atlantic slave trades. The result was the creation of a network of Kru diaspora communities in Cape Coast, Ascension Island, Fernando Po, and the Cape of Good Hope. By the 1860s, their service on Royal Navy ships was officially extended to include the Indian Ocean. Kru were hired for the purpose of assisting in the suppression of the slave trade to the Middle East, and later, the Mascarene Islands and sections of the east coast of Africa. Their ability to man surfboats and small watercraft became even more significant due to a shortage of Royal Navy ships in the region. As such, Kru found themselves on the front lines of intercepting slave *dhows* (slave ships) as a coalition of British naval ships and launch boats were required to fulfil their mission.

Kru were hired in the Royal Navy for similar reasons that European merchants hired them based on climatic concerns, diseases, hardworking demeanour, challenging landings, and cheap labor. Kru were thought to handle working in tropical climate with better rigour than the British.[297] They were also thought to be less susceptible to diseases, which led to a high volume of death amongst British sailors on the West Coast of Africa.[298] The Kru put their knowledge of landing watercraft in heavy surf and fog to use when delivering crewmembers ashore or when collecting water, food, and fuel for the ship. Kru worked for slightly less wages than their British counterparts and rendered voyages even more profitable in terms of prize earnings from the capture of slaver crews.

Rather than forming Krutowns as they had in the Atlantic, in the Indian Ocean Royal Navy ships became the diaspora spaces where the Kru were able to evolve their seaborne practices first developed on the Kru Coast. Kru service on Royal Navy ships in the Indian Ocean between 1862 and 1881 was based on an itinerary that included Simon's Town in South Africa, Zanzibar, Mombasa, the Seychelles, Aden, Basra, Bombay, and Trincomalee, among other locations.

---

[297] Holman, *Travels*, 63; Bold, *Merchant's and Mariner's*, 122; Rockwell, *Sketches*, 258.
[298] Curtin, "White Man's Grave," 94–110; Curtin, "End," 63–88.

As their diaspora network expanded, the Kru maintained a unique identity as evidenced through their Kru mark, hospital records, muster lists, gravestones, and mastery of their surfboats and other watercraft in naval contexts.

Atlantic Ocean Network

Royal Navy service provided the rationale for the creation of Krutowns in many of the ports where they labored in the Atlantic.[299] Following Freetown, communities developed along the West African coast at Cape Coast, on the Atlantic islands on Ascension Island and Fernando Po, and at the Cape of Good Hope in Simon's Town. Kru communities were established adjacent to naval bases as part of the Royal Navy's suppression strategy to maintain a steady labor pool of seamen. Their newly-formed communities were modelled after Krutown in Freetown. Headmen continued to structure labor relations with the British in their diaspora communities as their duties evolved to include increased service on steamships, which in turn created new jobs in engine rooms and coaling ships in port.

Freetown

Freetown remained the main port of Royal Navy operations between 1808 and 1840. The premier Court of Mixed Commission was based there and prize slave ships and their crews captured in the Bights of Benin and Biafra continued to be delivered to Freetown for adjudication. However, the great distance between Freetown and the slaver regions on the West African coast proved challenging for the limited number of West Africa Squadron ships and captures remained rather limited until the 1840s. Eventually, a Vice Admiralty Court was established in St. Helena for greater expediency in the adjudication of slaver crews in the southern Atlantic.[300]

The typical size of a Royal Navy crew could range between 60 and about 120 crewmembers.[301] It is widely held that Kru sailors accounted for between 10 and 15 members on each vessel.[302] However, as shown in Table 2.3, the number of Kru sailors on board could be augmented depending on manpower needs to well

---

299 Fraenkel, *Tribe*, 76.
300 Pearson, "Waterwitch," 112.
301 Ibid., 115.
302 Ibid., 115.

over 20 personnel, thereby potentially making up one-third of the crew on the low end of the range and one-sixth on the high end when their numbers are compared with total crew. Robert Burroughs has suggested that by the mid-1840s, the annual size of the West Africa Squadron was 36 vessels, which accounted for 15 percent of all Royal Navy warships in commission.[303] West Africa Squadron vessels were manned by some 4,000 personnel or one-tenth of the total naval workforce in the period.[304] Even if only 10 Kru served on a portion of these vessels annually, the number of Kru serving in the squadron in the 1840s alone would potentially be in the thousands. However, estimates of the annual number of Kru serving on European vessels and shoreside contracts in the nineteenth century that range between 5,000 and 20,000 migratory laborers reveal that Kru serving in the Royal Navy accounted for a small percentage of the overall Kru labor force.[305] The higher pay in the Royal Navy compared with merchant vessels and land-based jobs suggests there may have been greater competition amongst the Kru to obtain these contracts. Shipboard work also required less manpower compared with land-based porters and those engaged in infrastructural projects, which depended on greater numbers for timely completion. Moreover, service in the Royal Navy may have signalled prestige and membership in a special group amongst Kru as evidenced in their adoption of the common British naval practice of tattooing the arm with the image of an anchor.[306]

Cape Coast

Bilateral treaties between the British and other European nations and Brazil, and the location of Courts of Mixed Commission and Vice Admiralty Courts throughout the Atlantic, framed the itineraries and experience of the Kru serving on Royal Navy ships.[307] One of the first communities Kru established in a British workplace following Freetown was a community at Cape Coast on the Gold

---

[303] Robert Burroughs and Richard Huzzey, eds., *The Suppression of the Atlantic Slave Trade: British Policies, Practices and Representations of Naval Coercion* (Manchester: Manchester University Press, 2018), 6; David Eltis, *Economic Growth and the Ending of the Transatlantic Slave Trade* (New York: Oxford University Press, 1987), 92 (table 2), 94.
[304] Ibid., 6.
[305] Davis, *Ethnohistorical*, 49. See Chapter 6 for overview of figures.
[306] Clarke, "Sketches," 355.
[307] Allain, "Nineteenth Century," 359; John Beeler, "Maritime Policing and the Pax Britannica: The Royal Navy's Anti-Slavery Patrol in the Caribbean, 1828–1848," *The Northern Mariner* 16, no. 1 (2006): 2.

Coast. Their service on Royal Navy ships ensured that they sailed between Freetown and Cape Coast en route to the Bights of Benin and Biafra in pursuit of slave ships. While there is no evidence that they established a quarter known as Krutown as they had in Freetown, Thomas Baynes writing for *The Encyclopedia Britannica* described their community as a "colony of Kroomen" living in quarters adjacent to Cape Coast Castle in 1833.[308] The earliest available figure regarding the size of the community dates to 1868 when there were 16 Kru listed as living in the colony at Cape Coast.[309] Kru loaded and unloaded cargo on their surfboats and served in a military capacity stationed at Cape Coast Castle and the adjacent barracks.[310] They would have been responsible for watering and transporting supplies for the onward journey to the Bights or return to Freetown. Their permanent presence reveals their great value to the Royal Navy because they lived amongst local Fante seafarers who performed similar jobs and had served with the British for centuries in the region.

Hospital ordinance records reveal that the Kru were important enough to warrant distinction in their policy. Should Kru laborers suffer an injury on the job, they were admitted to the Government Hospital in Cape Coast (and all locations in the Gold Coast). They were charged a special fee compared with Royal Navy officers and seamen. An ordinance entitled "Rates Payable for Kroomen" in 1887 specified that the Royal Navy was to pay a fee for injured Kru for every day spent in the hospital:

> When any Krooman in the service of any person shall have been admitted as a patient into any Government Hospital by a Surgeon in charge, even though not upon the request of such Krooman's employer, there shall be payable by such employer in respect of such Krooman the sum of One shilling for each day of residence in such Hospital.[311]

Whether a shoreside laborer or seaman in the Royal Navy, their employer was responsible for paying one shilling per day for hospitalization. By comparison,

---

308 Thomas Spencer Baynes, "Cape Coast Castle – Cape Colony," in *The Encyclopedia Britannica: A Dictionary of Arts, Sciences and General Literature, Ninth Edition*, vol. 5 (New York: Henry G Allen and Company Publishers, 1833), 41.
309 J.J. Crooks, *Records Relating to the Gold Coast, 1750–1874* (1973; repr., London: Routledge, 2016), 354.
310 Kru service in the campaign against the Asante will be discussed in Chapter 4.
311 William Brandford Griffith, "Government Hospitals No.2," Ordinance 4, *Ordinances of the Settlements on the Gold Coast and of the Gold Coast Colony, in Force April 7th, 1887, with an Appendix containing the Rules, Orders in Consul, and Proclamations of Practical Utility and an Index* (London: Waterlow & Sons, 1887), 641.

British masters paid a fee of 10s., officers 7s. 6d. and seamen 4s. per day.³¹² Perhaps the lower fee was an incentive for British captains to employ Kru without fear of the heavy costs associated with hospital care. Moreover, the fact that the Kru were allotted special mention in the ordinance and assigned a fee that differed from British seamen demonstrates that the Kru had established a distinct identity in Cape Coast and elsewhere. Gradually, it became a common feature in hospital ordinances in West Africa to give the Kru special mention.

Ascension Island

A far more significant site for Kru labor was Ascension Island, which became an important port in Royal Navy operations when they occupied it in 1815 in response to Napoleon's banishment to St. Helena.³¹³ It served as the naval headquarters supply depot and medical base for the Royal Navy in the Atlantic, supplying the West Africa Squadron's northern and southern routes. Located nearly midway between Africa and Brazil, its strategic position enabled naval vessels to pursue slave ships far out to sea in all directions. The food, ship, and fuel stores that were supplied from Britain became a vital lifeline for British ships sailing in the vast Atlantic. Andrew Pearson has shown that following the completing of their contract on HMS Waterwitch, several Kru disembarked on Ascension Island.³¹⁴ This is significant because it shows that Kru remained on the island before transiting to another ship or perhaps returning to Freetown and that they gained employment beyond their villages on the Kru Coast and Freetown.

At Georgetown, much like at Cape Coast, Kru formed an independent colony in Garrison Station in the port. In their quarter, they lived in sheds adjacent to the lodgings of British seamen. This space enabled the Kru to speak their language, sing Kru work songs, and maintain cultural practices in diaspora.³¹⁵ Unlike Freetown, where there were many quarters inhabited by a range of African communities including Yoruba and Congolese, in Garrison, Kru formed the only unique African community. Due to the island's lack of resources and small population, Kru were required to perform shoreside duties. Their duties in-

---

312 Ibid., 641.
313 Ascension Island Government website, accessed November 18, 2018, http://www.ascension-island.gov.ac/the-island/history/.
314 Pearson, "Waterwitch," 115.
315 H. Davy, "Voyage of H.M.S. Thunderer to the Mauritius and Back, Notes by Mr. H. Davy, Master, R.N.–1843," in *The Nautical Magazine and the Naval Chronicle for 1844, A Journal of Subjects Connected to Maritime Affairs* (London: Simpkin, Marshall, and Co., 1844), 427.

cluded loading and unloading cargo, coaling ships, constructing the observatory, and providing portage services moving equipment from the coast to Green Mountain.[316]

Kru were so integral to operations on the island that the Royal Navy constructed Krooman's Hospital following the establishment of Georgetown Hospital in 1833.[317] It was classified as a government hospital and not only provided service for Kru seamen, but also functioned as an isolation center for disease-ridden British seamen arriving on Royal Navy ships.[318] The name of the hospital reveals the high value placed on Kru seamen in the Royal Navy and that the Kru formed a distinct community on the island given there was a hospital for them. Alternatively, it may also reveal that the Kru were segregated and not encouraged to receive care alongside British seamen. The British relied on Kru seamen for their labor on the island, but did not perceive them as equals.

Although the Kru population on Ascension Island remained small compared with that of Freetown, it formed a vital component of the total population. From only 50 Kru on the island in 1830, the population rose to between 70 and 80 in 1877 (Table 3.1).[319] The Statesman's Year Book for 1899 suggests that the Kru population increased to an estimated maximum of 177.[320] Based on these figures, the Kru accounted for one-third of the population in 1830, 26.6 percent in 1877, 35.4 percent in 1899, and 36.8 percent of the total population in 1905. Statistics show that Kru seamen formed a significant part of the total population of the island between 1830 and 1905. Their service in the Royal Navy ensured that they continued to circulate between Ascension Island, Freetown, Fernando Po, and the Bights in the northern routes and between St. Helena, Simon's

---

316 Isobel Black Gill, *Six Months in Ascension: An Unscientific Account of a Scientific Expedition By Mrs. Gill* (London: John Murray, 1878), 96.
317 "Hospital, Ascension Island," *London Illustrated News*, February 28, 1874, 20; Ascension Island Heritage Society, accessed June 15, 2016, http://www.ascension-island.gov.ac/heritage-amble/; http://www.pdavis.nl/GreenMountain.htm.
318 "Hospital, Ascension Island," *London Illustrated News*, 28 February 1874, 20; Ascension Island Heritage Society, accessed June 16, 2016, http://www.ascension-island.gov.ac/heritage-amble/; http://www.pdavis.nl/GreenMountain.htm.
319 William Henry Bayley Webster, *Narrative of the Voyage to the Southern Atlantic Ocean in the Years 1828, 29,30 Performed in H.M. Sloop Chanticleer, Under the Command of the Late Captain Henry Foster, F.R.S. & c. By Order of the Lords Commissioners of the Admiralty. From the Private Journal of W.H.B. Webster, Surgeon of the Sloop. In Two Volumes* vol. 1 (London: Richard Bentley, 1834), 64.
320 J. Scott Keltie, ed., *The Statesman's Year-Book: Statistical and Historical Annual of the States of the World for the Year 1899* (London: MacMillan and Co., 1899), 180.

Town, and the Angolan coast in the southern routes resulting in the formation of their own quarter.

Table 3.1: Kru population in Ascension Island.

Year	Total Population	Kru Population
1830	150	50
1877	300	70–80
1899	500	177
1905	450	166

Source: Gill, *Six Months*, 134; Webster, *Narrative*, 384; *Baily's Magazine of Sports and Pastimes* 23 (London: A.H. Baily and Co., 1873), 290; Keltie, *The Statesman's Year-Book*, 180; Army and Navy Calendar for 1882/83–1893/94 (1894), 133; J. Scott-Keltie, ed., *The Statesman's Year-Book* (London: Macmillan and Co., 1905), 192.

Fernando Po

Although Freetown remained the main port where slaver ships were delivered for adjudication in the Mixed Commission Court, it was believed by some to be too distant from the epicenter of illegal slave trading and the British sought the establishment of a port in closer geographical proximity. In 1827, Britain negotiated with Spain to obtain Fernando Po so as to establish a Mixed Commission Court for the purposes of more expedient adjudication in the region.[321] The island became the staging point for Royal Navy operations in the suppression of slave trade in the Bights for a time. Almost immediately after Britain acquired Fernando Po, Kru were hired for the construction of the British naval station at Clarence Cove.[322] Clarence Town, the main settlement on the island, was founded by Captain W.F. Owen the same year.[323] Kru engaged in their regular work as boatmen and longshoreman moving cargo between ship and shore in surfboats and other variety of watercraft. Eventually, one of their primary duties was to provide coal

---

[321] John Lipski, "The Spanish of Equatorial Guinea: Research on La Hispanidad's Best-Kept Secret," *Afro-Hispanic Review* 21, no. 1–2 (2002): 76; Martin Lynn, "John Beecroft and West Africa, 1829–54," (unpublished Ph.D. thesis, University of London, 1979), 19–39.
[322] Alfred Burdon Ellis, *West African Islands* (London: Chapman and Hall, 1885), 70.
[323] Martin Lynn, "Commerce, Christianity and The Origins of 'Creoles' of Fernando Po," *The Journal of African History* 25, no. 3 (1984): 258; Richard Francis Burton, *Abeokuta and the Camaroons Mountains: An Exploration*, vol. 2 (London: Tinsley Brothers, 1863), 49.

for Royal Navy vessels docked in Clarence Cove.[324] The advent of steamships created new jobs that were dominated by Kru workers including the coaling of Royal Navy ships, as one captain proclaimed: "when coaling at Clarence Cove… The filling of the coal bags on shore was done by the Kroomen."[325] Coaling seems to have been solely performed by Kru. Similar to their multifaceted jobs in Freetown, they were tasked with clearing land, cutting, transporting, and sometimes floating timber in their surfboats.[326] Kru worked on the local steamer transporting inhabitants of the island along the coast and on rivers.[327] Indeed, Kru residing in Fernando Po had the opportunity to work both Royal Navy and commercial contracts in agriculture.[328]

By 1832, the Kru community in Clarence Cove was mixed with other "free negroes" and numbered 2,000.[329] "Free Negroes" included black settlers from Sierra Leone and possibly other African peoples including the Yoruba, who in some cases were recaptives.[330] The Kru were designated as distinct from other Africans, most probably because of their frequent employment with the British and the British reliance on their skill set. Although the precise number of Kru in this community is unknown, they formed a crucial part of British military and labor operations in Fernando Po. While the height of Royal Navy activity occurred between 1827 and 1830, anti-slaving raids temporarily ceased altogether as main operations shifted back to Freetown following an outbreak of malaria on the island.[331] However, many Kru remained on the island as the Royal Navy con-

---

324 Parliamentary Papers, Session 6 February – 5 August 1873, vol. 8 (1873), 186–187. HMS Rosamond had a crew of 23 seamen, which included six Krumen or just over 25 percent of the total. See also Parliamentary Papers, Session 6 February – 5 August 1873, vol. 8 (1873), 186–187; Sir Henry Huntley, *Seven Years' Service on the Slave Coast of Western Africa*, vol. 1 (London: Thomas Cautley Newby, 1850), 210.
325 Parliamentary Papers, Session 6 February-5 August 1873, vol. 8 (1873), 186–187; Also see Parliamentary Papers, Correspondence Respecting Affairs in the Cameroons, Enclosure 1, no. 25 "Captain Brook to Rear-Admiral Salmon" (1885), 22; ADM 101/132/2, Folios 14–24.
326 Leonard, *Records*, 155; FO 47/30.
327 Sundiata, "Rise," 32.
328 Ibid., 70; Leonard, *Records*, 155. Chapter 4 examines the nature of their labor in agricultural production on the island.
329 Richard Lander and John Lander, *Journal of an Expedition to Explore the Course and Termination of the Niger, with a Narrative of the Voyage down that River to its Termination*, 3 vols. (London: John Murray, 1832), 2: 296.
330 Thomas Jefferson Bowen, *Central Africa: Adventures and Missionary Labors in Several Countries in the Interior of Africa* (New York: Southern Baptist Publication Society, 1857), 217–218.
331 Andrew Pearson, *Distant Freedom: St. Helena and the Abolition of the Slave Trade 1840–1872* (Oxford: Oxford University Press, 2016), 83; Susana Castillo-Rodríguez, "The First Mission-

tinued to use Clarence Town as a strategic port for refuelling their vessels with coal and garnering supplies.

A distinct "Kroo Town" developed in Clarence Town from 1841.[332] Like their diaspora community in Freetown, the Kru community in Clarence Town was led by a "head Krooman."[333] Apart from organizing labor on Royal Navy ships and agricultural labor, his duty was to negotiate contracts for ship captains who sought Kru seamen for their vessels.[334] Their community was almost entirely male as most of its members were described as living "singly" in 1842.[335] It is not known if Kru women were included in the population figures provided below. However, in 1848, the *Edinburgh New Philosophical Journal* carried a story about Kru men having concubine relationships with the indigenous Bubi women much to the dislike of European missionaries.[336] In reality, Kru may have intermarried and had children with these women to create a new creole generation. Such relations added to the tense relations between the Kru and local Bubi as Kru who attempted to settle in the interior were met with physical violence and forced to return to Clarence Town.[337] Based on such a response, the Bubi most certainly perceived the Kru as foreigners who attempted to acquire their traditional land.

In 1843, a Spanish expedition led by Captain Lerena resulted in a permanent Spanish presence on the island.[338] The British handed authority back over to the Spanish, yet, British diplomat John Beecroft was named Governor by the Spanish and also became the British Consul of the Bights of Benin and Biafra between 1849 and 1854.[339] Based in Clarence Town, Kru served on British vessels including HMS Antelope and HMS Rosamond. In 1850, Sir Henry Huntley described the

---

ary Linguistics in Fernando Po," in *Colonialism and Missionary Linguistics*, eds. Klaus Zimmermann and Birte Kellermeier-Rehbein (Berlin: Walter de Gruyter, 2015), 76.
332 CO 82/9, "John Clarke to the British Foreign and Anti-Slavery Society," November 2, 1841.
333 Rev. Hope Masterson Waddell, *Twenty-nine Years in the West Indies and Central Africa: A Review of Missionary Work Adventure 1829–1858 By the Rev. Hope Masterson Waddell* (London: T. Nelson and Sons, Paternoster Row Edinburgh, 1863), 297.
334 Ibid., 297.
335 Anonymous, *Baptist Missionary Herald* 37 (September 1841): 132.
336 Thomas Richard Heywood Thomson, "The Bubis, or Edeeyah of Fernando Po," *The Edinburgh New Philosophical Journal* 44 (1848): 240; Ibrahim K. Sundiata, *From Slaving to Neoslavery: The Bight of Biafra and Fernando Po in the Era of Abolition, 1827–1930* (Madison: University of Wisconsin Press, 1996), 86.
337 For more discussion on tensions between Kru and the Bubi peoples see Ibrahim K. Sundiata, *From Slaving*, 86–87; Sundiata, "Rise," 25–42; Castillo-Rodríguez, "First Missionary," 75–106.
338 Castillo-Rodríguez, "First Missionary," 83.
339 Ibid., 76.

crew of HMS Rosamond: "twenty-three, three of whom were officers and six were Kroomen to conduct the vessel... for the *Rosamond* was fast gaining upon the retreating vessel."[340] Kru accounted for nearly 25 percent of the crew on HMS Rosamond, which is very much in line with our analysis of Royal Navy ships in 1819–20 as shown in tables 2.2 and 2.3.[341] Their lasting presence on Royal Navy vessels transiting through Clarence Town demonstrates the important role Fernando Po continued to serve in British operations even after the handover to the Spanish.

The arrival of Spanish missionaries meant that some Kru workers were exposed to Catholicism perhaps for the first time. Most of the missionaries they had encountered in Freetown and Monrovia belonged to Protestant denominations. Beyond attempting to convert Kru workers, Catholic missionaries sought to decipher linguistic structures informing the Kru language. In 1843, Catholic missionary, Gerónimo M. Usera y Alarcón, found two Krumen who were willing to speak with him.[342] In the process, the two Krumen converted to Catholicism. In 1852, Gerónimo M. Usera y Alarcón recounted the details of their baptism:

> Pues bien, los dos negro *Crumanes* que tripulaban la primera canoa que en Fernando Póo abordó la bergantin *Nervion*, eran los mismos que el 1.° de mayo de 1844 recibian el santo Bautismo en la Real Capilla, eran mis dos hijos espirituales Felipe Quir y Santiago Yegüe.[343]

Following their baptism, the two Krumen (Crumanes in Spanish) were given the names Felipe Quir and Santiago Yegüe.[344] They had manned the canoes on the Nervion, a Spanish naval vessel, and continued their tradition of transporting people and commodities from ship to shore and vice versa with the Spanish in Fernando Po. Quir and Yegüe became fluent in Spanish following instruction by a teacher named José Mariano Vallejo.[345] Even though only two Kru are mentioned in the sources, the episode is significant. Kru had been largely resistant to literacy and conversion to Christianity on the Kru Coast and in Freetown until the later decades of the nineteenth century.[346] Quir and Yegüe are two of earliest

---

340 Huntley, *Seven Years' Service*, 210.
341 Pearson, "Waterwitch," 116.
342 Gerónimo M. Usera y Alarcón, *Observaciones al llamado Opúsculo sobre la Colonizacion de Fernando Póo* (Madrid: Aguado, 1852), 26–27. See also Castillo-Rodríguez, "First Missionary," 75–106.
343 Usera y Alarcón, *Observaciones*, 27.
344 Ibid., 26–27.
345 Ibid., 26–27.
346 Fox, *Brief History*, 608–609.

known cases of Kru converts to Christianity in a diaspora community.[347] Their willingness to learn to read and write in Spanish and convert to Catholicism demonstrates that Kru were affected by a range of European influences in their diaspora community in Fernando Po. Increased contact with missionaries inaugurated a trend towards conversion to Christianity amongst the Kru in the second half of the nineteenth century on the Kru Coast and in their diaspora communities.

Table 3.2[348] shows that the population varied between 1832 and 1901. The initial population between 1827 and 1832 was upwards to 2,000 inhabitants. However, the Kru population fell after 1834 when British activity came to a temporary halt on the island because of a shift in anti-slaving Royal Navy activity back to Freetown. In 1838, British interest in the agricultural viability of the island was renewed and the Kru population increased. Kru serving on Royal Navy ships docked at Clarence Town sailed to Freetown following the capture of a slave ship before returning to Fernando Po. Much like their routine movement between Ascension Island and Freetown, the cyclical trajectory between Clarence Town and Freetown shows that Kru not only migrated between their homeland on

---

[347] Although missions were established in the Colony of Liberia as early as the 1830s, there was little conversion amongst the Kru in their homeland on the Kru Coast until the 1860s. The establishment of Wesleyan and Methodist mission schools in Kru villages, the publication of Bishop Payne's *Dictionary of the Grebo* in 1860, and the rise of prominent evangelical leader William Wadé Harris were the main factors that led the spread of Christianity on the Kru Coast in the later decades of the nineteenth century. See David A. Shank, *Prophet Harris: The "Black Elijah" of West Africa* (Leiden: Brill 1994), 40, 101; Ben Stimpson, "William Wade Harris: The 'Black Elijah' of West Africa," *Church History* 4 (2007), 4; Sheila S. Walker, *The Religious Revolution in the Ivory Coast – The Prophet Harris and the Harrist Church* (Chapel Hill: University of North Carolina Press, 1983), 3–16.

[348] Huntley, *Seven Years' Service*, 1:167; *Baptist Missionary Herald* (September 1841), 133; Hutchinson, *Impressions*, 180; Peter Lund Simmons, *Tropical Agriculture: A Treatise on the Culture, Preparation, Commerce, and Consumption of the Principal Products of the Vegetable Kingdom* (London: E & F.N. Spoon, 1877), 246; Gerónimo M. Usera y Alarcón, *Memoria de la isla de Fernando Poo* (Madrid: T. Aguado, 1848), 13; J. Scott Keltie, ed., *The Statesman's Year Book* (New York: St. Martin's Press, 1897), 959; Don Joaquin J. Navarro, *Apuntes Sobre El Estado de la Costa Occidental de Africa Y Principalmente de las Posesiones Españoles en Golfo de Guinea* (Madrid: Imprenta Nacional, 1859), 159–160; Lynn, "Commerce," 259, 261; Reclus, *Universal Geography*, 503; Sundiata,"Rise," 28–29; Sundiata, *From Slaving*, 57; *Baptist Missionary Herald* September (1841): 132; "Fernando Po," 182–187 *The Missionary Herald*, September (1846), 186–187; CO 82/9, "John Clarke to the British Foreign and Anti-Slavery Society," November 2, 1841, The National Archives, Kew. Simmons' figure of 2000 Kru includes Kru circulating between the Oil Rivers, the Bight of Benin, and Fernando Po. The number 993 includes Kru in all regions of Fernando Po. See Manuel De Teran, *Síntesis Geográfica de Fernando Póo* (Madrid: Institut d'Etudes Africains, 1962), 85.

Table 3.2: Kru population in Fernando Po.

Year	Total Population	Population of Clarence Town	Kru Population
1832	2,000	1,500	1,000
1835		1,500	1,000
1838			300
1841		873	192
1843			209
1846		1,027	50
1848		900	
1856		982	380
1858			209
1872	15,000		2,000
1877		1,106	
1885		1,284	
1901	30,000		993

the Kru Coast and workplace, but increasingly between diaspora communities in regular intervals.

The establishment of Krutown in Fernando Po owed its existence to both Royal Navy anti-slave trade operations and employment on plantations with the West Africa Company.[349] The initiative to hire Kru for agricultural contracts in the 1840s lasted decades as Élisée Reclus commented on Kru laborers in 1899: "the trade of Fernando-Po is in the hands of the English and Portuguese dealers... The land is divided into large estates, and cultivated by the Kroomen."[350] It seems that black settlers from Sierra Leone also made their way to Fernando Po and hired Krumen to work their plantations.[351] They cultivated palm oil, yams, corn, rice, plantains, and cocoa following its introduction from Brazil in 1854.[352]

In contrast with the respect held for Royal Navy contracts, some Kru were discontent with their treatment on plantations. In 1841, the Baptist Missionary

---

349 MSN/MN 5014/1–20, William E. Hearsey, Jr. Letters, Rare Books and Special Collections, University of Notre Dame, United States.
350 Élisée Reclus, *Africa and Its Inhabitants*, vol. 2, ed. A.H. Keane (London: Virtue and Company, 1899), 118.
351 Ibid., 118; Ellis, *West African Islands*, 60.
352 Parliamentary Papers, vol. 35 (London: H.M. Stationary Office, 1842), 607; Ibrahim K. Sundiata "Prelude to Scandal: Liberia and Fernando Po, 1880–1930," *The Journal of African History* 15, no. 1 (1974): 98.

Society reported one story regarding Kru labor on an English owned plantation in which "two headmen named Freeman and Tom Jack were cruelly tortured by John Scott."[353] In response to the incident, some Kru migrated into the interior and formed an independent community. Kru were accustomed to high wages and standard treatment as stipulated in their contracts. Mistreatment was met with resistance in the form of an exodus away from the main port town in Clarence Town. Their new settlement consisted of 400 Kru laborers in the North-West Bay of the island.[354] However, they clashed with local Bubi villagers who perceived the Kru as encroaching on their territory and bringing competition in the fish market as they both sold fish locally and to passing ships.[355] Moreover, the Kru leader of their new community known as Baffler supposedly forced the Bubi to provide them with women.[356] The West Africa Company captured Baffler, deported him to Freetown, and replaced him with a new leader.[357] Some Kru were enticed back to Clarence Town with the promise of higher wages, which included 2s. 6d. per day for headmen, 2s. 2d. for regular adults, and 1s. per day for adolescents.[358] The payment system based on hierarchal pay was still very much in play. This episode is unique because rarely did Kru diaspora communities feature breakaway communities that left their original workplaces.

Simon's Town

One of the most significant Kru diaspora communities in the Atlantic was founded at the Cape of Good Hope naval station in Simon's Town. The station formed an important node in the suppression of the trans-Atlantic slave trade in the southern Atlantic. The British occupied Simon's Town in 1806 and established a naval base in 1814.[359] One of the main functions of the port was refitting

---

353 Baptist Missionary Society, John Clarke, Journal vol. 1 (1 series), 320. Also see Sundiata, "Rise," 33.
354 CO 82/11, John Clarke to the British and Foreign Anti-Slavery Society, November 2, 1841. Also see Sundiata, "Rise," 31.
355 Nuria Fernández Moreno, "Bubi Government at the End of the 19th Century: Resistance to the Colonial Policy of Evangelization on the Island of Bioko, Equatorial Guinea," *Nordic Journal of African Studies* 22, no. 1–2 (2013): 27.
356 Sundiata, "Rise," 31.
357 Ibid., 31.
358 Ibid., 31.
359 Albert Thomas, "'It Changed Everybody's Lives': The Simon's Town Group Areas Removals," in *Lost Communities, Living Memories: Remembering Forced Removals in Cape Town*, ed. Sean Field (Cape Town: David Philip, 2001), 83.

Royal Navy ships. Simon's Town was linked to southern Atlantic itineraries including St. Helena, Ascension Island, and the Angolan coast from Malemba in the north to Elephant Bay in the south.[360] Simon's Town was so important that it became the base of Royal Navy Operations being combined with the West Africa Station in Freetown between 1832 and 1841 before it combined with the East Indies Station in 1865. Eventually, it became its own separate station in 1867 and by 1870 it was absorbed by the West Africa Station. Despite unfavorable currents and the great distance of 3500 kilometers between the Cape and the Congo delta, it served the important role of readying vessels for patrols in the southern Atlantic between Angola and Brazil.[361]

The 1839 Palmerston Act enabled all Portuguese slave vessels to be detained and delivered to Mixed Commission Courts, and later, British Vice Admiralty Courts in St. Helena and Cape Town. Most significantly, it opened up Portuguese ships to capture south of the equator and explains the increase in slave ship captures that followed over the next decade. Equipment clauses that were inserted into treaties meant that ships fitted with slave equipment and whose nationality could not be determined could be detained and their crews tried even if they were not carrying slaves.[362] Building on the Palmerston Act, in 1845, the Aberdeen Act concentrated even more sharply on quelling the Angola-Brazilian slave trade.[363] Pearson has shown that HMS Waterwitch and HMS Madagascar, both of which carried Kru, periodically made land assaults on slave factories and barracoons on the Kabenda.[364] Slave ship crews were frequently delivered to the Vice Admiralty Court in James Town, St. Helena for trial. The formerly enslaved awaited redeployment on British ships and were often sent to the Caribbean to work as indentured laborers on plantations or were released in Benguela and Loanda in West Central Africa.[365]

Kru came to form a vital part of operations in Simon's Town in Cape Colony. In 1838, they arrived on HMS Melville for service on Royal Navy ships engaged in

---

360 Pearson, "Waterwitch," 106.
361 Albert Bergman, *On Board the "Pensacola": The Eclipse Expedition to the West Coast of Africa* (New York: n.p., 1890), 38; "St. Helena," *The Asiatic Journal and Monthly Register for British and Foreign India, China and Australasia* 3 (1830): 70. For more discussion on the slave ship network in the southern Atlantic between Angola and Brazil see Daniel B. Domingues da Silva, "The Atlantic Slave Trade from Angola: A Port-by-Port Estimate of Slaves Embarked, 1701–1867," *The International Journal of African Historical Studies* 46, no. 1 (2013): 105–122.
362 Allain, "Nineteenth Century," 366.
363 Pearson, "Waterwitch," 106.
364 Ibid., 107.
365 Ibid., 116.

the suppression of the slave trade in the southern Atlantic.[366] 1838 also marked the British abolition of apprenticeship in Cape Colony and the Caribbean and informed the context for hiring the Kru.[367] Slavery had been permitted in Simon's Town since 1743 when the Dutch East India Company used Simon's Town as a winter anchorage.[368] The abolition of slavery and apprenticeship created increased working opportunities for the Kru in the region. In terms of the viability of the port, it fared better than St. Helena and Ascension Island, which both lacked protected harbors and were subject to heavy swells that limited ship maintenance. As such, Simon's Town became the main port where Royal Navy ships were refitted and repaired. Supplies including water and food were widely available and the naval base had a medical facility.[369] As Pearson has noted, landings, however, remained difficult due to heavy seas and an anti-clockwise system of winds and currents.[370]

Kru served as contract workers tasked with coaling ships, clearing and mooring. Being at the crossroads of the Atlantic and Indian Oceans, Kru were hired on board ships sailing itineraries in both oceans. Once again, their superb seamen skills meant their labor was in high demand by the British. Initially, they were housed in a building exclusively reserved for Krumen in the West Dockyard that became known as the Warrant Officer's Club in the twentieth century.[371] During this period, they also continued to dominate the fishing industry selling to local markets.[372] In 1883, Kru were described as living in the "native quarter."[373] Some Kru continued to reside in the dockyard, while others made their homes on the hillside of the native quarter. By at least the 1890s, they established "Kroo Town" near the local railway station built from tents.[374] The area was

---

366 Arthur Davey, "Kroomen: Black Sailors at the Cape" (Unpublished paper, 1992), 9.
367 For a discussion on the abolition of slavery in Cape Colony see John Edwin Mason, *Social Death and Resurrection: Slavery and Emancipation in South Africa* (Richmond: University of Virginia Press, 2003), 38.
368 Michael Whisson, *The Fairest Cape? An Account of the Coloured People in Simonstown* (Johannesburg: The South African Institute of Race Relations, 1972), 4.
369 Pearson, "Waterwitch," 111.
370 Ibid., 111.
371 Whisson, *Fairest Cape?*, 6; Lynn Harris, "'A Gulf Between the Mountains': Slavers, Whalers, and Fishers in False Bay, Cape Colony," in *Sea Ports and Sea Power: African Maritime Cultural Landscapes*, ed. Lynn Harris (Greenville, NC: Springer, 2016), 35; Parliamentary Papers, "West Coast of Africa and Cape of Good Hope Station," vol. 42 (1883), 64.
372 Thomas, "It Changed Everybody's Lives", 84.
373 Parliamentary Papers, "West Coast of Africa and Cape of Good Hope Station," vol. 42 (1883), 64.
374 Arthur Davey, "The Kroomen of Simon's Town," *Simon's Town Historical Bulletin* XVI, no. 2 (1990): 51.

located apart from both the dockyard and the native quarter. Their decision to establish living quarters apart from the British and other African laborers reveals the Kru's urge to maintain distance between their community and other laboring groups. While statistics for the population of Krutown in the nineteenth century are scarce, the population was 115 in 1890.[375] Although not as grand in scale as the Krutown in Freetown or Fernando Po, Kru continued their tradition of creating diaspora communities in British ports.

The headman system remained very important for British-Kru relations in Simon's Town. In 1901, a Kruman was convicted of the attempted murder of his boss, Mr. Pinkham, master of the Admiralty coal hulk called the Nubian. Pinkham had a staff of seven Krumen in charge of coaling ships. The headman was given the task of flogging the convicted Kruman.[376] This episode demonstrates that the hierarchal order governing headman-laborer relations remained firmly in place.

In contrast to Kru working in Freetown and Fernando Po, their entire population in Simon's Town was employed by the Royal Navy and resembled their community in Ascension Island. The Kru depicted in Figure 3.1 are dressed in naval attire complete with a hat. The three Kru standing in front of the others may signify that they were headmen and had a higher naval rank.[377]

Similar to those who adopted Christianity in Fernando Po, Kru seamen in Simon's Town showed an increased tendency towards conversion in their diaspora community. Kru attended St. George's Naval Church at the Dockyard where they were baptized. St. Francis Church contains the burial records, dated 1859 and 1861, of the wives of two of the Kru.[378] Information found on gravestones in Seaforth Cemetery indicates that some Kru living in Simon's Town were by 1880 baptized and Christian.[379] Perhaps, working in the Royal Navy played a role in their decision to convert because of the influence of their British colleagues who would have been Christian. While only speculative, it may be that their service in the Royal Navy was a factor in the growing number of conversion rates to

---

[375] The population of 115 Kru is an approximate number based on the figures provided by Arthur Davey. See Davey, "Kroomen of Simon's Town," 51.
[376] Joline Young, "The West African Kroomen and their Link to Simon's Town," *South African History Online*, accessed on June 17, 2016, http://www.sahistory.org.za/archive/west-african-kroomen-and-their-link-simons-town-joline-young.
[377] "Kroomen Stationed in Simon's Town," 1889, Simon's Town Museum, accessed on May 1, 2017, http://www.simonstown.com/museum/stm_hist_miscellaneous.htm.
[378] Davey, "Kroomen of Simon's Town," 51.
[379] Seaforth Cemetery, accessed on May 1, 2017, https://blog.ecu.edu/sites/expeditionsouthafrica/seaforth-cemetery/.

Figure 3.1: Kru stationed in Simon's Town, c. 1889.
Source: "Kroomen in the West Dockyard" c. 1889, Simon's Town Museum, accessed on May 1, 2017, http://www.simonstown.com/museum/stm_hist_miscellaneous.htm. Courtesy of the collection of Simon's Town Museum.

Christianity amongst the Kru in their diaspora and homeland communities in the second half of the nineteenth century.

A significant number of Kru have gravestones in the Garden of Remembrance in Simon's Town. Lynn Harris has compiled a list of Kru buried in the cemetery, which have been organized into a table here (Table 3.3). In total, 89 Krumen are commemorated in the Garden of Remembrance at Seaforth, Simon's Town, and in the Commonwealth Cemetery in Dido Valley. Twenty-six more appear in Naval Hospital and Burial records, bringing the total Kru to 115.[380] Gravestone records show which Royal Navy ships the Kru served on while based in Simon's Town. These records illustrate that Kru life expectancy was between 18 years and 33 years. Their age is significant because it provides a glimpse of the average age of the workers and shows that the majority of Kru serving on Royal Navy ships were adults rather than *kofa* or adolescent workers. Their low life expectancy rate was most probably based on the dangerous conditions associated with the nature of their work in the Royal Navy.

The gravestones show the geographical extent of Kru service on sea routes in the Atlantic and Indian Oceans as well as the Mediterranean Sea. Personal infor-

---

380 Davey, "Kroomen of Simon's Town," 51.

Table 3.3: Kru gravestones in Simon's Town, South Africa.

Ship Affiliation	Service Action	Kru
HMS Pandora	Royal Navy gunboat that served in West Africa and Mediterranean squadrons in the 1860s	Tom Sharp, died 1880 J.M. Massey, died 1880 Tom Cockroach, died 1881 Black Whale, died 1880 Jack Glasgow, died 1881 Jack Smart died 30/10/1880
HMS Flora	Zulu Wars, served as a guard, store and receiving ship in Simon's Town from the 1850s	Jim Brown, died 18/4/1882, age 26 Tom Freeman, died 6/12/1884, age 23 Jack Never, died 26/11, 1893, age 22 Ben Jumbo, died 16/7, 1881, age 30 Tom Dollar, died 11/1883, age 40
HMS Raleigh	Squadron in Bombay, Madeira, Falkland Islands, Calcutta, Cape Town, Gibraltar, Ascension Island	Jack Johnson, died 7/7/1886, age 26 Charles Cole, died 3/4/1888, age 25 Jack Everyday, died 25/10/1885, age 25 Jim Brown, died 2/4/unknown Ben Roberts, died 7/10/1890, age 25 Joseph Mannie, died 15/9/1888, age 27 Jack Purse, died 28/4/1886, age 22
HMS Penelope	Anglo-Egyptian War in 1882. A receiving ship in 1888 and a Boer War orison hulk in 1897.	Ben Johnson, died 29/4/1889 George Baker, died 29/11/1890 Jim Daws, died 10/7/1890 Tom D., died 4/1896 John Bull, died 28/4/1890 Sim Reeves, died 11/8/1890 Tom Tree, died 18/9/1890 Jack Smart no. 2, died 24/9/1880, age 22 Tom Peter no.8, died 8/1893 Jack Andrews, died 9/1893 Flying Jim, died 3/12/1889 Sam Lewis, died 9/10/1889 Dick Dead Eye, died 21/8/1890 Tom Poorfellow, died 28/4/1889, age 24
HMS Boadicea	Slave Trade Raids around Zanzibar in 1890s. Flagship of the East India Station	George Moses, died 16/1/1882 Dick Dallik, died 26/7/1882, age 28
HMS Curacoa	Cape and West Africa Stations in the 1880s	Jim Crow, died 7/4/1890
HMS St. George	West Africa Station	Bob Roberts, died 8/6/1896, age 22 Tom Bowling, died 4/1896 John Westlake, died 7/1895
HMS Watchful	Gunboat in Royal Navy in the 1880s	Tom Peters no. 5, died 18/8/1886, age 18

Table 3.3: Kru gravestones in Simon's Town, South Africa. *(Continued)*

Ship Affiliation	Service Action	Kru
HMS Rapid	Cape of Good Hope Station and missions in Mediterranean countries including Corfu, Albania, and Malta	John Bull, died 11/3/1886, age 26
HMS Alecto	Anti-slavery service of the coast of West Africa	Tom Pea Soup, died 23/4/1886, age 21
HMS Simoon	British War against the Ashante in 1873. A Hospital and water supply ship for troops.	Jim Crow, died 23/10/1904

Source: Harris, "Gulf Between the Mountains," 35.

mation therein reveals that the Kru returned to their community in Simon's Town following the completion of their contracts. The existence of Kru gravestones and Krutown suggest they had established a diaspora community by the 1880s when the first gravestones were produced. Despite its distant location, the Kru community in Simon's Town remained intimately connected with other Kru communities in the Atlantic as they circulated between ports.

The Kru diaspora in the Atlantic grew in tandem with the expansion of Royal Navy activities in the era of the suppression of the trans-Atlantic slave trades. Since Royal Navy ships almost entirely hired the Kru in Freetown, it can be deduced that those serving and living in Royal Navy ports were for the most part Proper Kru, Grebo, and Bassa Kru-speaking seamen. Although the ships eventually returned to Freetown in most cases, each port remained interconnected and became a place where Kru could seek new contracts or permanently remain.

Indian Ocean Network

The Indian Ocean slave trade grew in scale over the course of the nineteenth century and led to the employment of Kru seamen. Paul Lovejoy has estimated that the export of enslaved East Africans was 1,651,000 in the nineteenth century.[381] The main ports for acquiring slaves included Zanzibar, Pemba Island, Lamu, and Kilwa, whose primary exports also included cloves, ivory, copal, and coconut

---

381 Lovejoy, *Transformations*, 151.

oil.[382] Roughly half of the enslaved were sent northward in the slave trade to the Arabian Peninsula, Persia, and the Ottoman Empire to serve as domestic servants, soldiers, farm workers, concubines, pearl divers, and laborers on date plantations.[383] Slave disembarkation ports included Muscat, Soor, and Persian Gulf towns such as Bussorah and Mohamrah in Persia.[384] Perisan, Omani, and Ottoman caravans arrived, purchased the enslaved, and then dispersed as far abroad as Turkey.[385] The other half remained on plantations in East Africa. Data suggests that the nineteenth century represented a sharp increase in the number of enslaved African exports compared with earlier centuries, which was a result of East Africa and the Persian Gulf's inclusion into an emerging global capitalist economy.[386]

However, the Royal Navy's involvement in quelling the Indian Ocean slave trade was minimal before the 1860s. Despite the tightening succession of restrictions enabled by the Moresby Treaty (1822) and Hammerton Treaty (1845), Matthew Hopper has suggested that the East African slave trade peaked in the 1870s, which coincided with the greatest deployment of Kru sailors in the Indian

---

[382] Edward Alpers, *The Indian Ocean in World History* (Oxford: Oxford University Press, 2014), 53, 95; Howell, *Royal Navy*, 3; Matthew Hopper, "The African Presence in Eastern Arabia," in *The Gulf in Modern Times, People, Ports, and History* (New York: Palgrave-Macmillan, 2014), 327–350; Frederick Cooper, *Plantation Slavery on the East Coast of Africa* (New Haven: Yale University Press, 1977); Abdul Sheriff, "The Slave Trade and Its Fallout in the Persian Gulf," in *Abolition and Its Aftermath in Indian Ocean Africa and Asia*, ed. Gwyn Campbell (New York: Routledge, 2005), 106.
[383] Edward Alpers, "Recollecting Africa: Diasporic Memory in the Indian Ocean World," *African Studies Review* 43, no. 1 (2000): 83–99; Edward Alpers, *East Africa and the Indian Ocean* (Princeton: Markus Wiener Publications, 2009), 68–69; Behnaz A. Mirzai, "African Presence in Iran: Identity and its Reconstruction," *Outre-Mers revue d'histoire* 89, no. 335–336 (2002): 229–246; Behnaz A. Mirzai, *A History of Slavery and Emancipation in Iran, 1800–1929* (Austin: University of Texas Press, 2017), 33–90; Ralph Austen, "The Mediterranean Islamic Slave Trade Out of Africa: A Tentative Census," *Slavery & Abolition* 13, no. 1 (1992): 214–248; Gwynn Campbell, *Structure of Slavery in Indian Ocean Africa and Asia* (London: Routledge, 2004), 58; Matthew Hopper, "East Africa and the End of the Indian Ocean Slave Trade," *Journal of African Development* 13, no. 1 (2011): 27–54.
[384] Captain G.L. Sullivan, *Dhow Chasing in Zanzibar Waters: And on the Eastern Coast of Africa* (London: Frank Cass & Co. Ltd, 1873), 344.
[385] Ibid., 399; Vijayalakshmi Teelock and Abdul Sheriff, "Slavery and the Slave Trade in the Indian Ocean," in *The Transition from Slavery in Zanzibar and Mauritius* by Abdul Sheriff, Vijayalakshmi Teelock, Saada Omar Wahab, and Satyendra Peerthum (Oxford: African Books Collection, 2016), 35.
[386] Sheriff, *Slaves*, 21.

Ocean.[387] Although Britain's main concern in the Indian Ocean was protecting their sea routes to India, they were also influenced by the rejuvenated call for the abolition of slave trading by the British public during the 1850s and 1860s. Similar to British abolitionist narratives in the 1780s, David Livingstone and Richard Burton's writings on the horrors of the slave trade created a sense of urgency towards the abolition of the East African slave trade.[388]

The greatest challenge was that the Royal Navy was ill-equipped and designated few ships for anti-slavery patrols. In 1858, the East African coast was patrolled by a single ship, HMS Lyra. Based in Bombay, and later Trincomalee (Sri Lanka), the East Indies Station was responsible for Royal Navy operations in Indian Ocean waters between Mozambique and Rangoon. The relocation of the East Indies Station from Trincomalee to China in 1864 resulted in even less availability of resources towards the suppression of the slave trade. Hopper has proposed that because of the great distance and lack of resources only between seven and 11 Royal Navy ships were ever dedicated to anti-slave trade patrols in the Indian Ocean between 1865 and 1874.[389]

The lack of resources necessitated the use of a coalition of launch boats on Royal Navy ships in order to successfully engage slave ships. As such, the demand for Kru seamen, whose mastery of small watercraft was well known, increased in the Indian Ocean. In 1861, Rear-Admiral Walker requested that the Admiralty grant him use of Kru seamen at Cape Station (as Simon's Town was also known) for service on Royal Navy ships sailing the Indian Ocean. Beginning in January 1862, Royal Navy ships in the Indian Ocean were authorized to carry Kru.[390] There had already been 56 Kru serving on Royal Navy ships in the Indian Ocean who embarked at Cape Station even before the official request. However, Kru employment in the Indian Ocean became more systematized as they were

---

387 Gerald S. Graham, *Great Britain in the Indian Ocean* (Oxford: Oxford University Press, 1967), 196–210; J.B. Kelly, *Britain and the Persian Gulf* (Oxford: Oxford University Press, 1968), 411–451; Matthew Hopper, "Slavery and the Slave Trades in the Indian Ocean and Arab Worlds: Global Connections and Disconnections," 'Slaves of One Master:' Globalization and the African Diaspora in Arabia in the Age of Empire, November 7-8, 2008, Yale University, New Haven, Connecticut, 5.
388 See David Livingstone, *Last Journals*, vol. 2, ed. Horace Waller (Edinburgh: Edinburgh University Press, 1874), 212; Richard Francis Burton, *The Lake Regions of Central Equatorial Africa*, vol. 1 (London: Longman, 1860), 99; Richard Francis Burton, *The Lake Regions of Central Equatorial Africa*, vol. 2 (London: Longman, 1860), 368, 377.
389 Matthew Hopper, *Slaves of One Master: Globalization and Slavery in Arabia in the Age of Empire* (New Haven, CT: Yale University Press, 2015), 153.
390 Howell, *Royal Navy*, 41–42; ADM 123/48, "Admiralty (Romaine) to Rear-Admiral Walker, Number M 39," January 30, 1862, The National Archives, Kew, United Kingdom.

recruited for the specific task of manning launch boats and intercepting slave ships.[391] Kru embarked Royal Navy ships bound for the Indian Ocean in Freetown and Simon's Town.[392] Following their departure, they anchored at Zanzibar, next to HMS London, a floating station known as the East Africa Station that served as a depot. They then circulated between ports and islands, which included Mozambique, Madagascar, Mombasa, Aden, Comoros, Seychelles, Mauritius, Bombay, Trincomalee, and the Persian Gulf anchorages.

In 1862, 15 Kru served on HMS Gorgon and 51 on HMS Lyra. By 1863, a total of 100 Kru were working on various Royal Navy ships engaged in the suppression of Indian Ocean slave trade.[393] Although this number was much smaller than the number of Kru serving on Royal Navy ships in the Atlantic, the ratio of Kru to total crew seems to have been much higher in some cases. By then, the Kru were in high demand and there was a British initiative for the Kru to become officers.[394] There is no evidence that they became officers in the nineteenth century, but headman did reach the rank of eighth class in the Royal Navy.[395]

Captain G.L. Sullivan's account provides evidence of the ships upon which Kru served and the itineraries they sailed. After hiring Kru seamen at Freetown and Simon's Town on HMS Daphne, they sailed to Mauritius, Bombay, and Aden.[396] Kru on HMS Pantaloon tendered at Aden, the Seychelles, the Coco-de Mer Latham Islands, and Zanzibar before returning to East India Station in Bombay on May 11, 1866.[397] Sullivan reveals a third sailing route between Cape St. Andrews, Madagascar, and Trincomalee, Ceylon (Sri Lanka).[398] A fourth route was a roundtrip voyage from Aden to the Seychelles and Comoros Islands.[399]

Captain Sullivan provided further details on Royal Navy vessel allocation in various regions of the Indian Ocean. These included the following list:
– On the Arabian coast, from Ras-el-Had to Haura, one vessel and two steam launches.
– Red Sea, one vessel and two launches.

---

391 Howell, *Royal Navy*, 42.
392 Ibid., 41; ADM 123/48, "Admiralty (Romaine) to Rear-Admiral Walker," no. M 39, 30 January 1862, The National Archives, Kew, United Kingdom.
393 ADM 8/141 and ADM 8/142, "List Books, Cape of Good Hope Station," The National Archives, London, United Kingdom; Howell, *Royal Navy*, 42.
394 Howell, *Royal Navy*, 42; ADM 1/5768, "Notes on African Slave Trade, Captain E. Wilmot," 1861, The National Archives, Kew, United Kingdom.
395 See Chapter 2.
396 Sullivan, *Dhow Chasing*, 91.
397 Ibid., 93.
398 Ibid., 127.
399 Ibid., 137.

- From Cape Guardafui to Formosa Bay, one vessel and one launch – but removed during monsoon.
- From Formosa Bay to Cape Delgado, one vessel and one launch.
- From Cape Delgado to Macalonga River, one vessel and one launch.
- From Macalonga River to Inhambane, one vessel and one launch.
- From Commoro Islands to N.W. coast of Madagascar, one vessel and two launches.[400]

The Royal Navy formed what it conceptualized as a spider's web in the Indian Ocean as a practical means of patrolling vast distances. The coalition of vessels and small watercraft placed the Kru on the front lines of abolitionism as they operated launch boats and risked their lives boarding slave *dhows*.[401] In an episode off the east coast of Africa in the Indian Ocean, the heroic actions of several Krumen on board HMS Dryad are recorded as they chased down a *dhow* slave ship. HMS Dryad was engaged in the pursuit of a slave ship near Ras Madraka in which it ran aground. Three launches were dispatched to rescue the enslaved Africans on board and the Kru played a crucial role in rescuing a total of 58 Africans. Headman Jim George and Peter Warman swam back through the surf to the third boat and helped pull slaves from the *dhow*. For his efforts, Jim George was awarded a medal of honor; a bronze medal by the Royal Humane Society.[402] The names of specific Kru sailors were celebrated, which may have enabled the nineteenth-century British public to appreciate the great risks that were associated with service in the Royal Navy. Individual stories of Kru sailors resonated with nineteenth-century British authors who frequently crafted seamen tales, which referenced the Kru, for a readership who craved "exotic" characters and foreign adventures.[403]

The Kru headman system continued to structure labor relations between the British and Kru in the context of their Indian Ocean service. Every Royal Navy ship carried approximately 12 Kru seamen including a headman, second head-

---

400 Ibid., 199.
401 Howell, *Royal Navy*, 22; ADM 123/178, "Commander Oldfield to Captain Crawford," no. 3, March 23, 1861.
402 ADM 127/40, "Acting Lieutenant Henn to Commander Colomb, 6 May 1869, and Admiralty to Commodore Heath," no. P270, September 21, 1869; Howell, *Royal Navy*, 71.
403 For the body of Victorian and contemporary literature featuring Kru characters see Dickens, "Our Phantom Ship," 363–378; Dickens, "Cheerily, Cheerily!", 25–31; William Henry Giles Kingston, *The Two Whalers; Or, Adventures in the Pacific* (London: Society for Promoting Christian Knowledge, 1885), 61; Morley Roberts, "A Steerage Passage," in *Land-Travel and Sea-faring* (London: Lawrence and Bullen, 1891), 7; Adam G. Marshall, *Nemesis: The First Iron Warship and Her World* (Singapore: National University of Singapore, 2016), 37.

man, and 10 regular seamen. Smaller ships carried eight Kru consisting of a headman, second headman, and six seamen. Rear-Admiral Walker made a request to exceed this number and hire a greater number of Kru sailors.[404] The dominant role of the second Kru headman seems to have been more common in the Indian Ocean context as compared with the Atlantic suppression of the slave trade. One reason may have included the greater number of steamships in operation in the 1860s, which expanded the types of jobs performed by the Kru. In some cases, a greater number of workers may have necessitated the need for greater supervision, and hence a second headman. Alternatively, the British may have preferred hiring a second headman for purposes of completing tasks with greater efficiency regardless of the size of the Kru labor force.

Table 3.4 shows the number of Kru serving on each Royal Navy vessel in the Indian Ocean during the 1860s.

Table 3.4: Kru on Royal Navy Ships in the Indian Ocean, 1862–1869.

Year	Name of Ship	Number of Kru Serving
1862	HMS Gorgon	15
1862	HMS Lyra	15
1862–1869	HMS Star	10–15
1862–1869	HMS Nymph	10–15
1862–1869	HMS Dryad	10–15
1862–1869	HMS Daphne	10–15

Source: Howell, *Royal Navy*, 5, 51; Sullivan, *Dhow Chasing*, 91.

Zanzibar

Kru were allowed shore leave when anchored off the coast of Zanzibar. In 1866, they were noted as seeking a copy of a Bible in an unnamed church by Reverend Halcombe. While in his church, Halcombe observed on April 1, 1866 that the Kru were "baptized at Sierra Leone... they were men of 30, with the Kroo mark down the forehead and nose."[405] They maintained the Kru mark that distinguished them from other Africans. Moreover, these Krumen had been baptized and converted to Christianity. These two phenomena reveal both continuity and transfor-

---

404 Howell, *Royal Navy*, 42.
405 Halcombe, *Mission Life*, 58–59.

mation in the Kru free wage labor diaspora as traditional practice was kept and conversion to Christianity was becoming more common amongst Kru sailors.

Grave Island Cemetery, a naval cemetery, and its register document the Kru presence in Zanzibar (Table 3.5). Gravestones provide details on a sailor's date of death, ethnicity, and the vessel they served upon. Inscribed beside all of their names is the label "Krooman", which clearly preserved their unique identity and speaks to the nature of their service in the Royal Navy.[406] Moreover, their English names are written on the headstones and show that they maintained a dual identity throughout the nineteenth century.

Following the capture of a slave *dhow*, the enslaved Africans on board were disembarked in Zanzibar as well as the Seychelles, Aden, Cape of Good Hope, Mombasa, Mauritius, and Bombay.[407] Between 1861 and 1872, the Royal Navy delivered 2,409 captive Africans to the Seychelles. In 1864, approximately 2,000 Liberated Africans disembarked in Bombay.[408] The condition of the enslaved was not always known after they were released. Much like the recaptives in the Atlantic who were delivered and released in Freetown, Liberated Africans in the Indian Ocean found themselves in a foreign environment with an uncertain future that could very easily have turned them into recaptives.[409] Slave ship crews were often condemned to prison in Zanzibar.

Table 3.5: Kru gravestones in Grave Island Cemetery, Zanzibar.

Name	Date of Death	Ethnicity	Ship Affiliation
KG William	1873	Krooman	HMS Glasgow
King George	September 16, 1874	Krooman	HMS Vulture
Tom Walker	December 19, 1898	Krooman	HMS Fox
John William	July 19, 1899	Krooman	HMS Trush

Source: Zanzibar National Archive, File AA12/6. British Consulate Records. "Register of Graves, Grave Island Cemetery."

---

406 Zanzibar National Archive, File AA12/6, British Consulate Records, "Register of Graves, Grave Island Cemetery."
407 Howell, *Royal Navy*, 69–70; CO 167/522, "Foreign Office (Otway) to Under-Secretary, no. 6426 Mauritius," June 5, 1869, The National Archives, Kew, United Kingdom.
408 Clifford Pereira, "Black Liberators: The Role of Africans & Arabs sailors in the Royal Navy within the Indian Ocean 1841–1941" (paper presented at UNESCO Symposium on 'The Cultural Interactions Resulting from the Slave Trade and Slavery in the Arab-Islamic World, Rabat, May 18, 2007), 4.
409 British and Foreign State Papers, 1822–1823, "Inclosure – Evidence of Quashie Sam" (London: James Ridgway and Sons, 1850), 522.

By the 1880s, Kru had been mostly replaced by "Seedies" and Somali workers.[410] This was much to the dissatisfaction of Captain Lushington who vehemently claimed "12 Seedies equals 8 Kroomen."[411] The decision to replace the Kru was based on the time and cost required to transfer them between Freetown, Simon's Town and East Africa. The Indian Ocean slave trade was winding down by the 1880s, yet some Kru continued to serve in the region as evidenced by their gravestones in Zanzibar. Christopher Lloyd has suggested that the slave trade effectively ended in 1883, however, Hopper has shown that illegal slave trading continued well into the twentieth century to the Arabian Peninsula.[412] The Brussels Conference in 1888–1890 sought to quell the last bastions of the trade by providing the British with the right to search all ships suspected of trafficking slaves in the Red Sea, Persian Gulf, and southwestern Indian Ocean region off the coast of Mozambique and to deliver crews for adjudication before mixed tribunals.[413]

Kru played a vital role in Royal Navy operations in the Indian Ocean between 1862 and 1881. Despite their small number of between 10 and 15 Kru on each ship, the British relied on their manning skills on launch boats in pursuit of slave ships, perhaps to a greater degree than those serving in the Atlantic. While the Kru never formed Krutowns in Indian Ocean ports as they had in the Atlantic, they carried their diaspora on the decks of Royal Navy ships. Their service in the region was captured in narratives of the period and continues to be remembered on gravestones. Since Kru serving on Royal Navy ships were hired in Freetown and Simon's Town, Proper Kru, Grebo, and Bassa seafarers most certainly accounted for the majority of Kru in the region. Their experience in the Royal Navy in the Atlantic and Indian Oceans would gradually expand to include service in expeditions and naval brigades as they engaged in British military campaigns in Asia and Africa.

---

[410] "Seedies" was the name assigned to Liberated Africans who served on ships along the east coast of Africa. The term "seedies" derives from the word *sayyids*. See Stanziani, *Sailors*, 63; ADM 127/1, "Admiralty to Commodore Heath, number M73," April 7, 1870, The National, Kew, Archives, United Kingdom; Howell, *Royal Navy*, 72.
[411] ADM 1/6220, "Minute, V. Lushington," June 9, 1871; Howell, *Royal Navy*, 72.
[412] Hopper, *Slaves*, 159.
[413] Allain, "Nineteenth Century," 380, 382.

Chapter 4
Kru Labor in Expeditions and Military Campaigns

Beginning in the 1820s, Kru expanded their wage-earning opportunities in British expeditions of exploration and diplomacy in West Africa and West Central Africa. The British depended on Kru pilotage, porterage, and general labor in Hugh Clapperton's second expedition to Sokoto (1825–1827), and a series of Niger River expeditions including those led by Richard and John Lander (1830), Macgregor Laird, Richard Lander, and R.A.K. Oldfield (1832–1833), William Allen, Henry Dundas Trotter, and Bird Allen (1841–1842), and William Balfour Baikie (1854). Based on their valuable services, they were later employed on David Livingstone's Zambezi Expedition (1858–1864). Kru continued to rely on their mastery of watercraft as they navigated rivers, collected food and water, and transported European crew ashore for trade and negotiations with local polities. Often, the British provided additional financial incentives including gratuities to ensure that the Kru remained for the duration of the expeditions.[414] After all, the Kru had garnered a favorable reputation seaside and shoreside and remained in control of their labor to the extent that they would refuse work or leave workspaces if contractual terms and conditions were not to their satisfaction.[415] Perhaps most significantly, the expeditions opened the way for a greater British presence in the Niger Delta and increased palm oil production, which led to the creation of several Kru diaspora communities in Bonny and Calabar.

During the same period, Kru duties in the Royal Navy were extended to include service in military campaigns in Asia and Africa including the First Opium War (1839–1842), occupation of Lagos (1851–1852), campaign against Asante (1873–1874), Anglo-Zulu War (1879), and Sudan Campaign (1884–1885). Service in the First Opium War in China expanded their labor to the Pacific Ocean where they continued to serve on Royal Navy ships thereafter. Their participation in the assault on Lagos resulted in British control and the eventual establishment of a Kru diaspora community that lasted well into the twentieth century. While their role in expeditions largely depended on their mariner skills, the opportunity to serve in naval brigades on battlefields truly represented a new facet in the Kru labor experience. Moreover, their role in transporting military equipment and soldiers ashore, porterage, and engaging in battles at the front reveals the com-

---

414 Allen and Thomson, *Narrative*, 1: 494–495.
415 *The Church Missionary Review* 32, no. 12 (1881): 725; Frost, *Work*, 72.

plex nature of European colonial processes that unfolded in Asia and Africa in the nineteenth century.

Expeditions

Kru laborers played important roles in British expeditions in Africa. They cut paths, carried materials, manned and piloted British ships, and sailed vessels along two of Africa's most important rivers, the Niger River and the Zambezi River. The expeditions were largely inspired by European ideologies rooted in the desire to increase trade in the African interior, spread Christianity, and, from their perspective, inspire a higher level of civilization based on European social and economic values.[416] The primary concern of the Kru remained earning wages on contract, and they seem to have given little attention to the political impact of their involvement on local societies.

Clapperton's Second Expedition, 1825–27

Kru served on Hugh Clapperton's second expedition to the Sokoto Caliphate between 1825 and 1827. During the first expedition that began in Tripoli, Clapperton established diplomatic relations in Borno and the Sokoto Caliphate after crossing the Sahara under the command of Major Dixon Denham between 1822 and 1825.[417] Clapperton's second expedition arose from a mutual desire between the British and the Sultan of the Sokoto Caliphate, Muhammed Bello, to open up commercial trade with one another. On his voyage back to West Africa, he landed in Freetown for the purpose of acquiring Kru seamen. On October 27, 1825, Clapperton reported that he hired Kru in Freetown:

---

[416] For a discussion on ideologies informing colonial endeavor in Africa see Lewis H. Gann and Peter Duignan, *Colonialism in Africa, 1870–1960* (London: Cambridge, 1969), introduction; Frederick Lugard, *The Rise of Our East African Empire* (Edinburgh: W. Blackwood and Sons, 1893), 1:585–587, 2:69–75; Rudyard Kipling, "The White Man's Burden," *McClure's Magazine* 12, no. 4 (1899): 290.

[417] E.W. Bovill, ed., *Captain Clapperton's Narrative*, in *Missions to The Niger: The Bornu Mission, 1822–25*, Part 3, vol. 4 (Cambridge: Cambridge University Press, 1966); Dixon Denham, Hugh Clapperton, and Walter Oudney, *Narrative of Travels and Discoveries in Northern and Central Africa in the years 1822, 1823, and 1824*, 2 vols. (London: Darf Publishers Ltd., 1826); Bruce Lockhart and Lovejoy, *Hugh Clapperton*, 1.

H.M. Government however most wisely and humanely ordered that every ship serving on the African station shall be allowed a certain number [of hired men] to be paid and victualed on board for those duties during the time she is on the station-every merchant ship is obliged to do the same... I have also for the purpose of being able to land at all places and at all times hired – 14 – the head man of whom is called Tom Freeman.[418]

Their duties were to assist in the collection of water, wood, and landing along the coast as they approached Badagry in the Bight of Benin.[419] Clapperton was aware of the necessity of hiring Kru on his voyage because of their positive reputation, and due to the high mortality rates affecting British seaman in West Africa.[420] The headman, Tom Freeman's labor gang included: "Bottle of Beer, Black Will, Prince Will, Jack Monday, Ben Coffee, Jim George, Tom Nimblo, Jack Tartar, Yellow Will, Jack Morgiana, Jack Purser, Tom Briggs, and Peter Johnson."[421] Kru workers in Clapperton's expedition continued to depend on their headman. There were 14 Kru laborers in total, which suggests the manpower required was on par with the number of Kru serving on Royal Navy ships during the period.

Clapperton landed at Badadgy on December 7, 1825 and made his way overland and crossed the Niger at Bussa. Kru played a fundamental role in porterage and the manning of watercraft. Clapperton realized that the Niger and neighboring rivers formed a larger network of waterways that had the potential to establish a network of trading posts that would link the British on the West African coast with the Sokoto Caliphate in the interior.[422] Unfortunately, Clapperton arrived in Kano, the major emporium of the interior, at a time when the Caliphate was at war with Borno, which Clapperton also intended to visit. When it was discovered that Clapperton had presents for Shehu al-Kanemi, the ruler of Borno, that included firearms, he was detained and during his internment in Sokoto died of disease.[423]

---

418 Bruce Lockhart and Lovejoy, *Hugh Clapperton*, 83.
419 Ibid., 82–83.
420 Ibid., 83.
421 Ibid., 83.
422 Ibid., 12.
423 Ibid., 53.

Lander Brothers' Expedition, 1830

Following his death in 1827, his assistant, Richard Lemon Lander, returned to the coast and later published Clapperton's journals and his own account in 1829.[424] Almost immediately upon his return to Britain, Lander was commissioned to lead a new expedition, together with his brother John, and in 1830 they left Britain on the brig Alert. Like Clapperton, the Lander brothers hired Kru seamen for their expedition. They landed at Badagry on March 22, 1830, and made their way to Bussa, from where they traveled down the Niger towards the delta.[425] Their mission, too, was far from successful, since they were imprisoned and were only freed in the Niger Delta when a Portuguese ship purchased their liberty. From a European perspective, however, they demonstrated that the Niger River did indeed flow into the Atlantic Ocean in the many rivers that were now recognized as the delta of the Niger.

The Kru played an important role in navigation. One of their duties included piloting the Alert and its smaller craft through potentially challenging sub-marine terrain. Richard Lander explained that their duty was to "sound the bar of the river, in order to know whether there was sufficient depth of water for the vessel to pass over it."[426] The Kru also engaged in towing the Alert with smaller craft as the anchor was raised.[427] In typical Kru fashion, Lander noted that they manned each craft with six rowers while on the Niger.[428]

Laird Expedition, 1832–33

British interest in establishing the Niger as commercial hub continued to gain momentum and in 1832, Macgregor Laird, supported by Liverpool merchants, sent two ships, the Alburkah and the Quorra, to the Niger. The Quorra had 26 crewmembers and the Alburkah had 14, both included Kru, although their exact numbers were not provided.[429] Laird noted the "dexterity of the Kroomen

---

424 Ibid., 82–83.
425 Richard and John Lander, *Journal*, 1: 41.
426 Ibid., 3: 252.
427 Ibid., 283.
428 Ibid., 284.
429 MacGregor Laird and R.A.K. Oldfield, *Narrative of an Expedition into the Interior of Africa, By the River Niger in 1832, 1833 and 1834 in the Steam-Vessels Quorra and Alburkah* vol. 2 (London: Richard Bentley, 1837), 302; John W. Davies, "On the Fever in the Zambesi: A Note from Dr.

is exemplified in their diving, and their power of remaining under water for a considerable time."[430] Their skills were useful for the maintenance of the hull, which required Kru to venture beneath the ship for the purposes of cleaning it.

As was the case on previous expeditions, the primary function of Kru workers was cutting wood, gathering supplies, and tendering crew members and goods ashore on small craft.[431] Occasionally, they were also sent to trade ashore, acquiring food for the crew including meat and livestock to be slaughtered.[432] Laird's expedition had not proven to be an immediate commercial success, but the mission was in part driven by a desire to establish commercial relations with Igbo, Igala, and Edo traders on the Niger in palm oil that it was hoped would ultimately quell the trans-Atlantic slave trade.

In terms of navigation, Laird's experimentation with steamship technology marked the beginning of a new era in the British Empire in West Africa. Steamship prototypes had been in use since 1819, but the Alburkah and Quorra were the first multi-purpose armed steamships to make an oceanic voyage, predating the Nemesis, which was the first iron steamship solely designed for warfare.[433] Laird eventually founded the African Steamship Company in 1852.[434] Faster travel periods and a flat-bottomed hull that enabled travel in shallow rivers played a major role in British expeditions into the interior of West Africa. Moreover, as mentioned above, it created new jobs for the Kru such as firestokers and coalers, and increased the demand for them in supplying wood for the ships.

Niger Expedition, 1841–42

Kru returned for service on the Niger in the expedition of 1841–1842. In 1840, Thomas Fowell Buxton, Member of Parliament, abolitionist and founder of the

---

Livingstone to Dr. M'William June 3rd 1861," *Transactions of the Epidemiological Society of London* 1 (1863): 239.
430 Laird and Oldfield, *Narrative*, 303.
431 Ibid., 302; William Simpson, *A Private Journal Kept During the Niger Expedition: From the Commencement in May 1841, Until the Recall of the Expedition in June 1842 By William Simpson* (London: John F Shaw, 1843), 69–70.
432 Laird and Oldfield, *Narrative*, 2:133.
433 Peter Ward Fay, *The Opium War, 1840–1842: Barbarians in the Celestial Empire in the Early Part of the Nineteenth Century and the War by Which They Forced Her Gates Ajar* (Chapel Hill: University of North Carolina, 1975), 260–263; Lincoln P. Paine, *Warships of the World to 1900* (Boston: Houghton Mifflin Harcourt, 2000), 115.
434 Peter N. Davies, *The Trade Makers: Elder Demspter in West Africa, 1852–1872, 1973–1989* (Oxford: Oxford University Press, 2017), xxvi.

Society for the Mitigation and Gradual Abolition of Slavery (later known as the Anti-Slavery Society), began organizing the largest expedition on the Niger yet undertaken.[435] Buxton's vision for increased commerce and the promotion of Christianity in West Africa was rooted in similar principles informing the establishment of Freetown some five decades earlier.[436] Reverend J.F. Schon and Reverend Samuel Ajayi Crowther joined the expedition and were responsible for assessing the disposition of African rulers in the interior to receiving the gospel.[437] Three ships sailed for the Niger including HMS Albert commanded by Captain H.D. Trotter, HMS Wilberforce commanded by Captain William Allen, and HMS Soudan commanded by Bird Allen. The goal of the expedition was to establish a model farm or trade center and mission in Lokoja at the confluence of the Niger River and Benue River.[438]

Prior to the expedition, Captain Trotter recognized the need to offer the Kru higher wages than those offered on Royal Navy ships in order to entice Kru to join the expedition. Unlike their service on Royal Navy ships where they could receive additional prize money following the capture of a slave ship, there was no such opportunity on the expedition. Trotter claimed that higher wages would "ensure getting the best description of men."[439] He suggested giving those Kru who completed the expedition one month's wages as a gratuity.[440] The gratuity was not to exceed a total of £200 and was to be distributed amongst Kru laborers.[441] Trotter was concerned Kru seamen would abandon the expedition in search of better economic opportunities. Eleven men were designated as stokers on the ships and the remainder were tasked with landing boats and shoreside duties.[442] In total, £500 was allotted for Kru employment in expedition expenses.[443]

---

[435] Junius P. Rodriguez, *Slavery in the Modern World: A History of Political, Social and Economic Oppression*, vol. 1 (Santa Barbara: ABC-CLIO, 2011), 156.
[436] Suzanne Schwarz, "Commerce, Civilization and Christianity: The Development of the Sierra Leone Company" in David Richardson, Suzanne Schwarz, and Anthony Tibbles eds., *Liverpool and Transatlantic Slavery* (Liverpool: Liverpool University Press, 2007), 270.
[437] Kenneth Dike, "Origins of the Niger Mission 1841–1891," A paper read at the Centenary of the Mission at Christ Church, Onitsha, on November 13, 1957 (Ibadan: Ibadan University Press, 1962), 6.
[438] Whitford, *Trading Life*, 129.
[439] Allen and Thomson, *Narrative*, 1: 494.
[440] Ibid., 495.
[441] Ibid., 497.
[442] Parliamentary Papers, vol. 2, no. 15, "Niger Expedition," Colonial Office, R. Vernon Smith, January 1841, 13, 1842.
[443] Allen and Thomson, *Narrative*, 1: 491.

On June 26, 1841, Kru were hired on HMS Wilberforce and HMS Albert in Freetown.[444] The muster list suggests that 108 "Men entered in Africa," which included the Kru who were dispersed amongst the vessels. Forty-four were assigned on HMS Albert, 37 on HMS Wilberforce, 18 on HMS Soudan, and nine on a fourth vessel, Amelia.[445] Some of the names of Kru crewmembers were listed on the ships' manifests. Jack Be-Off on HMS Albert was listed as being born in Kru Country, and held the rank of Ordinary seaman. Two other Kru included Andrew Williams, an Able seaman, and James Carol, a stoker.[446] The ships sailed for the Niger on August 20, 1841. They performed the same types of jobs they had in previous expeditions, manning small craft along the river, collecting timber for fuel, fresh water, and supplies.[447] They were responsible for providing a portion of the food for the crew and fished in the lagoons and river.[448] They were also tasked with unique duties, as demonstrated by a Kru seaman who dug the grave of a fallen crewmember.[449]

As was the case on all previous expeditions, the headman system remained integral for the completion of daily operations. Several headmen were hired on HMS Wilberforce including Wilson who led a gang of eight Kru laborers.[450] Jack Andrews headed another gang, whose duty was to assist in working small vessels.[451] His gang included Jack Frying-pan, King George, Prince Albert, Jack Sprat, Bottle-of-Beer, Tom Tea-Kettle, Prince of Wales, Duke of York, and Sam Lewis.[452] The expedition produced a model farm for a Niger mission, albeit the mission did not develop further until Crowther's return in 1854.[453] Treaties between the British and rulers in Aboh and Idah towards the abolition of the slave trade were signed and they granted permission for the presence of missionaries. However, mortality rates were high amongst the British sailors. Fifty-four crew of the total of 162 crewmembers were dead from malaria within weeks of

---

444 Simpson, *Private Journal*, 128, 18, 22, 68–70. Simpson suggests that the number of Kru employed amounted to 120.
445 Allen and Thomson, *Narrative*, 1:461.
446 Ibid., 465.
447 James Frederick Schön and Samuel Crowther, *Journals of the Rev. James Frederick Schön and Mr. Samuel Crowther: Who, Accompanied the Expedition Up the Niger, in 1841, in Behalf of the Church Missionary Society* (London: Hatchard and Son, 1842), 150; Simpson, *Private Journal*, 47.
448 Allen and Thomson, *Narrative*, 1:167.
449 Schön and Crowther, *Journals*, 164.
450 Simpson, *Private Journal*, 58.
451 Allen and Thomson, *Narrative*, 1:77.
452 Ibid., 77–78.
453 Dike, "Origins," 9.

the voyage up the Niger. In contrast, Kru seamen experienced a very low mortality rate on the expedition. Only four Kru laborers died from malaria including one on HMS Albert, two on HMS Wilberforce, and one on HMS Soudan.[454]

Baikie Expedition, 1854

High mortality rates amongst British sailors and low economic returns in the 1841–1842 expedition meant that there was little interest amongst the British government in funding another expedition in the Niger until more than a decade had passed. In 1854, the British embarked on another expedition with the goal of increasing the number of trading stations on the Niger and establishing missions. John Beecroft was assigned to command the expedition, but he died in Fernando Po before ascending the Niger. In his stead, Dr. William Balfour Baikie, a surgeon and naturalist, commanded the expedition in the steamer, Pleiad. He sailed up the Niger and then up the Benue, surpassing all previous expeditions in terms of distance.

Advances in medicine with the development of quinine meant that an antimalarial drug could be taken as a prophylactic for the first time. Although Jesuits in the sixteenth century and indigenous populations in South America, Central America, the Caribbean, and parts of West Africa had known about the medicinal properties of cinchona bark, it was not used in the large-scale production of medicine until the mid-nineteenth century.[455] The Niger Expedition provided the opportunity to test the viability of quinine amongst British sailors.[456] Quinine became available in the 1850s for regular use and played a major role in lowering

---

[454] Allen and Thomson, *Narrative*, 506; John Beecroft, "On Benin and the Upper Course of the River Quorra, or Niger, by Captain Becroft," *Journal of the Royal Geographical Society of London* 11 (1841): 184, 189. Kru served on the Ethiope steamer in April 1840. Commanded by Captain Beecroft, they sailed in Fermoso River (Benin River) before finding it impassable and, in May 1840, sailed the Niger River.

[455] Philip Curtin, *The Image of Africa: British Ideas and Action, 1780–1850*, vol. 1 (Madison: University of Wisconsin, 1973), 81; Philip Curtin, *Disease and Empire: The Health of European Troops in the Conquest of Africa* (Cambridge: Cambridge University Press, 1998), 5, 21, 113, Curtin, "End," 63–88; Alexander Bryson, "Prophylactic Influence of Quinine," *Medical Times and Gazette* 7 (January 7, 1854): 6–7; J.O. M'William, *Medical History of the Expedition to the Niger during the years 1841–1842 comprising An Account of the Fever* (London: John Churchill, 1843), 10.

[456] Curtin, *Image of Africa*, 81; Bryson, "Prophylactic Influence," 6–7; M'William, *Medical History*, 10.

fatalities. As a result, there was not a single death amongst British sailors due to malaria for the first 118 days of the expedition.[457]

Based on high mortality rates amongst British sailors in past expeditions, the British government hired as many African laborers as possible. Unlike previous expeditions in which Kru laborers were hired in Freetown, Kru were hired directly on the Kru Coast.[458] The Kru formed half of the complement on the voyage up the Niger in the 1854 expedition: 33 in a total crew of 66.[459] Samuel Crowther observed the Kru paddling canoes between ship and shore, collecting wood, and purchasing food and beer from local Igbo traders.[460] Ultimately, Baikie's efforts led to the creation of trading posts and missions in Onitsha, Gbebe, and Lokoja.

Opening up the Niger led to the increased employment of Kru workers in the Niger Delta in the palm oil industry. The demand for palm oil in British factories rose and more ships were devoted to the trade in the mid-nineteenth century.[461] Used as a lubricant for machinery as well as for soap, candles, and the palm kernals for margarine and cattle feed, palm oil grew in demand.[462] The shift to so-called "legitimate trade" was meant to encourage Kru, Yoruba, and other traders on the west coast of Africa to earn profits from palm oil production rather than from slave trading, which abolitionists believed to be mutually exclusive.[463] How-

---

[457] Dike, "Origins," 10.
[458] William Balfour Baikie, *Narrative of an Exploring Voyage Up to the Rivers Kuora and Binue Commonly Known as the Niger and Tsadda in 1854* (1856; repr., London: Psychology Press, 1966), 18, 366.
[459] Davies, "On the Fever in the Zambesi," 241.
[460] Samuel Crowther, *Journal of an Expedition up the Niger and Tshadda Rivers Undertaken by Macgregor Laird in Connection with the British Government in 1854* (London: Church Missionary House, 1855), 8, 43, 66, 87, 89, 94, 130.
[461] David Northrup, "The Compatibility of the Slave and Palm Oil Trades in the Bight of Biafra," *The Journal of African History* 17, no. 3 (1976): 359, 360.
[462] Martin Lynn, "From Sail to Steam: The Impact of the Steamship Services on the British Palm Oil Trade with West Africa, 1850–1890," *The Journal of African History* 30, no. 2 (1989): 228.
[463] Kristin Mann, "Owners, Slaves and the Struggle for Labour in the Commercial Transition in Lagos," in *From Slave Trade to 'Legitimate' Commerce: The Commercial Transition in Nineteenth Century West Africa*, ed. Robin Law (Cambridge: Cambridge University Press, 2002), 195–214; Robin Law, "The Politics of Commercial Transition: Factional Conflict in Dahomey in the Context of Ending the Slave Trade," *The Journal of African History* 38, no. 2 (1997): 213–333; Martin Lynn, *Commerce and Economic Change in West Africa: The Palm Oil Trade in the Nineteenth Century* (Cambridge: Cambridge University Press, 2002), 34–104; Northrup, "Compatibility," 353.

ever, the transition caused an increase in local slavery as the enslaved were redirected to agricultural production in the Bight of Biafra.[464]

Bonny and Calabar

During this transitional period, Kru remained on wage labor contracts with the British and founded diaspora communities in the Niger Delta. Palm oil production in Bonny played a major role in Kru migration. By the 1850s, there were between 500 and 600 Kru working on agricultural contracts in Bonny.[465] Many Kru were hired specifically for the transport of palm oil on British vessels.[466] Kru worked on contracts that lasted between six months and a year before returning to Freetown where many had been hired or to their homeland on the Kru Coast.[467] In 1850, the Petrel carried 63 Kru workers for contracts in palm oil agriculture.[468] Demand was so high that up to 200 vessels engaged in the palm oil trade were said to employ Kru annually.[469]

Kru were hired for their ability to navigate unpredictable waters with adverse sub-marine terrain including sandbars. Using their surfboats as they had for centuries on the Kru Coast, Kru were recorded as transporting individuals, loading and unloading cargo including palm oil and missionary goods, and manning small boats upon the arrival of mail steamers arriving at Bonny.[470] Kru living in Bonny made for a labor pool that offered hundreds of Kru workers.[471] Gangs of Kru laborers were hired out from Bonny for service along the many riv-

---

[464] Kristin Mann, *Slavery and the Birth of an African City: Lagos, 1760–1900* (Bloomington: Indiana University Press, 2007), 1–8, 51–130; Lovejoy, *Transformations*, 160–184.
[465] Accounts and Papers, vol. 9, Session 4 February-August 8, 1851, "Enclosure 1, in No. 50, Colonial Land and Emigration Office" (June 8, 1850), 450.
[466] Ibid., 450.
[467] Ibid., 450.
[468] Ibid., 450.
[469] British and Foreign State Papers, 1861–1862, vol. 52, "Reports from Naval Officers. West Coast of Africa Station," no. 62, Commodore Edmonstone to Rear-Admiral Sir H. Keppel," January 4, 1861, 538.
[470] Whitford, *Trading Life*, 287; Adolphe Burdo, "Travels in Central Africa," *The Christian World Magazine and Family Visitor* 17 (London: James Clarke and Company, 1881): 154; British and Foreign State Papers, 1861–1862, vol. 52, "Captain Walker to Mr. Hamilton, Abstract of Journal of Steam-Ship *Sunbeam* During the Expedition Up the River Niger in 1861," (September 28, 1861), 598.
[471] Peter N. Davies, ed., *Trading in West Africa, 1840–1920* (London: Croom Helm, 1976), 30.

ers and tributaries that make up the Niger Delta as the British traded and loaded ships at Bonny, Opobo, Calabar, and elsewhere.

Table 4.1 shows Kru wages earned on British commercial contracts in the Bight of Biafra. The location and duration of contracts determined wage rates. The pay rates and rank are not always provided in the sources and so information is both sporadic and inconsistent. Table 4.1 shows an approximation of Kru wage rates on commercial vessels in the Bights of Benin and Biafra. As the nineteenth century progressed, Kru had the opportunity to earn higher wages while engaged in commercial labor for the British. The Kru headman continued to receive a percentage of wages from his labor gang, and therefore, his wages increased depending on the size of the labor force. Kru were also guaranteed that all travel expenses including return passage were covered. The low salaries for the year 1899 did not specify the length of the contract. However, the table shows that headmen continued to make up to three times higher salary than regular workers.

Table 4.1: Kru Wages in the Bight of Biafra.

Year	Rank	Duration of Contract	Location	Pay Rate/ Month	Advance
1860s-1870s	Boatmen	6 months	Bight of Biafra	£1 5s	10s
1860s-1870s	Headman	6 months	Bight of Biafra	£2 10s	£1
1899	Headman	NA	Calabar	30s	None
1899	Ordinary	NA	Calabar	10s	None

Source: Smith, *Trade*, 100–103; "Negro Civilization," *Journal of Health*, 259; Frost, *Work*, 26; Guinness, *New World*, 213; Colonial Reports, no. 315, "Southern Nigeria, Report for 1899–1900" (London: Darling & Son, 1901), 26.

Wages were not only dependent on rank but may have also been affected by the location of their embarkation. In 1863, Richard Burton observed the following correlation between embarkation and pay rates:

> When shipped at S'a Leone for merchant service, their wages are more than those who embark at Cape Palmas; nominally the former now receive 30s., the latter $2 per month in goods, which reduce it to $1. Some picked gig-crews in the Oil Rivers, receive $5, besides additional clothes and caps; the average pay is from $3 to $4.[472]

---

[472] Richard Francis Burton, *Wanderings in West Africa from Liverpool to Fernando Po*, 2 vols. (London: Tinsley Brothers, 1863), 26.

According to Burton, Kru hired in Sierra Leone had the opportunity to earn a higher wage rate than those hired in their homeland on the Kru Coast near Cape Palmas. However, Burton shows that Kru already based in their diaspora communities in the Niger Delta were hired for work on the Oil Rivers at a higher salary than in all other locations. Perhaps, the British were willing to pay a little more because they did not have to worry about additional expenses incurred on the voyage from Freetown or Cape Palmas to the Niger Delta.

Headmen continued to play an important role in the organization of the Kru workforce. Jane Martin has suggested that the headman changeover process in Calabar occurred every twelve months. A second headman returned to the Kru Coast or Freetown and recruited a labor gang every six months. The newly-hired gang went to Calabar and familiarized itself with the work routine by learning from the gang that was already there. A full changeover took place every October.[473] Over the course of the nineteenth century, the Kru seem to have developed a unique process of selecting a second headman to return and recruit gang laborers to replace the existing ones, such as the case in Calabar.[474]

In Calabar, Kru living and working quarters were associated with a building known as the "Kroo House."[475] It was located on a stretch of beach next to the boatshed and marine stores. This building most probably served as lodgings for some Kru workers and a storage space for their marine equipment. Although not a quarter, the fact they had their own residence named after them signifies that they formed a distinct community in Calabar and played a fundamental role in marine and agricultural operations.

Zambezi Expedition, 1858–1864

The lasting impact of Kru participation in British expeditions was not limited to West Africa, as they also served in David Livingstone's Zambezi Expedition between 1858 and 1864. Similar to British expeditions on the Niger, Livingstone's expedition was rooted in the British desire to establish trading posts and missions in the African interior.[476] The British government and subscriptions raised

---

[473] Martin, "Krumen," 405.
[474] Ibid., 405.
[475] *Foreign Office Diplomatic and Consular Reports on Trade and Finance No. 1834: Africa: Report for the Year 1895–1896 of the Administration of the Niger Coast Protectorate* (London: Majesty's Stationary Office, 1897), 130.
[476] David Livingstone, *Missionary Travels and Researches in South Africa* (London: John Murray, 1857), 92.

£5,000 for the expedition. Livingstone served as British Consul, whose task was to establish trade on the Zambezi.[477]

Livingstone sailed on HMS Pearl on March 10, 1858 from Liverpool to Quelimane to undertake an exploratory journey up the Zambezi River. Kru, who were hired in Freetown, assembled and manned the Ma-Robert, a 75-foot long paddle wheeled flat-bottomed steam boat intended to carry 36 men up the Zambezi River.[478] Similar to their role in the Niger expeditions, Kru continued to serve as boatmen, collected wood, and provided ship maintenance. New duties included keeping night-watch and serving as cooks.[479]

Livingstone offers a brief glimpse into the lives of those Kru who served. Two Kru on the expedition were mentioned by name. Tom Coffee served as engineer's mate.[480] A Kru named Tom Jumbo supposedly served to reassure the local inhabitants of the benevolent intentions of Livingstone's expedition, even though he spoke a completely different language.[481] However flawed, Livingstone hoped that by employing the Kru as mediators they would garner trust between themselves and the Shupanga, Tsonga, and Shona along the route. Thomas Baines described the Kru as being "lent" for their services, which suggests that they were valuable for operations on board the Ma-Robert and shoreside.[482]

One challenge during the expedition was that the Ma-Robert kept running aground. Kru helped to keep the boat on course as one passenger observed: "Kroomen going into water willingly... Grounded again-then a third and fourth time; very trying to their tempers."[483] The Ma-Robert was unable to navigate the cataracts on the Shire River. As a result, Livingstone had to make his way to Lake Nyassa by way of an overland trek.[484] Kru did not accompany Livingstone on the trek. Initially, Livingstone commented favorably on their work ethic claim-

---

[477] A.D. Roberts, "Livingstone, David (1813–1874)," *Oxford Dictionary of National Biography* (Oxford: Oxford University Press, 2004) online, n.p, accessed August 10, 2018, https:// http://www.oxforddnb.com/.

[478] Donald Simpson, *Dark Companions: The African Contribution to the European Exploration of East Africa* (London: Paul Elek Limited, 1975), 39.

[479] G.W. Clendennen and D.H. Simpson, "African Members of the Zambezi Expedition, 1861–1864: A Prosopographical Foray," *History in Africa* 12 (1985): 29–49; Livingstone, *Expedition*, 59; Edward C. Tabler, *Baines on the Zambezi, 1858 to 1859* (Johannesburg, SA: Brenthurst Press, 1982), 93, 97, 117; Livingstone, *Narrative*, 95, 96.

[480] Simpson, *Dark Companions*, 41.

[481] Ibid., 41.

[482] Tabler, *Baines*, 62.

[483] Simpson, *Dark Companions*, 41.

[484] "Letters Relating to Dr. Livingstone," *Proceedings and Monthly Record of Geography* 40 (1866): 307–308.

ing: "The Kroomen all worked admirably."[485] Despite their important role in operations, the Kru fell out of favor with Livingstone after one Kru was supposedly accused of theft. This was followed by a strike amongst the Kru who refused to work in response to the accusation, which led to their condemnation by Livingstone.[486] Livingstone also condemned the Kru for their inability to march on long treks, which was likely the result of their unwillingness to cooperate with him following the strike. Since the next phase of the expedition would be an overland trek, he thought the Kru unfit.[487] On July 29, 1859, the Kru were dismissed and set sail on HMS Persian to Freetown.[488] They were replaced by eight Kololo laborers. Livingstone concluded: "Disciplined Europeans are much better than Kroomen."[489]

Despite their usefulness and hard work, the Kru were viewed with suspicion and condemned if they dared to challenge British authority. Livingstone's remarks upon hiring Kru reveal the Victorian racist perceptions that informed his perspective: "We have twelve Kroomen, who seem docile and willing to be taught."[490] From Livingstone's perspective, Kru on the expedition were like children who required European instruction and were at odds with their traditional reputation as hardworking and industrious. There was also an economic aspect to their dismissal. Livingstone complained that while the Kololo ate local "country food" in the region, Kru insisted on their "man of war's allowance of beef, biscuit, tea, sugar, etc."[491] Kru were accustomed to a higher standard of treatment in the Royal Navy, which they expected on the expedition. Livingstone seems uncomfortable with their expectations. He implies that expenditures could be cut with the dismissal of Kru seamen.

Ultimately, the expedition did not succeed as parts of the Zambezi proved unnavigable. The expedition was recalled by the British government in 1863 be-

---

485 Simpson, *Dark Companions*, 41.
486 David Livingstone and Charles Livingstone, *Narrative of an Expedition to the Zambesi and Its Tributaries: And of the Discovery of the Lakes Shirwa and Nyassa, 1858–1864* (New York: Harper & Brothers, 1866), 96–103; William Garden Blaikie, *The Personal Life of David Livingstone* (New York: Harper Brothers, 1881), 257; Sjoerd Rijpma, *David Livingstone and the Myth of African Poverty and Disease: A Close Examination of his Writing on the Pre-Colonial Era* (Leiden: Brill, 2015), 121.
487 Livingstone, *Narrative*, 96.
488 Ibid., 96–103; Rijpma, *David Livingstone*, 121; Sir Reginald Coupland, *Kirk on the Zambesi* (Oxford: Clarendon Press, 1928), 98.
489 J.P.R. Wallis, ed., *The Zambezi Expedition of David Livingstone, 1858–1863*, vol. 1 (London: Chatto & Windus, 1956), 104–105, 325; Rijpma, *David Livingstone*, 175–176.
490 Blaikie, *Personal Life*, 248.
491 Wallis, *Zambezi Expedition*, 104–105, 325.

cause the economic and political prosperity of the region was questioned. There was no opportunity for Kru to establish diaspora communities along the Zambezi River as there had been in the Niger Delta. Despite Livingstone's negative attitude towards the Kru, employment opportunities with the British increased as they were hired in military campaigns in the decades that followed.

In all of the expeditions under question, Kru were hired in Freetown or in Cape Palmas, which meant that the expeditions were most likely comprised of Proper Kru, Grebo, and Bassa laborers. Similar to their relationship on the Kru Coast, the British continued to rely on Kru surfboats and seafaring skills while maneuvering sub-marine terrain, conducting trade and obtaining supplies in riverine environments.

Military Campaigns and Naval Brigades

Kru served in various British military campaigns in Asia and Africa in the nineteenth century. Their contribution played a significant role in the consolidation of British influence, and ultimately the establishment of British colonial rule in both continents. Their function was to serve in Royal Navy brigades as porters, stevedores, boat transporters, soldiers, and to assist with firing rockets, artillery, and Gatling guns. Kru service in military operations expanded the geographical breadth of their diaspora in the African continent and Pacific Ocean.

First Opium War, 1839 – 42

In one of their first known military engagements, Kru served in Britain's campaign against the Chinese in the First Opium War. Since the 1620s, when the British arrived at the Canton River, the East India Company traded silver for such items as silk, porcelain, and tea with Guangzhou merchants. Once the British understood the great value placed on opium, they sought to control the opium trade from India to China.[492] The British held a monopoly over the opium trade until 1834, and, in 1839, Commissioner Lin was sent on behalf of the Emperor and ordered to halt the trade in the region. Fifteen hundred tons of opium were destroyed and Western traders were placed under house arrest.[493] Conflict

---

[492] Daniel Headrick, *Power Over Peoples: Technology, Environments, and Western Imperialism, 1400 to the Present* (Princeton: Princeton University Press, 2012), 198.
[493] Ibid., 199.

between the British and Chinese ensued and the East India Company set up a Secret Committee, which ordered six new steamers ready for combat. These included the Nemesis, Phlegethon, Ariadne, Medusa, Pluto, and Proserpine.[494]

The Nemesis embodied new steamship technology as it was the largest iron steamer built in the period and because of its flat bottom and six-foot draft it was able to sail up rivers and across oceans in deep and shallow waters with equal proficiency. Weaponry included a rocket-tube, ten small cannons, five six-pounders, and two pivot-mounted 32-pounders.[495] Although the Nemesis was commissioned by the Secret Committee of the East India Company, it was commanded by Royal Navy Commander William Hall. Both the British Royal Navy and the East India Company sought to quell Chinese opposition to British influence and stabilize the opium trade in their favor. Whereas Kru had hitherto been involved in the suppression of the trans-Atlantic slave trades, they now also served on a ship engaged in a war for control of commerce.

Kru served on the Nemesis between 1840 and 1842 for the duration of the itinerary from St. Thomas to the Canton River.[496] William Dallas Bernard and Sir William Hutcheon Hall reported that three Krumen boarded the Nemesis in St. Anne on the island of St. Thomas and participated in the China Wars.[497] Kru were drawn from the pool of laborers working in St. Thomas (São Tomé as it was known in Portuguese).[498] São Tomé and Principe served as refueling ports for Royal Navy ships engaged in anti-slaving activities in the Atlantic.[499] Some Kru remained on the islands and cut timber for the purposes of coaling.

---

494 Ibid., 200.
495 Ibid., 200.
496 Fay, *Opium War, 1840–1842*, 260–263.
497 William Dallas Bernard and William Hutcheon Hall, *Narrative of the Voyages and Services of the Nemesis, from 1840–1843; And of the Combined Naval and Military Operations in China: Comprising a Complete Account of The Colony of Hong Kong, And Remarks on The Character and Habits of the Chinese from Notes of Commander W.H. Hall, R.N. by W.D. Bernard, ESQ, A.M. Oxon, In Two Volumes* vol. 1 (London: Henry Colburn, 1844), 28. Kru were noted for their service in the Opium Wars; see *The Mariner's Church Gospel Temperance Soldier's and Sailor's Magazine* 30, no. 3093 (1843): 40. St. Thomas was the English name given the Portuguese island of São Tomé. Kru were hired as agriculturalists on São Tomé by a mix of British and Portuguese planters. The Kru who returned to the United Kingdom was also confirmed in a magazine; see *The Mariner's Church Gospel Temperance Soldier's and Sailor's Magazine* 30, no. 3093 (1843): 40. For more information on Nemesis see Fay, *Opium War*, 260–263.
498 Bernard and Hall, *Narrative*, 23. Kru were employed for agricultural labor contracts on São Tomé in the 1870s. There was a proposal to hire Kru laborers for a period of ten years. See Minutes of Evidence Taken Before The Royal Commission of Fugitive Slaves, Lieutenant V.L. Cameron, May 2, 1876, 61.
499 Bernard and Hall, *Narrative*, 23.

There is no clear indication as to why Kru were not hired in Freetown or in Cape Colony in southern Africa. It may be that the captain decided to increase the size of his crew en route in order to meet ship maintenance demands. As expert divers and swimmers, Kru were employed on the Nemesis based on their ability to perform laborious duties, including cleaning barnacles under the hull of ships.[500]

The Nemesis was the first iron steam frigate to circumnavigate the Cape of Good Hope before heading to Cape Delagoa. The itinerary included anchorage at Ceylon (Sri Lanka) and Singapore, before sailing towards its final destination in China.[501] The Nemesis arrived in Macao in November 1840 and by early 1841 it was engaged in attacks on forts on the Bogue River, the main defenses protecting Guangzhou. The Nemesis engaged Chinese war junks and fire rafts (rafts laden with oil-soaked cotton and gunpowder) before taking control of the Grand Canal at the Yangzi River.[502] By July 1842, following attacks on Chinese forts at Wusong, near Shanghai, the British took Zhenjiang up the Yangzi and effectively blocked the Grand Canal, which was China's main channel of trade between Beijing and the central and southern provinces. As a result, in August 1842, the Treaty of Nanjing was signed by the Chinese and British, which transferred the island of Hong Kong to Britain, opened five ports to foreign trade, and set import duties.[503]

Serving on the Nemesis in Pacific waters expanded the geographical breadth and military nature of the Kru labor network. Until this voyage, Kru are not known to have sailed east of Simon's Town in the Cape of Good Hope. It is likely they performed the task of manning boats and transporting British seamen and war materials from ship to shore on the smaller boats, as they were generally hired for their ability to handle small craft. They were also likely to serve as "powder monkeys", meaning gunners' assistants whose job it was to replenish fresh gun powder to the gunners firing the canons.[504] Two of the three Kru who embarked the ship in St. Thomas survived the conflict and made the return voyage to Freetown, while the third Kru had been killed in action in China, which suggests that beyond boating their involvement most probably had a military

---

500 Ibid., 26.
501 Nathan Hale, ed., *The Monthly Chronicle of Events, Discoveries, Improvements, and Opinions* 2, no. 1 (Boston: S.N. Dickinson, 1841): 86.
502 Headrick, *Power*, 204.
503 Ibid., 204.
504 See Costello, *Black Salt*, 55.

component.⁵⁰⁵ In typical fashion, the surviving Kru were provided with return transport home via Calcutta.

The fact that Kru were sought for service on the Nemesis is significant. By 1840, they had developed a strong reputation based on their skills as seamen, which led to their selection for the voyage on the Nemesis to China. Kru continued to serve on Royal Navy ships in Hong Kong and along the Chinese coast thereafter. In 1861, 21 of them were listed as serving on HMS Algerine in Hong Kong following the Second Opium War 1857–60.⁵⁰⁶ While little documentation exists providing details on their daily experiences on the Nemesis and HMS Algerine, the fact they served on these ships reveals that the Kru labor network had expanded to include Pacific waters in the Far East. Their service in the Opium War marks the first known case in which Kru participated in a British military campaign against a sovereign polity and adds an important nuance to the nature of their military service, which would gradually lead to Kru serving on the front lines in future campaigns.

Occupation of Lagos, 1851–52

Beginning in the 1850s, Kru participated in succession of British military campaigns in Africa. In 1851, Kru served in the assault on Lagos. While the British suggested that the reason for the attack was to end illegal slave trading and local slavery that persisted in the region, a more pertinent reason seems to have been to establish Lagos as a British port for trade and commerce.⁵⁰⁷ Conflict between multiple claimants for the position of Oba of Lagos and Kosoko's refusal to sign a treaty that would have abolished slave trading with John Beecroft who was waiting for an agreement aboard HMS Bloodhound proved to be the main factors that influenced the British decision to intervene.⁵⁰⁸ Another factor was an increase in slave exports from Lagos to Cuba, the southern United States,

---

505 Bernard and Hall, *Narrative*, 26, 471.
506 Daniel Owen Spence, *A History of the Royal Navy: Empire and Imperialism* (London: I.B. Taurus, 2015), 227; Pereira, "Black Liberators," 3.
507 See Mann, *Slavery*, 1–8, 51–130; Biko Agozino, *Pan-African Issues in Crime and Justice* (London: Taylor and Francis, 2017), 224; Johnson U.J. Asiegbu, *Nigeria and its British Invaders, 1851–1920* (Lagos: Nok Publishers International, 1984), 3–40.
508 Robert Smith, "To the Palaver Islands: War and Diplomacy on the Lagos Lagoon in 1852–1854," *Journal of the Historical Society of Nigeria* 5, no. 1 (December 1969), 3; Robert Smith, "The Lagos Consulate, 1851–1861," *The Journal of African History* 15, no. 3 (1974), 398.

and Brazil even after the Palmerston Act and Aberdeen Act had sought to quell the illegal slave trades to the Americas.

During the campaign, Kru served on HMS Teazer, HMS Penelope, and HMS Sampson under Lieutenant Corbett, Captain Lyster, and Captain Jones.[509] On December 26, 1851, Captain Jones led a military force of 400 soldiers and officers ashore in boats that were manned by Kru.[510] Their role was to transfer the landing parties ashore and guard the launch boats as the soldiers and other Kru proceeded to the front.

Surgeon Samuel Donnelly provides a valuable record that demonstrates the extent of Kru participation in the battle (Table 4.2). In the document titled "List of Officers, Seamen, Marines, and Kroomen, belonging to H.M.S. *Sampson*, killed and wounded at Lagos on Dec. 26, 1851," Donnelly reported that a Kruman named Jumbo received a "wound of the right shoulder."[511] The fact that Kru were designated their own category on the list demonstrates their significant role in Royal Navy operations in the battle.

Table 4.2 shows Kru serving on each craft belonging to HMS Sampson. They accounted for 11.1 percent of the crew carried on the 1st Lifeboat, 11.4 percent on the 2nd Lifeboat, 9.5 percent on Pinnace, 12.5 percent on the 1st Cutter, 14.2 percent on the 2nd Cutter.[512] A larger number of Kru manned the small craft belonging to HMS Penelope as they accounted for 24.6 percent on the whaler, 20.5 percent on the 1st Lifeboat, 20 percent on the 2nd Lifeboat, 14.2 percent on the Pinnace, ten percent of the 1st Cutter, and ten percent of the 2nd Cutter.[513] In total, 14 Kru served on the watercraft belonging to HMS Sampson out of a total of 134 crewmembers engaged in the battle, which shows that they formed 10.4 percent of the force. Forty-one Kru out of a total of 223 crewmembers landed watercraft belonging to HMS Penelope, which reveals they formed 18.3 percent of the total landing force.[514] Overall, 55 Kru engaged in the assault out of a total of 357 crewmembers thereby forming 15.4 percent of the total landing complement. Their duties transporting ammunitions, crew, and guarding the surfboats served a crucial function in the attack on Lagos.

---

509 William Ernst Ward, *The Royal Navy and the Slavers: The Suppression of the Atlantic Slave Trade* (London: Allen & Unwin, 1969), 212, 215; Accounts and Papers, Inclosure 7 in No. 70, "Lewis T. Jones, Captain H.M.S. Sampson," (1852), 202.
510 Ward, *Royal Navy*, 212, 215.
511 Accounts and Papers, Inclosure 7 in No. 70, "Lewis T. Jones, Captain H.M.S. Sampson," (1852), 202.
512 Ibid., 203.
513 Ibid.
514 Ibid.

Table 4.2: Kru serving on HMS Ships in the assault on Lagos.

Ship	Type of Watercraft	Number of Kru	Total Crew
HMS Sampson	1st Lifeboat	4	36
	2nd Lifeboat	4	35
	Pinnace	2	16
	1st Cutter	2	21
	2nd Cutter	2	14
	1st Gig	0	7
	2nd Gig	0	5
HMS Penelope	Whaler	19	77
	1st Lifeboat	7	34
	2nd Lifeboat	7	35
	Pinnace	4	28
	1st Cutter	2	20
	2nd Cutter	2	20
	1st Gig	0	9
Total		55	357

Source: Accounts and Papers, Inclosure 7 in No. 70, "Lewis T. Jones, Captain H.M.S. Sampson" (1852), 202.

The treaty handing authority over land in Lagos to the British was signed by John Beecroft, Henry William Bruce, Oba Akitoye, and Chief Ashogbon aboard HMS Penelope on January 1, 1852.[515] Based on available sources, this was most probably the first time Kru served in a military capacity in a British campaign in Africa. Their role as guards and the fact some Kru were wounded and killed in the conflict shows that they were assigned a military function beyond transportation.

Kru began to work in Lagos following the British occupation in 1851 and its formal annexation in 1861. Lagos became the site of one of their largest diaspora communities and differed from those mentioned above in that their community developed as a direct result of a military campaign. Kru were responsible for manning the launch boats in HMS Brune, which was stationed at Lagos.[516] Kru migrant workers lived on Lagos Island next to Tinubu Square, which was initially formed in the 1870s.[517] Like other Krutowns and quarters, the location was ideal for its close proximity to the harbor where they labored. Moreover, in the 1850s

---

515 Ibid., 212, 215.
516 Sir William M.N. Geary, *Nigeria Under British Rule* (London: Routledge, 1927), 33.
517 Martin, "Krumen," 406, 412.

and 1860s it continued to serve as a stop for West Africa Squadron ships replenishing supplies while in search of slavers in the Bights. Sixty-six Kru children were recorded as being born in Lagos during the 1870s and 1880s.[518] While the male population continued to dominate the Kru community in Lagos, the birth of Kru children suggests that Kru women may have accompanied their husbands. Alternatively, Kru may have intermarried with local Yoruba women, and the children were recorded as Kru. Regardless, it shows the growth of the Kru diaspora community towards a permanent presence.

The acting Governor of Nigeria estimated the "floating Kroo population" in Lagos to be 1,200 in 1897. While many Kru transited through the port on ship contracts, the increase in population may have been related to the construction of the port in Lagos.[519] Kru were engaged in shoreside and seaborne labor with some only able to find work in domestic service. They also contributed to the construction of infrastructure including roads and buildings in Lagos, and most notably, Lagos Port and the railway north of the port.[520] The British had come to rely on Kru labor in Lagos as they had throughout West Africa.

Similar to the Gold Coast, Kru were distinguished as a distinct community in documents pertaining to hospitalization in Lagos. Kru working as pilots in the harbor and in local factories were required to pay for their stay in the Colonial Hospital in Lagos a total "sum of Four shillings and two pence for each of the first five days of his residence in the said Hospital, and the sum of One shilling and three pence for each subsequent day."[521] Ordinance No.1 also reveals that the Kru were making wages in order to pay for their stay in the hospital. The fact the Kru were distinguished from servants and designated their own quarter reveals that they maintained their unique identity while in the Colony of Lagos.

Kru were also distinguished by the British through their inclusion in the procession in Port Lagos in 1897 honoring Queen Victoria's Diamond Jubilee. The Kru are visible in a photograph and report under the title "portraits of local people."[522] Categorizing the Kru as local people meant that their diaspora community in Lagos was both distinct and sizeable. Kru serving in the Royal Navy

---

[518] Mann, *Slavery*, 189.
[519] Schmidt, "Kru Mariners," 110–123.
[520] Mann, *Slavery, 189*; "Southern Nigeria, Report for 1899–1900," 26.
[521] George Stallard and Edward Harrinson Richards, *Ordinances and Orders, and Rules Thereunder, in Force of the Colony of Lagos on December 31, 1893*, "Hospital Fees for Kroomen and Servants, no.1 1881" (London: Stevens, 1894), 412.
[522] Trustees of the British Museum. "Diamond Jubilee – Procession of Kroo boys on the Marina Lagos." British Museum, registration number Af, A51.71; also posted in Asiri Magazine on June 15, 2017, accessed October 28, 2017, http://asirimagazine.com/en/.

wore white on this special occasion of Queen Victoria's Diamond Jubilee as a form of commemoration.

By the early twentieth century, Kru were requested to serve on labor contracts in Lagos as boatmen for periods of six months, with a chance to renew for 12 months. As was the case in boarding in Freetown, Kru were given an advance of £1 for each headman who could earn £2 10s. per month and 10s. for every Kru boatman on £1 5s. per month.[523] The decision to hire the Kru in Lagos was based on the Governor's previous experience of drawing on Kru labor in the Gambia.[524] The wage rate reveals that the headman structure that became institutionalized in Freetown was still very much in play as regular laborers were expected to provide their headmen with a portion of their earnings a century later.

Asante Campaign, 1873–74

While the short and long-term effects of the assault on Lagos can be said to have influenced Kru employment, the Anglo-Asante War in 1873–74 involved Kru but did not have an immediate impact on Kru employment in the region. Rather, the sizeable Kru diaspora communities that were founded in Accra and Sekondi in the twentieth century were the product of later developments.[525] A series of battles had unfolded in the Gold Coast between the British and the Asante since the 1820s, most notably when the British were defeated in 1822 at the Battle of Nsamankow. The Second Anglo-Asante War ended in 1864 in a stalemate.

---

[523] Smith, *Trade*, 100–103; "Negro Civilization," *Journal of Health*, 259; Frost, *Work*, 26; Guinness, *New World*, 213; Colonial Reports, no. 315, "Southern Nigeria, Report for 1899–1900" (London: Darling & Son, 1901), 26.

[524] Frost, *Work*, 26.

[525] An interview with Ga community leader A Bonso III (Stool Secretary) and Okyeeme Abeka Gikafo (Chief Linguist) on December 20, 2012 revealed that the Kru formed a sizeable community in the James Town quarter of Accra in the early twentieth century. According to oral tradition, the Kru paid a form of tribute to the Ga chiefs who administered James Town in exchange for land for the establishment of Krutown. This was a unique economic arrangement compared with other Krutowns, such as the one established in Freetown, where they were not required to pay tribute to local Mende and Temne chiefs. Their duties included loading and unloading ships in the harbor using their surfboats. They also performed manual labor contributing to the construction of the sewer system. During the time of the interview, Krutown was completely abandoned and in a state of ruin. Many Kru had returned to their communities in Liberia or scattered throughout Accra decades earlier when contracts became too few.

The Third Anglo-Asante War commenced in 1873 led by General Garnet Wolseley with a force of 2,500 British troops that were augmented with several thousand African and Indian troops against the Asante. Kru served with the British in the campaign against the Asante between 1873 and 1874. Similar to their role in Lagos, they were employed for their ability to land supplies and military personnel in the face of adverse sea conditions. Henry Brackenbury recognized the need for Kru expertise in piloting surfboats carrying military equipment when he lamented about the "difficulty… in the landing and storage of supplies and stores."[526] This campaign was augmented by a large body of Kru hired at Cape Palmas, meaning they were most probably Grebo, to serve as carriers on board HMS Ambriz.[527] Beyond landing supplies, their function was to carry the heavy equipment and ammunition towards the front.[528] They served alongside carriers from Accra (presumably Fante).[529] They far outnumbered their counterparts, the "Accramen," by 500 percent. According to George Dobson, the British "fed" and "properly led" the Kru.[530]

However, Kru formed but one component of a mixed force, as reported by Henry Stewart in 1879:

> The forces at his disposal consisted of only 20 royal marine artillery, under Lieutenant Allen; 169 royal marine light infantry, from H.M.S. *Simoon*, under Captain Crease; 500 bluejackets and marines… 200 West India negro troops… 20 Kroomen and 126 Houssas, under Lieutenant Richmond; besides a few armed police, and 300 labourers with axes to clear a path.[531]

The British drew their forces from their various ports in the Caribbean, Bight of Biafra, and towns on the Kru Coast. Kru were tasked with cutting paths through

---

[526] Henry Brackenbury, *The Ashanti War: A Narration Prepared from the Official Documents by Permission of Major-General Sir Garnet Wolseley By Henry Brackenbury*, vol. 1 (London: William Blackwood and Sons, 1874), 164.
[527] Charles Rathbone Low, *A Memoir of Lieutenant-General Sir Garnet J. Wolseley. By Charles Rathbone Low* (London: Richard Bentley & Son, 1878), 95. Cape Palmas is the heart of the Grebo region and therefore it seems that Grebo would most likely make up the greatest proportion of hired laborers.
[528] George Armand Furse, *Military Transport: H.M. Stationary Office, 1882* (London: W. Clowers & Sons, 1882), 45; Low, *Memoir*, 146.
[529] George Dobson, "The River Volta, Gold Coast, West Africa By Mr. George Dobson of Cardiff Read to the Members, in the Library, January 29th 1892, at 7:30 pm," *The Journal of Manchester Geographical Society* 8 (Manchester, 1892): 21.
[530] Ibid., 21.
[531] Henry Stewart, *Our Redcoats and Bluejackets: War Pictures, forming a Narrative of the Naval and Military History of England from 1793* (London: Ballantyne Press, 1879), 350.

the dense jungle on the way to Kumasi and served in the naval brigade on the war front. Every Royal Navy ship had its own brigade, which was a ground combat force made of crewmembers whose role was to assist British land forces in battle. The British defeated the Asante at the Battle of Amoaful on January 31, 1873 and occupied the capital Kumasi before burning it. In July 1874, the Treaty of Fomena was signed. Victory can be attributed to the use of quinine and the Gatling gun, which provided an advantage over the Asante. Little is known about the Kru's first-hand experiences at the front and if they served in a role beyond delivering equipment. However, based on available evidence, this was most probably the first episode in which Kru travelled from the coast to the war front in a British military campaign and set the stage for further involvement in future campaigns.

Anglo-Zulu War, 1879

Kru continued to serve on front lines in conflict in an even greater capacity during the Anglo-Zulu War in 1879. The British attempted to annex the Zulu state, which was not completed until 1887.[532] Factors that influenced the conflict included British tensions with Boer settlers, the goal of avoiding bush conflict with the Zulu in the way they had encountered the Xhosa, the desire to quell the threat of Portuguese expansion who sought to control the Port Delgoa region in the east, and the need to protect the sea route between the Indian and Atlantic Oceans.[533] British colonial administer Sir Henry Frere was tasked with the goal of uniting South Africa under a British confederation despite the great challenges of uniting independent black states, the Boer republics, and British colonies. Looking to the British Governor of Natal and the Transvaal, Sir Theophilus Shepstone, for valid reasons to invade Zulu territory, Frere ultimately based his decision to attack on the number of firearms accumulating in Zulu territory and incursions they made in the adjacent lands. Furthermore, the British had a direct stake in the region following the annexation of the Transvaal into a formal British colony in 1877, which created shared borders with the Zulu.[534] An ultimatum

---

[532] For information on the Anglo-Zulu wars see Carolyn Hamilton, ed., *The Mfecane Aftermath: Reconstructive Debates in Southern African History* (Witswatersrand: Wits University Press, 1995), 1–12, 395–416; Harold E. Raugh, Jr., *Anglo-Zulu War 1879: A Selected Bibliography* (New York: Scarecrow Press, 2011), 1–74.
[533] Ibid., 287, 293, 303.
[534] Joyce Bowman, "Reconstructing the Past Using the British Parliamentary Papers: The Anglo-Zulu War of 1879," *History in Africa* 31 (2004): 121.

was sent to Zulu King Cetshwayo in December 1878, which required him to disband his army or face the British military. Knowing the terms would not be accepted, an army led by Lord Chemsfield was prepared and the war commenced.

In early January 1879, Kru arrived on Royal Navy ships on the coast at Durban. Royal Navy ships that carried Kru included HMS Active, HMS Tenedos, HMS Boadicea, and HMS Forester. HMS Active was ordered to sail from the Cape to Durban with 42 Kru on board.[535] Kru stationed in Simon's Town provided the bulk of Kru engaged in the conflict. Others made their way from Freetown to the Cape for assignment on the ships. Given their location of embarkation, Kru serving were most certainly Proper Kru, Grebo, and Bassa seamen. Similar to their role in the Asante campaign, they carried artillery supplies ashore and served as porters.[536]

HMS Active's naval brigade included 14 Kru, ten of whom had been honored with the South African Medal in 1878.[537] They were recognized for their contributions in several battles preceding the outbreak of the Anglo-Zulu War, including the Battle of Quintana against the Xhosa and battles against the Galeka and Gaika.[538] A total of 76 medals were given with the 1877–1878 clasp. Fifty-three went to Royal Navy seamen, 13 to the Royal Marines, and ten to Kru.[539] Although their names were not recorded, the appearance of ten "Kroomen" in the South African Medal Roll reveals the important role they served in Royal Navy brigades.[540]

Following their landing in Durban, under the direction of Commander Henry Campbell, HMS Active's naval brigade made their way to the front by steamer, marching, and railway assisting with the transport of two 12-pound guns and a Gatling gun.[541] One war correspondent noted that: "Onlookers during the disembarkation of the Navals were highly amused, when Kroomen (native sailors) came ashore, to note the astonishment of the local natives, who spoke to them in Zulu but elicited only replies in English."[542] This episode shows the great dif-

---

535 Sir Henry Hallam Parr, *A Sketch of the Kafir and Zulu Wars: Guadana to Isandhlwana* (London: C. Kegan & Co., 1880), 36; Dutton, *Forgotten Heroes*, 376.
536 *The Graphic* (August 16, 1879): 507.
537 John Laband and Ian Knight, *The War Correspondents, The Anglo-Zulu War* (KwaZulu-Natal: Jonathan Ball, 1996), 13; Dutton, *Forgotten Heroes*, 374.
538 Dutton, *Forgotten Heroes*, 374.
539 Ibid., 374.
540 Ibid., 374.
541 Ibid., 13.
542 W.H. Clements, *The Glamour and Tragedy of the Zulu War* (London: John Lane, The Brodley Head, 1936), 20.

ference between Kru and the indigenous population in appearance, dress, and language. Indeed, the divide was so great that they were paid wages to fight against the Zulu and ensure the colonial conquest of the Zulu state. The naval brigade arrived at the Lower Tugela River and was assigned to Colonel Pearson's Number One Column. On January 22, 1879, the Kru fought at the Battle of Inyezane. Two Kru named Jack Lewis and Jack Ropeyarn were recorded as being wounded in the battle and were sent to Fort Eshowe to recover until March 1879.[543]

Figure 4.1 is a portrait of the British line at the Battle of Inyezane. The image depicts the members of HMS Active's naval brigade dressed in blue uniforms with white sailor caps. Both the colour of their uniform and distinct shape of their cap distinguished them from regular armed forces servicemen who wore red uniforms and white helmets. Within the naval brigade, Kru were distinguished from British members by the satchel worn over their shoulder. The satchel most likely contained ammunition or other materials related to their duties. Four Kru are shown servicing the artillery gun. They were responsible for loading artillery and ammunitions and operating rockets. As the illustration shows, their role in the Anglo-Zulu War had evolved from transporting military supplies to engaging in battles on the front. Kru risked their lives alongside their British counterparts.

Ultimately, the war concluded in August 1879 and Cetshwayo was exiled to Cape Town before his eventual reinstallment in the Natal, albeit in a limited capacity in 1883. Due to conflict between Zulu factions, the Natal was not fully absorbed until 1887. Significantly, Kru service complicates any straightforward racial notions regarding British colonialism, highlighting that the colonial process involved a plethora of manpower drawn from various indigenous peoples in Africa and Asia. While the British held power and directed operations, Kru served in the Royal Navy and engaged in conflict with whomever was required regardless of the ethnic group in question, which was perhaps rooted in an impulse stemming from competition between their autonomous communities on the Kru Coast.

---

[543] Parliamentary Papers, "Letter of Henry F. Norbury, Staff Surgeon, RN to Director-General, Medical Department of the Navy," January 24, 1879, vol. 54, *Further Correspondence Respecting the Affairs of South Africa*, 174.

Figure 4.1: The Zulu War – the naval brigade landed from the HMS Active, c. 1879.
Source: "The Zulu War –The Naval Brigade Landed from the HMS Active," *The Graphic* 15 (February 22, 1879), 150. Courtesy of ©Illustrated London News Ltd/Mary Evans.

Sudan Campaign, 1884–85

In what became their most publicized contribution in a British military campaign in the nineteenth century, Kru formed a major part of the Nile fleet sent to reinforce General Charles Gordon in Khartoum between 1884 and 1885. An outpost for the Ottoman Empire via Egyptian rule since 1820 when the Sudan region was occupied, taxation and enslavement led to discontent among the local populace. The arrival of the British in Egypt in 1873 led to the installation of Gordon as Governor of Sudan. His anti-slavery campaign and advocacy for the spread of Christianity were seen as a threat and local inhabitants took up resistance led by Sudanese Islamic cleric, Muhammad Ahmad. On June 29, 1881, he declared himself Mahdi (the Guided One or Redeemer) and urged jihad against Anglo-Egypt authorities.[544] The Mahdist Revolution led to the creation of an army and Islamic state led by the Mahdi. Mahdi's army secured control of Khartoum in 1882 and in 1883 successfully defended an assault by a British-Egyptian military expedition led by British Colonel William Hicks, which resulted in the evacuation of British forces until the military campaign to secure Khartoum commenced in 1884 led by Gordon.

---

544 References to the Mahdi in Islam can be found in compilations in the Hadith.

The Kru's duty was to operate small craft that would transport fresh supplies and reinforce Egyptian garrisons in service of the British who had been cut off from General Gordon's men by Mahdi's forces.[545] The British built eight hundred "whaling gigs," which were wooden boats that were 30 feet long and carried two sailors and ten soldiers. Sailing up the Nile, Donald Featherstone described their boats as follows: "Like beads on a string, they were towed upstream to Wadi Halfa by paddle steamers chartered from Thomas Cook."[546]

Kru served as auxiliaries on steamships performing coaling activities and navigating the Nile. Like all previous campaigns, they were hired for their boat manning skills, this time in the cataracts of the Nile to the north of Khartoum.[547] Working in labor gangs, Kru were tasked with hauling the whaling boats through difficult stretches of the Nile, along with Sudanese laborers and Egyptian soldiers. Under sail, the whaleboats could reach speeds of six knots and, in the absence of wind, the Kru had to row the boats using six men.[548]

Three hundred Kru were sought for the expedition. Headmen received 2s. 6d. per day, second headman, 2s. per day, and regular workers 1s. per day.[549] The minimal length of their contract was six months. Kru embarked in Freetown and Cape Palmas before they transited through Gibraltar (a major port on route from West Africa to Britain and the Mediterranean) and landed at Alexandria. Given their ports of embarkation, Kru serving most certainly included Proper Kru, Grebo, and Bassa. They then took the railway to Assouit where they set sail up the Nile. In total, 261 Kru served in the campaign.[550]

Unlike their service in the Anglo-Asante War and the Anglo-Zulu War, Kru only helped to transport supplies and were not directly involved in military battles with the Mahdists. However, Kru served an important role in the transportation of supplies and troops in the Sudan Campaign. Although small in number, the British relied on the Kru's ability to pilot small craft through the cataracts. The siege on Khartoum ended on January 28, 1883, but not before the beheading

---

545 Emilius Albert De Cosson, *Days and Knights of Service with Sir Gerald Graham's Field Force at Suakin* (London: John Murray, 1886), 327.
546 Donald Featherstone, *Khartoum, 1885: General Gordon's Last Stand* (Oxford: Osprey Publishing, 1993), 56.
547 Alex Macdonald, *Too Late for Gordon and Khartoum: the Testimony of an independent Eye-Witness of the Heroic Efforts for the Rescue and Relief. With Maps and Plans and Several Unpublished Letters of the Late General Gordon* (London: Spottiswoode and Co., 1887), 45–46.
548 Featherstone, *Khartoum*, 56.
549 Macdonald, *Too Late for Gordon*, 46.
550 Kru routinely anchored at Gibraltar on route to Britain. For evidence of Kru seamen in Gibraltar see *The Nautical Magazine: A Journal of Papers on Subjects Connected with Maritime Affairs* (London: Simpkin, Marshall, and Co., 1855): 348; Macdonald, *Too Late for Gordon*, 46.

of Gordon and heavy losses. Resistance continued and the Mahdi continued to battle the Anglo-Egyptian Army until they were defeated on September 2, 1898 at Karari. On January 19, 1899, the Condominium Agreement created joint administration of the Sudan by the British and Egyptian governments.

Kru service in expeditions and military campaigns reveals the complex nature of British colonialism in Africa. The British were concerned with garnering influence over vast regions of the continent at the expense of their European rivals including the French, Germans, and Portuguese. While expeditions provided the blueprint for permanent incursions, British military campaigns in Africa opened indigenous peoples to colonization, a process which was intensified following the Berlin Conference in 1884 and 1885. In this context, Kru labor has political implications that may be perceived as complicit with colonialism and the racism underscoring the European mantra of the three "C's" (Civilization, Christianity, and Commerce), which drove the colonial project.[551] It is reasonable to assume that the Kru had few qualms about fighting an ethnically different indigenous people in the same way they had no hesitation in engaging in the trans-Atlantic slave trades. In Africa, ethnic differences seem to have been as divisive a factor as race was between Europeans and Africans. In short, individuals from outside one's ethnic group were fair game for enslavement and military conquest. What seems most probable is that the Kru were simply willing to serve on any contract with the British that ensured wages. Their entrepreneurial impulses continued to guide them during the era of European colonial conquest in Africa and Asia in the nineteenth and twentieth centuries.

---

551 For a discussion on the ideologies informing European colonial endeavor in Africa see Gann and Duignan, *Colonialism*, introduction; Lugard, *Rise*, 1: 585–587, 2: 69–75; Kipling, "White Man's," 290.

Chapter 5
Kru Labor in the British Caribbean

Beyond the expansion of Kru labor in the Royal Navy, expeditions, and military campaigns, Kru accepted the opportunity to work in agricultural and marine labor in the British Caribbean. The British understood that Emancipation in 1834 and the cessation of Apprenticeship in 1838 caused a labor shortage in some British colonies that led the British to experiment with indentured labor on plantations in the Caribbean.[552] While most indentured workers came from the Indian sub-continent, there were efforts to require Liberated Africans taken off slave ships to serve as indentures in the Caribbean.[553] By contrast, the Kru willingly agreed to the terms of free wage labor contracts and went to the Caribbean, although their numbers were not sufficient to meet the labor needs of the British colonies. They were one of many African and Asian groups who went to the Caribbean during the 1840s under contract alongside Indian, Chinese, Indonesian, Igbo, Yoruba, and Congolese workers.[554] Kru employment in Trinidad, Jamaica, and British Guiana was dominant between 1841 and the 1890s.

The nature of Kru contracts and their laboring activities on wharves, canals, and estates in Trinidad, Jamaica, and British Guiana shows that the Kru extended their diaspora in the Caribbean. Surfboats and other small watercraft remained foundational to their marine activities while Kru also increased their role in agricultural labor for a time. They established villages that resembled Kru-

---

[552] "Topic: Labour Problem and African Immigrants," West Indies Committee Papers 1833–1843 Box 4, Folder 1, Minutes July 1833-June 1843, Resolutions of the Standing Committee of West India Planters: On Immigration, February 18, 1842, 109. West Indiana Special Collections Library, The University of the West Indies, Trinidad and Tobago.
[553] Daniel Domingues da Silva, David Eltis, Philip Misevich, and Olatunji Ojo, "The Diaspora of Africans Liberated from Slave Ships in the Nineteenth Century," *Journal of African History* 55, no. 3 (2014): 347–369; Richard Anderson, "The Diaspora of Sierra Leone's Liberated Africans: Enlistment, Forced Migration, and 'Liberation' at Freetown, 1808–1863," *African Economic History* 41 (2013): 101–138.
[554] For a discussion on the diversity of African and Asian laborers who migrated to the Caribbean on contracts see David Hollet, *Passage from India to El Dorado: Guyana and the Great Migration* (Madison: Associated University Press, 1999), 85, 321; Walton Look Lai, *Indentured Labour, Caribbean Sugar: Chinese and Indian Migrants to the British West Indies, 1838–1918* (Baltimore: John Hopkins University Press, 1993), 154–270; K.O. Laurence, *A Question of Labor: Indentured Immigration into Trinidad and British Guiana, 1875–1917* (Kingston: Ian Randle, 1994), 8–38; Juanita De Barros, *Reproducing the British Caribbean: Sex, Gender, and Population Politics after Slavery* (Chapel Hill: University of North Carolina Press, 2014), 16–39.

https://doi.org/10.1515/9783110680331-010

towns in West Africa albeit on a smaller scale. Settlement patterns and the Kru mark continued to signify Kru identity in the Caribbean. However, some of the economic structures that had governed Kru communities in West Africa did not survive in the Caribbean. Factors including the decline of headmen and traditional channels of gift-giving, the purchase of privately owned land, and intermarriage with Creole women inhibited their regular return to the Kru Coast and undermined the long-term stability of Kru diaspora communities in the Caribbean, thereby altering the pattern of Kru migration.

Policy and Immigration

In the post-slavery period, the British government provided economic initiatives for West Africans to work in the Caribbean plantation setting. British planters understood hiring migrant workers as a strategic maneuver to compete with slave-produced crops in French, Spanish, and Dutch domains. In 1842, the planters' position was clearly expressed by the Standing Committee of West Indian Planters:

> That in addition to the immediate and direct advantages which West India Colonies would derive from such a Free Immigration of Labourers from British Settlements on the Coast of Africa as would render the supply of labour sufficient, the most effective means of abolishing the Slave Trade would be afforded; for, by an adequate supply of labour, the British Planters would be enabled to compete with the grower of Sugar by Slave Labour, and the motives for continuing the Slave Trade would no longer exist.[555]

The challenge the British planters faced was how to produce crops at competitive prices using free labor over slave labor. Their remedy was believed to reside in the immigration of workers in their colonies so that the supply of labor equaled the demand.[556] Workers were sought from Sierra Leone and the Kru Coast based on their previous work experience with the British and for their ability to work in tropical climates. Freetown was the main hub for acquiring Kru labor in the initial stages of British Caribbean immigration.[557] However, Michael Craton has suggested the reason for encouraging migrant workers from West Africa, India, and

---

[555] "Topic: Labour Problem and African Immigrants," West Indies Committee Papers 1833–1843 Box 4, Folder 1, Minutes July 1833-June 1843, Resolutions of the Standing Committee of West India Planters: On Immigration, February 18, 1842, 109. West Indiana Special Collections Library, The University of the West Indies, Trinidad and Tobago.
[556] Ibid., 109.
[557] Schuler, "Kru Emigration," 164.

China was also meant to secure the planters' hegemony over emancipated African descendants (Creoles) by creating competition for jobs and inserting a new class between the planters and former slaves.[558] Regardless, from the planters' perspective the common denominator was rooted in the need to continue to make a profit following Emancipation and the ending of Apprenticeship in 1838.

Between 1834 and 1917, the British Caribbean received 300,000 immigrants of which only a tiny minority, about four percent, came from Africa.[559] There are discrepancies as to the number of Kru who entered Jamaica, Trinidad, and British Guiana. Trinidadian historian Donald Wood has suggested that between 1,000 and 2,000 Kru entered the British Caribbean between 1840 and 1860.[560] G.W. Roberts provides an even more conservative figure, estimating that only 400 Kru laborers immigrated to the West Indies.[561] Records suggest that in the 1840s and 1850s, 2,421 migrant laborers from the Kru Coast went to the British and French Guianas, however.[562] In 1848, Acting Governor of Sierra Leone, Benjamin Pine, claimed that 500 Kru workers went to Demerara in British Guiana, 200 to Jamaica, and 150 to Trinidad.[563] Pine's figures may only be accurate until 1848 as Kru continued to arrive in the British Caribbean until 1853.

Schuler provides the best estimate of the number of Kru landing in British Guiana based on ship records. Schuler's ship muster lists show that 989 Kru arrived in British Guiana between 1841 and 1853.[564] Their number may have been even higher because some officials did not distinguish Kru workers from other

---

558 Michael Craton, "Reshuffling the Pack: The Transition from Slavery to Other Forms of Labor in the British Caribbean, ca. 1790–1890", *New West Indian Guide* 68, no. 1–2 (1994): 41. See also Mary Turner, "Chattel Slaves into Wage Slaves: A Jamaican Case Study," in Malcolm Cross and Gad Heuman, eds., *Labour in the Caribbean: From Emancipation to Independence* (London: Macmillan, 1988), 14–31; Richard B. Sheridan, "Changing Sugar Technology and the Labour Nexis in the British Caribbean 1750–1900, with Special Reference to Barbados and Jamaica," *Nieuwe Wesr-Indische Gids* 63 (1989): 59–93; Monica Schuler, "The Recruitment of African Indentured Labourers for European Colonies in the Nineteenth Century," in *Migration: Indentured Labour Before and After Slavery*, ed. Pieter C. Emmer (Dordrecht: Nijhoff, 1986), 125–161.
559 Schuler, "Kru Emigration," 155–156.
560 Donald Wood, "Kru Migration to the West Indies," *Journal of Caribbean Studies* 2, no. 2–3 (1981): 266–282.
561 George W. Roberts, *The Population of Jamaica* (Cambridge: Cambridge University Press, 2013), 110.
562 Schuler, "Kru Emigration," 155.
563 Accounts and Papers, Papers Relative to the Emigration of Labourers from Sierra Leone and St. Helena to the West Indies, "Despatch from the Acting Governor Pine to Earl Grey," Government House, Sierra Leone, June 5, 1848, vol. 8, no. 1 (1850), 643, The National Archives, Kew, United Kingdom.
564 Schuler, "Kru Emigration," 165.

Africans. When combined with the numbers offered by Pine, Schuler's figures reveal that the number of Kru entering British Guiana was in line with Donald Wood's estimates of between one and two thousand Kru. Schuler claims that British Guiana had the second largest Kru population outside of Freetown in the period.[565] Therefore, their settlements in Berbice, Essequibo, and Demerara represent important nodes in the Kru free wage labor diaspora in the British Caribbean.

Kru are sometimes distinguished in ship emigration records while in other instances they are not and were included under the general category of African immigration. Although their contracts were significantly longer in duration (five years) than they had previously accepted in the Royal Navy (three years), Kru were given special privileges including free return passage to Freetown and the Kru Coast following the completion of contracts, which was not always the case for Liberated Africans who went to the Caribbean under contract.[566] Based on their history as preferred workers on British contracts in West Africa, Kru, perhaps more than any other immigrants to the West Indies, "felt themselves in a position to state terms" to their employers.[567] Based on past labor experiences, the power dynamics between the British and Kru, as compared with the British and other laboring groups in the Caribbean, remained unique.

Although Kru had ventured into Caribbean waters as early as the 1830s on board Cuban slave ships that were sometimes seized and delivered to British authorities in Havana, British contracts offered between 1841 and 1853 created new opportunities for their employment. The several thousand Kru who worked in the British Caribbean were drawn by contracts promising higher wages than previously offered as compensation for the lengthy duration of five years (in some cases shortened to three years). Kru who accepted these contracts engaged in seaborne and agricultural labor that bore both similarities and differences to the nature of their work on the Kru Coast and in their diaspora communities in West Africa.

Trinidad, Jamaica and British Guiana became the workplaces in Britain's "experiment" with Kru labor in the Caribbean.[568] In the early 1840s, the British

---

565 Ibid., 155–156.
566 CO 111/210, no. 107, "Henry Light to Lord Stanley," May 16, 1844.
567 West India Committee Papers, "Report of the Committee Appointed to Confer with Her Majesty's Government, [and], Meeting of Merchants, held in Bishopgate Street, on the 26th Oct 1842," A. Colvile, February 22, 1843, Box 4, Folder 1 (1843), 3, West Indiana Special Collections Library, The University of the West Indies, Trinidad and Tobago.
568 *The Economist*, January 15, 1848, in *The Economist Weekly Commercial Times, Bankers Gazette*, and *Railway Monitor*, vol. 6 (London: Economist Office, 1848), 60.

hoped to develop a labor scheme between Freetown, the Kru Coast, and their colonies in the Caribbean. They sought Kru labor in ports and plantations.[569] The first Kru arrived in the Caribbean in 1841 before any formal act of legislature had been created regarding the terms of their employment.

On May 21, 1841, Kru landed in Jamaica on board the Hector along with an unnamed barge. Sixteen Krumen disembarked in Port Royal.[570] The length of their informal contract was initially for one year.[571] The British hoped that by bringing a Kru headman, he would recognize the benefits and encourage a steady flow of recruits to immigrate to Jamaica on contract.

Within a year, in 1842, a series of acts calling for the regulation of Kru workers and African migrants to Jamaica focused on their role as farm workers. The call for labor was mandated in the *Laws of Jamaica*, which sought to direct the flow of immigrant laborers towards cultivation on plantations.[572] The laws governing the length of contracts and free return passage were enacted in 1843.[573] Contract periods were raised from one year to five years and if that number was exceeded with two additional years the Kru were required to give six months notice in order to receive free passage home.[574]

However, the impulse to hire the Kru for plantation labor in Jamaica failed to generate the steady flow of workers that the British government had anticipated. Kru immigration from West Africa to Jamaica ended in 1843 with Kru arriving on the Glen Huntley.[575] The Kru seemed to be disinterested in the plantation contracts offered in Jamaica as compared with those in Trinidad and British Guiana. Some Kru found the voyage too long as it could take up to one week longer to travel from Sierra Leone to Jamaica as compared with the 28 days to sail to Tri-

---

[569] House of Commons Papers, Select Committee on West Coast of Africa, "Copy of Mr. Barclay's Address to the Headman of the Villages in Sierra Leone Freetown, Sierra Leone 12 April 1841, Appendix to Report from the Select Committee on West Coast of Africa," no. 24 (1841), 467, The National Archives, Kew, United Kingdom.
[570] Ibid., 467.
[571] Ibid., 467. Initially, the British experimented with different contract lengths as short as one year before implementing contracts that ranged between three and five years.
[572] "The Acts of Jamaica Passed in the Year Annual Laws of Jamaica, Cap 51 Act to make Provision for the Introduction of Emigrants to this Island, 1842," in *The Laws of Jamaica* (Kingston: Government Printer, 1843), 116.
[573] Parliamentary Papers, "Papers Relative to Emigration," no. 52, Enclosure no. 10, vol. 8, April 20, 1843, p. 142.
[574] Ibid., 143.
[575] Accounts and Papers, vol. 35, "Correspondence Relative to the Emigration of Labourers to the West Indies and the Mauritius, From the West Coast of Africa, the East Indies, and China, R. Bruce, Agent General of Immigration, King's House, May 13, 1843," in *Papers Relative to the Emigration from the West Coast of Africa to the West Indies* (London: W. Clowes and Sons, 1844), 21.

nidad and British Guiana.[576] Census records in Jamaica do not distinguish between the Kru and other African immigrants. As such, the exact number of Kru who immigrated is unknown. Only a single account in *Littell's Living Age* in 1884 referenced the failed attempt of the British authorities to procure a steady flow of Kru workers on Jamaican plantations whose population dwindled by the 1880s.[577]

Kru immigration to Trinidad occurred on a slightly larger scale than to Jamaica. The first Kru workers arrived in Trinidad from Sierra Leone on a merchant vessel named the Elizabeth and Jane in January 1841.[578] Sixteen Krumen out of a total of 180 laborers landed at Port of Spain.[579] In 1843, a second Kru labor gang arrived on the Senator.[580] Although the exact number of Kru on board is not known the total crew numbered 102, including 12 delegates and 90 workers.[581] The arriving Kru had high monetary expectations for working in Trinidad. In 1843, Captain Denman noted that Kru laborers demanded an advance payment

---

576 Accounts and Papers, vol. 31, Emigration, Session February 3-August 12,1842, Correspondence Relative to Emigration, no. 13, "Copy of the Despatch from Lord John Russell to John Carr, Esq. or the Officer Administering the Government of Sierra Leone, Enclosure in No. 13, Extract of a Letter from Mr. Marryat to Lord John Russell," 469. The Elizabeth and Jane made the journey from Sierra Leone to Trinidad in 28 days, while the Superior took 36 days to land in British Guiana. This was abnormally long perhaps due to weather and sea conditions and should have taken roughly the same amount of time as Trinidad.
577 E. Pluribus Unum, *Littell's Living Age*, 5th series, vol. 46 (Boston: Littell and Co., April-June 1884), 40.
578 General Report of the Emigration Commissioners, vol. 1, no. 2 "Copy of the Despatch from Lieutenant-Governor Sir Henry MacLeod to Lord John Russell, 20 May 1841," 47. The number of Kru on board is provided. However, in many documents, the name of the merchant ship is not mentioned. This was not uncommon as the ship that accompanied the Hector to Jamaica was also an unnamed brig. However, a description in another source described the Kru and other African workers landing in Trinidad from Sierra Leone on a vessel called the Elizabeth and Jane. See Accounts and Papers, vol. 31, Emigration, Session February 3 – 12 August 1842, Correspondence Relative to Emigration, no. 13, "Copy of the Despatch from Lord John Russell to John Carr, Esq. or the Officer Administering the Government of Sierra Leone, Enclosure in No. 13, Extract of a Letter from Mr. Marryat to Lord John Russell," 469.
579 Parliamentary Papers, "No. 5, Paris 17 June 1842, No. 5 Letter from S. Cipriani to Messrs. Jos Marryat & Sons 17 June 1842," in *Irish University Press Series of British Parliamentary Papers Report from the Select Committee on the West Coast of Africa Together With Minutes of Evidence Select Committee on the West Coast of Africa Appendix and Index Part II, 1842* (Shannon: Irish University Press, 1968), 480.
580 E. Littell, *Littell's Living Age*, vol. 8 (1846): 188.
581 Ibid., 188.

of T20.00 (Trinidadian dollars) before their departure.[582] Kru felt it was their right to ask for an advance, which was standard practice on British contracts in West Africa.[583]

British officials and the plantocracy in Trinidad seem to have been very interested in acquiring thousands of Kru workers. As part of their strategy, Captain Denman proposed bringing over a headman to observe the working conditions in Trinidad.[584] Similar to British officials in Jamaica, the West Indies Committee hoped that the headman would be impressed with the working conditions and would encourage a regular flow of Kru laborers. The proposal suggested that the Kru embark directly from their homeland on the Kru Coast, although in the 1840s, Kru were hired on the Kru Coast as well as in Freetown.[585]

By 1852, the British began to attribute their success in sugar cultivation in Trinidad to the immigrants brought to work the plantations, including the Kru. The West Indies Committee recognized that immigrant labor was at the heart of British enterprise in the Caribbean because it lowered the costs of production.[586] While the precise number of Kru workers who immigrated to Trinidad for contracts is unknown, Dr. Louis De Verteuil suggested that "several hundred" Kru workers made the journey.[587]

Censuses in the nineteenth century rarely distinguished the Kru from other African laborers in Trinidad. A census in 1891 shows that Africans accounted for 1,288 or 1.8 percent of the total population. Although Kru are not identified as a unique group in the census, they formed a small segment of the population as their presence was singled out by several sources. Since all African immigration had ceased in 1861, any Kru laborers that had immigrated to Trinidad were elderly in the census year of 1891 and only formed a small group within the total number of African immigrants.[588]

---

[582] Parliamentary Papers, "Evidence of the Honorable Captain Denman R.N.," Acting Committee November 14, 1843, vol. 6 (1843), 119–120.
[583] Ibid., 119–120.
[584] Ibid., 119–120.
[585] CO 111/210, no. 107, "Henry Light to Lord Stanley," May 16, 1844.
[586] West India Committee Papers, "The West India Committee Minutes from 9 January 1852–19 February 1857," Acting Committee January 9, 1852, Box 4, Folder 3, (1852), 1, West Indiana Special Collections Library, The University of the West Indies, Trinidad and Tobago.
[587] Louis De Verteuil, *Trinidad: Its Geography, Natural Resources, Administration, Present Condition, and Prospects* (1855), 2nd ed. (London: Cassel and Company, 1884), 341.
[588] Trinidad Registrar-General's Department, *Census of the Colony of Trinidad, 1891* (Port of Spain: U.S. Government Printing Office, 1892), vii, 26; Daniel Hart, *Trinidad and the Other West India Islands and Colonies*, 2nd ed. (Trinidad: The Chronicle Publishing Office, 1866), 66.

The majority of Kru laborers were destined for British Guiana. Sixty Kru laborers among a total Kru of 226 African laborers were landed in British Guiana at the port in Demerara on September 22, 1841 on the Superior.[589] Kru were hired both in Freetown and on the Kru Coast. However, in 1844, there was a conscious shift towards hiring the Kru directly on the Kru Coast. R.G. Butts, planter and representative of Berbice and Demerara planters, proposed a labor scheme between the Kru Coast and British Guiana due to a supposed dislike of Liberated Africans hired at Freetown, who the planters regarded as less productive and skilled as compared to the Kru.[590] The Kru had been noted for their "prodigious capacity and organization for work," a perception that informed the planters' decision to only hire Kru workers.[591] The British thus sent delegates to the Kru Coast to acquire laborers for contracts in British Guiana. They were selected from the colonial immigration department and from the body of labor recruiters for planters and headmen. Butts met with King Freeman, who agreed to send his attendant and son as delegates to British Guiana at the rate of £1 per month for one year.[592]

Cape Palmas, Grand Cess, and Settra Kru became the main villages on the Kru Coast for recruitment in British Guiana. The Proper Kru from Settra Kru, Kru from Grand Cess, and Grebo laborers from Cape Palmas came to form the demographic composition of the Kru working in British Guiana. A direct connection between Grand Cess and Berbice (British Guiana) was established by Jack Purser, a merchant from Settra Kru, who worked as a sub-agent for emigration. He requested that his son, who had worked in Berbice, return to the Kru Coast in order to share his experiences of working in British Guiana. As was the case in West Africa, connections between diaspora communities and specific villages on the Kru Coast can be traced, which reveals the demographic composition of the Kru diaspora in British Guiana.

By 1846, the British government reassessed the strategies used to attract Kru labor in British Guiana. Five-year contracts were largely replaced by three-year contracts. Some reports also suggest that salaries were higher at £1 per month as compared with lower rates back in West Africa.[593] From the Kru perspective,

---

[589] Schuler, "Kru Emigration," 165; Frost, *Work*, 166.
[590] CO 111/123, "H. Light to Lord Stanley, 30 September 1844, enclosing R.G. Butts to H.E.F. Young, 23 July-7 August 1844, no. 200," The National Archives, Kew, United Kingdom; CO 111/121, "Light to Stanley enclosing Butts to Young, 13 March 1845, no. 57," The National Archives, Kew, United Kingdom.
[591] Schuler, "Kru Emigration," 155–156.
[592] Ibid., 166–167.
[593] Ibid., 171.

contracts in British Guiana enabled young Krumen to gain experience and an "education" in long-distance migratory labor.[594] Workers were offered a pay rate of 8d. per day and free passage to British Guiana.[595]

In 1850, there remained a strong market for Kru labor in British Guiana. Incentives including free passage home, advance payments, and higher wages than those offered in West Africa continued to be offered by the British. Kru now had the option of remaining for a period of five years with free passage home or three years without paid passage.[596] The option for free return passage following a five-year contract may have enticed some Kru to remain for the longer contract. Direct appeals on the Kru Coast continued to attract workers for several years as emigration from the Kru Coast to British Guiana continued until 1853. The final voyage from the Kru Coast to British Guiana was made on the Elphinstone in 1853, decades before the ending of Indian and Chinese migrant labor in the British Caribbean.[597] Mounting tensions and the frequent outbreak of war between the Kru and Liberian settler communities in Kru territory was probably a factor which led the Kru to use a portion of the funds from their workers who had served in British Guiana towards their war effort against the Liberian settlers.[598]

Nature of Employment

Kru workers continued their tradition of working in wharves in the British Caribbean. The first Kru workers who arrived in Trinidad in January 1841 were selected by British contractors to work at the wharf of Port of Spain. Their duties included serving as stevedores, loading and unloading cargo.[599] Kru were also responsible for manning ferries and tenders (small boats) transporting people, raw materials, and commodities between ship and shore.[600]

---

594 Ibid., 167–168.
595 West India Committee Papers, "General, Communicated by the Demose," Oct 8, 1844, SC 89, Box 4, no. 2 (1844), 206. West Indiana Special Collections Library, The University of the West Indies, Trinidad and Tobago.
596 Accounts and Papers of the House of Commons, vol. 9, Enclosure in no. 19, no. 340 Downing Street (July 5, 1850): 401–403, The National Archives, Kew, United Kingdom.
597 Schuler, "Kru Emigration," 171.
598 Ibid., 172; Jo Mary Sullivan, Settlers in Sinoe County, Liberia, and their Relations with the Kru, c. 1835–1920 (Boston: unpublished Ph.D. thesis, 1978), 209–219.
599 Parliamentary Papers, "No. 5 Letter from S. Cipriani to Messr, J. Marryat and Sons," June 17, 1842, vol. 12 (1842), 480.
600 *Trinidad Royal Gazette* 7, no. 3, March 18, 1846.

Similarly, Kru who arrived in Port Royal, Jamaica, several months later in May 1841, were employed in the dockyards.[601] Immediately following their arrival, Robert Montgomery Martin reported that the Kru were employed at the wharves in both Port Royal and Kingston.[602] They performed the same duties as in Port of Spain, moving cargo on small craft. Kru labor in Trinidad and Jamaica was an extension of their work with the British in Freetown and other diaspora communities in West Africa.

Kru who landed in Demerara in September 1841 were employed in marine labor that was slightly different from their work on the dockyards in Trinidad and Jamaica.[603] Rather than working on the dockyards, Kru were required to sail flatboats while transporting crops and individuals on canals between the plantations and ships.[604] An intricate system of canals enabled the transport of commodities directly between plantation and ship in many cases without having to employ porters to deliver goods to the dockyards before loading them on vessels.

In 1841, Henry Light provided details on the Kru's occupation as boatmen on estates in British Guiana who were "separated in squads" and paid at a rate of between $10.00 and $12.00 per month, which was more than double what they made for marine services in the Oil Rivers at the best of times.[605] Agent-General James Hackett described the Kru as "free agents" who "remained unindentured" making their "own bargains for daily, weekly, or monthly work."[606] Kru were at liberty to decide where they wanted to work in British Guiana. Most significantly, they were not indentured, meaning they had mobility and could move between dockyards, estates, and other work environments. Based on their long history of

---

[601] House of Commons Papers, Select Committee on West Coast of Africa, Appendix no. 24, "Copy of Mr. Barclay's Address to the Headman of the Villages," vol. 12 (1842), 467.
[602] Robert Montgomery Martin, ed., "West Indies," *The Colonial Magazine and Commercial Maritime Journal* 6 (1841): 118.
[603] Schuler, "Kru Emigration," 155–156; Frost, *Work*, 166.
[604] Accounts and Papers, Emigration, Session 3 February to 12 August 1842, vol. 21, Correspondence Relative to Emigration, Enclosure in No. 8 Government House, Demerara 6 June 1841, Henry Light (London: William Clowes and Sons, 1842), 373.
[605] Accounts and Papers, Emigration, Session 3 February to 12 August 1842, vol. 21, Correspondence Relative to Emigration, 1842, Enclosure in No. 8 Government House, Demerara 6 June 1841, Henry Light (London: William Clowes and Sons, 1842), 373. For a comparative salary range see salaries offered in the Niger Delta in Chapter 4.
[606] Accounts and Papers, Emigration, Session 3 February to 12 August 1842, vol. 21, Correspondence Relative to Emigration, 1842, Extract Minute from the Proceedings of the Immigration Committee, Tuesday the 25th May 1841, James Hackett, Agent-General (London: William Clowes and Sons, 1842), 368.

employment with the British, Kru continued to occupy a privileged position in British Guiana. The rules described by Hackett as applying to the Kru were completely different from those that applied to Indian and Chinese indentured laborers, who were compelled to remain on their assigned estates by virtue of their contracts, through fines and the threat of violence.[607]

Many Kru elected to continue their traditional job in surfboats and other watercraft moving cargo on rivers and canals as shown in Table 5.1. As such, Kru had the ability to service a number of estates and were most certainly hired in small groups in order to complete jobs efficiently. It is not clear from the list, however, who the headmen were but the hierarchal structures informing Kru labor were very much intact upon their arrival in British Guiana. As Table 5.1 shows, Kru also maintained their practice of using English names in their workplaces.

Table 5.1: Kru working sea transport in Demerara, 1842.

Kru not living on any particular Estate		
Kingson	Jim George	John Davis
Tom Walker	Salt Water	Sea Breeze
Jack Passer	Seargent	Tom Lee
Big Gum	George Andrews	Yellow Will
Peter Jumbo	Tom Nimmey	Peter Warman
Thomas Nimmey	Tom Freeman	Jim Freeman
John Grey	Tom Toby	Tom Brown
Bottle Beer		

Source: Accounts and Papers, Emigration, Session 3 February to 12 August 1842, vol. 21, Correspondence Relative to Emigration, 1842, Enclosure in No. 8 Government House, Demerara 6 June 1841, Henry Light (London: William Clowes and Sons, 1842), 372.

The note accompanying the list of Krumen explained their role:

> The above [Kru] being principally boatmen, and very intelligent and active people, were all readily engaged to work on board the steamers and drohergs [droghers] belonging to estates at a high rate of wages, none of them receiving less than at a rate of 10 dollars per month, besides houses, food &c.[608]

---

[607] For a discussion on the differences between free wage labor and indentured labor in the British Caribbean see Northrup, *Indentured*, 4–10; Mahmud, "Cheaper than a Slave," 215–243.
[608] Accounts and Papers, Emigration, Session 3 February to 12 August 1842, vol. 21, "Correspondence Relative to Emigration, 1842," Enclosure in No. 8 Government House, Demerara 6

Kru served as boatmen on steamers and droghers and received housing and food in addition to a salary of $10.00 per month.[609] Their specialization in manning craft ensured that they experienced a degree of mobility and pay rate that distinguished their service from other immigrant laborers in British Guiana.

Besides continuing their tradition of seaborne labor, Kru also performed agricultural labor on estates in Trinidad, British Guiana, and Jamaica. While they had worked on plantations in Fernando Po as early as the 1830s, their numbers were small and any large-scale plantation work did not commence until the later decades of the nineteenth century. It was hoped by planters that the Kru would adapt quickly to the task system working in groups as they had under headmen on ships and shoreside in Freetown.[610]

In Trinidad, Kru found employment on Belmont Estate, Bellevue Estate, and Beauxjour Estate, among others. Belmont Estate was located close to Port of Spain, Bellevue Estate was near Freeman's Bay in Oropuche, and Beauxjour Estate was in the southwestern region of the island in South Naparima.[611] The Kru labored in sugarcane, cocoa, and later, coffee production. Kru workers were initially sent to a specific estate and later had the opportunity to switch locations.

In 1842, a letter from S. Cipriani, the owner of the Beauxjour Estate, reveals the number of Kru laborers on his estate and their wage rate:

> The Kroomen who went from Sierra Leone to Trinidad were on their arrival engaged by me, and employed on the Beauxjour Estate, South Naparima, a property I own in partnership with Mr. M.P. Begné; their number, I believe, was 16. In consequence of a dispute among themselves, some left the estate a few months after; the remainder are still on it. The rate of wages out of crop is 40 cents per task; during crop they receive 50 or 60; they

---

June 1841, Henry Light (London: William Clowes and Sons, 1842), 372. A drogher was a small freight barge used to transport sugar, cotton, rum, and lumber in the West Indies.

609 Accounts and Papers, Monthly Return of African Emigrants located in District G, County of Essequibo, August 1, 1841, A.W. Lyons, Stipendiary Magistrate, District G, Affairs of British Guiana, General Report of the Emigration Commissioners, vol. 1 (London: H.M. Stationary Office, 1842), 55.

610 Parliamentary Papers, "No. 5, Paris 17 June 1842 no. 5, Letter from S. Cipriani to Messrs. Jos Marryat & Sons, 17 June 1842," Irish University Press Series of British Parliamentary Papers Report from the Select Committee on the West Coast of Africa Together With Minutes of Evidence Select Committee on the West Coast of Africa Appendix and Index Part 2, 1842 (Shannon: Irish University Press, 1968), 480.

611 Parliamentary Papers, "No. 5 Letter from S. Cipriani to Messr, J. Marryat and Sons," June 17, 1842, vol. 12, 480.

also receive an allowance of salt fish. They did not contract to work for any given time; they were employed in field labour.[612]

The pay rate model in Trinidad differed from the Kru's past experience working on commercial and Royal Navy ships. Whereas the Kru received standard wages on commercial vessels every month and wages were determined by rank in the Royal Navy, in Trinidad, their wages on estates were seasonal, increasing, and decreasing depending on crop cycles. Their pay rate at 40¢ per task in out of crop season and between 50¢ and 60¢ per task during crop season was described as much higher than what they could receive in Sierra Leone, which was given as 4d. per day during the same period.[613] Equally significant, the above passage also shows that the Kru left estates for work elsewhere on the island where "they did not contract to work for any given time." The Kru were promised return passage to Sierra Leone after three or five years of service. However, once they arrived on the island they were not obliged to remain on a single estate for the duration of the contract and they most probably shifted between marine and estate labor depending on the season and the availability of jobs.

In British Guiana, Kru served on the following plantations in Essequibo: Plantation Hamburg, Bathsheba's Lust, Lima, Reliance, Land of Plenty, Aberdeen; and in Demerara: La Resouvenir, Helena, Enmore, Greenfield, Turkeyen, Annandale, and Dochfour.[614] Their primary duties included harvesting the sugar cane.[615] In 1841, five Kru laborers were recorded at Plantation Hamburg

---

[612] Parliamentary Papers, "No. 5, Paris 17 June 1842 No. 5 Letter from S. Cipriani to Messr, Jos Marryat & Sons 17 June 1842," Irish University Press Series of British Parliamentary Papers Report from the Select Committee on the West Coast of Africa Together With Minutes of Evidence Select Committee on the West Coast of Africa Appendix and Index Part 2, 1842 (Shannon: Irish University Press, 1968), 480.

[613] William Hardin Burnley, *Observations on the Present Condition of the Island of Trinidad and the Actual State of the Experiment of Negro Emancipation* (London: Longman, 1842), 71. The Kru had some experience with task pay in Freetown in the 1790s before their pay became standardized on British commercial and Royal Navy ships in the early nineteenth century. They also received task-based pay for domestic work performed for settlers. However, in Freetown their pay rate was not informed by crop cycles to the same degree as it was in Trinidad. See Ludlam, "Account," 48.

[614] Accounts and Papers, Emigration, Session 3 February to 12 August 1842, vol. 21, "Correspondence Relative to Emigration, 1842, Enclosure in No. 8 Government House, Demerara 6 June 1841 Henry Light (London: William Clowes and Sons, 1842), 370–371.

[615] H. Barkly, *Fifth Report from the Select Committee on Sugar and Coffee Planting: Together with the Minutes of Evidence and Appendix* (March 18, 1848), 24; Cruickshank, "African Immigrants," 81.

in Essequibo.[616] Their tasks are described as jobbing and performing field labor for which they received a salary of $11.00 per month, notably higher than the neighboring plantation at Bathsheba's Lust, where African workers received between $8.00 and $10.00 per month. The Kru were further given an allowance of salt fish and allotted provision grounds for cultivation on estate grounds.[617]

Jobbing could include maintenance of estate buildings or digging new canals to connect and expand the network of estates with waterways.[618] One official described a gang of ten Kru laborers building a canal on Montrose Estate in 1844.[619] In 1848, H. Barkly noted the Kru's strong work ethic: "All the canes on the estate, making 360 hogsheads… were cut by 16 Kroomen from the day of their arrival; an extent of work which had never been done by any number of slaves."[620] Based on their positive reputation, they received contracts in the timber trade in British Guiana, which required floating timber downriver to awaiting vessels, much like their role in Sierra Leone.[621]

Evidence for Kru agricultural labor in Jamaica shows that the Kru presence was small in scale. In 1843, an unknown number of Kru workers arrived in Jamaica on the Glen Huntley.[622] They landed in Montego Bay to be employed in agricultural labor.[623] However, in the case of Jamaica, specific estate names where the Kru worked remains unknown in contrast to their worksites in Trinidad and British Guiana.

---

616 Monthly Return of African Emigrants located in District G, County of Essequibo, 1 August 1841, A.W. Lyons, Stipendiary Magistrate, District G, Affairs of British Guiana, General Report of the Emigration Commissioners, I (London: H.M. Stationary Office, 1842), 55.
617 Ibid., 55.
618 Accounts and Papers, vol. 35, "Copy of a Despatch from Governor Light to Lord Stanley, no. 8, May 13, 1843," *Papers Relative to Emigration from the West Coast of Africa to the West Indies* (1843), 72.
619 Accounts and Papers, Colonies: Emigration, vol. 35, Session 1, February-September 1844 Papers Relative to Emigration from the West Coast of Africa to the West Indies (1844), 72, The National Archives, United Kingdom.
620 Ibid., 24; Walter Rodney, *A History of the Guyanese Working People, 1881–1905* (Baltimore: John Hopkins University, 1981), 252.
621 W.H. Campbell, "The Forests of British Guiana, Appendix III," *Proceedings of the Royal Colonial Institute* (London: The Institute, 1874), 153.
622 Accounts and Papers, vol. 35, Correspondence Relative to the Emigration of Labourers to the West Indies and the Mauritius, From the West Coast of Africa, the East Indies, and China, R. Bruce, Agent General of Immigration, King's House, May 13, 1843. Papers Relative to the Emigration from the West Coast of Africa to the West Indies (London: W. Clowes and Sons, 1844), 21.
623 Ibid., 21.

Settlement Patterns

The Kru formed several diaspora communities in Trinidad. The British government gave land for Kru settlements. These lands were Crown lands that were set aside for immigrant worker villages.[624] The primary example of such a scheme was the establishment of "Krooman's Village." Similar to Krutowns in West Africa, "Krooman's Village" was established in Trinidad for the purpose of providing a steady labor pool for the British.[625] The settlement was located within the vicinity of Freeman's Bay in Oropuche. In 1855, De Verteuil described Krooman's Village as one among many African settlements adjacent to the village of St. Mary's.[626] Based in their village, Kru worked as agricultural laborers on nearby plantations including Bellevue Estate and Otaheiti Estate.[627] With access to Freeman's Bay, the location of their village also enabled them to continue to load and unload cargo between British ships and shoreside using small craft, most probably including surfboats carved from local woodlands. Krooman's Village in Trinidad represents the expansion of Kru diaspora communities first founded in West Africa to include the Caribbean.

Two other Kru settlements existed in Trinidad: one near Cipriani Estate, Beauxjour, in South Naparima, and the other adjacent to Belmont Estate.[628] The number of Kru living in these settlements remains unknown but the concentration of Kru laborers in each region may date as early as 1842.[629] Kru were en-

---

[624] CO 295/261, "Sub Indendant of Crown Land Report, 1871," The National Archives, Kew, United Kingdom; "No. 5, Paris 17 June 1842 No. 5 Letter from S. Cipriani to Messrs. Jos Marryat & Sons 17 June 1842," Irish University Press Series of British Parliamentary Papers Report from the Select Committee on the West Coast of Africa Together With Minutes of Evidence Select Committee on the West Coast of Africa Appendix and Index Part II, 1842 (Shannon: Irish University Press, 1968), 480.
[625] *Trinidad Royal Gazette* 12, no. 2, January 1, 1851- December 31, 1851, 2.
[626] Verteuil, *Trinidad*, 313–314.
[627] *Trinidad Royal Gazette* 12, no. 2, January 1, 1851- December 31, 1851, 2.
[628] CO 295/261, "Sub Indendant of Crown Land Report, 1871," The National Archives, Kew, United Kingdom; "No. 5, Paris 17 June 1842 No. 5 Letter from S. Cipriani to Messrs. Jos Marryat & Sons 17 June 1842," Irish University Press Series of British Parliamentary Papers Report from the Select Committee on the West Coast of Africa Together With Minutes of Evidence Select Committee on the West Coast of Africa Appendix and Index Part II, 1842 (Shannon: Irish University Press, 1968), 480.
[629] "No. 5, Paris 17 June 1842 No. 5 Letter from S. Cipriani to Messrs. Jos Marryat & Sons 17 June 1842," Irish University Press Series of British Parliamentary Papers Report from the Select Committee on the West Coast of Africa Together With Minutes of Evidence Select Committee on the West Coast of Africa Appendix and Index Part 2, 1842 (Shannon: Irish University Press, 1968), 480.

couraged to move closer to Belmont because of its proximity to Port of Spain and the hope that the Kru would begin regular immigration if their Kru headman could have his own residence built in the area.[630] A Kru headman requested a piece of land be set aside for his gang of Kru workers to reside near Port of Spain, which may have been an attempt to replicate a miniature Krutown like those back in West Africa.[631]

Reverend Alexander Kennedy described the diverse African groups who resided in Belmont between 1836 and 1849:

> Belmont was, to a large extent, peopled by African settlers, brought hither by English vessels... They worked for the Government as free labourers – on the roads, the Savannah and Public Gardens. They were allowed to settle on the east of the Dry River, principally in Belmont, which became known as Freetown Valley – the free Africans having settled there. Among the settlers were the following tribes: the Mandingo, Eboe, Kramanti, Kroomen, Congo and Yarraba.[632]

All Africans are described as working as free laborers on the construction and maintenance of roads, the savannah, and public gardens. The African groups mentioned made for a diverse labor force. The area where they resided in the vicinity of Belmont Estate was named Freetown Valley, which most certainly reveals a connection with Freetown, where the majority were hired. More significantly, the mix of workers resembled Freetown as each group had its own quarter.

A major concern of both the British government and planters was to avoid a population of squatters. Giving the Kru and their fellow migrant workers the opportunity to live in villages reduced the problem of squatters on estates and in ports.[633] In *Notice to Emigrants to the Island of Trinidad*, W. Hamilton revealed that the Kru were to be "furnished with a house and provision grounds."[634] Those Kru living in Krooman's Village and Freetown Valley were provided with lodgings and land as part of their contractual labor.

---

630 *Caribbean Societies* no. 2 (1985): 50–51.
631 David Hollett, *Passage from India to El Dorado: Guyana and the Great Migration* (Teaneck, NJ: Fairleigh Dickinson University Press, 1999), 85.
632 C.B. Franklin, *After Many Days: A Memoir. Being a Sketch of the Life and Labours of Rev. Alexander Kennedy, First Presbyterian Missionary to Trinidad, Founder of Greyfriars Church, and its Pastor for Fourteen Years: January 1836-December 1849. With an Introduction by Rev R.E. Welsh* (Port of Spain: Franklin's Electric Printery, 1910), 76.
633 Ibid., 341.
634 W. Hamilton, Papers Relative to the Affairs of Trinidad, March 18, 1841, General Report on the Emigration Commissioners, vol. 1, Papers Relative to the West Indies, 1841–1842 (London: William Clowes and Sons, 1842), 48.

Communal land schemes resulted in Kru settlements that ensured traditional social, political, and economic structures would continue to inform Kru labor relations. Initially, Kru headmen remained responsible for organizing labor and continued the practice of exacting a portion of their labor gang's salary as was protocol in West Africa. They remained integral to ensuring the flow of Kru workers to Trinidad, Jamaica, and British Guiana. Upon their return to the Kru Coast, they continued to give a portion of their salary to the *krogba* of their village.

However, several developments would gradually limit Kru immigration and undermine the authority of headmen in the British Caribbean. Most significantly, the opportunity for Kru to purchase private property enabled Kru laborers to gain unprecedented economic, social, and political autonomy. Besides the creation of communal land schemes, the Colonial Office encouraged the Kru to purchase their own private land plots.[635] The British hoped that by presenting the opportunity to own land, African migrant workers including the Kru would consider permanent settlement in Trinidad.

The price of land in Trinidad as authorized by the British colonial government was "one Pound per Acre."[636] Land purchases were to be paid in cash and were to range in size between 40 and 50 acres.[637] At £1 per acre, a 40-acre lot cost £40. Kru who worked at a rate of approximately 2 shillings per day could make £1 in ten days (20 shillings equalled £1) and roughly £3 in a month.[638] It took Kru workers between 13 and 14 months to afford the cost of a lot. In 1855, De Verteuil reported that a migrant worker in Trinidad had the opportunity "to commute his return passage in exchange for £5 in money and five acres of land."[639] The financial incentive and ability to own land were appealing for some Kru.

Similarly, Kru in British Guiana were encouraged to purchase land plots. Upon their arrival in the early 1840s, they were housed in estate lodgings and cottages.[640] However, by the 1850s, Crown lands were available for purchase in plots of less than 100 acres in the Canal No. 1 district, along the Demerara

---

635 CO 295 /132–133 (1840), 181.
636 Ibid., 190.
637 Ibid., 190.
638 Ibid., "Lots, Living quarters and Pay Rate," 135.
639 Verteuil, *Trinidad*, 348.
640 Accounts and Papers, Emigration, Session 3 February to August 12, 1842, vol. 21, Correspondence Relative to Emigration, 1842, Enclosure in No. 8 Government House, Return of Emigrants from Sierra Leone working as Labourers or Trademen in District E County of Demerara July 1, 1841, J.O. Lockhart Mure Stipendiary Justice of the Peace, District E (London: William Clowes and Sons, 1842), 378.

River, where the Kru largely resided.[641] According to J.A. Veerasawmy in 1919, "many Kroomen and Oku people from Oruba [Yoruba] from West Africa, and Congoes were settled there" in the 1890s.[642] Veerasawmy estimated their population to have grown from 100 in 1891 to 1,000 by 1911.[643] The size of the Kru community at Canal No. 1 is unknown, but a large community of African laborers consisting of Yoruba, Kongo, and Kru continued to live in the vicinity into the early twentieth century.[644]

The ability to purchase private property reveals a major transformation in the Kru diaspora. In 1853, John Brummel suggested that land purchase enabled Kru workers to gain a new identity in British Guiana.[645] Their independence may explain why some Kru laborers were recorded as being reluctant to give a percentage of their wages to headmen in the Kru villages and to the Kru *krogba* on the Kru Coast upon completion of contracts.[646] Brummel contended that land ownership became a way of liberating Kru from the traditional gift-giving protocol altogether since they remained in British Guiana and effectively ended ties with their homeland.[647] The opportunity to own land individually differed from their experience on the Kru Coast where land was communally owned by their respective *dako* and where they remained subject to the authority of the *krogba*. The combination of the Kru's ability to own land outside of the communal village and complete task-based work on an individual basis as jobbers enabled the Kru to function beyond traditional societal norms. Employment could be obtained without having to wait for a headman to secure a contract. As a result, the practice of giving a portion of their wages to headmen gradually became redundant. Similarly, the authority of the *krogba* on the Kru Coast was maintained through gift-giving rituals associated with homecomings. In the British Caribbean, there was no equivalent figure that structured relations in their com-

---

641 Josephine Boenisch, "Ethnic Differences in Peasant Agriculture: The Canals Poulder" (Master's thesis, McGill University, 1971), 28.
642 J.A. Veerasawmy, "The Noitgedacht Murder," *Timehri* 6, Third Series (1919): 116. See also Boenisch, "Ethnic Differences," 28; Brian L. Moore, *Cultural Power, Resistance, and Pluralism: Colonial Guyana, 1838–1900* (Montreal: McGill Press, 1995), 139, 144; B.W. Higman, Carl Campbell and Patrick Bryan, *Slavery, Freedom and Gender: The Dynamics of Caribbean Society* (Kingston: University of the West Indies Press, 2003), 138, 144.
643 Veerasawmy, "Noitgedacht Murder,"116.
644 See E.P. Skinner, "Ethnic Interaction in a British Guiana Rural Community: A Study in Secondary Acculturation and Group Dynamics" (Ph.D. dissertation, Columbia University, 1955), 258.
645 John Brummell, *British Guiana: Demerara after Fifteen Years of Freedom, by a Landowner. By John Brummell* (London: T. Bosworth, 1853), 78.
646 Ibid., 77.
647 Ibid., 78.

munities. Both the decline of the headmen's authority and the absence of the *krogba* played a role in creating an unprecedented sense of Kru individualism.

The demographic imbalance between Kru males and females was another factor that influenced the development of Kru communities in Trinidad and British Guiana. Very few Kru women made the voyage to the Caribbean and none were recorded as having joined Kru workers in Jamaica. In 1841, the Superior carried the wives of several Kru workers to British Guiana.[648] A report by W.M. Humphrys, Agent-General for Immigration, in 1844, described the arrival of the Arabian in 1843 containing 48 immigrants, 15 of whom were Krumen accompanied by a single Kru woman.[649] British colonial and consular authorities provided various incentives to increase Kru female immigration in Trinidad and British Guiana. In 1844, free passages were offered to those Kru who brought their wives.[650] The British government certainly seemed to think that the option of bringing wives would result in a permanent labor force, as demonstrated by their desire for every ship sailing from Freetown to contain a manifest of one-third women.[651] Despite these incentives, few Kru women migrated. Similar to Kru communities in West Africa, those in Trinidad and British Guiana were overwhelmingly male. The main factor discouraging Kru women to immigrate may have been the three to five-year duration of contracts and the long distance between the Kru Coast and the Caribbean.

Based on the low number of Kru women in Caribbean, the Kru diaspora was transformed through intermarriage with Creole women.[652] Many of the Kru who migrated were young laborers and unmarried, which also explains the low numbers of Kru women who immigrated to British Guiana. An unmarried Kru woman found it much more difficult to survive if she was not supported by a husband. With few Kru women available, Kru males married beyond their community. Single Kru men were reported to be more likely to settle permanently in British Gui-

---

[648] Parliamentary Papers, House of Commons and Command, "Affairs of British Guiana Immigration Office, September 23, 1841," vol. 29 (1842), 113.

[649] Accounts and Papers, Colonies, Emigration, vol. 35, Session 1 February-5 September 1844, Papers Relative to Emigration from the West Coast of Africa to the West Indies, Enclosure in No. 13 Immigration Agent's Office, Georgetown, Demerara, September 19, 1843, W.M. Humphrys, Agent-General for Immigration (1844), 89, The National Archives, United Kingdom.

[650] Kuczynski, *Demographic Survey* 1: 83. For more discussion on incentives see Frost, *Work*, 21.

[651] Parliamentary Papers, Acting Committee November 14, 1843, "Evidence of the Honourable Captain Denmase R.N.," November 1843, 6, 119–120.

[652] Parliamentary Papers, House of Commons and Command, vol. 29, "Affairs of British Guiana Immigration Office September 23, 1841" (London: HM Stationary Office, 1842), 113.

ana as compared with those Kru who had wives back in Freetown or the Kru Coast.[653]

Creole women outnumbered men in British Guiana, as reported by the Commissioners of Immigration in 1850: "British Guiana, where it so happens that of the African race there are more females than males, and that Africans coming to this colony without their wives readily form alliances with the Creole population."[654] These unions resulted in a new generation marked by what Stuart Hall terms "hybridity" as plural societies with multiple ancestral origins creolized.[655] Kru laborers were among many laboring groups in British Guiana, and in the second half of the nineteenth century a new generation of creolized Kru became the norm.

Despite these changes within Kru communities, a traditional practice that endured was the Kru mark. According to Henry Kirke in 1898, "men, with... tattooes on their noses and cheeks... tireless oarsmen... they roused their spirits by chanting wild Kroo songs, which marked the time to the measured beat of the oars."[656] Kirke's comments reveal that the Kru continued to practice their tradition of scarification, although Kirke refers to the scars as "tattooes," in British Guiana. He also showed that Kru identity continued to be intimately bound with marine service and that paddling continued to be marked by song. However, due to their low numbers and intermarriage with the Creole population, the Kru eventually disappeared as a distinct ethnic group in the twentieth century. The ability to study their diaspora in the Caribbean with a degree of certainty is mostly limited to the nineteenth century.[657]

In the British Caribbean, Kru continued to engage in the labor they were familiar with on marine vessels in dockyards, estates and rivers in Trinidad, Jamaica and British Guiana. The establishment of Krooman's Village in Trinidad enabled the Kru to maintain a cultural space with a distinct identity alongside Indian, Chinese, Yoruba, and Congolese workers for a period that lasted several decades. In British Guiana, Kru seemed to have had a greater degree of mobility in terms of contracts and living quarters than elsewhere in the British Caribbean.

---

[653] Accounts and Papers, Sugar Growing Colonies, "Despatch from Governor Barkly to Earl Grey," September 25, 1850, vol. 9, no. 49, 1851, 188.
[654] Accounts and Papers, vol. 9, Enclosure in no. 49, W.B. Wolseley, Acting Secretary, "Minute of the Proceedings of the Commissioners of Immigration Correspondence, at a Meeting Held at the Guiana Public Buildings, Tuesday, 20 August 1850," 189.
[655] Hall, "Cultural Identity," 235.
[656] Kirke, *Twenty-Five Years*, 171–172.
[657] The one exception being the use of genealogies, which may reveal the descendants of the Kru workers.

While they maintained the tradition of the Kru mark that distinguished them from other laborers, their community was transformed through the ability to own private land and obtain contracts independent of headmen. The relationships the Kru formed with Creole women and the decision of many Kru to remain in mixed ethnic communities along the Demerara River and elsewhere led to their creolization and eventual absorption. One crucial distinction between the Kru experience in the British Caribbean and West Africa was that while the Kru were assimilated into an emerging creole society in the former, their diaspora communities in West Africa continued well into the twentieth century and, in some cases, the twenty-first century.

Chapter 6
Growth in Diaspora and Decline in the Homeland

For a greater part of the nineteenth century, the Kru homeland and diaspora were deeply influenced by the social, political, and economic forces enacted by the Liberian state.[658] From its founding in 1822, the colony of Liberia excluded the Kru from citizenship. Thereafter, the Kru had to contend with the interests of the American Colonization Society in order to continue their labor migration with the British. The capital, Monrovia, became the unique site of two Kru diaspora communities that were linked with the British trade network and European factories, yet founded independently. Surfboats remained at the center of Kru activity in Monrovia as they transported people and commodities ship and shoreside and continued to obtain contracts for service on ships sailing the coast.

As the ACS established colonies in the vicinity of the Kru Coast in the 1830s, a series of treaties were negotiated to maintain peace between their communities and the Kru amid mounting tensions. However, the establishment of the Liberian state in 1847 increased political tensions through state-sanctioned land acquisition and the implementation of Port of Entry Laws, which imposed a tax on Kru laborers. Liberian State measures fostered competition between the British and French, which compelled some Kru to accept an increase in French contracts in Grand Bassam in order to evade an oppressive regime of taxation.[659] Legislation impeded the authority of the *krogba* and headmen, and by the 1870s led to a shift in the Kru economy towards increased palm oil production. Equally disruptive was the state strategy to support missions on the Kru Coast, which resulted in greater conversion rates to Christianity amongst the Kru. In response to all of these factors, Kru migration to their diaspora communities in ports in West Africa increased in the later decades of the nineteenth century.[660]

---

[658] The ACS sponsored colony in Cape Mesurado was known as the colony of Liberia, or simply Liberia, in the period between 1822 and 1846. See Tom Shick, "A Quantitative Analysis of Liberian Colonization From 1820 to 1843 with Special Reference to Mortality," *The Journal of African History* 7, no. 1 (1971): 45.

[659] Henry Astbury Leveson, *The Forest and the Field* (London: Chatto and Windus, 1874), 272.

[660] Davis, *Ethnohistorical*, 47.

Colony of Liberia

The creation of the colony of Liberia was welcomed by many American planters as an ideal opportunity for dealing with the United States' growing free Black population. Their population had more than tripled from 59,466 in 1790 to 186,466 in 1810.[661] By 1816, their number had increased to more than 200,000 compared with 1.5 million enslaved Africans.[662] Free Blacks were thought by some to pose a direct threat to the social order informed by the plantocracy in the southern states.[663]

At the heart of this colonial project was the ACS. Founded in 1816, it was an association whose proclaimed aim was "to colonize, with their own consent, on the coast of Africa or in such other place as Congress shall deem expedient, the people of colour in our country."[664] Founder of the ACS, Virginia federalist, Charles Fenton Mercer, applied for federal funds via the Virginia Assembly in order to establish the colony of Liberia at Cape Mesurado.[665] ACS agents closely observed the Colony of Sierra Leone and hoped to create a vibrant settlement of their own at Cape Mesurado that would foster trade and growth for a settler population.

Cape Mesurado was selected as the ideal location for trade and colonial expansion because it had served as a regular port-of-call for American commercial ships for at least a decade and European vessels for several centuries.[666] Kru seamen were recorded as being hired on European merchant ships at the Cape since at least the first decade of the nineteenth century.[667] Cape Mesurado served as a frequent port-of-call for Royal Navy ships engaged in the suppression of the trans-Atlantic slave trades where Kru seamen were regularly hired for service.

---

[661] Thomas Shick, *Behold the Promised Land* (Baltimore: John Hopkins Press, 1980), 13.
[662] Charles I. Foster, "The Colonization of Free Negroes, in Liberia, 1816–1835," *The Journal of Negro History* 38, no. 1 (1953): 41.
[663] For a discussion on the politics informing the creation of the colony of Liberia and the ACS see George W. Brown, *The Economic History of Liberia* (Washington: Washington Associated Publishers, Inc., 1941), 9–10; Early Lee Fox, *The American Colonization Society, 1817–1840* (1919; repr., Whitefish, MO: Kessinger Publishers, 2007), 1–25; Allan Yarema, *The American Colonization Society: An Avenue to Freedom?* (Lanham: University Press of America, 2006), 1–14; Philip John Staudenraus, *The History of the American Colonization Society*, vol. 1 (Madison: University of Wisconsin Press, 1958), 1–75.
[664] Brown, *Economic History*, 9–10; Fraenkel, *Tribe*, 4.
[665] Mary Tyler McGraw, "Free Blacks and African Colonization, 1816–1832," *Journal of American Studies* 21, no. 2 (1987): 208.
[666] Swan, "Memoranda," 318–320.
[667] Fraenkel, *Tribe*, 71, 77.

The first settlers landed at Cape Mesurado on January 7, 1822. ACS agents labelled the settlers "Americo-Liberians" (a term with which they self-identified) in the colony based on their heritage in the Americas and their association with the newly formed colony of Liberia.[668] They received plots of land from ACS agents, established stores, and constructed buildings.[669] Agents provided tools to the settlers for cultivation.[670] When the colonists arrived at the Cape, there was a Kru migrant settlement in the southwest corner of Bushrod Island.[671] ACS agent, Jeduhi Ashmun estimated the Kru population on Bushrod Island to be 50.[672] Fraenkel suggests that the Kru community dated to at least the first decade of the nineteenth century.[673] In 1822, Ashmun noted the following:

> It is proper, in this place, to avert to a small hamlet placed on the beach one mile to the northward of the settlement, belonging to a people entirely distinct in origin, language and character, from all their neighbours. These are the Kroomen, well known by foreigners visiting the coast, as the watermen and pilots of the country. They originate from a populous maritime tribe, whose country is Settra-Kroo, near Cape Palmas.[674]

Ashmun was well aware of their reputation as seamen for hire. Their community was distinct from Krutown in Sierra Leone because it had developed independent of the British. The possibility of working for wages had led Kru residing between the Cestos and Grand Cess Rivers in the Proper Kru region to go west to Cape Mesurado, and find employment on British, French, Dutch, German, and American vessels and in factories.[675]

The composition of the Kru community gradually shifted in the nineteenth century as other *dako* besides the Proper Kru came to represent the majority

---

668 Shick, *Behold*, 72; Thomas Sabin, "The Making of the Americo-Liberian Community: A Study of Politics and Society in Nineteenth Century Liberia" (Ph.D. thesis, Columbia University, 1974), 81.
669 Paul Finkelman, ed., *Encyclopedia of African-American History, 1619–1895: From the Colonial Period to the Age of Frederick Douglass*, vol. 2 (Oxford: Oxford University Press, 2006), 58.
670 Gershoni, *Black Colonialism*, 10; Richard West, *Back to Africa: A History of Sierra Leone and Liberia* (London: Jonathan Cape, 1970), 108–111.
671 Breitborde, "Structural," 70, 71, 112–114.
672 Jehudi Ashmun, *History of the American Colony in Liberia from December 1821 to 1823* (Washington: Way & Gideon, 1826), 7.
673 Fraenkel, *Tribe*, 71.
674 Ashmun, *History*, 6.
675 Svend E. Holsoe, "A Study of Relations between Settlers and Indigenous Peoples in Western Liberia, 1821–1847," *African Historical Studies* 4, no. 2 (1971): 342; Ralph Randolph Gurley, *Life of Jehudi Ashmun, Late Colonial Agent: With an Appendix contacting Extracts from His Journal and Other Writings; with a Brief Sketch of the Life of the Rev. Lott Cary* (New York: Leavitt, Lord and Co., 1835), 160, 238–239.

Figure 6.1: Krootown, Monrovia, c. 1886. Source: Johann Büttifoker, "Kroo Town bei Monrovia, mit einer Gruppe von Krunegern. Maker," 1886, accessed on June 1, 2017, https://www.pinterest.com/pin/460774605603362096/.

of laborers in Monrovia including Jloh Kru from Sasstown and Gbeta Kru from Picaninny Cess on the Kru Coast.[676] Tonkin and Davis have suggested that their towns on the Kru Coast developed in the nineteenth century. The Jloh are believed to have migrated from east of the Cavalla River at an unknown date before eventually being associated with the creation of Sasstown around 1840.[677] The Gbeta Kru formed the town Picaninny Cess to the northwest of Grand Cess. They are believed to have emigrated from the St. John River in Bassa country before establishing themselves in Picaninny Cess.[678]

Kru were one migrant community amongst indigenous populations in the vicinity of Cape Mesurado which included the Dei, Gola, and Kondo. Samuel Wilkeson made an early reference to "Krootown" in 1825.[679] However, it was not until the 1830s that there were frequent references to a Monrovia Krutown in the *African Repository* and other writings of the period. The earliest known photograph dates to 1886 (Figure 6.1).[680]

Similar to the Krutown that developed in Freetown, Kru resided next to the waterside on the bank of the Mesurado River (Figure 6.2), which was essential due to the nature of their work. They fished for subsistence and sold their catch locally. Although, in 1872, Kru were discouraged from selling fish at the market because authorities were concerned about flooding the market and

---

676 Fraenkel, *Tribe*, 77.
677 Davis, *Ethnohistorical*, 106–107; Tonkin, *Narrating*, 22.
678 Davis, *Ethnohistorical*, 130.
679 Samuel Wilkeson, *A Concise History of the Commencement, Progress and Present Condition of the American Colonies in Liberia* (Washington: Madisonian Office, 1839), 20. Although Wilkeson published his book in 1839, he refers to Krootown in a section referring to events in 1825.
680 "Municipal Legislation at Monrovia," *African Repository* 12, no. 5 (1836): 163; *African Repository* 48 (1872): 186; *A Manual to Accompany Colton's Missionary Map of the World* (New York: G.W. & C.B. Colton & Co., 1878), 53; "Elevation of the Natives," *African Repository* 51, no. 2 (1875): 125.

Figure 6.2: Krootown, Monrovia c. 1903.
Source: Unknown Photographer. Krootown, Monrovia, Postcard, Union Postale Universelle, 1903.

they confiscated fish sold in the colony during that period.[681] As seen in Figure 6.2, living on the riverbank allowed Kru easy access to European and American ships for trade and employment. The size of the Kru population in Monrovia in the early nineteenth century is unknown. Yet, it is reasonable to suggest that the population was far less than the number of Kru in Freetown because they were not employed on steady contracts with the British in Monrovia. Rather, their employment more closely resembled their hiring practices on the Kru Coast, which depended on passing or docking ships. Büttikofer estimated the population to be 1,000 in the 1880s.[682] Similar to Freetown, Krutown was administered by a headman known as the "Kru Governor".[683] They played a similar role in Monrovia organizing labor and maintaining order.

Eventually, a second Krutown developed on the other bank of the Mesurado River.[684] It was smaller and was more akin to a makeshift settlement than an official Krootown. In 1886, Büttikofer differentiated the two communities:

> Whereas the Krootown at Monrovia supplies the Dutch factory with labourers and sailors, the Woermann factory draws the same almost exclusive from the other, which therefore is also called German Krootown. It is smaller though, and now also built anew, as a couple of years ago the town stood quite close to the mouth of the river on the so-called *Kroo-point*.[685]

Beyond supplying British ships with seamen, both Krutowns catered to the labor demands of Dutch and German factories by supplying workers. The establishment of German Krootown suggests that Kru continued to live close to their workplaces and were willing to create new communities in any location where they

---

681 Anonymous, "Liberian Intelligence," *African Repository* 48, no. 6 (1872): 186.
682 Büttikofer, *Travel*, 49.
683 Fraenkel, *Tribe*, 89.
684 Büttikofer, *Travel*, 49.
685 Ibid., 50.

had the opportunity to earn steady wages. Their duties included transporting cargo from factory to ship before departure for Europe. Kru residing in German Krootown supplied docked ships with coal that was stored in the Woermann factory. Kru worked at many Woermann factories on the African coast between Monrovia and Swakopmund in South West Africa.[686] German companies tended to hire Kru laborers in Monrovia, which meant that most Kru working on contract came from the Proper Kru, Gbeta, and Jloh *dakwe*.[687]

Monrovia became the capital of the colony of Liberia in 1824, whose Constitution written in 1825 provided ACS agents with the power to enforce laws, defined Americo-Liberian settler rights, and laid the legal framework for future colonies.[688] Under the Constitution, the ACS would appoint a governor to head each colony as they were established on the coast, gradually forming a commonwealth. Americo-Liberian settlers could run for office, and it was their responsibility to elect a deputy governor in each settlement. The Constitution stipulated that as each colony was formed it would be allocated ten seats in a commonwealth government and the deputy governor held the power to enact laws, which could be subject to a veto by the governor.[689] However, Kru, Dei, Gola, and Kondo were excluded from the Constitution and, consequently, tensions between Americo-Liberians and indigenous peoples grew.

Besides Americo-Liberians, Liberated Africans were given the rights and benefits of citizenship. They established settlements in the colony, served in militias, and worked as domestic laborers in Americo-Liberian households.[690] They also labored as farmers and sold their produce in local markets.[691] Claude Clegg III has argued that their communities served as a "buffer zone" between Amer-

---

[686] Kru worked on Woermann factories in Victoria, Doula, Cape Lopez, Gabon and Swakopmund. See Theodor Bohner, *Die Woermanns* (Berlin: Brüke zur Heimat, 1935), 133.
[687] Sundiata, "Rise," 28.
[688] John Bernanrd Blamo, "Nation-Building in Liberia as Revealed by Symbol Analysis," (Ph.D. thesis, Boston University, 1969), 43; Huberich, *Political*, 1: 212–213, 272–286, 2: 1029.
[689] Gershoni, *Black Colonialism*, 12; Archibald Alexander, *A History of Colonization on the Western Coast of Africa* (1846; repr., New York: Negro Universities Press, 1969), 569.
[690] Harrison Akingbade, "The Liberian Settlers and the Campaign Against the Slave Trade, 1825–1865," *Africa Rivista trimestrale di studi e document tazione dell'Istituto italiano per l'Africa e l'Oriente* 38, no. 3 (1983): 342, 345; A. Doris Banks Henries, *The Liberian Nation* (New York: Herman Jaffe Publishers, 1954), 58; Anonymous, "Hostile Movement among the Natives of the Dey Country," *Liberian Herald* 3 (1832): 3; Anonymous, "Mechlin to Gurley, April 1832," *African Repository* 8, no. 5 (1832): 130–136.
[691] Anonymous, *African Repository* 8, no. 3 (1833): 93–94.

ico-Liberians and indigenous populations.[692] Ashmun established a settlement for Liberated Africans called New Georgia on Bushrod Island, separate from Krutown and Americo-Liberians.[693]

Friction between Americo-Liberian settlers and Kru erupted in periodic skirmishes in 1825 in direct response to the Constitution.[694] Despite their differences, ACS agents and Americo-Liberian settlers understood the economic value of hiring Kru whom they viewed as "serviceable."[695] In 1826, the "Kroo nation" signed treaties with ACS agents in Monrovia. The Kru received an annual tribute of 100 bars of iron in order to keep the peace and in recognition of their invaluable potential as a workforce.[696] Moreover, their recognition as a "nation" shows that the Kru had carved out a distinct homeland and diaspora in the nineteenth century that was recognized by ACS agents and Europeans alike.

Controlling the flow of Kru labor was a primary concern in the colony of Liberia. In 1835, Monrovia Town Council passed an ordinance declaring procedures that all Kru laborers had to follow upon their arrival at Krutown. In 1836, the ordinance was published and stated the following:

> All Kroomen... residing, or who may hereafter reside at Krootown, on this side of the Mesurado river, shall pay annually, to the Town of Monrovia, the sum of one dollar and fifty cents, as a tax, and do any fatigue duty that may be required of them by the President of the Town Council... That all Kroomen... arriving at thus place for the purpose of laboring or residing, shall report themselves within five days after their arrival, to the President of the Town Council; and receive a certificate, – which certificate shall grant them permission to reside in Krootown, and for which certificate they shall pay the sum of one dollar and fifty cents.[697]

Kru had to pay an annual fee and obtain a certificate in order to reside in Monrovia. All Kru and other indigenous peoples who resided in Monrovia and were not employed by its citizens could be arrested and forced to serve hard labor.[698] The ordinance affected the mobility of the Kru diaspora community who had lived in the vicinity of Monrovia for decades before the arrival of the Americo-Li-

---

692 Claude Andrew Clegg III, *The Price of Liberty: African Americans and the Making of Liberia* (Chapel Hill: University of North Carolina Press, 2009), 94.
693 Ibid., 93.
694 Jehudi Ashmun, "Relations of the Colony with Kroomen," *African Repository* 2, no. 3 (1826): 96–97.
695 Ibid., 96.
696 Ibid., 96–97.
697 Anonymous, "Municipal Legislation at Monrovia," *African Repository* 12, no. 5 (1836): 163.
698 Huberich, *Political*, 2: 508; Fraenkel, *Tribe*, 13.

berian settlers. The council wanted to control their labor to ensure that the colony generated an income through taxation.

The ACS held legal authority over Kru laborers in the colony. Fines were listed as follows: "And be it further resolved, That no person or persons, are permitted to employ, Kroomen… without they have complied with the above resolution, unless they become responsible for their tax."[699] Kru laborers risked a $2.00 fine for failure to produce a work certificate and forced removal from the settlement. If they were unable to pay the fine, they were to perform public labor until it was paid.[700] Americo-Liberians, European and American ship captains who employed the Kru without proper documentation would be fined and forced to pay their tax.[701] The colony's taxation policy was a precursor to state taxation legislature in the republic era following independence.

ACS expansion increased in the 1830s as settler colonies were established on the Kru Coast. Each colony was funded by state chapters of the ACS. "Maryland in Africa" colony was founded near Cape Palmas, and was supported by the Maryland Colonization Society in 1833.[702] In 1834, the New York and Pennsylvania societies established colonies near Bassa Cove. In 1837, the Mississippi and Louisiana societies founded the colony of Greenville at the Sinoe River.[703] The colony of Greenville forced Kru to vacate their land and move across the river to Blue Barre in 1837.[704] Two British traders, David Murray and Jack Purse, who traded in Settra Kru, created petitions and appealed to the British to protect them against Liberian encroachment, although the British government seems to have provided no assistance.[705] British employment and trade were central to the Kru economy. The risk of displacement threatened to undermine their free wage labor cycle.

In 1837, the Legislative Council ordered a trade policy on the coast that limited all trade to six official ports of entry in Harper, Grenville, Buchanan, Marshall, Monrovia, and Robertsport.[706] The policy was the precursor to the succession of Port of Entry Laws in 1849, 1859, 1865, and 1891, in the republic era that placed customs on all trade. The policy elevated tensions with British traders.

---

[699] "Municipal Legislation," 163.
[700] Ibid., 163.
[701] Ibid., 163.
[702] William D. Hoyt, Jr., "John McDonogh and Maryland Colonization in Liberia, 1834–1835," *The Journal of Negro History* 24, no. 4 (1939): 440–453.
[703] Ibid., 228.
[704] Davis, "Liberian," 235; Fraenkel, "Social Change," 156.
[705] Davis, "Liberian," 235; FO 47/5, "Hamilton to Palmerstone May 9, 1851."
[706] Brown, *Economic History*, 127.

Laurie Hamilton and Hatton Cookson of London were two firms operating on the Kru Coast.[707] Hamilton agent, David Murray, employed Kru in a factory in Settra Kru. In one episode, Ranger, a Hamilton-owned brig, was seized in Buchanan by Liberian authorities for not paying customs.[708] The incident not only intensified relations between the Kru and the Liberian colony, but also increased British traders' resentment towards the Liberian colonial government. Customs threatened both Kru and British trader returns.

The ACS proposed to establish the Commonwealth of Liberia in 1838 by uniting the autonomous colonies that dotted the coast.[709] Headed by Thomas Buchanan, head of the ACS envoy, a commonwealth was formed gradually. The commonwealth did not consider the possibility of citizenship for the Kru and other indigenous peoples until 1841, at which time there was a proposal for citizenship for those Kru who had lived in an ACS colony for a minimum of three years.[710] They had to be "civilized," which meant converting to Christianity and abandoning "all the forms, customs and superstitions of heathendom."[711] Americo-Liberians equated civilization with Christianity at the expense of indigenous religious practices. Despite the opportunity for the Kru to become citizens, they largely refused to convert to Christianity. Their response may have been a form of resistance against Americo-Liberian colonization, which required them to submit to the terms and conditions defined by the interests of the ACS and Americo-Liberian settlers.

"Mississippi in Africa," joined the commonwealth in 1842 and became the main hub of Sinoe County. Based in Cape Palmas, "Maryland in Africa" remained independent until 1857, after which it entered the Republic of Liberia as Maryland County.[712] Each colonial settlement gradually gained territory as a result of treaties with the local populations including the Kru.[713] Figure 6.3 is a map of the Commonwealth of Liberia in 1839, which illustrates the extent of ACS colonies between the Gallinas River in the west and the region to the east of Harper in Maryland Colony.

---

707 Anonymous, "Message of Governor Roberts to the Legislative Council, January 9, 1843," *African Repository* 19, no. 6 (1843): 176–184; Davis, "Liberian," 231.
708 Davis, "Liberian," 231.
709 Gershoni, *Black Colonialism*, 12. For an analysis of Maryland Colony see Hannah Abeodu Bowen Jones, "The Struggle for Political and Cultural Unification in Liberia, 1847–1930" (Ph.D. thesis, Northwestern University, 1962), 7; a study on Mississippi Colony includes Sabin, "Making of the Americo-Liberian Community," 81.
710 Huberich, *Political*, 2: 724.
711 Ibid., 724; Fraenkel, *Tribe*, 13.
712 Fraenkel, *Tribe*, 15.
713 Ibid., 15–16.

Part of the Liberian strategy to secure authority over the Kru Coast was to establish missions in all of the colonies. A variety of denominations responded, including Methodist, Baptist, Roman Catholic, Wesleyan, and Presbyterian missionaries. By 1838, Methodists had constructed missions in Sinoe County on the Kru Coast.[714] Missionaries were dealing with a sizeable Kru population. In 1840, Presbyterian missionaries Pinney, Canfield, and Alward published their population estimates on the main trading towns on the Kru Coast. The layout of Grand Cess was observed by Canfield:

> Grand Sesters [Grand Cess] is 40 or 50 miles above Cape Palmas... There is one large town of near 500 houses, and some six and seven smaller towns are in the immediate neighborhood. We judge the entire population to be not far from five or six thousand... [715]

While Grand Sesters (Grand Cess) was reported to have a population of between five and six thousand, the wider population in the region was estimated at between 10,000 and 12,000 inhabitants.[716] Proper Kru towns including Little Kru, Nana Kru, King William's Town, Settra Kru, and Krubah were estimated to have between 400 and 600 inhabitants each.[717] In 1866, *The Missionary Magazine* later reported: "They [Kru] lay off their towns at right angles, and place each principal street under a chief or headman."[718] Kru organized the physical layout of their villages based on traditional hierarchal structures that also enabled for easy access to labor pools.

The entire Kru Coast was estimated to have a population of between 30,000 and 40,000.[719] When these numbers are compared with the number of Kru migrant laborers working abroad, which was estimated to be between 5,000 and 20,000 a year, the percentage of workers ranges from 16.6 percent upwards to 66.6 percent of a population of 30,000, and between 12.5 percent and 50 percent of a population of 40,000.[720] The numbers of between 5,000 and 20,000 laborers are reasonable when the whole Kru-speaking region between Cape Mesurado and the Bandama River is taken into account. It cannot be known, however, what percentage of the Kru Coast estimates provided by Pinney, Canfield and Al-

---

714 J. Wold, *God's Impatience in Liberia* (Grand Rapids, MI: Eerdmans, 1968), 58; Lawrence Breitborde, *Speaking Social Identity: English in the Lives of Urban Africans* (Berlin: Walter de Gruyter, 1998), 144.
715 Pinney, Canfield and Alward, "Report," 213.
716 Ibid., 212.
717 Ibid., 182.
718 "Miscellany," *The Missionary Magazine* no. 46 (1866): 120.
719 Ibid., 183; *The Missionary Chronicle* no. 11 (1843): 6.
720 Davis, *Ethnohistorical*, 49.

Figure 6.3: Map of the Commonwealth of Liberia, 1839.
Source: S. Augustus Mitchell, *Map of Africa: Map of Liberia*, no. 17, 1839. Engraved by J.H. Young. American Colonization Society, Library of Congress, Washington, D.C., United States.

ward were male. Since workers purchased multiple wives it is reasonable to assume females outnumbered males.

In 1842, a Methodist mission was built in the vicinity of Cape Palmas.[721] "Coloured ministers" were sent by Presbyterian missions to Settra Kru and Sinoe (Greenville) in 1842.[722] In spite of these developments, the Kru remained largely resistant to conversion during the colonial era between 1822 and 1846. They may have perceived the missions as part of the ACS's attempt to dominate their society and force them into the commonwealth. In 1844, one report concluded: "there never was an instance known of a Krooman being converted."[723]

Americo-Liberians sought to become active trading partners with Europeans in camwood, palm oil, and gold, which effectively displaced the Kru's traditional role as intermediaries in trade with Europeans along the Kru Coast. Conflict between these communities was exacerbated further by the Liberian colonial gov-

---

[721] Breitborde, *Speaking Social*, 144.
[722] Bliss, "Board of Foreign Missions," 247; *Annual Report of the Board of Foreign Missions of the Presbyterian in the United States of America* 4 (New York: Presbyterian Church, 1841), 9.
[723] Pedro de Zulueta, *Trial of Pedro de Zulueta, Jun., on a Charge of Slave Trading* (London: C. Wood and Company, 1844), 77.

ernment's attempt to abolish the slave trade. The slave trade provided the Kru with a source of revenue that was deemed illegitimate because it could not be taxed by the Liberian government. Another source of tension was created by Americo-Liberian expansion in the vicinity of the Kru Coast, which led to a shortage of Kru land for cultivation and village development.[724] The government's attempt to tax Kru laborers and limit their employment opportunities to mandated ports created a further rift between Kru and the Americo-Liberian communities, who in contrast were not taxed in ports.[725]

In 1845, the Peace and Friendship Treaty called for the Kru to pledge to end their participation in slave trading.[726] The treaty stated the following conditions:

> [The Kru]… bind themselves to abstain from all participation, direct or indirect, in the slave trade, that no foreign officer, agent or subject, except of the colony of Liberia, or the American Colonization Society, shall purchase, have, or in any way, by sale, lease or gift, obtain right to, or claim upon, the Kroo territory."[727]

As evidenced in the above passage, the Kru remained engaged in slave trading on the Kru Coast as late as 1845. Their continued participation in the slave trade was understood by commonwealth authorities as a hindrance to moral and economic progress. Kru were further instructed to not consider selling their lands to a foreign power. Based on the Kru's long-established practice of working on British contracts, the Liberian Commonwealth was naturally concerned that the Kru would form an alliance with the British and seek a British protectorate in their homeland. In the emerging political system, Kru remained at the mercy of the commonwealth government. They could not purchase land and did not have equal access to or protection of the law. As such, the option of leaving the Kru Coast for work abroad with the British or French may have seemed increasingly appealing.

The Liberian Commonwealth created stratified communities. Americo-Liberian settlers held little regard for the Dei, Gola, Condo, and Kru, who they perceived as "uncivilized" based on their non-Christian religious traditions and minimal attire.[728] In contrast, Dei including King Peter, Bristol, and Getumbe were recorded as not wanting to participate in attacks on the Americo-Liberian

---

[724] Zulueta, *Trial*, 29.
[725] Brown, *Economic History*, 127.
[726] Frost, *Work*, 32; Brooks, *Kru Mariner*, 84, 90.
[727] Davis, *Ethnohistorical*, 46; Anonymous, *African Repository* 21, no. 2 (1845): 41.
[728] Gershoni, *Black Colonialism*, 1–10; Huberich, *Political*, 2: 724; Fraenkel, *Tribe*, 13.

settlers because they were "brothers based on same skin colour."⁷²⁹ Their perspective suggests an affinity with the Americo-Liberians based on racial connections, as compared with regular tensions between Dei and Kru, which was rooted in ethnic differences. A socio-economic hierarchy emerged that positioned Americo-Liberians as the dominant group at the expense of indigenous populations. Liberated Africans found themselves in the middle, and sided with Americo-Liberians in times of conflict with the Kru.⁷³⁰ However, the ACS recognized the Kru's important role in commerce and trade in the commonwealth.⁷³¹ Yuketiel Gershoni has argued that the creation of Liberia occurred through "a process of colonization."⁷³² Although his position holds merit, Gershoni tends to place complete blame on the Americo-Liberian settlers rather than recognizing the role of the ACS as being responsible for fomenting a system of oppression against indigenous peoples.

Transformations on the Kru Coast

On July 26, 1847, officials of Liberia declared independence and adopted a republican constitution, which divided the country into three counties: Montserrado (between the Farmington and Mano Rivers), Grand Bassa (between the Farmington and Sanguin Rivers), and Sinoe Country (between the Sanguin and Grand Cess Rivers). Two districts were also created which included Marshall and Cape Mount. The Kru Coast was included in Sinoe County. Liberian authority in the region which had hitherto been rather minimal soon grew in intensity following independence.

Kru, Dei, Gola, and other indigenous peoples were not mentioned in the 1847 Liberian Constitution and no funds were allotted for their communities.⁷³³ In contrast, Americo-Liberian settlements were assigned the status of townships with access to federal government and county financial assistance.⁷³⁴ The dis-

---

729 Ashmun, *History*, 24; "Statement of Getumbe Recorded by E.W. Blyden," vol. 15/1, 1870–1871, letter nos. 04853–5, *American Colonization Society Papers*, Library of Congress, Washington D.C., United States.
730 Akingbade, "Liberian Settlers," 342, 345; Henries, *Liberian Nation*, 58; "Hostile Movement," 3; Anonymous, *African Repository* 8, no. 5 (1832): 131.
731 Davis, *Ethnohistorical*, 46; *Missionary Register*, vol. 34 (London: Seeley, Jackson & Halliday, 1846): 19.
732 Gershoni, *Black Colonialism*, 1–10.
733 Ibid., 13; Fraenkel, *Tribe*, 18–19.
734 Ibid., 19.

crepancy in access to government funds contributed to uneven economic development between Americo-Liberian townships and aboriginal villages in the second half of the nineteenth century.

Controlling coastal trade was a primary concern for the Liberian government. On December 26, 1849, the first Port of Entry Act was created with intention of limiting all trade to specific ports in Americo-Liberian communities, which included Monrovia, Buchanan, Greenville, and Marshall.[735] The legislation stated: "no vessel, which shall arrive from any foreign port, or the cargo on board, shall be entered elsewhere than at one of the ports of entry established by the government."[736] Foreign traders had to supply a manifest with destinations for their cargoes in Liberia and the persons co-signed to the delivery.[737] European-owned factories could gain exemption in exchange for a fee.[738] The Liberian government did not have the military manpower to rigidly enforce the Act. British and French traders largely ignored the laws, and continued to trade in ports of their choosing, much to the displeasure of the Liberian state.

Tensions between Kru and Americo-Liberian community of Greenville erupted in 1855. Kru villages including Settra Kru, Little Kru, Blue Barre, Buto, and Tasi formed an alliance against the Americo-Liberian community in Greenville. The immediate cause for the conflict was the seizure of three Kru laborers working on the British brig Ariel in Sino Bay. In 1856, the conflict was described in the *African Repository:*

> Fisherman from Blue Barre seized a canoe and 3 Croomen working for the British ship, Ariel, in Greenville harbor. County sheriff went to secure their release, but as he was leaving their village, a few mysterious fires broke out. There followed a dispute about who set them: Blue Barre said that the settlers did, settlers thought natives did or pretext for commencing hostilities. They then murdered a few settlers and attacked settlements (Readsville, Bluntsville, Louisa, and Upper Tannersville). Combining with the Booloo and Sinou tribes, they attacked Lexington. Settlers lost 8 killed and 6 wounded. Took place in Nov., 1855.[739]

The establishment in Greenville had forced the Kru to relocate across the Sinoe River and create a new settlement called Blue Barre. The *African Repository* report may have overlooked the possibility that the Fisherman was actually Kru.

---

735 FO 47/3, "Hamilton to FO January 3, 1850"; FO 47/3, "Roberts to Palmerston February 6, 1850"; Davis, "Liberian," 234.
736 Davis, "Liberian," 234.
737 Ibid., 234.
738 FO 47/7, "Roberts to Earl of Malmesbury, July 21, 1852"; FO 47/7, "Malmesbury to Roberts October 12, 1852"; FO 47/7, "Roberts to Malmesbury October 13, 1852"; Davis, "Liberian," 234.
739 Anonymous, *African Repository* 32, no. 2 (1856): 59–60.

After all, many Fishermen belonged to the Kabor and Gbeta *dakwe*.[740] Since Kru villages were in competition, it is not surprising that they would seize the three Kru workers who belonged to another *dako*. In the aftermath of their forced removal to Blue Barre, they may have perceived the three Kru as taking their jobs after being offered employment via Americo-Liberian agents in Greenville. Regardless of who fired the shots first during their release, the Americo-Liberians or the Fisherman, Kru responded by attacking Americo-Liberian communities including Readsville, Bluntsville, Louisiana, and Upper Tannersville before surrounding Greenville.[741]

The Liberian government in Monrovia sent a military force to assist Greenville. Outnumbered and outgunned, the Kru surrendered. The government demanded that the Kru make payments for damages incurred during their assault on the settlements. Liberian authorities forced Kru to pay fines by placing an embargo on all foreign trade between Sanguin and Little Kru on the Kru Coast. Foreign traders were given until May 1856 to close operations. Unable to trade, Kru communities complied and the incident came to be known as the Sino War.[742] The Sino War ultimately arose from the ability of Americo-Liberian traders to displace the Kru as intermediaries in trade between coastal and interior communities.

Within a year, in 1856, hostilities between the Grebo peoples, who lived between the Grand Cess and Cavalla Rivers, and Americo-Liberian settlers evolved into a revolt. Americo-Liberian communities were dependent on the Grebo for their food supplies and local trade. Similar to the Proper Kru, Grebo served as middlemen in trade with the interior. Americo-Liberians sought to regulate and control prices on trade items such as rice, which equated to lower profits.[743] However, the greater issue was over land acquisition. Americo-Liberian settlers forcibly acquired land near Cape Palmas and established Harper. On December 22, 1856, Governor Drayton ordered the removal of Grebo peoples from Cape Palmas with an offer to purchase their towns.[744] He had heard the rumor that Grebo had massacred colonists with no evidence to support the claim. The Grebo refused to leave and Drayton ordered an attack. Americo-Liberians frequently em-

---

740 Sullivan, "The Kru," 282.
741 Davis, "Liberian," 236; "Message of President Roberts to the Legislature, 20 December 1855," in Holsoe, "Study," 166; "Roberts to ACS," *African Repository* 32, no. 2 (1856): 60; FO 47/11, "Newham to FO, 31 December 1855"; *African Repository* 32, no. 2 (1856): 59–60.
742 Davis, "Liberian," 237.
743 Harrison Ola Abingbade, "The Settler African Conflicts: The Case of the Maryland Colonists and the Grebo, 1840–1900," *The Journal of Negro History* 66, no. 2 (1981): 93.
744 Ibid., 96.

ployed a strategy of divide and rule aligning themselves with one Grebo village over another in times of conflict as was the case when they supported Padee against the Naffau.[745] Drayton allied with the Rocktown and Cavalla people against the Grebo at Cape Palmas, who were their traditional enemies. In co-ordination with Cavalla and Rocktown forces, the colonial militia burnt their houses and killed Grebo in four settlements in Garaway.[746] The Grebo responded by setting fire to the Protestant Episcopal Mission at Mount Vaughn near Harper.[747]

Drayton appealed to the Monrovia government for assistance. On February 11, 1857, Liberia sent a force of 115 men commanded by General J.J. Roberts. The use of heavy artillery forced the Grebo to sign a treaty. On February 26, 1857, head of the Palmas Grebo and chiefs of the Garaway Grebo agreed to a treaty, which forced them to reside on the banks of the Hoffman River about four kilometers from their village at the Cape. The treaty was called the "Treaty of Peace, Friendship and Indemnification, between Liberia, State of Maryland in Liberia, and the Cape Palmas and Garaway Tribes."[748] The conditions stipulated that Americo-Liberians "settle on the Hoffman River, north of Harris' house."[749] The treaty demanded that the Grebo provide 12,000 pounds of rice or the equivalent value in cattle to the colonial government in Harper within seven months. In return, the Grebo were given a payment in goods that equated to $1000.00.[750] The seventh stipulation declared that any future disputes were to be taken before the administration in Harper for settlement.[751] On April 6, 1857, the colony of Maryland was annexed by Liberia and became Maryland County. Based on their reliance on Liberian military forces, the conflict precipitated their amalgamation in the state.

In Liberia, a larger state with more counties and a growing population equated to an even greater potential to generate state revenue. As such, in 1859, the Liberian Legislature passed a new series of Port of Entry Laws. The laws ensured customs duties were collected from American and European ships trading on the Liberian coast.[752] However, in 1859, unlike the Port of Entry Act in 1849, the laws did not specify ports. Rather, Liberian authorities attempted to intercept ships and impose customs in all ports where possible. However, the state still lacked

---

745 Ibid., 95.
746 Ibid., 96.
747 Ibid., 96.
748 *British and Foreign State Papers, 1856–1857*, vol. 48 (London: William Ridgeway, 1866), 586.
749 Ibid., 586.
750 Ibid., 586.
751 Ibid., 578.
752 Davis, *Ethnohistorical*, 47.

the military manpower to strictly enforce the laws. It was not until 1865 that all unregulated trade ceased, specific ports of entry were selected, and the law was fully implemented.[753]

The Port of Entry Law of 1865 was written by President Daniel B. Warner (1864–1868) and limited all foreign trade and export to six towns including Harper, Marshall, Buchanan, Greenville, Monrovia, and Robertsport.[754] All of these ports were Americo-Liberian settlements. Kru villages along with all indigenous settlements were excluded.[755] Significantly, Liberian traders were exempted from restrictions, and could call at any port of their choosing.[756] Although the laws limited trade to specific ports much in the same way legislature had attempted to influence trade in 1837 and 1849, unlike previous legislature in which ship captains landed and presented their itineraries, in 1865, trade was concentrated exclusively in the mandated ports.

One of the aims of the new law was to impede unregulated British and French trade on the Liberian coast. The new regulations led to a decline in foreign trade on the Kru Coast and became a major impetus for Kru migration.[757] The Kru's response to the laws was mixed. Settra Kru complied, but Picaninny Cess, Grand Cess, and Sasstown continued to trade illegally.[758] Kru residing in Krutown in Monrovia had no choice but to comply. Their location in the capital made it extremely difficult to circumnavigate the new laws.

Headmen experienced a major shift in their ability to negotiate contracts as a result of Port of Entry Law. Wages for contracts were negotiated between the headman and the employer before reporting to Liberian government officials. The shipper and laborer were required to pay a tax both at departure from and return to Liberia.[759] Upon departure and return, employers paid a fee at a rate of $1.00 per Kru worker and $2.00 per stevedore to the Liberian government.[760] The process for hiring Kru required that European and American ship captains submit "order books" containing the number of workers for contract, their special skills, work history, and information on whether or not they had

---

[753] Ibid., 47; W.A. Johnson, "Port Regulations of Liberia," *African Repository* 35, no. 4 (1859): 117–118.
[754] Davis, *Ethnohistorical*, 47; Johnston, *Liberia*, 1: 392–393.
[755] Ibid., 47; Ibid., 392–393.
[756] "Message of President Warner to the Legislature 6 December 1864," in Holsoe, "Study,"167.
[757] Davis, "Struggle," 239.
[758] "Message of President Warner to the Legislature, 10 December 1868," in Holsoe, "Study," 168; FO 47/24, "King Tobey Settra Kru to FO, 12 December 1894."
[759] Davis, *Ethnohistorical*, 49.
[760] Martin, "Krumen," 13–14.

paid their taxes on previous contracts. Liberian authorities recorded the number of laborers and determined the amount of tax to be paid.[761] The headman hoped to secure the highest wages possible as they were now responsible to pay taxes to the Liberian government.[762]

The evolution of the headman's "book" or reference letter from its initial use on the Kru Coast as a means of securing contracts was transformed for use by the Liberian state to ensure they controlled Kru labor. Headmen faced the double task of negotiating beneficial wages with ship captains in a regulated system governed by the Liberian state. Their once powerful role was diminished as they sought approval on two levels before contracts could commence. Furthermore, headmen were still responsible for giving a portion of their earnings to the *krogba* upon the completion of a contract. The situation was even worse for regular Kru laborers who earned lower wages than the headman, and had to follow homecoming protocol.

Faced with increased taxation, it proved to be more profitable for many Kru migrant laborers to remain in their diaspora communities. The Port of Entry Laws seemed to have an immediate effect. In 1866, *The Spirit of Missions* reported: "They [Kru] have... ceased to work on board of ships, and are occupied chiefly in trade on their own account or as agents of foreigners."[763] The population of Grand Cess remained about the same as it was reported in 1840 at about 12,000 inhabitants, which suggests many Kru remained in their laboring communities for the time being.[764] Regardless of whether Kru decided to abandon migrant labor or remain in their diaspora communities, a disruption in the power relations that governed the relationship between the *krogba*, headmen, and regular workers perpetrated through state regulation and taxation threatened to undermine the Kru economy and social structure.

Port of Entry Laws not only influenced Kru migrant workers to remain in their diaspora communities, but also increased employment opportunities with the French amongst Kru speaking peoples to the east of the Cavalla River beyond the rigid policies of the Liberian government. While the Kru had traded with the French for centuries on the Kru Coast, beginning in the 1860s they found a new wave employment on French contracts in ports to the east of

---

[761] Ibid., 49.
[762] Ibid., 49. Greenville operations appears in the FO 47/36, "Minutes of the Kroo Labour Conference," October 1, 1902.
[763] Anonymous, "Full Description of Our African Field," *The Spirit of Missions* 31 (1866): 76.
[764] Ibid., 76.

Cape Palmas in territory that would become Côte d'Ivoire.⁷⁶⁵ The result was twofold: increased employment and competition between the British and French as they vied to hire the Kru on labor contracts and the creation of a Kru wage labor diaspora and network with the French in the Atlantic.

Where there had been minimal Kru employment with the French in the early decades of the nineteenth century, the Anglo-French Treaty in 1845 ensured that the French Navy would supply 26 ships off the coast of West Africa in the attempt to stamp out the trans-Atlantic slave trades. The opportunity to obtain contracts with the French led Kru-speaking peoples in the region to migrate to Grand Bassam where they were routinely hired to work in such places Libreville, Brazzaville, Dahomey, Ouidah, and even as far abroad as Panama and French Guiana.⁷⁶⁶ By the 1860s, the Kru formed a large diaspora community in Grand Bassam amongst Alladian, Appolonian, Fante, and Nzima populations.⁷⁶⁷ In 1863, Captain A. Vallon observed the role of the Kru in Grand Bassam: "Dans le dagereux brisant de Grand-Bassam, un Krouman, porteur d'un magnifique poisson pris dans la lagune, essayait d'atteindre une embarkation du *Dialmath*."⁷⁶⁸ Even more significant is that the Dialmath was one of the French Navy ships that embarked Kru in Grand Bassam and sailed for Libreville,

---

765 Des Bruslons, *Dictionnaire Universel*, 1059; Martinière, *Le Grand Dictionnaire*, 72; *Dictionaire Universel de Commerce*, 640; Charles Athanase Walckenaer, *Histoire Générale Des Voyages ou Nouvelle Collection des Relations de Voyages Par Mer*, vol. 19 (Paris: Chez Lefèvre, 1830), 180.
766 Henry H. Bucher, "Liberty and Labor: The Origins of Libreville Reconsidered," *Bulletin de l'Institut Foundamental d'Afrique Noire*, 2nd series, 41, no. 3 (1979): 478–496; Peter P. Hinks and John R. McKivigan, *Encyclopedia of Anti-Slavery and Abolition*, vol. 2 (Westport: Greenwood, 2007), 432; Jeffrey Gunn, "Homeland, Diasporas and Labour Networks: The Case of Kru Workers, 1792–1900" (Ph.D. dissertation, York University, 2019), 237–241; John Hope Franklin, *George Washington Williams: A Biography* (Durham: Duke University Press, 1998), 201; Catherine Coquery-Vidrovitch, *Brazza et la Prise de Possession du Congo: La Mission de l'Ouest Africain, 1883–1885* (Paris: Mouton et Cie, 1971), 1–30; Bruce Whitehouse, *Migrants and Strangers in an African City: Exile, Dignity, Belonging* (Bloomington: Indiana University Press, 2012), 31; Behrens, *Les Kroumen*, 74, 80; A. Vallon, "La Côte Occidentale," in *Revue Maritime et Coloniale*, vol. 9 (Paris: Ministère de la Marine, 1863), 373–394; Schuler, "Kru Emigration," 174–183; Charles Rogers, "Report on the Panama Canal," *The Panama Canal* (Washington: Government Printing Office, 1889), 43; Charles Rogers, "Progress at Panama," *Popular Science* 32 (1888): 453; Gary G. Kuhn, "Liberian Contract Labor in Panama, 1887–1897," *Liberian Studies Journal* 6, no. 1 (1975): 43–52.
767 Walckenaer, *Histoire Générale*, 272; Henrique, *Les Colonies* 5: 203–204; Monica Blackmun Visonà, *Constructing African Art Histories for the Lagoons of Côte d'Ivoire* (London: Routledge, 2017), 51, 121.
768 Vallon, "La Côte Occidentale," 388; "Établissements de la Côte D'Or et du Gabon," in *Revue Maritime et Coloniale*, vol. 9 (Paris: Ministère de la Marine, 1863), 41.

which shows a clear connection between Kru diaspora communities.[769] Kru resided in a quarter of the "native village."[770] Kru or Kroumen, as they were more commonly known to the east of the Cavalla River, consisted of a number of Kru-speaking peoples including Grebo, Bété, Godié, and Dida laborers. Like the Kru working in Freetown, they too would have easily been able to distinguish community members based on dialect and village affiliation, while accepting the general label Kroumen in their workplaces.

Kru were hired for loading and unloading cargoes and were once again called upon to utilize their seamen skills transporting commodities and crew between shore and ship.[771] Working in Grand Bassam freed the Kru from Liberian regulation and taxation that burdened those who continued to seek contracts in their homeland on the Kru Coast. In Grand Bassam, their reputation for being "efficient and obedient" enabled the Kru to find increased employment on French contracts.[772]

As shipborne employment opportunities on the Kru Coast in Liberia became less attractive, Kru turned to agricultural production as an increasingly important source of income. The agricultural viability of Liberia as a mass exporter of crops had been under consideration since its formation. As early as the 1830s, one report proposed an agricultural system directed by Americo-Liberians as follows: "The Liberians might adopt the system, of procuring the aborigines, to aid in the cultivating their lands, with advantage and success. Such a connexion, between the colonists and them, was one of mutual dependence."[773]

The Liberian government's main concern was the lack of a labor force to produce agricultural commodities. Kru had traded in agricultural products for centuries in rice, plantain, grains, palm oil, and malagueta pepper.[774] Their experience made them the prime candidates for laborers tasked with the cultivation of Americo-Liberian lands. The proposal reveals the power dynamics in the relationship between Americo-Liberians, the owners of the land, and Kru, who worked the land. Increasingly, trade with Europeans was conducted by Americo-Liberian traders rather than Kru. The Liberian state was clearly forming a hi-

---

769 Vallon, "La Côte Occidentale," 388; "Établissements," 41, 55.
770 Visonà, *Constructing*, 51, 121.
771 Leonard Chenery, *The West Coast of Africa: From Sierra Leone to Cape Lopez, Part 2* (Washington: Government Printing Office, 1875), 125.
772 Robert Hamill Nassau, *My Ogowe: Being a Narrative of Daily Incidents During Sixteen Years in Equatorial West Africa* (New York: Neale Publishing Company, 1914), 398.
773 Anonymous, *African Repository* 8, no. 2 (1832): 53.
774 Elbl, "Portuguese Trade," 516; Parliamentary Papers 12 (1842): 607.

erarchal system that placed Americo-Liberian and Kru in a co-dependent albeit uneven economic relationship.

However, it wasn't until the 1870s that the Kru Coast became the epicenter of Liberian palm oil production. The main palm oil and palm kernel trading depots were located in a series of villages on the Kru Coast and included Trade Town, New Cess, Trade Town Point, Timbo, Grand Collah, Settra Kroo, River Cess, Waupee, Nana Kroo, Neffu, and Sassa Town.[775] Kru were responsible for producing the palm oil and transporting it to Americo-Liberian settlements for sale to European traders.[776] European merchant ship captains praised the Kru for their ability to heat palm oil and pour it into casks before carefully transporting it on their surfboats and loading cargo ships.[777]

Kru participation in the Liberian palm oil industry led to a transformation in relationship between the *krogba*, headmen, and laborers that had developed on the Kru Coast. In some cases, the *krogba* agreed to "furnish the labour" for Americo-Liberian estates and factories that were established close to the vicinity of a Kru village.[778] This is significant in labor relations because it meant the *krogba* was tasked with supplying a labor force and not headmen who had traditionally been responsible for providing labor gangs on contracts with the British. *Krogba* negotiated the terms of the contracts. Since gift-giving protocol associated with the homecoming of migrant workers was in decline due to the impact of Port of Entry Laws, the *krogba* could potentially earn a higher profit by taking a cut of the workers' wages and cutting out headmen who served as the middleman in migrant labor. The change represents a shift in the hierarchal labor system that developed between the Kru and British, and more closely resembles earlier trade practices on the Kru Coast.

While Kru engaged in state-driven agricultural production, their communities saw a rise in the presence of missions. Until the 1870s, Kru conversion to Christianity had been a slow process. As late as 1851, William Fox lamented: "Next to the Mohammedans, I believe the Kroomen are the most difficult to be brought under the influence of the gospel."[779] In the first half of the nineteenth century when the Kru diaspora cycle was in full effect, Kru may have seen little need to convert to Christianity and viewed it as an Americo-Liberian attempt to exact socio-political influence over their communities on the Kru Coast.

---

[775] Anonymous, "Liberian Intelligence," *African Repository* 48, no. 6 (1872): 186.
[776] Ibid., 186.
[777] Martin, "Krumen," 411.
[778] Gurley, *Life of Jehudi Ashmun*, 331.
[779] Fox, *Brief History*, 609.

President Joseph Roberts (1848–1856 and 1872–1876) recognized the political advantage of establishing missions on the Kru Coast. He proposed increasing the number of missions for the purpose of "introduce[ing] into degraded and benighted Africa the blessings of Civilization and Christianity."[780] Despite their inclusion in the state, Liberia did not yet have complete authority over Kru communities. Roberts hoped to work in tandem with missionaries in order to garner Christian converts that would lead to improved relations between Kru and the Liberian state. The government used a divide and rule policy by forming alliances with some Kru villages over others, while defending those communities with missions at all costs.[781]

Wesleyan and Methodist mission schools were established in Kru villages including Sinoe, Ebenezer, Settra Kru, Nana Kru, and Little Kru on the Kru Coast.[782] Reverend Edwin Munsell Bliss described an evangelical process based on "farming, teaching and preaching."[783] Each mission focused on literacy, religious study, and maintenance through agriculture. Sunday was recognized as the Sabbath in the town of Ebenezer, and the chief had instructed the Kru to attend church service rather than work.[784] In Cape Palmas, *Dictionary of the Grebo*, published by Bishop Payne in 1860, played a role in spreading the gospel amongst Kru-speaking peoples in the decades that followed. Grebo spoke Kru and Payne hoped that many Kru would have access to the Bible via this dictionary.[785] Missionaries were gradually garnering influence amongst the Kru.

Kru in diaspora communities in West Africa may have also played a role in the expansion of Christianity through their homecomings. Mary A. Sharp's mission in Krutown, Monrovia, played a significant role in converting Kru. Established in 1878, Miss Sharp's Mission, as it was known, served as a religious and educational institution.[786] While preachers had attempted to convert the Kru in

---

[780] Ibid., 237.
[781] Ibid., 237; FO 47/7, Roberts to Malmesbury, July 27, 1852.
[782] Reverend Eugene R. Smith, ed., *The Gospel in All Lands* (New York: Methodist, 1890), 41–42; Reverend Edwin Munsell Bliss, ed., *The Encyclopedia of Missions: Descriptive, Historical, Bibliography, Statistical. With a Full Assortment of Maps, a Complete Bibliography, and Lists of Bible Versions, Missionary Societies, and a General Index*, vol. 2 (New York: Funk and Wagnalls, 1891), 389.
[783] Bliss, *Encyclopedia of Missions*, 389.
[784] Ibid., 389.
[785] David A. Shank, *Prophet Harris: The "Black Elijah" of West Africa* (Leiden: Brill, 1994), 40.
[786] John Morrison Reid, *Missions and Missionary Society of the Methodist Episcopal Church* (New York: Eaton and Mains, 1895), 247; "Kroo boys, Miss Sharp's Mission, Monrovia," *Liberia Graphic* (1900): 8; "Bishop Taylor in Liberia," *The African Repository* 62, no. 3 (1885): 87.

Krutown as early as 1837, there is no evidence they had garnered any converts.[787] Missions not only encouraged conversion to Christianity, but also provided education. Sharp provided "school work for the Kroos."[788] Sharp's mission was also a center for baptisms. A Kru male and female were among 16 converted by Miss Sharp in 1885.[789] As converts, they could have possibly influenced family members to follow suit during their homecoming visits to the Kru Coast. An example is found in those Kru who formed part of the Methodist settlement called Jekwikpo. Many Jloh Kru, known as Jloh Methodists, had converted while on contracts on the West African coast and remained on the mission grounds after the death of the missionaries.[790]

By the 1880s, it seems that missionary efforts were paying off as religious conversion characterized many Kru communities on the Kru Coast. Missions were located in nearly every town on the Kru Coast including in Sasstown, Niffoo, Nanna Kroo, Settra Kroo, Garaway, and Grand Sesters.[791] Minister J. Wold suggested the Kru Coast experienced the "greatest rate of conversion to Christianity in Liberia."[792] With a weakening economy that threatened to displace the traditional power dynamics between *krogba*, headmen, and workers, Kru may have been more receptive to Christianity and, in particular, missionary institutions that provided the opportunity to gain security and social standing in the emerging society that was influencing their villages.[793]

Borders

Following the Berlin Conference between 1884 and 1885, in which European powers sought to establish formal colonies over vast regions of Africa, the primary concern for Liberia immediately became defining the extent of its national borders. Treaties between the Gola, Vai, and British in the region of the Gallinas

---

[787] "Monrovia, December 21, 1836," *African Repository* 12, no. 7 (137): 221.
[788] Reid, *Missions*, 247.
[789] Anonymous, "Bishop Taylor in Liberia," *African Repository* 61, no. 3 (1885): 86–87.
[790] Tonkin, *Narrating*, 22.
[791] Smith, *The Gospel*, 41–42; see also *The Ninth Annual Report of the Board of Foreign Missions of the Presbyterian Church in the United States of America* (New York: Presbyterian Board, 1846), 14–16.
[792] Breitborde, *Speaking Social*, 82.
[793] One of the most important works of historical fiction that engages with the complex relationship between Europeans and indigenous communities through colonialism is Chinua Achebe's *Things Fall Apart* (London: Heinemann, 1958).

secured the Liberian border with Sierra Leone in the west.[794] Although British ships continued to trade without paying proper taxes to Liberian authorities, they recognized Liberian claims to the region.[795]

The border in the east was of much more concern because both the French and Liberia had claims to the territory between the Cavalla River and San Pedro River. The Liberian government believed that the only way to secure their borders was to establish new settlements in the region. It had been part of the colony of Maryland and continued to be counted as belonging to Maryland County at least in theory, but claims to the east of the Cavalla River remained contentious with the French. In 1884, President Johnson's expansionist position was clearly stated when he proclaimed "the first and principal measure to be adopted... is the establishment of the settlements."[796] Johnson suggested creating a new settlement at the mouth of the San Pedro River, which required treaties with local communities in the region.[797] He requested the ACS to encourage a new wave of Black immigrants and financial aid from the United States for the purpose of settlement in the region. President Johnson selected Cavalla and Nifu as two new ports of entry in 1885.[798] The race to secure Liberian borders has been recognized by Gershoni who argued: "The plans of President Johnson and decisions of the Legislature were in fact aimed at implementing effective control and seem to be an unequivocal response to the February 1885 resolutions of the Berlin Conference."[799]

However, the ACS's response was one of disinterest. Liberia's poor economy after 1871, when it was forced to take a loan from the United States coupled with the ending of the Civil War in 1865, meant that immigration from America slowed. The other obstacle was that the French had made agreements in the same region with Grebo and other Kru-speaking peoples near Bereby, east of the Cavalla River.[800] In 1886, Liberia decided to enforce their port of entry policy and tax all Grebo entering and exiting the mouth of the Cavalla River. Shortly

---

[794] "Message of the President of Liberia, 5 December 1862," Presidential Message, Liberian National Archives.
[795] FO 403/6, "Smith to Lewis [Liberian Secretary of State], December 17, 1860"; FO 403/6, "Smith to Hill [Governor of Sierra Leone], 22 December 22 1860."
[796] "Inaugural Address of President Johnson, January 7, 1884," 118, Liberian National Archives.
[797] Ibid., 119.
[798] "Message of President Johnson to the Legislature, 1884," Holsoe, "Study," 170.
[799] Ibid., 298.
[800] "Legislation of the U.S., Monrovia, to the Secretary of State, Washington, December 7, 1885, no. 149, and Message of the President of Liberia, 18 December 1885," Enclosure No. 6, Diplomatic, 6, both in Diplomatic Dispatches from U.S. Ministers to Liberia, 1863–1906, vol. 10, May 4, 1885 – January 9, 1891.

thereafter, a Grebo revolt unfolded in the town of Half Cavalla near the Cavalla River. The Grebo sought protection against Liberian forces by requesting that the British governor in the Gold Coast intervene and form a protectorate in the region.[801] One rationale used by the Liberian government in support of their land claim was to include the region between the Cavalla and San Pedro River as part of the Kru Coast. Grebo inhabited the region on either side of the Cavalla River. They were known as Kroumen in Côte d'Ivoire and continue to identify as such in the twenty-first century.[802]

During this period, the reconceptualization of Kru Coast boundaries was politically and economically motivated. While the Liberian government regarded the Kru Coast as within Liberian borders in hopes of generating revenue through taxation, French and American officials extended the conceptual boundaries of the Kru (known as Krouman or Croumanes in French) homeland to include the towns to the east of the Cavalla River.[803] By 1874, Henry Leveson identified the towns of Cavalli, Half Bereby, Grand Lahou, and Grand Bassam, all in French territory, as belonging to the Kru Coast.[804] The urge to identify Grebo as Kru was most certainly an economic strategy to ensure that British, French, and Americans continued to hire their preferred Kru laborers beyond the restrictions imposed through Liberian customs and taxation.

In 1885, Élisée Reclus published a map of the Kru Coast or "Kru Territory" in which he limited the region between the Sinoe and King William's Town. When compared with earlier maps, Figure 6.4 reveals that the Kru homeland underwent several conceptual phases of expansion and contraction. Reclus limited the Kru homeland within Liberia compared with Leveson who extended it much further east to Grand Bassam.[805] Indeed, Kroumen were hired in Cavally, Tabou, Bereby, San Pedro, Drewin, Sassandra, and Lahou at the Bandama River. Similarly, Francis Bacon defined the Kru Coast as the "one country" that extended 100 miles in the interior between Little Kroo and Tabou, east of

---

[801] FO 47/20, "King of Chiefs of Cavally to the Governor of the Gold Coast, 27 January 1887," The National Archives.
[802] Kroumen formed 8.5 percent of the total population in a demographic survey conducted in 2018. Accessed on May 1, 2017, https://www.indexmundi.com/cote_d_ivoire/demographics_pro file.html.
[803] Reclus, *Universal Geography*, 233–234; Société de Géographie, *Comptes Rendus des Séances de la Société de Géographie et De La Commission Centrale* (Paris: Société de Géographie, 1897), 260–261; Chenery, *West Coast*, 114, 118.
[804] Henry Astbury Leveson, *The Forest and the Field* (London: Chatto and Windus, 1874), 272.
[805] Ibid., 272.

the Cavalla River.[806] Tabou were perceived by some as belonging to the Kru Coast alongside Proper Kru and Grebo communities.[807]

While it is problematic that the Kru homeland experienced periods of expansion and contraction based on the exterior perception of European traders and the Liberian government who were informed by their own economic and political agendas, what is for certain is that those individuals who identified as Kru or at the very least spoke Kru continued to trade and find employment within and sometimes beyond these geographical parameters. What remained constant in map productions in the nineteenth century was the inclusion of what is claimed by Kru oral traditions as the original five Proper Kru villages.[808] Much in the same way that nations and homelands have been described by Benedict Anderson as "imagined communities," the Kru homeland could be perceived as larger or smaller in geographic scale depending on whose perspective informed its construction.[809] Dimensions may have varied depending on whether Proper Kru, Grebo, Bassa, Godié, and Bété peoples or European ship captains were tasked with providing the details. Maps of the period can at best provide historians with an approximate sample of the Kru homeland when language and occupation are variables. However, understanding that the Kru Coast consisted of various segments of Kru-speaking peoples provides for more accurate analysis.

In 1891, French Minister of Colonies, Noël Ballay, presented French claims to the region between the Cavalla River and San Pedro River. France intended to establish a protectorate over the territory and agreed to void their treaties with Buto, Garawe, and other Grebo and Kru villages west of the Cavalla River in return for Liberia ending its claims on the territory between the Cavalla and San Pedro Rivers.[810] On December 8, 1892, the Liberian government and the French signed an agreement that set the boundary at the Cavalla River.[811]

---

[806] Bacon, "Cape Palmas," 196.

[807] Ludlam, "Account," 43–44; *The Knickerbocker* 33 (1849): 337. See Ronald Davis map of Kru Coast in Davis, *Ethnohistorical*, v.

[808] Interviews with Chief Davis, Smith, and Deputy Governor Worjloh revealed that the Proper Kru towns were perceived as the heartland of the Kru homeland. See also Connelly, "Report," 38–40.

[809] Benedict Anderson, *Reflections on the Origins and Spread of Nationalism* (New York: Verso, 1991), 5–8. See also McEvoy, "Understanding," 62–80.

[810] "John Russwurm to J.H.B. Latrobe, 30 December 1845," *African Repository* 22, no. 8 (1846): 205; Bernand Schnapper, *La Politique et le commerce Français dans le Golfe de Guinée de 1838 à 1871* (Paris: Mouton, 1961), 19, 42.

[811] Yuketiel Gershoni, "The Drawing of Liberian Boundaries in the Nineteenth Century: Treaties with African Chiefs versus Effective Occupation," *The International Journal African Historical*

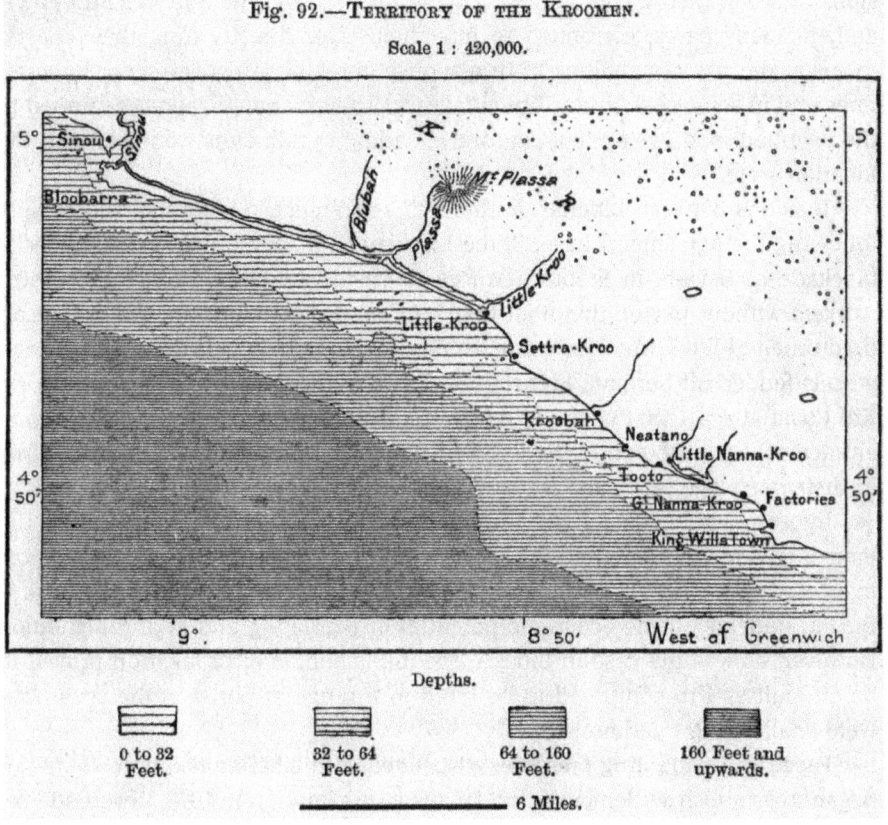

Figure 6.4: Kru Coast, 1885.
Source: Reclus, *Universal Geography*, 219.

During the same period of negotiations with the French, the Liberian government tightened its Port of Entry Laws. In 1891, the Liberian Legislature established the African Shipping Bureau. Kru labor was even more forcefully regulated, recorded, and taxed by the Liberian government.[812] While Kru were limited to where they could trade and hire themselves out for foreign contracts, Americo-Liberians were not restricted by the Port of Entry Laws and could trade in any port. Such restrictions and unequal treatment of Kru workers fuelled ten-

---

Studies 20, no. 2 (1987): 306; Pete John Murdza, Jr., "The Tricolor and the Lone Star: A History of Franco-Liberian Relations 1847–1903 (Ph.D. thesis, University of Wisconsin, 1979), 347.
812 Martin, "Krumen," 416.

sions between their communities.⁸¹³ Many Kru violated the Port of Entry Laws, and, in many cases, continued to hire themselves directly from their coastal towns at the risk of penalties.⁸¹⁴ In response, the Liberian government imposed fines and in some cases burnt Kru villages.⁸¹⁵ Their marginalization continued in the twentieth and twenty-first centuries, leading to numerous conflicts with the Liberian state.⁸¹⁶

Tensions between Liberian authorities and French traders did not subside following the agreement. In 1893, the Liberian ship the Goronommah formed a blockade at Cavalla in French territory to ensure no ships could offload Kru workers without paying the labor tax.⁸¹⁷ In another incident, the Goronommah fired on and killed Kru on a canoe serving the Ambriz in Settra Kru.⁸¹⁸ Liberian vessels fended off German, French, and British ships attempting to trade on the Kru Coast at ports that were not recognized by the Port of Entry Laws. Liberian enforcement contributed to the decline of the Kru economy and regular returns in their free wage labor diasporas.

Interested in increasing the profitability of Kru labor, on January 11, 1894, the French government in Grand Bassam sought to regulate Kru workers by imposing tax at a rate of ₣25 per laborer.⁸¹⁹ Governor of Côte d'Ivoire, Louis-Gustave Binger, understood the economic potential of regulating and taxing Kru labor. However, as was the case in Liberia, the implementation of taxation proved to be difficult as Kru continued to be hired in a range of ports on the coast that were challenging to administer.

Faced with mounting pressures associated with Liberian taxation, some Kru began to establish settlements along rivers in the interior. In 1893, Reverend Ezekiel Smith observed their migration into the interior: "They [Kru] are beginning to settle along the rivers of the country and spreading themselves interiorward, where they engage in trade and farming."⁸²⁰ Some Kru embarked on an internal migration as a result of the dire economic situation created by the Port of Entry Laws. Unlike their migration 100 years earlier from the Kru Coast to Freetown,

---

813 Davis, *Ethnohistorical*, 47; Behrens, *Les Kroumen*, 85.
814 Ibid., 48.
815 Ibid., 47.
816 For a discussion on the Kru Revolts in 1915 and 1930 see Davis, *Ethnohistorical*, 51–64.
817 Davis, "Liberian," 244; FO 47/18, "W.H. Willcocks, acting British vice-consul, to FO, 18 November 1893."
818 Davis, 245; FO 47/19, "Cardew to FO, 16, 17, and 24 November, 1894."
819 Archives Nationales, Section d'Outre-Mer Côte d'Ivoire, Vol. 14, 1a, Grand-Bassam, January 11, 1894. See also Behrens, *Les Kroumen*, 90.
820 Anonymous, *African Repository* 48, no. 2 (1872): 52; "Address of Rev. Ezekiel E. Smith," *Liberia* 2 (1893): 29.

which accelerated and expanded the Kru free wage labor diaspora, Kru migrated in retreat out of necessity in the name of subsistence and survival in unfamiliar territory.

While some Kru continued to engage in direct trade with Europeans and Americans on the Kru Coast at the risk of financial penalties, many Kru decided to migrate for work and remain in the diaspora communities they had forged under British employment in Freetown, Lagos, Cape Coast, and later, Accra. Other Kru went to Monrovia and although it was within the authority of the Liberian government, they may have thought they would fare better with more ship traffic in the port than in their homeland communities based on the restrictions. All of these communities experienced rapid population growth from the 1890s when the Port of Entry Laws were rigidly enforced. By the early twentieth century, the Kru population in Lagos rose to 2,680 while Freetown had 1,551, Accra 13,000, and Monrovia 8,000.[821]

The social, economic, and political relationship between the Kru and the colony of Liberia between 1822 and 1846, and the Liberian state between 1847 and 1900, deeply impacted the Kru diaspora and created an unstable environment in their homeland that was forced to adapt to capitalist trade and colonial forces. The succession of Port of Entry Laws between 1837, 1849 1859, 1865, and 1891 gradually undermined the authority of *krogba* and headmen. Kru society had formed such a dependency on British free wage labor contracts that intervention by the Liberian state threatened to undermine their economy and the socio-political power structures that informed their communities. Moreover, the increased presence of missions on the Kru Coast and the shift to agricultural production were part of the Liberian strategy to extend political influence in the region.

The Liberian government's attempts to legislate restrictions on Kru trade through taxation inadvertently increased competition between the British and French. French contracts resulted in the establishment of a Kru diaspora community in Grand Bassam and elsewhere. Although Kru formed a diaspora with the French, it was never on the same global or numerical scale as with the British. Far more Kru served with the British in a variety of commercial and military contexts in Africa, Asia, Europe, and the Americas. The evolution of headmen under the British hiring system that emerged in the early nineteenth century in Freetown became the model for their employment that influenced other Europeans

---

821 Estimates found in Martin, "Krumen," 406, 412; Crooks, *Records Relating*, 354.

including the French and Germans as well as the Americans in terms of pay structures, contract length, and the hierarchal nature of their service.[822]

---

[822] Kru served on US Navy ships in the Atlantic tasked with intercepting slave ships in two periods between 1820 and 1822 and between 1840 and 1861. Kru rank and pay in the US Navy was directly influenced by the Royal Navy from whom the US took their lead in anti-slaving operations in the Atlantic. For a history of Kru service on US Navy vessels see Donald L. Canney, *African Squadron: The U.S. Navy and the Slave Trade, 1842–1861* (Washington D.C.: Potomac Books, 2006), 68; John Pentangelo, "Sailors and Slaves: USS Constellation and the Transatlantic Slave Trade," in *Navies and Soft Power: Historical Case Studies of Naval Power and the Nonuse of Military Force*, ed. Bruce A. Elleman and S.C.M. Paine (Newport: Naval War College Press, 2015), 7; Charles Rockwell, "Sketches of Foreign Travel and Life at Sea," *African Repository* 18, no. 11 (1842): 277–278; William Elliot Griffs, *Matthew Calbraith Perry, A Typical Naval Officer* (Boston: Cupples and Hurd, 1890), 307–308; *Correspondence Relative to the Naval Expedition to Japan 1852–1854* (1855), 2; Herbert Gilliland, ed., *USS Constellation on the Dismal Coast: Willie Leonard's Journal, 1859–1861* (Columbia, SC: University of South Carolina Press, 2013), 3. *1852–1854* (1855), 2; Herbert Gilliland, ed., *USS Constellation on the Dismal Coast: Willie Leonard's Journal, 1859–1861* (Columbia, SC: University of South Carolina Press, 2013), 3.

Conclusion
Kru Free Wage Laborers in Global History

Following the water trails of Kru surfboats through time has reconfigured the fragmented history of the Kru into a coherent diaspora framework. The migration of Kru workers from their homeland communities on the Kru Coast under British employment represents a movement of free wage labor that resulted in the formation of a diaspora in Africa, the British Caribbean, and wherever the Kru served on ships sailing the Atlantic, Indian, and Pacific Oceans. Significantly, Kru laborers engaged in a voluntary diaspora. Regardless of whether they worked in a diaspora community or solely on a ship, they routinely returned to their homeland on the Kru Coast between contracts. Their diaspora is qualified as a free wage labor diaspora because they were paid for their labor and had the choice to work. Further, the definition of Kru workers expanded in the nineteenth century as the conceptual boundaries of the Kru Coast came to include a range of peoples who spoke Kru. While not always a marker of ethnicity, language was one of the binding forces that enabled Kru beyond the Proper Kru settlements to claim Kru ethnicity.

The Kru story began in the heart of the Kru homeland, where some of the Proper Kru and neighboring trading towns between the Cestos and Grand Cess Rivers traced their origins to at least the sixteenth century, and most probably earlier. Portuguese accounts of surfboats in the region suggest that contact with the Kru was established as early as the fifteenth century. Although their communities were politically autonomous and competed for trade with Europeans, the name "Kru" or "Crou" associated with the Proper Kru *dako* disseminated and became a general label used by Europeans to identify peoples living in the coastal vicinity. Over time, other Kru *dakwe* emerged including the Kabor, Gbeta, Jloh, Sasstown (or Pahn), Grand Cess (or Siklio) and the interior *dakwe* Matro, Bolo, Nanke, and Bwa. By the nineteenth century, Kru-speaking peoples on the West African coast between Cape Mesurado and the Bandama River including the Grebo, Bassa, Krahn, Bété, Godié, and Dida, among others, were recognized as Kru by European and American employers. Collectively, they accepted the label Kru while trading on the coast and in their workplaces. On one hand, they were indifferent to how they were externally classified, however, on the other, being recognized as Kru carried a positive reputation in the nineteenth century and ensured access to contracts. As such, it is our position that the label "Kru" is but one layer informing Kru identity, which must also include dialect, *dako*, secret society membership (if applicable) and village. Understanding the specificities informing various sub-groups of Kru-speaking peoples allows for greater precision of analysis and for deeper meanings in their diaspora to emerge.

Analysis of Kru labor has required the use of a wide range of multilingual primary and secondary sources, physical sources, and Kru oral traditions. English, French, Dutch, German, Portuguese, and Spanish sources offer unique insight on various segments of the Kru-speaking populations on the Kru Coast and in their diaspora communities. Sources as diverse as postcards, gravestones, photographs, oral tradition, court cases, ordinances, Admiralty files, primary published ship captain and traveller accounts, missionary records, ship records, estate records, work songs, medal rolls, and oil paintings, several of which appear here for the first time in secondary published form, provide a sense of the geographical extent and multifaceted nature of the Kru diaspora. Indeed, our goal has been to build on the foundational research of Brooks, Behrens, Fraenkel, Tonkin, Davis, Massing, Martin, Frost, Schuler, and others, by extending analysis to include the full scope of Kru labor in the Atlantic, Indian, and Pacific Oceans. Recovering the Kru voice through interviews with Kru community members in Liberia and Sierra Leone has provided invaluable information on their diaspora communities, Kru women and headmen, information which would otherwise remain inaccessible. Moreover, understanding how the Kru remember their past adds new layers of meaning in the historiography and vitality to the analysis of their diaspora.

Pedagogically, Kru labor intersects and fits into several strands of the discipline of History including African History, British History, Atlantic History, Indian Ocean History, Wage Labor History, British Caribbean and French Caribbean History, Maritime History, Mission History, Colonial History, and Transnational History. Kru labor and their diaspora add valuable nuances in discussions centered on race, ethnicity, class, colonialism, free labor, and the Atlantic and Indian Ocean worlds. Moreover, the Kru case provides a deeper understanding of the social, economic, and political impact of the introduction of outsourced wage labor in West Africa as African communities shifted their economies towards Atlantic commerce from the fifteenth century. Kru labor speaks to the historical contribution of African labor in the making of the global economy that has significantly benefited from African resources.

The Kru free wage labor diaspora was distinct from the larger trans-Atlantic diasporas, which transported 12.8 million enslaved Africans to the Americas. The nature of the Kru free wage labor diaspora presented in this book resonates with aspects of the parity trade relations proposed by John Thornton, which existed between Europeans and Africans until the mid-nineteenth century.[823] While Kru were never in a position of authority over the British, they were empowered to decide which contracts they would accept and they were paid wages for their labor based on contractual terms.

The Kru Coast's natural environment consisting of rocky sub-sea terrain and adverse surf conditions gave the Kru an advantage and placed them in a position to negotiate trading terms with European traders who struggled to carry out trade operations between ship and shore. As fishermen, Kru developed the necessary seamen skills through use of their surfboats, which enabled them to find employment on European merchant vessels sailing the West African coast from at least the seventeenth century. Whether traversing high surf, paddling out to sea, landing supplies or navigating riverine systems, Kru surfboats and other small watercraft lay at the center of their labor experience at all stages of their diaspora thereafter.

Throughout the various phases of their diaspora, Kru underwent a number of social, economic, and political transformations at home and abroad. During the initial phase of Kru trade with the British and other Europeans, the emergence of trade-men, "talk-men," and interpreters, the advent of the Kru mark and, most significantly, the evolution of the lead paddler to headman, were key developments that marked their transition towards the Atlantic economy. These developments were in response to European trade. While the Kru traded in rice, palm oil, and ivory, the slave trade played a significant role in their economy from at least the seventeenth century. They continued to trade in slaves on the Kru Coast and serve on Cuban slave ships on the West African coast until the mid-nineteenth century.

Kru labor experienced a catalyst moment with the founding of Freetown in 1792. Population statistics reveal that growth of their community was related to their service in the Royal Navy following the British decree to abolish the trans-Atlantic slave trade and an increase in shoreside contracts. Freetown became the epicenter of Royal Navy activity as the Kru were offered contracts, which lasted three years with a monthly salary that exceeded all other contracts. Kru served on the front lines of British abolitionism in the Atlantic intercepting slave ships, releasing enslaved Africans and delivering slave ship crews to Sierra Leone for trial at the Vice Admiralty Court, and later, the Court of Mixed Commission. By 1816, they had established their own distinct community in a district known as Krutown, which provided the British with a readily available pool of laborers for ship and shoreside contracts. Krutown became the site of socio-eco-

---

823 Thornton, *Africa*, 1–10, 13–71.

nomic transformations including the institutionalization of the position of headman, restructuring of the age-grade system to meet the manpower demands of the British, and new responsibilities for women in the household and market. Headmen played a crucial role in organizing labor gangs, ensuring wages were distributed, and maintaining discipline amongst workers. As such, they were paid more than regular workers and served as the link between British captains and Kru workers. Hierarchal order was further entrenched following the creation of the Krutown Headman who served as administrator with the British, overseeing all contracts and the conduct of Kru community.

The homecoming experience developed into a crucial component in the Kru's diaspora cycle as they circled between their community in Freetown and their villages on the Kru Coast. The result is that direct links between *dakwe* on the Kru Coast and Krutown can be firmly established. While the Proper Kru formed the majority of laborers in Freetown as demonstrated in the naming of the streets after the original five settlements, members of the Grand Cess *dakwe*, Grebo, and Bassa peoples were also present in the nineteenth century. Moreover, homecoming protocol, which included presenting gifts to the *krogba* and purchasing wives, became crucial components of the Kru economy.

The Kru free wage labor diaspora grew as Kru shifted their labor towards Royal Navy contracts and so-called "legitimate" trade in palm oil production. As such, a succession of Krutowns and laboring communities were established on the West African coast as the Kru migrated for work. Service in the Royal Navy enabled the Kru to establish settlements in Cape Coast, Ascension Island, Fernando Po, and Simon's Town in the Cape of Good Hope. Their duties included coaling ships and intercepting slave ships before sailing to Freetown. In the case of Fernando Po, Kru also performed agricultural labor. Population statistics show that the Kru community in Ascension Island and Fernando Po continued to experience growth in the nineteenth century. Ordinances reveal that the Royal Navy had to pay for sick or injured Kru while they received care in "Krooman's Hospital" in Garrison. Their designation in records demonstrates their importance in the Royal Navy.

Between 1862 and 1881, Kru were hired on Royal Navy ships in the Indian Ocean to assist in the suppression of the slave trade. Kru played a major role in capturing slave *dhows*. The shortage of Royal Navy ships meant that Kru were tasked with manning the launch boats aboard each vessel, which enabled a larger coalition to form. Kru operated out of Simon's Town in South Africa, Zanzibar, the Seychelles, Aden, Basra, Bombay, and Trincomalee. Although Kru did not form Krutowns in Indian Ocean ports, they were identified as Kru in Zanzibar because of their Kru mark and continue to be remembered on gravestones. Even when they did not form distinct communities, their bodies bore the mark of their diaspora.

Their role as stevedores, porters, and boatmen engaged in so-called "legitimate trade" in palm oil led to the creation of Kru diaspora communities in Bonny and Calabar. Headmen continued to organize and ensure labor gangs circulated between the Kru Coast and the Oil Rivers annually. During the same period, the establishment of new coastal communities on the Kru Coast in the nineteenth century led to the formation of new *dako* including Jloh and Gbeta. They all spoke Kru, and their villages, which were adjacent to the Proper Kru, extended to the Cestos River in the west and Grand Cess in the east. In all cases, *dakwe* on the Kru Coast continued to inform the demographic composition of each diaspora settlement. Jloh from Sasstown and Gbeta from Picaninny Cess were the most common Kru working in Monrovia, while Grand Cess Kru formed the majority in Cape Coast. Workers from Settra Kru were hired for contracts in Calabar and Bonny, and Kru in Ascension Island, Fernando Po, Simon's Town, and Lagos were most frequently hired in Freetown and belonged to the Proper Kru and Grand Cess *dakwe*. They were also accompanied by Bassa and Grebo laborers. All of their settlements were interconnected as Kru circulated on contract between their homeland on the Kru Coast and diaspora communities. By the close of the nineteenth century, some of their diaspora communities displaced the Kru Coast as the main centers of employment.

Kru participation in expeditions, Royal Navy service in the Indian Ocean, and in military campaigns played a role in the British consolidation of its empire in Africa and Asia. During expeditions between the 1820s and 1860s, Kru served as boatmen and porters who were frequently charged with collecting wood and water for the crew. Their services contributed to the functioning of the expeditions. Perhaps even more significant, Kru service in the Royal Navy was extended to include military campaigns. Their duties included serving as porters, boatmen, gunners, and auxiliary soldiers in naval brigades. The nature of their service adopted a military dimension as they served on the front lines in the Anglo-Zulu War and were awarded medals for their service during the period. Rather than forming diaspora communities, Royal Navy ships became the cultural spaces where Kru maintained traditional practices and were also able to evolve their seaborne practices first developed in their homeland on the Kru Coast. Their role in expeditions and military campaigns shows that Kru were concerned with the economic terms of their contracts and less so with the lasting social, economic, and political effect of engaging in conflict with those outside their communities. The politically autonomous nature of their villages on the Kru Coast, which fostered competition in trade and periodic conflict, most certainly informed their worldview towards other Africans. Moreover, their role reveals the complex nature of European colonial processes in Africa and Asia.

The Kru free wage labor diaspora expanded to include the British Caribbean. Beginning in 1841, Kru migrated to Jamaica, Trinidad, and British Guiana for contracts on estates and wharves that promised higher wages than those earned on the west coast of Africa. Service in Jamaica was short-lived and few records survive of their service beyond the wharf in Kingston and their landing in Montego Bay. Much more can be said of their experience in Trinidad where they worked on several estates in Port of Spain and Oropuche. Similarly, Kru circulated between estates in Demerara, Berbice, and Essequibo in British Guiana. They continued their tradition of manning small craft as they transported people and commodities from estate to ship. Their contracts were between three and five years in length. As an incentive, they were offered higher wages than could be earned in West Africa. The Kru free wage labor diaspora was maintained in Trinidad with the creation of "Krooman's Village" and other communities that resembled Krutowns in West Africa, but on a smaller scale. In British Guiana, Kru formed a community in Canal No.1 where they resided alongside Yoruba laborers. They continued to apply the Kru mark, which distinguished Kru from other laboring groups including Yoruba and Liberated Africans. Kru bound for British Guiana were hired in Freetown, Settra Kru, and Grand Cess, which shows that the majority belonged to the Proper Kru and Grand Cess *dakwe* and most certainly included Bassa and Grebo laborers.

Despite these continuities, Kru laborers underwent a process of creolization. Their ability to purchase land was a major factor. On the Kru Coast where land was communally owned by their respective *dako*, Kru remained subject to the authority of the *krogba*. In Trinidad and British Guiana, this was not the case. The combination of the Kru's tendency towards task-based work on an individual basis as jobbers and the opportunity to own land outside of the communal village allowed the Kru to function beyond traditional societal norms. The hierarchal order informing the relationship between Kru worker, headman, and *krogba* became obsolete as many Kru decided to remain in Trinidad and British Guiana indefinitely following the completion of their contract. By circumnavigating the traditional protocol of gift-giving for the *krogba* and paying a percentage of their wages to their headman, Kru laborers gained a new-found sense of economic independence. Another factor in their creolization was intermarriage with Creole women. As such, their descendants were frequently classified as "Africans" rather than Kru or confused with Yoruba laborers in demographic surveys. The result was that the Kru free wage labor diaspora in the British Caribbean was short-lived, and these factors led to their disappearance as a distinct ethnic group in Trinidad and British Guiana by the early twentieth century.

By the close of the nineteenth century, Kru diaspora communities in West Africa experienced growth, while employment in their homeland on the Kru Coast declined. ACS agents and Americo-Liberian settlers aimed to profit from Kru labor as early as the 1830s when all Kru laborers were made to pay a head tax while working in Krutown in Monrovia. Following independence in 1847, the succession of Port of Entry Laws had a major effect on the Kru economy. Kru headmen acquired new state responsibilities ensuring each worker was properly taxed before they could embark and disembark vessels. This created pressure on headmen to secure higher wages in order to avoid lower net wages. The Kru Coast economy was forced to shift towards its secondary industry in palm oil production, which placed Kru in a subservient role to Americo-Liberian settlers and the Liberian state that controlled sales on the Kru Coast. Conversion rates to Christianity surged as a result of the growing missionary presence on the Kru Coast that aimed to influence their socio-cultural practices.

Competition between the British, French, Germans, Americans, and Liberians for Kru labor increased. Increased taxation via Port of Entry Laws imposed by the Liberian government and mounting conflict were responsible for the lack of opportunities on the Kru Coast as Kru workers sought to make a living abroad free from government interference. Many Kru decided to immigrate to their diaspora communities in Freetown, Cape Coast, Lagos, and elsewhere. Others accepted French contracts and formed a new diaspora community in Grand Bassam. While economic incentives to work abroad increased, there was little desire to return and hand over a portion of their earnings to both their *krogba* and the Liberian state. Moreover, conflict with Americo-Liberian settler communities and the loss of land that transpired created an unstable socio-economic environment on the Kru Coast that further marginalized the Kru in relation to the Liberian state.

In the late nineteenth century, the nature of Kru identity evolved to encompass a greater range of Kru speaking peoples as they emigrated for contracts. Kru Coast boundaries were at the heart of the conflict between the Liberian and French government to secure the border between Liberia and Côte d'Ivoire. In 1891, Liberian authorities perceived the Kru Coast as the expanse of land that extended eastwards to the San Pedro River. There was an attempt to extend Port of Entry Laws in the region and tax laborers. However, the Liberian government was only able to secure the region to the west of the Cavalla River. The French understood that the region was inhabited by Kroumen in the towns to the east of Cavalla River, which included Cavally, Bereby, Tabou, and Drewin, among others. These were the main trading villages where laborers were traditionally employed by French merchants. The British generally hired the Kru on the Kru Coast to the west of the Cavalla River or in diaspora communities such as in Freetown. The boundaries of the Kru Coast were politicized and depending on who was responsible for providing the dimensions it could be as large as the region between the Mesurado River and Bandama River or limited within the Liberian national borders created in 1893. In the latter, when language remains the deciding variable, the Kru Coast encompassed the region between Cape Mesurado and the Cavalla River in Liberia and the area between the Cavalla River and Bandama River in Côte d'Ivoire. While the Kru Coast experienced periods of growth and contraction in the nineteenth century depending on sources, the peoples therein spoke Kru and were able to identify each other by *dako* affiliation, dialect, and the location of their villages.

The data presented suggests that the Kru free wage labor diaspora was often contradictory and overlapping in nature. Kru served an abolitionist function on board British Royal Navy ships tasked with intercepting slave ships, while simultaneously serving on Cuban slave ships bound for Havana. Kru loaded enslaved Africans in the Rio Pongo and the Gallinas and continued to engage in the slave trade on the Kru Coast until at least the 1850s. Similarly, Kru participated in military and exploration campaigns that paved the way for British colonial conquest in Africa. Their contradictory impulses revealed their tendency to make a living by all available means.

The power dynamics governing the economic relationship between the British and the Kru were structured differently than the systems informing master and slave relations in the Americas. While enslaved Africans could negotiate and possess a degree of mobility within the framework of slavery, Kru remained free and in control of their bodies and labor for which they were paid. They answered to their headmen and worked within the parameters established in British contracts, but were never enslaved in the process. Much like their transition from childhood to adulthood through Kru age-sets, adolescent Kru understood that they first had to learn the necessary skills to become regular laborers, which could be a physically and emotionally demanding transition.

Despite racist undertones that informed their working relationship with the British, the ship became a cultural space where the Kru could perform both within and outside racial parameters. Peter Linebaugh and Marcus Rediker's (2000) examination of alternative societies where rigid class hierarchies informing power-relations amongst the ship crew had the potential to become fluid depending on the circumstances in question resonates with the nature of Kru service on British Royal Navy ships. The Kru were able to take full advantage of the fluid order which defined their roles on ships despite the racial hierarchies that contextualized the period.[824] The British came to depend on the Kru, particularly in the Indian Ocean, when they were tasked with manning Royal Navy launch boats as part of a wider coalition in pursuit of slave *dhows*. They frequently led the charge, boarded slave ships and put their lives at risk for which they were awarded medals. As such, Royal Navy ships created a fluid space that could not contain the Kru within a rigid racial system.

While the Liberian state played a significant role in the decline of the Kru economy in the later decades of the nineteenth century, Kru had positioned themselves on a course for economic disaster long before. Although they continued to trade with Europeans and Americans on the Kru Coast, the Kru economy developed a dependency on British contracts. The risk of losing the revenue generated from the homecomings of migrant workers threatened to undermine the social, economic, and political structures that informed Kru societies in the nineteenth century. Traditional age-sets were geared towards fulfilling British labor contracts. Profits earned affected social status, the ability to meet bride-price demands necessary for marriage, and maintained the authority of the *krogba*. The Kru failed to diversify their homeland economy to the extent that was needed given the encroaching Liberian state. Once the Liberian state imposed regulatory measures to interrupt the free flow of laborers, their entire social, economic, and political structures began to collapse and they were forced to develop alternative strategies of survival that ultimately led their homeland into a state of decline and marginalization in the twentieth century. Like many global indigenous peoples, the weakening of the Kru's economy expedited their forced assimilation into the nation-state apparatus, which valued their labor but not their political will.

In conclusion, the Kru developed a strategic engagement with British employment in shipping contexts in West Africa. The transformations which occurred within Kru communities along the Kru Coast, in Freetown, and the migratory culture that emerged is comparable with other African communities such as the Cabenda, Vai, and the Nyamwezi caravan culture that came to fruition in the nineteenth century in East Africa, albeit on a much grander scale.[825] While Kru did not occupy a position of authority, their labor force became vital to British commercial operations in West Africa. Tracing the Kru free wage labor diaspora from the Kru Coast to the Atlantic, Indian, and Pacific Oceans reveals the active role they played in the expansion of British trade and military cam-

---

824 Peter Linebaugh and Marcus Rediker, *The Many Headed Hydra: Sailors, Slaves, Commoners, and the Hidden History of the Revolutionary Atlantic* (Boston: Beacon Press, 2000), 13–14.
825 See Rockel, *Carriers*, 4–5.

paigns and calls for a rethinking of African agency in the development of global capitalism. Their case remains an early example of the outsourcing wage labor model that has come to dominate work environments in the twenty-first century. Perhaps no other African ethnic group occupied such a versatile and important social and economic role in British commercial and military interests in the nineteenth century as the Kru did.

Appendix A
Muster Lists, 1819–20

The tables presented in Appendix A reflect the pay for Kru serving in the Royal Navy. The information comes from the ADM 30/26 series "Muster Lists of Kroomen Serving on Various Ships, 1819–1820." The columns are divided into African Names, Rank, Full Wages, and Net Wages (also spelled Neat and Nett in some instances). In some cases, there is an Advance column and in-kind payment column usually under the heading Tobacco. In terms of naval rank, "Ord" refers to ordinary seamen who carried the rank of eighth class seamen. These individuals were the headmen who received higher wage rates. "Sm" refers to Kru who carried an eleventh class rank. Salaries were paid in pounds, shillings, and pence. For example, £4 1s. 1d. means 4 pounds, 1 shilling, and 1 pence.

HMS Whistle

Table A.1: Pay list for Africans employed on board His Majesty's Brig "Whistle", November 10, 1819 to January 19, 1820.

African Names	Rank	Slopes supplies by the Navy Board	Full Wages	Net Wages
Thom Nimma	Ord	18s 4d	£3 19s 8d	£3 1s 4d
Prince Will	Ord	18s 4d	£3 19s 8d	£3 1s 4d
John October	Ord	18s 4d	£3 19s 8d	£3 1s 4d
Dick Williams	Ord	18s 4d	£3 19s 8d	£3 1s 4d
Jon Many	Ord	18s 4d	£3 19s 8d	£3 1s 4d
Jon Arab	Ord	18s 4d	£3 19s 8d	£3 1s 4d
Thom Stuart	Ord	£1 0s 1d	£2 16s 6d	£1 10s 5d
Charles Smith	Sm	18s 0d	£1 6s 6d	8s 6d
Ben Coffee	Sm		£4 8s 6d	£3 18s 8d
Tom Freeman (2)	Sm		£4 8s 6d	£3 18s 8d
Big William	Sm		£4 8s 6d	£3 15s 6d
John Freeman	Sm		£4 8s 6d	£3 15s 6d
Total				£48 3s 0d

Source: ADM 30/26, "Muster list of Kroomen Serving on Various Ships," The National Archives, Kew, United Kingdom.

HMS Myrmidan

Table A.2: November 26 to December 20, 1819

African Names	Rank	Full Wages	Net Wages
Thomas Reed	Ord	£1 1s 6d	£1 1s 6
John Freeman	Ord	£1 1s 6d	£1 1s 6d
Grando	Ord	£1 1s 6d	£1 1s 6d
Tom Toby	Ord	£1 1s 6d	£1 1s 6d
Jim George	Ord	£1 1s 6d	£1 1s 6d
Sam Coffee	Ord	£1 1s 6d	£1 1s 6d
Jack Freeman	Ord	£1 1s 6d	£1 1s 6d
Jim Centire	Ord	£1 1s 6d	£1 1s 6d
Bottled Beer	Ord	£1 1s 6d	£1 1s 6d
Tom Walker	Sm	18s 9d	18s 9d
Jack Haulauney	Sm	18s 9d	18s 9d
James Pallas	Sm	18s 9d	18s 9d
Ben Coffee	Ord	£1 1s 6d	£1 1s 6d
Boy Lancho	Sm	18s 9d	8s 9d
Total		£12 9s 3d	£12 9s 3d

Source: ADM 30/26, "Muster list of Kroomen Serving on Various Ships," The National Archives, Kew, United Kingdom.

HMS Myrmidan

Table A.3: December 21 1819 to July 29, 1820

African Names	Rank	Two Months Advance	Full Wages	Net Wages
Thomas Reed	Ord	£1 1s 6d	£4 2s 4d	£3 0s 10d
Jon Pallas	Sm	18s 9d	£3 14s 3d	£2 15s 6d
Ben Williams	Sm	18s 9d	£3 12s	£2 13s 3d
Jack Savee	Ord	£1 1s 6d	£4 2s 4d	£3 0s 10d
Jack Luisefoot	Ord	£1 1s 6d	£4 2s 4d	£3 0s 10d
Chaus Tobacco	Sm	11s 9d	£3 12s	£2 13s 3d
Jack Reed	Sm	11s 9d	£3 12s	£2 13s 3d
Bill Williams	Ord		£2 8s	£2 8s
King George	Ord		£2 0s 4d	£2 0s 4d
Bottled Beer	Sm		£1 15s 3d	£1 15s 3d
Galley Will	Sm		£1 15s 3d	£1 15s 3d
Boy Tom	Sm		£1 15s 3d	£1 15s 3d

Table A.3: December 21 1819 to July 29, 1820 *(Continued)*

African Names	Rank	Two Months Advance	Full Wages	Net Wages
Bill Thomas	Sm		£1 15s 3d	£1 15s 3d
Limon Row	Sm		£1 15s 3d	£1 15s 3d
John Reed	Ord		£1 18s 6d	£1 18s 6d
Jas Freeman	Sm		£1 13s 9d	£1 13s 9d
Tom Freeman	Sm		£1 13s 9d	£1 13s 9d
Total				£38 8s 4d

Source: ADM 30/26, "Muster list of Kroomen Serving on Various Ships," The National Archives, Kew, United Kingdom.

HMS Tartar

Table A.4: Pay list for Africans employed on His Majesty's Ship *Tartar* Commissioner Sir George Collier, January 14, 1820 to June 3, 1820

Men's Names	Rank	Full Wages	Net Wages
Ben Freeman (1)	Ord	£6 1s 8d	£6 1s 8d
Tom Freeman	Ord	£6 1s 8d	£6 1s 8d
Tom Jack	Ord	£6 1s 8d	£6 1s 8d
Will Freeman	Ord	£6 1s 8d	£6 1s 8d
Jack Aboo	Ord	£6 1s 8d	£6 1s 8d
Tom Freeman (2)	Ord	£6 1s 8d	£6 1s 8d
Tom Lee	Sm	£5 6s 6d	£4 16s 8d
Jack Fletcher	Ord	£6 1s 8d	£6 1s 8d
Bob Williams	Sm	£5 6s 6d	£4 16s 8d
Gar Will	Ord	£6 1s 8d	£6 1s 1d
Bottle of Beer	Sm	£5 6s 6d	£4 16s 8d
Will Grey	Ord	£6 1s 8d	£6 1s 8d
Jac Freeman	Ord	£6 1s 8d	£6 1s 8d
Jac George	Ord	£6 1s 8d	£5 11s 10d
Will Jumbo	Sm	£5 6s 6d	£5 6s 6d
Sam Louise	Sm	£5 6s 6d	£4 16s 8d
Total		£93 10s 10d	£90 11s 10d

Source: ADM 30/26, "Muster list of Kroomen Serving on Various Ships," The National Archives, Kew, United Kingdom.

Appendix B
Interviews

Interviews were conducted in Freetown, Monrovia, and Accra in December 2012. Information pertaining to the date and location of the interview and the name and age of the interviewee are listed below.

I Freetown, Sierra Leone

Interview 1
December 4, 2012
Interviewee: Chief Tuleh Davis
Location: King William Street, Freetown, Sierra Leone
Age: unknown
Audio File: 06

Interview 2
December 5, 2012
Interviewee: Chief Tuleh Davis
Location: King William Street, Freetown, Sierra Leone
Age: unknown
Audio File: 07

Interview 3
December 12, 2012
Interviewee: Rev. Joseph Kamara
Location: St. Thomas Kroo Church
Age: 57
Audio File: 15

Interview 4
December 13, 2012
Interviewee: Mr. Doe Smith (Retired Lawyer/Son of Headman)
Location: Krutown
Age: 90
Audio File: 18

II Monrovia, Liberia

Interview 5
December 11, 2012
Interviewee: S. Tugbe Worjloh (Deputy Governor)
Location: New Krutown
Age: 76
Audio File: 9 – 11

Interview 6
December 11, 2012
Interviewee: Reverend Gibson (Kru Chairman)
Location: New Krutown
Age: 69
Audio File: 12 – 13

III Accra, Ghana

Interview 7
December 20, 2012
Interviewee: Okyeeme Abeka Gikafo (Chief Linguist)
Location: Jamestown, Accra
Age: 84 years old
Audio File: 14
and
Interviewee: A Bonso III (Stool Secretary)
Location: Jamestown, Accra
Age: 58 years old
Audio File: 14

Glossary of Kru Language Terms

Bo, Boviowah or Gbo	Secret society practiced by the Kru.
Bodio	An officer in Bo secret society. The *bodio* kept fetishes and was a high priest.
Borh	Soldiers.
Claho	Possible ancestors of the Kru who migrated hundreds of kilometers from the West African interior before settling in the region that eventually became known as the Kru Coast.
Dako	A territorial unit composed of various *pantons* sharing political officers based on a collective historical tradition. The six coastal *dako* consisted of Kabor, Jloh, Gbeta, Sasstown (or Pahn), Grand Cess (or Siklio), and Proper Kru or "Five Tribes." The interior *dako* consisted of Matro, Bolo, Nanke, and Bwa.
Dea	Village.
Deyâbo	Doctors in Bo secret society.
Fishmen	People living in the same vicinity as the Kru along the Kru Coast. They were distinguished from the Kru as subsistence fishermen, as compared with the Kru who were traders with Europeans. The Kru and Fishmen frequently engaged in confrontation according to sources.
Gbaubi or gbo bi	A figure known as the "father of the army" who held nearly equal authority as the *krogba*.
Gbau	The warrior class in Bo secret society.
Giwon	Meaning "leopard's mouth," a building housing fetishes, war trophies, and objects important to the *dako*.
Gnekbade	Elders in Bo secret society.
Ibadio	Function of council to the dual leadership of the War King and the Peace King. An officer in the Sedibo whose equivalent figure is the Tibawah.
Kafah	Scouts.
Kedibo	The young men in Bo society.
Klao	The origins of the name Kru are believed to have been derived from Klao or Krao according to oral traditions.
Kofa	Age-set composed of young adolescent boys.
Krogba	The highest officer in a *dako* was known as the "father of the town" who was democratically selected by a group of *panton nyefue*.
Kru	A term denoting the peoples who live on the Kru Coast of Liberia between the Cestos River and Cape Palmas. In the nineteenth century, the term was applied to peoples living between Cape Mesurado in Liberia and the Bandama River in Côte d'Ivoire. Alternative and interchangeable names include Carou, Carow, Croo, Crewmen, Crou, Croumen, Kharoo, Klao, Krao, Krau, Krewmen, Kroo, Krooboys, Kroomen, Krou, Kroumen.
Kwi	Poro bush spirit honored by wearing a mask. Also known as Nyessoa.
Nyaswa	The most revered Poro bush spirit honored by wearing a mask.
Panton	The name given to a patrilineage in Kru society.

Panton Nyefue	The head of the *panton* who was the eldest member deemed physically and mentally fit to hold the position.
Sedibo	The soldier class composed of middle-aged men in Bo secret society.
Tibawah	Function of council to the dual leadership of the War King and the Peace King. An officer in the Sedibo whose equivalent figure is the Ibadio.
Torh	War.
Worabanh	Served as the military leader in times of war.

Bibliography

Primary Sources

The National Archives, Kew
Admiralty Record Office. ADM 30/26. "Muster List of Kroomen Serving on Various Ships." June 12, 1819 – June 2, 1820.
Admiralty Record Office. ADM 8/126–139. List Books. 1845–1860.
Admiralty Record Office. ADM 8/141. List Book. 1862.
Admiralty Record Office. ADM 8/142. List Book. 1863.
Admiralty Record Office. ADM 123/23. "Enclosure in Hammerton to Rear-Admiral Dacres." April 9, 1846.
Admiralty Record Office. ADM 123/178, "Coghlan to Secretary to the Government, Bombay," number 14 (secret). November 1, 1860.
Admiralty Record Office. ADM 123/178. "Commander Oldfield to Captain Crawford, Number 3." March 23, 1861.
Admiralty Record Office. ADM 123/48. "Admiralty (Romaine) to Rear-Admiral Walker, Number M 39." January 30, 1862.
Admiralty Record Office. ADM 101/132/2/Folios14–24. Surgeon General Remarks. 1861.
Admiralty Record Office. ADM 1/5768. "Notes on African Slave Trade, Captain E. Wilmot." 1861.
An Act for the Abolition of the Slave Trade 1807.
Colonial Office Records. CO 111/180. Despatches. September-October 1841.
Colonial Office Records. CO 111/182. Despatches. January-July 1841.

British Library
Clarkson Papers, 1792.
The Graphic
The Illustrated London News

School of Oriental and African Studies, University of London
London Gazette. February 21, 1879.

National Maritime Museum
NMM, ZBA 2465.

The National Archives of Trinidad and Tobago
Trinidad Royal Gazette. 1838–1880.

West Indiana Special Collection Library, The University of the West Indies, St. Augustine, Trinidad and Tobago

West India Committee Records. Resolutions of the Standing Committee of West India Planters: on Immigration, "Topic: Labour Problem and African Immigrants. February 18, 1842." July 1833-June 1843.

West India Committee Records. A. Colvile. "Report of the Committee Appointed to Confer with Her Majesty's Government, [and], Meeting of Merchants, held in Bishopgate Street, on the 26th Oct 1842." February 22, 1843.

West India Committee Records. "Topic: Labour Problem and African Immigrants." July 1833-June 1843.

West India Committee Records. "Report of the Committee Appointed to Confer with Her Majesty's Government, [and], Meeting of Merchants, held in Bishopgate Street, on the 26th Oct 1842." February 22, 1843.

West India Committee Records. Acting Committee. "Evidence of the Honourable Captain Denmase R.N." November 14, 1843.

West India Committee Records. "Evidence of the Honourable Captain Denmase R.N." Chairman Charles Cane, pp. 119–120. 697 h and 6977–7000. November 14, 1843.

West Indies Committee Records. Acting Committee. "General, Communicated by the Demose." October 8, 1844.

West India Committee Records. "The West India Committee Minutes from 9 January 1852–19 February 1857." Acting Committee, January 9, 1852. Box 4, Folder 3, 1852.

Liberian Collections Library, Indiana University, Bloomington, Indiana

Monrovia Journal. Liberia Accounts. 1841–1848.

Library of Congress, Washington D.C., United States

The African Repository and Colonial Journal.

Letter Books of Commodore Matthew Perry. "Matthew Perry to Abel Upshuir, 13 April 1843." M206. March 10, 1843 – February 20, 1845.

Commodore Benjamin Cooper, Squadron Letters, roll 104, no. 57. September 3, 1849.

Sierra Leone Public Archives, Fourah Bay College, Freetown, Sierra Leone

Abolition of the Slave Trade Act, 1807.
Blue Books. 1878–1900.

Newspapers
African Standard
Sea Magazine
Sierra Leone Weekly News
The Seaman
The Sierra Leone Daily Mail
The Weekly Mirror
The West Africa Mail and Trade Gazette

The University of Notre Dame, Rare Books and Special Collections
William E. Hearsey, Jr. Letters. MSN/MN 5014–1 to MSN/MN 5014–20. 1865–1876.

Walter Rodney National Archives, Georgetown, Guyana
1840–1860.
Colonial Policy Minute Papers. 1838–1860.
Governor's Correspondence, Immigration Department Correspondence and Reports. 1841–1848.
The British Guiana Official Gazette. 1845–1860.

Simon's Town Museum, South Africa
Photograph. Kroomen in the West Dockyard, c. 1889.

Zanzibar National Archives
File AA12/6. British Consulate Records. "Register of Graves, Grave Island Cemetery."

Published Primary Sources

Alexander, Archibald. *A History of Colonization on the Western Coast of Africa.* 1846. Reprint, New York: Negro Universities Press, 1969.

Allen, William, and Thomas Richard Heywood Thomson. *Narrative of the Expedition to the River Niger, in 1841.* 2 vols. London: R. Bentley, 1848.

Annual Report of the Board of Foreign Missions of the Presbyterian in the United States of America. Vol. 4. New York: Presbyterian Church, 1841.

Anonymous. "A New Temperance Sailors' Home Wanted." *The Mariner's Church Gospel Temperance Soldiers' and Sailor's Magazine* 30, no. 3093 (1843): 40.

Armistead, Wilson. *A Tribute for the Negro: Being a Vindication of the Moral, Intellectual and Religious Capabilities of the Coloured Portion of Mankind.* Manchester: William Irwin, 1848.

Ashmun, Jehudi. *History of the American Colony in Liberia from December 1821 to 1823.* Washington: Way & Gideon, 1826.

Ashmun, Jehudi. "Relations of the Colony with Kroomen." *African Repository* 2, no. 3 (1826): 96–97.

Atkins, John. *A Voyage to Guinea, Brasil, and the West-Indies: In His Majesty's Ships, the Swallow and Weymouth. Describing the Several Islands and Settlements, Viz, Madeira, the Canaries, Cape de Verd, Sierraleon, Sesthos, Cape Apollonia, Cabo Corso, and Others on the Guinea Coast; Barbadoes, Jamaica, &c. in the West-Indies. The Colour, Diet, Languages, Habits, Manners, Customs, and Religions of the Respective Natives and Inhabitants. With Remarks on the Gold, Ivory, and Slave-trade; and on the Winds, Tides and Currents of the Several Coasts.* London: C. Ward and R. Chandler, 1735.

Bacon, Francis. "Cape Palmas and the Mena, or Kroomen." *The Journal of the Royal Geographic Society* 12 (1842): 196–206.

Baikie, William Balfour. *Narrative of an Exploring Voyage Up to the Rivers Kuora and Binue Commonly Known as the Niger and Tsadda in 1854*. 1856. Reprint, London: Psychology Press, 1966.

Barbot, Jean. *A Description of the Coasts of North and South Guinea, and of the Ethiopia Inferior, Vulgarly Angola... And a New Relation of the Province of Guiana, and of the Great Rivers of Amazons and Oronoque in South-America*. London: A. & J. Churchill, 1732.

Barret, Paul. *L'Afrique Occidentale: La Nature et L'Homme Noir*. Vol. 2. Paris: Challamel, 1888.

Baynes, Thomas Spencer. "Cape Coast Castle – Cape Colony." In *The Encyclopedia Britannica: A Dictionary of Arts, Sciences and General Literature, Ninth Edition*. Vol. 5. New York: Henry G Allen and Company Publishers, 1833.

Beecroft, John. "On Benin and the Upper Course of the River Quorra, or Niger, by Captain Becroft." *Journal of the Royal Geographical Society of London* 11 (1841): 184–189.

Bergman, Albert. *On Board the "Pensacola": The Eclipse Expedition to the West Coast of Africa*. New York: n.p., 1890.

Bernard, William Dallas, and William Hutcheon Hall. *Narrative of the Voyages and Services of the Nemesis, from 1840–1843; And of the Combined Naval and Military Operations in China: Comprising a Complete Account of The Colony of Hong Kong, And Remarks on The Character and Habits of the Chinese from Notes of Commander W.H. Hall, R.N. by W.D. Bernard, ESQ, A.M. Oxon, In Two Volumes*. Vol. 1. London: Henry Colburn, 1844.

Binger, Louis Gustave. *Du Niger au Golfe de Guinée, par le Pays de Kong et le Mossi*. Paris: Hachette et Cie, 1892.

Blaikie, William Garden. *The Personal Life of David Livingstone*. New York: Harper Brothers, 1881.

Bliss, Reverend Edwin Munsell, ed. *The Encyclopedia of Missions: Descriptive, Historical, Bibliography, Statistical. With a Full Assortment of Maps, a Complete Bibliography, and Lists of Bible Versions, Missionary Societies, and a General Index*. Vol. 2. New York: Funk and Wagnalls, 1891.

Bold, Edward. *The Merchant's and Mariner's African Guide*. Salem: Cushing and Appleton, 1823.

Bosman, William. *A New and Accurate Description of the Coast of Guinea*. London: J. Knapton, 1705.

Bouët-Willaumez, Édouard. *Commerce et Traite des Noirs aux Côtes Occidentales D'Afrique*. Paris: Imprimerie Nationale, 1848.

Bowen, Thomas Jefferson. *Central Africa: Adventures and Missionary Labors in Several Countries in the Interior of Africa*. New York: Southern Baptist Publication Society, 1857.

Brackenbury, Henry. *The Ashanti War: A Narration Prepared from the Official Documents by Permission of Major-General Sir Garnet Wolseley By Henry Brackenbury*. Vol. 1. London: William Blackwood and Sons, 1874.

Bridge, Horatio. *Journal of an African Cruiser*. Edited by Nathanial Hawthorne. London: Wiley and Putnam, 1845.

Brummell, John. *British Guiana: Demerara after Fifteen Years of Freedom, by a Landowner. By John Brummell*. London: T. Bosworth, 1853.

Bryson, Alexander. "Prophylactic Influence of Quinine." *Medical Times and Gazette* 7 (January 7, 1854): 6–7.

Bryson, Alexander. *Report on the Climate and Principle of Diseases of the African Station*. London: William Clowes and Sons, 1847.

Buckler, Henry. *Central Criminal Court. Minutes of Evidence, Taken in Short-Hand*. No. 618. London: George Herbert, 1836.

Burdo, Adolphe. *The Niger and the Benueh; Travels in Central Africa*. Translated by Mrs. George Sturge. London: Richard Bentley and Son, 1880.

Burdo, Adolphe. "Travels in Central Africa." *The Christian World Magazine and Family Visitor* 17 (1881): 154.

Burnley, William Hardin. *Observations on the Present Condition of the Island of Trinidad and the Actual State of the Experiment of Negro Emancipation*. London: Longman, 1842.

Burton, Richard Francis. *Abeokuta and the Camaroons Mountains: An Exploration*. Vol. 2. London: Tinsley Brothers, 1863.

Burton, Richard Francis. *The Lake Regions of Central Equatorial Africa*. 2 vols. London: Longman, 1860.

Burton, Richard Francis. *Wanderings in West Africa from Liverpool to Fernando Po*. 2 vols. London: Tinsley Brothers, 1863.

Büttikofer, Johann. *Travel Sketches from Liberia: Johann Büttikofer's 19th Century*. Edited by Henk Dop and Phillip Robinson. Leiden: Brill, 2012.

Campbell, W.H. "The Forests of British Guiana, Appendix III." *Proceedings of the Royal Colonial Institute*. London: The Institute, 1874.

Canot, Théodore. *Revelations of a Slave Trader; or Twenty Years' Adventures of Captain Canot*. London: Richard Bentley, 1854.

Carnes, J.A. *Journal of a Voyage from Boston to the West Coast of Africa; with a full Description of the Manner of Trading with the Natives on the Coast*. Boston: J.P. Jewett and Co., 1852.

Chenery, Leonard. *The West Coast of Africa: From Sierra Leone to Cape Lopez, Part 2*. Washington: Government Printing Office, 1875.

Childe, Timothy. *A System of Geography: Or, A New and Accurate Description of the Earth, In All of its Empires, Kingdoms, and States, Part of the Second, Containing the Description of Asia, Africa, and America*. London: Printed for Timothy Childe, 1701.

Clarke, Reverend J. "The West African Company." *Anti-Slavery Reporter* 2, no. 16 (Wednesday, August 11, 1841): 170.

Clarke, Robert. "Sketches of the Colony of Sierra Leone and Its Inhabitants." *Transactions of the Ethnological Society of London* 2 (1863): 320–363.

Clarkson, John. "Governor Clarkson's Diary, November 6 1792." In *Sierra Leone After A Hundred Years*, edited by Ernest Graham Ingham, 16–137. London: Seeley, 1894.

Cleland, James. *Enumeration of the Inhabitants of the City of Glasgow and County of Lanark. For the Government Census with Population Statistical Tables Relative to England and Scotland*. 2nd ed. Glasgow: John Smith & Son, 1832.

Cobbett, William. "Evidence in Support of the Statement, January to June 1802." In *Cobbett's Annual Register (Political Register)*. Vol. 1. London: Cox and Baylis, 1802.

Coke, Thomas. *An Interesting Narrative of a Mission, Sent to Sierra Leone, in Africa: By Methodists, in 1811: to Which is Prefixed, An Account of the Rise, Progress, Disasters,*

and Present State of that Colony: the Whole Interspersed with a Variety of Remarkable Particulars. London: Paris & Son, 1812.
Colomb, Philip Howard. *Slave-Catching in the Indian Ocean: A Record of Naval Experiences*. London: Longmans, Green and Co., 1873.
Connelly, Reverend James M. "Report of the Kroo People." *American Colonization Thirty-Ninth Annual Report* (1856): 38–40.
Corry, Joseph. *Observations on the Windward Coast of Africa; the Character, Religion, Customs, &C. Of the Natives, with a System Upon Which They May Be Civilized, and a Knowledge Attained in the Interior of This Extraordinary Quarter of the Globe, and Upon the Natural and Commercial Resources of the Country*. London: G. and W. Nicol, 1807.
Crowther, Samuel. *Journal of an Expedition up the Niger and Tshadda Rivers Undertaken by Macgregor Laird in Connection with the British Government in 1854*. London: Church Missionary House, 1855.
Cugoano, Ottobah. *Thoughts and Sentiments on the Evil and Wicked Traffic of The Slavery and Commerce of the Human Species, Humbly Submitted to The Inhabitants of Great-Britain, By Ottobah Cugoano, A Native of Africa*. London: n.p., 1787. Eighteenth Century Online. Accessed July 7, 2014.
Dapper, Olfert. *Naukeurige Beschrijvingen der Afrikaensche Gewesten*. Amsterdam: Jacob Van Meurs, 1668.
Davies, John W. "On the Fever in the Zambesi: A Note from Dr. Livingstone to Dr. M'William June 3rd 1861." *Transactions of the Epidemiological Society of London* 1 (1863): 235–242.
Davies, William. *Extracts from the Journal of the Rev. William Davies, 1st, when a Missionary at Sierra Leone, Western Africa; Containing some Account of the Countrey, etc.* New York: Wesleyan Printing Office, 1835.
Davy, H. "Voyage of H.M.S. Thunderer to the Mauritius and Back, Notes by Mr. H. Davy, Master, R.N.–1843." In *The Nautical Magazine and the Naval Chronicle for 1844, A Journal of Subjects Connected to Maritime Affairs*, 70–78,138–145, 208–212, 384–391. London: Simpkin, Marshall, and Co., 1844.
De Cosson, Emilius Albert (F.R.G.S.). *Days and Knights of Service with Sir Gerald Graham's Field Force at Suakin*. London: John Murray, 1886.
De Marees, Pieter. *Beschryvinghe Ende Historische Verhael Van Het Gout Koninckrijck Van Gunea Anders de Gout-Custe de Mina Genaemt Liggende In Het Deel Van Africa*. S-Gravenhage: Martinus Nijhoff, 1912.
De Marees, Pieter. *Description and Historical Account of the Gold Kingdom of Guinea*. 1602. Edited by A. Van Dantzig and Adam Jones. London: British Academy, 1987.
Denham, Dixon, Hugh Clapperton, and Walter Oudney. *Narrative of Travels and Discoveries in Northern and Central Africa in the years 1822, 1823, and 1824*. 2 Vols. London: Darf Publishers Ltd., 1826.
Des Bruslons, Jacques Savary. *Dictionnaire Universel de Commerce*. Paris: Jacques Estienne, 1723.
De Sintra, Pedro. *The Voyages of Cadamosto*. Second Series. Translated by Gerald Crone. London: Hakluyt Society, 1927.
De Verteuil, Louis. *Trinidad: Its Geography, Natural Resources, Administration, Present Condition, and Prospects*. 1855. 2nd ed. London: Cassel and Company, 1884.
Dickens, Charles. "Cheerily, Cheerily". *Household Words* 15 (1852): 308–321.

Dickens, Charles. "Our Phantom Ship." In *A Collection of British Authors*. Vol. 112: *Household Words* 5 (1852): 363–378.

Dobson, George. "The River Volta, Gold Coast, West Africa By Mr. George Dobson of Cardiff Read to the Members, in the Library, January 29th 1892, at 7:30pm." *The Journal of Manchester Geographical Society* 8 (1892): 19–25.

Drake, Richard. "Revelations of a Slave Smuggler: being an Autobiography of Capt. Richard Drake, an African Trader for Fifty Years – from 1807 to 1857 [New York, 1860]." In *Slave Ships and Slaving with an Introduction by Capt. Ernest H. Pentecost, R.N.R.*, edited by George Francis Dow, 205–281. 1927. Reprint, Cambridge, MD: Cornell Maritime Press, 1968.

Durrant, William. "The Kru Coast, Cape Palmas and the Niger." In *Vacation Tourists and Notes of Travel in 1861*, edited by Francis Galton, 9–336. London: MacMillan and Company, 1862.

Ellis, Alfred Burton. *West African Islands*. London: Chapman and Hall, 1885.

"Établissements de la Côte D'Or et du Gabon." In *Revue Maritime et Coloniale*. Vol. 9. 31–65. Paris: Ministère de la Marine, 1863.

Falconbridge, Alexander. *An Account of the Slave Trade on the Coast of Africa*. 2nd edition. London: James Phillips, 1788.

Forbes, Lieutenant Frederick. *Six Months' Service in the African Blockade*. 1849. London: Dawsons, 1969.

Fox, William. *A Brief History of the Wesleyan Missions on the West Coast of Africa*. London: Aylott and Jones, 1851.

Franklin, C.B. *After Many Days: A Memoir. Being a Sketch of the Life and Labours of Rev. Alexander Kennedy, First Presbyterian Missionary to Trinidad, Founder of Greyfriars Church, and its Pastor for Fourteen Years: January 1836 – December 1849. With an Introduction by Rev. R.E. Welsh*. Port of Spain: Franklin's Electric Printery, 1910.

Fry, Henry. *The History of North Atlantic Steam Navigation: With Some Account of Early Ships and Shipowners*. London: S.L. Martson, 1896.

Furse, George Armand. *Military Transport: H.M. Stationary Office, 1882*. London: W. Clowers & Sons, 1882.

Gill, Isobel Black. *Six Months in Ascension: An Unscientific Account of a Scientific Expedition By Mrs. Gill*. London: John Murray, 1878.

Griffith, William Brandford. "Government Hospitals No.2," Ordinance 4. *Ordinances of the Settlements on the Gold Coast and of the Gold Coast Colony, in Force April 7th, 1887, with an Appendix containing the Rules, Orders in Consul, and Proclamations of Practical Utility and an Index*. London: Waterlow & Sons, 1887.

Griffiths, Ralph, and George Edward Griffiths, eds. "Exposure of the Slave Trade." *The Monthly Review* 1, no.1 (London: G. Henderson, 1833): 21–36.

Griffs, William Elliot. *Matthew Calbraith Perry, A Typical Naval Officer*. Boston: Cupples and Hurd, 1890.

Guinness, H. Grattan. *The New World of Central Africa: With a History of the First Christian in the Congo*. London: Hodder and Stoughton, 1890.

Gurley, Ralph Randolph. *Life of Jehudi Ashmun, Late Colonial Agent: With an Appendix contacting Extracts from His Journal and Other Writings; with a Brief Sketch of the Life of the Rev. Lott Cary*. New York: Leavitt, Lord and Co., 1835.

Hakluyt, Richard, ed. *The First Voyage Made by Master W. Towerson to the Coast of Guinea in the Yere 1555.* London: J. MacLehose and Sons, 1904.

Halcombe, Reverend J.J. *Mission Life: A Magazine of Information about Church Missions and the Countries in which They are Being Carried On.* London: Lothian and Co, 1866.

Hart, Daniel. *Trinidad and the Other West India Islands and Colonies.* 2nd ed. Trinidad: The Chronicle Publishing Office, 1866.

Hastings, A.C.G. *The Voyage of the 'Dayspring'.* London: John Lane – The Bodley Head, 1926.

Henrique, Louis. *Les Colonies Françaises.* Vol. 5. Paris: Maison Quantin, 1890.

Hewett, J.F. Napier. *European Settlements on the West Coast of Africa: With Remarks on the Slave Trade and the Supply of Cotton.* London: Chapman and Hall, 1862.

Holman, James. "Mr. Holman's Travels." *The Asiatic Journal and Monthly Register for British and Foreign India, China and Australasia* 14 (May-August 1834): 62–64.

Holman, James. *Travels in Madeira, Sierra Leone, Teneriffe, St Jago, Cape Coast, Fernando Po, Princess Island, Etc., Etc.* 2nd edition. London: Routledge, 1840.

Howe, George. "The Last Slave Ship." 1890. In *Slave Ships and Slaving with an Introduction by Capt. Ernest H. Pentecost, R.N.R.*, edited by George Francis Dow, 352–382. 1927. Reprint, Cambridge, MD: Cornell Maritime Press, 1968.

Howland, George. "Captain George Howland's Voyage to West Africa, 1822–1823." In *New England Merchants in Africa: A History Through Documents, 1802–1865.* Edited by Norman Bennett and George E. Brooks. Boston: Boston University Press, 1965.

Hume, David. *Essays: Moral, Political and Literary.* Vol. 21. London: n.p., 1741.

Huntley, Sir Henry. *Seven Years' Service on the Slave Coast of Western Africa.* Vol. 1. London: Thomas Cautley Newby, 1850.

Hutchinson, Thomas Joseph F.R.G.S. *Impressions of Western Africa.* London: Longman, 1858.

Hutchinson, Thomas Joseph F.R.G.S. *Ten Year's Wandering among the Ethiopians; with sketches of the Manners and Customs of the Civilized and Uncivilized Tribes, From Senegal to Gaboon.* London: Hurst and Blackett Publishers, 1861.

Ingham, Ernest Graham. *Sierra Leone After A Hundred Years.* London: Seeley, 1894.

Keltie, J. Scott, ed. *The Statesman's Year-Book: Statistical and Historical Annual of the States of the World for the Year 1899.* London: Macmillan, 1899.

Kingsley, Mary H. *Travels in West Africa.* New York: Macmillan, 1897.

Kingsley, Mary H. *West African Studies.* 1899. 3rd ed. London: Routledge, 2011.

Kingston, William Henry Giles. *The Two Whalers; Or, Adventures in the Pacific.* London: Society for Promoting Christian Knowledge, 1885.

Kipling, Rudyard. *From Sea to Sea* in *The Writings in Prose and Verse of Rudyard Kipling.* Vol. 16, Part 2. London: Charles Scribner's Sons Publications, 1899.

Kipling, Rudyard. "The White Man's Burden." *McClure's Magazine* 12, no. 4 (February 1899): 290.

Kirke, Henry. *Twenty-Five Years in British Guiana.* London: S. Low, Marsten, 1898.

Koelle, Sigismund. *Polyglotta Africana.* London: Church Missionary Society House, 1854.

Laird, MacGregor, and R.A.K. Oldfield. *Narrative of an Expedition into the Interior of Africa, By the River Niger in 1832, 1833, and 1834 in the Steam-Vessels Quorra and Alburkah.* Vol. 2. London: Richard Bentley, 1837.

La Martinière, Antoine Augustin Bruzen de. *Le Grand Dictionnaire Géographique et Critique.* Vol. 5. Paris: Gosse, 1735.

Lander, Richard, and John Lander. *Journal of an Expedition to Explore the Course and Termination of the Niger, with a Narrative of the Voyage down that River to its Termination.* 3 vols. London: John Murray, 1832.

Langdon, John. "Three Voyages to the West Coast of Africa, 1881–1884." In *Travel, Trade and Power in the Atlantic, 1765–1884*, edited by Betty Wood ad Martin Lynn, 165–284. Cambridge: Cambridge, 2002.

Latham, Robert Gordon. *The Ethnology of British Colonies and Dependencies.* London: J. Van Voorst, 1851.

Latimer, John. *The Annals of Bristol in the Eighteenth Century.* London: Butler & Tanner, 1893.

Leonard, Surgeon Peter. *Records of a Voyage to the Western Coast of Africa in His Majesty's Ship "Dryad," And of the Service on that Station for the Suppression of the Slave Trade, in the Years 1830, 1831, and 1832.* Edinburgh: William Tait, 1833.

"Letters Relating to Dr. Livingstone." *Proceedings and Monthly Record of Geography* 40 (1866): 307–308.

Leveson, Henry Astbury. *The Forest and the Field.* London: Chatto and Windus, 1874.

Livingstone, David. *Last Journals.* Vol. 2. Edited by Horace Waller. Edinburgh: Edinburgh University Press, 1874.

Livingstone, David. *Missionary Travels and Researches in South Africa.* London: John Murray, 1857.

Livingstone, David, and Charles Livingstone. *Narrative of an Expedition to the Zambesi and Its Tributaries: And of the Discovery of the Lakes Shirwa and Nyassa, 1858–1864.* New York: Harper & Brothers, 1866.

Lok, John. *The second voyage to Guinea set out by Sir George Barne, Sir John Yorke, Thomas Lok, Anthonie Hickman and Edward Castelin, in the yere 1554. The Captaine whereof was M. John Lok.* London: n.p., 1554.

Long, Edward. *The History of Jamaica, Volume 2: Reflections on its Situation, Settlements, Inhabitants, Climate, Products, Commerce, Laws and Government.* 1774. Montreal: McGill-Queens Press, 2003.

Lord, William Barry, and Thomas Baines. *Shifts and Expedients of Camp Life, Travel and Exploration.* London: Horace Cox, 1871.

Low, Charles Rathbone. *A Memoir of Lieutenant-General Sir Garnet J. Wolseley. By Charles Rathbone Low.* London: Richard Bentley & Son, 1878.

Lübelfling, Johann von. "Johann von Lübelfling's Voyage of 1599–1600." In *German Sources for West African History 1599–1669*, edited by Adam Jones. Wiesbaden: Steiner, 1983.

Ludlam, Thomas. "An Account of a Tribe of People called Kroomen, inhabiting a small District of the Grain Coast of Africa, between Cape Mount and Cape Palmas." In *The Sixth Report of the Directors of the African Institution Read at the General Annual Meeting*, 87–102. London: African Institute, 1812.

Ludlam, Thomas. "An Account of the Kroomen on the Coast of Africa." *The African Repository and Colonial Journal* 1, no. 2 (1825): 43–55.

Lugard, Frederick. *The Rise of Our East African Empire.* Edinburgh: W. Blackwood and Sons, 1893.

Lugenbeel, J.W. "Native Africans in Liberia-Their Customs and Superstitions." *African Repository* 28, no. 1, 6 (1852): 13–17, 171–174.

Macaulay, Kenneth. *The Colony of Sierra Leone Vindicated from the Misrepresentations of Mr. Macqueen of Glasgow.* London: Cass, 1826.

Macaulay, Zachary, ed. *The Christian Observer: Conducted by Members of the Established Church, Given by Disciples Divinity House* 15, no.11 (1816): 756.

Macdonald, Alexander. *Too Late for Gordon and Khartoum: the Testimony of an independent Eye-Witness of the Heroic Efforts for the Rescue and Relief. With Maps and Plans and Several Unpublished Letters of the Late General Gordon.* London: Spottiswoode and Co., 1887.

MacGregor, John. *Commercial Statistics: A Digest of the Productive Resources, Commercial Legislation, Custom Tarriffs, of All Nations. Including All British Commercial Treaties with Foreign States.* Vol. 5. London: Whittaker and Company, 1850.

Manning, Edward. "Six Months on a Slaver in 1860." 1879. In *Slave Ships and Slaving with an Introduction by Capt. Ernest H. Pentecost, R.N.R.* 310–351, edited by George Francis Dow, 310–351. 1927. Reprint, Cambridge, MD: Cornell Maritime Press, 1968.

Martin, Robert Montgomery, ed. *The Colonial Magazine and Commercial Maritime Journal* 6 (1841): 118–119.

McAllister, Agnes. *Lone Woman in Africa: Six Years on the Kroo Coast.* New York: Eaton and Mains, 1896.

M'William, J.O. *Medical History of the Expedition to the Niger during the years 1841–1842 comprising An Account of the Fever.* London: John Churchill, 1843.

Nassau, Robert Hamill. *My Ogowe: Being a Narrative of Daily Incidents During Sixteen Years in Equatorial West Africa.* New York: Neale Publishing Company, 1914.

Navarro, Don Joaquin J. *Apuntes Sobre El Estado de la Costa Occidental de Africa Y Principalmente de las Posesiones Españolas en Golfo de Guinea.* Madrid: Imprenta Nacional, 1859.

"Negro Civilization." *The Journal of Health and Disease* 1 (1846): 258–260.

Ogilby, John. *Africa: being an accurate description of the regions of Egypt, Barbary, Lybia, and Billedulgerid, the land of the Negroes, Guinee, Ethiopia, and the Abyssines, with all the adjacent islands... Collected and translated from most authentick authors... by John Ogilby.* London: T. Johnson, 1670.

Parr, Sir Henry Hallam. *A Sketch of the Kafir and Zulu Wars: Guadana to Isandhlwana.* London: C. Kegan & Co., 1880.

Pereira, Duarte Pacheco. *Esmeraldo de Situ Orbis.* Second Series. Vol. 79. Translated and edited by George H.T. Kimble. London: Hakluyt Society, 1936.

Pereira, Duarte Pacheco. *Esmeraldo de Situ Orbis: côte occidentale d'Afrique du sud marocain au Gabon.* Translated and edited by Raymond Mauny. Bissau: Centro de Estudos da Guiné Portuguesa, 1956.

Phillips, Thomas. "Journal." 1746. In *Slave Ships and Slaving with an Introduction by Capt. Ernest H. Pentecost, R.N.R.*, edited by George Francis Dow, 36–80. 1927. Reprint, Cambridge, MD: Cornell Maritime Press, 1968.

Pimentel, Manoel. *Arte de Navegar: Em que se Ensinam as Regras Praticas, E os Modos de Cartear, e de Graduar a Baleftilha por via de Numeros, e Muitos Problemas uteis á Navegaçaõ.* Lisboa: Francisco da Silva, 1746.

Pinney, Mr., Canfield, and Alward. "Report of Messrs Pinney, Canfield and Alward." *The Missionary Chronicle* 8 (1840): 213.

Raithby, John. *The Statutes Relating to the Admiralty, Navy, Shipping and Navigation in the United Kingdom from 9 Hen. III. to 3 Geo IV., inclusive with Notes.* London: George Eyre and Andrew Strahan, 1823.

Raleigh, Sir Walter. *The Discovery of Guiana*. 1595. Reprint, London: Cassell, 1887.
Ramsay, T.W. *Costumes on the Western Coast of Africa*. Np, 1830.
Rankin, F. Harrison. *The White Man's Grave: A Visit to Sierra Leone, in 1834*. Vol. 1. London: Richard Bentley, 1834.
Reclus, Élisée. *Africa and Its Inhabitants*. Vol. 2. Edited by A.H. Keane. London: Virtue and Company, 1899.
Reclus, Élisée. *The Universal Geography: Earth and Its Inhabitants*. Edited by A.H. Keane. London: J.S. Virtue & Co., 1885.
Reid, John Morrison. *Missions and Missionary Society of the Methodist Episcopal Church*. Vol. 1. New York: Eaton and Mains, 1895.
Roberts, Morley. "A Steerage Passage." In *Land-Travel and Sea-faring*, 1–31. London: Lawrence and Bullen, 1891.
Rockwell, Charles. *Sketches of Foreign Travel: And Life at Seal Including a Cruise on Board a Man-of-War, as Also a Visit to Spain, Portugal, the South of France, Italy, Sicily, Malta, The Ionian Islands, Continental Greece, Liberia and Brazil; And a Treatise of the Navy of the United States*. Boston: Tappan and Dennet, 1842.
Rockwell, Charles. "Sketches of Foreign Travel and Life at Sea." *African Repository* 18, no. 11 (1842): 273–286.
Rogers, Charles. *Intelligence Report on the Panama Canal*. Washington: Government Printing Office, 1889.
Rogers, Charles. "Progress at Panama." *Popular Science* 32 (February 1888): 447–455.
Schön, James Frederick, and Samuel Crowther, *Journals of the Rev. James Frederick Schön and Mr. Samuel Crowther: Who, Accompanied the Expedition Up the Niger, in 1841, in Behalf of the Church Missionary Society*. London: Hatchard and Son, 1842.
Scott, Walter. *The Edinburgh Annual Register, For 1825*. 18. Edinburgh: John Ballantyne and Company, 1826.
Simmons, Peter Lund. *Tropical Agriculture: A Treatise on the Culture, Preparation, Commerce, and Consumption of the Principal Products of the Vegetable Kingdom*. London: E. & F.N. Spoon, 1877.
Simpson, William. *A Private Journal Kept During the Niger Expedition: From the Commencement in May 1841, Until the Recall of the Expedition in June 1842 By William Simpson*. London: John F. Shaw, 1843.
Smith, Eugene R. *The Gospel in All Lands*. New York: Hunt and Eaton, 1893.
Smith, John. *Trade and Travels in the Gulph of Guinea, with an Account of the Manners, Habits, Customs, and Religion of the Inhabitants*. London: Simpkin & Marshall, 1851.
Société de Géographie. *Comptes Rendus des Séances de la Société de Géographie et de la Commission Centrale*. Paris: Société de Géographie, 1897.
Stallard, George, and Edward Harrinson Richards. *Ordinances and Orders, and Rules Thereunder, in Force of the Colony of Lagos on December 31, 1893*. London: Stevens, 1894.
Stephen, James. *The Slavery of the British West India Colonies Delineated, As it Exists in Both Law and Practice and Compared with the Slavery of Other Countries*. London: Joseph Butterworth and Son, 1824.
Stevens, Thomas. "Punjabee Well-Jumpers and Krooboy Divers." *Harper's Round Table* 8 (September 27, 1887): 766.

Sullivan, Captain G.L. *Dhow Chasing in Zanzibar Waters: And on the Eastern Coast of Africa.* London: Frank Cass & Co. Ltd., 1873.
Swan, Samuel. "Memoranda on the African Trade (1810–1811)." In *Yankee Traders, Old Coasters and African Middlemen: A History of American Legitimate Trade with West Africa in the Nineteenth Century.* Appendix J, edited by George E. Brooks, 313–343. Boston: Boston University Press, 1970.
Teage, Hilary. "The Slave Trade." *African Repository* 12, no. 5 (1836): 158–160.
"The Acts of Jamaica Passed in the Year 1842, Annual Laws of Jamaica, Cap 51. Act to make Provision for the Introduction of emigrants to this Island, 1842." In *The Laws of Jamaica.* Kingston: Government Printer, 1843.
The Navy List. London: John Murray, 1862.
The Ninth Annual Report of the Board of Foreign Missions of the Presbyterian Church in the United States of America. New York: Presbyterian Board, 1846.
"The Panama Ship Canal." *Scientific American Supplement* 11, no. 282 (May 1881): 4487–4489.
"The Panama Ship Canal." *Scientific American: Supplement* 26, no. 656 (July 28, 1888): 10471–10472.
The Queen's [or] King's Regulations and Admiralty Instructions for the Government of Her Majesty's Naval Service. Vol. 2. London: H.M. Station Office, 1879.
Thomas, Reverend Charles W. *Adventures and Observations on the West Coast of Africa and Its Islands.* New York: Derby and Jackson, 1860.
Thompson, George. *The Palm-Land, Or West Africa, Illustrated: Being a History of Missionary Labors and Travels with Descriptions of Men and Things in Western Africa.* 2nd ed. Cincinnati: Moore, Wilstach, Keys & Co., 1859.
Thomson, Thomas Richard Heywood. "The Bubis, or Edeeyah of Fernando Po." *The Edinburgh New Philosophical Journal* 44 (1848): 232–245.
Thorpe, Robert. *A Letter to William Wilberforce, ESq M.P., Vice President of the African Institution.* London: F.C. and J. Rivington, 1815.
Towerson, Williamson. "Voyage to Guinea in 1555." 1555. Accessed June 16, 2018. https://www.e-reading.club/chapter.php/80243/53/Kerr_-_A_General_History_and_Collection_of_Voyages_and_Travels%2C_Vol.VII.html.
Unum, E. Pluribus. *Littell's Living Age.* 5th series, 46 (1884): 40.
Usera y Alarcón, Gerónimo M. *Memoria de la isla de Fernando Poo.* Madrid: T. Aguado, 1848.
Usera y Alarcón, Gerónimo M. *Observaciones al llamado Opúsculo Sobre la Colonizacion de Fernando Póo.* Madrid: Aguado, 1852.
Vallon, A. "La Côte Occidentale." In *Revue Maritime et Coloniale.* Vol. 9. 373–394. Paris: Ministère de la Marine, 1863.
Villault, Nicolas. *Relation des costes d'Afrique, appellées Guinée: avec la description du pays, moeurs & façons de vivre des habitans, des productions de la terre, & des marchandises qu'on en apporte, avec les remarques historiques sur ces costes.* Paris: Chez Denys Thierry, 1669.
Waddell, Rev. Hope Masterson. *Twenty-nine Years in the West Indies and Central Africa: A Review of Missionary Work Adventure 1829–1858 By the Rev. Hope Masterton Waddell.* London: T. Nelson and Sons, Paternoster Row Edinburgh, 1863.

Wadstrom, Carl Bernhard. *An Essay on Colonization, Particularly Applied to the Western Coast of Africa, with some Free Thoughts on Cultivation and Commerce*. London: Wadstrom, 1794.

Walckenaer, Charles Athanase. *Histoire Générale Des Voyages ou Nouvelle Collection des Relations de Voyages Par Mer*. vol. 19. Paris: Chez Lefèvre, 1830.

Warren, C.E. *The Royal Navy List*. London: Witherby & Co., 1878.

Webster, Dan. *Report of the Secretary of State* (September 14, 1850), 75.

Webster, William Henry Bayley. *Narrative of the Voyage to the Southern Atlantic Ocean in the Years 1828, 29, 30 Performed in H.M. Sloop Chanticleer, Under the Command of the Late Captain Henry Foster, F.R.S. & c. By Order of the Lords Commissioners of the Admiralty. From the Private Journal of W.H.B. Webster, Surgeon of the Sloop. In Two Volumes*. Vol. 1. London: Richard Bentley, 1834.

Welsh, James. "A Voyage to Benin beyond the Countrey of Guinea made by Master James Welch, who set forth in the Yeere 1588." In *The Principle Navigations, Voyages, Traffiques and Discoveries of the English Nation*. Vol. 6. Edited by Richard Hakluyt. 450–451. London: J. MacLehose and Sons, 1904.

Whitford, John. *Trading Life in Western and Central Africa*. Liverpool: The "Porcupine" Office, 1877.

Wilkeson, Samuel. *A Concise History of the Commencement, Progress and Present Condition of the American Colonies in Liberia*. Washington: Madisonian Office, 1839.

Wilks, Samuel Charles, ed. *The Christian Observer: Conducted by Members of the Established Church, Given by Disciples Divinity House* 18, no. 11 (1819): 859.

Wilson, Reverend John Leighton. "Letter from Africa, No.1." *African Repository* 15, no. 16 (1839): 262–267.

Wilson, Reverend John Leighton. *Western Africa: Its History, Conditions and Prospects: With Numerous Engravings*. New York: Harper and Brothers, 1856.

Winterbottom, Thomas. *An Account of the Native Africans in the Neighbourhood of Sierra Leone*. London: C. Whittingham, 1803.

Zöller, Hugo. *Das Togoland und die Sklavenküste*. Berlin: Verlag von W. Spemann, 1885.

Zulueta, Pedro de. *Trial of Pedro de Zulueta, Jun., on a Charge of Slave Trading*. London: C. Wood and Company, 1844.

Secondary Sources

Abingbade, Harrison Ola. "The Settler African Conflicts: The Case of the Maryland Colonists and the Grebo, 1840–1900." *The Journal of Negro History* 66, no. 2 (1981): 93–109.

Achebe, Chinua. *Things Fall Apart*. London: Heinemann, 1958.

Adler, M.N., ed. *The Itinerary of Benjamin of Tudela*. New York: Philipp Feldheim Inc., 1907.

Agozino, Biko. *Pan-African Issues in Crime and Justice*. London: Taylor and Francis, 2017.

Akingbade, Harrison. "The Liberian Settlers and the Campaign Against the Slave Trade, 1825–1865." *Africa Rivista trimestrale di studi e document tazione dell'Istituto italiano per l'Africa e l'Oriente* 38, no. 3 (1983): 342.

Alpers, Edward. *East Africa and the Indian Ocean*. Princeton: Markus Wiener Publications, 2009.

Alpers, Edward. "Recollecting Africa: Diasporic Memory in the Indian Ocean World." In *Special Issue on the Diaspora*, edited by Judith Byfield. *African Studies Review* 43, no. 1 (2000): 83–99.
Alpers, Edward. *The Indian Ocean in World History*. Oxford: Oxford University Press, 2014.
Anderson, Benedict. *Reflections on the Origins and Spread of Nationalism*. New York: Verso, 1991.
Anderson, Richard. "The Diaspora of Sierra Leone's Liberated Africans: Enlistment, Forced Migration, and 'Liberation' at Freetown, 1808–1863." *African Economic History* 41 (2013): 101–138.
Anstey, Roger. *The Atlantic Slave Trade and British Abolition, 1760–1810*. London: MacMillan Press Ltd., 1975.
Asiegbu, Johnson U.J. *Nigeria and its British Invaders, 1851–1920*. Lagos: Nok Publishers International, 1984.
Austen, Ralph. "The Mediterranean Islamic Slave Trade Out of Africa: A Tentative Census." *Slavery & Abolition* 13, no. 1 (1992): 214–248.
Bangura, Joseph. *The Temne of Sierra Leone: African Agency in the Making of a British Colony*. Cambridge: Cambridge University Press, 2017.
Banton, Michael. *West African City: A Study of Tribal Life in Freetown*. London: Oxford University Press, 1957.
Beeler, John. "Maritime Policing and the Pax Britannica: The Royal Navy's Anti-Slavery Patrol in the Caribbean, 1828–1848." *The Northern Mariner* 16, no. 1 (2006): 1–20.
Behrendt, Stephen D. "Crew Mortality in the Transatlantic Slave Trade in the Eighteenth Century." *Slavery & Abolition* 18, no. 1 (1997): 49–71.
Behrens, Christine. *Les Kroumen de la Côte Occidentale d'Afrique*. Bordeaux: Centre d'études de Géographie Tropicale, 1974.
Biyi, Esu. "The Kru and Related Peoples, West Africa, Part I." *Journal of the African Society* 29, no. 113 (1929): 71–77.
Blackburn, Robin. *The Overthrow of Colonial Slavery, 1776–1848*. London: Verso, 1988.
Blamo, John Bernard. "Nation-Building in Liberia as Revealed by Symbol Analysis." Ph.D. thesis, Boston University, 1969.
Boenisch, Josephine. "Ethnic Differences in Peasant Agriculture: The Canals Poulder." Master's thesis, McGill University, 1971.
Bohner, Theodor. *Die Woermanns*. Berlin: Brücke zur Heimat, 1935.
Bovill, E.W., ed. *Captain Clapperton's Narrative*, in *Missions to The Niger: The Bornu Mission, 1822–25*, Part 3, Vol. 4. Cambridge: Cambridge University Press, 1966.
Bowman, Joyce. "Reconstructing the Past Using the British Parliamentary Papers: The Anglo-Zulu War of 1879." *History in Africa* 31 (2004): 117–132.
Braidwood, Stephen J. *Black Poor and White Philanthropists: London's Blacks and the Foundation of the Sierra Leone Settlement 1786–1791*. Liverpool: University of Liverpool, 1994.
Brathwaite, Kamau. *The Development of Creole Society in Jamaica, 1770–1820*. Oxford: Clarendon, 1971.
Breitborde, Lawrence Bart. *Speaking Social Identity: English in the Lives of Urban Africans*. Berlin: Walter de Gruyter, 1998.
Breitborde, Lawrence Bart. "Structural Continuity in the Development of an Urban Kru Community." *Urban Anthropology* (1979): 111–130.

Brooks, George E. *The Kru Mariner in the 19th Century: A Historical Compendium*. Newark, Delaware: Liberian Studies Monologue Series no.1, 1972.

Brown, Christopher Leslie. *Moral Capital: Foundations of British Abolitionism*. Chapel Hill: North Carolina Press, 2006.

Brown, George W. *The Economic History of Liberia*. Washington: The Associated Publishers, 1941.

Bruce Lockhart, Jamie, and Paul Lovejoy, eds. *Hugh Clapperton into the Interior of Africa: Records of the Second Expedition, 1825–1827*. Leiden: Brill, 2005.

Brunsman, Denver. *The Evil Necessity: British Naval Impressment in the Eighteenth-Century Atlantic World*. University of Virginia Press, 2013.

Bucher, Henry H. "Liberty and Labor: The Origins of Libreville Reconsidered." *Bulletin de l'Institut Foundamental d'Afrique Noire*. 2nd series. 41, no. 3 (1979): 478–496.

Buell, R.L. *The Native Problem in Africa*. Vol. 2. New York: MacMillan, 1928.

Burroughs, Robert, and Richard Huzzey, eds. *The Suppression of the Atlantic Slave Trade: British Policies, Practices and Representations of Naval Coercion*. Manchester: Manchester University Press, 2018.

Campbell, Gwynn. *Structure of Slavery in Indian Ocean Africa and Asia*. London: Routledge, 2004.

Canney, Donald L. *African Squadron: The U.S. Navy and the Slave Trade, 1842–1861*. Washington D.C.: Potomac Books, 2006.

Carey, Neil. "Comparative Native Terminology of Poro Groups." *Secrecy: The Journal of the Poro Studies Association* 1, no. 1 (2014): 1–21.

Carretta, Vincent. "Black Seamen and Soldiers." Review of *Black Salt: Seafarers of African Descent on British Ships*, by Ray Costello. *Eighteenth-Century Life* 38, no. 3 (Fall, 2014): 150–153.

Carretta, Vincent, ed. *The Interesting Narrative and Other Writings*. London: Penguin, 2003.

Carretta, Vincent, ed. *Thoughts and Sentiments on the Evils of Slavery and Other Writings*. London: Penguin, 1999.

Carrington, Selwyn H.H. *The Sugar Industry and the Abolition of the Slave Trade, 1775–1810*. Gainsville: University of Florida, 2002.

Castillo-Rodríguez, Susana. "The First Missionary Linguistics in Fernando Po." In *Colonialism and Missionary Linguistics*, edited by Klaus Zimmermann and Birte Kellermeier-Rehbein, 75–106. Berlin: Walter de Gruyter, 2015.

Cateau, Heather. "Itinerant Slaves: On the Plantation's Margins-Hired Slaves and Seamen." Paper presented at the Association of Caribbean Historians 35th Annual Conference. Universidad Interamericana de Puerto Rico, San Juan, Puerto Rico. April 28-May 2, 2003.

Christopher, Emma. *Slave Ship Sailors and Their Captive Cargoes, 1730–1807*. Cambridge: Cambridge University Press, 2006.

Clegg III, Claude Andrew. *The Price of Liberty: African Americans and the Making of Liberia*. Chapel Hill: University of North Carolina Press, 2009.

Clements, W.H. *The Glamour and Tragedy of the Zulu War*. London: John Lane, The Brodley Head, 1936.

Clendennen, G.W., and D.H. Simpson. "African Members of the Zambezi Expedition, 1861–1864: A Prosopographical Foray." *History in Africa* 12 (1985): 29–49.

Cobley, Alan. "Black West Indian Seamen in the British Merchant Marine in the Mid Nineteenth Century." *History Workshop Journal*, no. 58 (Autumn, 2004): 259–274.

Cohen, Abner. *Custom and Politics in Urban Africa: A Study of Hausa Migrants in Yoruba Towns.* London: Routledge, 1969.
Cooper, Frederick. "African Labor History." In *Global Labour History: A State of the Art*, edited by Jan Lucassen, 91–116. Bern: Peter Lang, 2006.
Cooper, Frederick. *Plantation Slavery on the East Coast of Africa.* New Haven: Yale University Press, 1977.
Coquery-Vidrovitch, Catherine. *Brazza et la Prise de Possession du Congo. La Mission de l'Ouest Africain, 1883–1885.* Paris: Mouton et Cie, 1969.
Coquery-Vidrovitch, Catherine, and Paul E. Lovejoy, eds. *The Workers of African Trade.* Beverly Hills: Sage Publications, 1985.
Costello, Roy. *Black Salt: Seafarers of African Descent on British Ships.* Oxford: Oxford University Press, 2012.
Coupland, Sir Reginald. *Kirk on the Zambesi.* Oxford: Clarendon Press, 1928.
Coupland, Sir Reginald. *The British Anti-Slavery Movement.* 2nd ed. London: Frank Cass & Co. Ltd, 1964.
Craton, Michael. "Reshuffling the Pack: The Transition from Slavery to Other Forms of Labor in the British Caribbean, ca. 1790–1890." *New West Indian Guide* 68, no. 1–2 (1994): 23–75.
Crooks, John Joseph. *Records Relating to the Gold Coast, 1750–1874.* 1973. London: Routledge, 2016.
Cruickshank, J.G. "African Immigrants After Freedom." *Timehri: The Journal of the Royal Agricultural and Commercial Society of British Guiana* 6, Third Series (1919): 74–85.
Curtin, Philip. *Death by Migration: Europe's Encounter with the Tropical World in the Nineteenth Century.* Cambridge: Cambridge University Press, 1989.
Curtin, Philip. *Disease and Empire: The Health of European Troops in the Conquest of Africa.* Cambridge: Cambridge University Press, 1998.
Curtin, Philip. *The Atlantic Slave Trade: A Census.* Madison: University of Wisconsin Press, 1969.
Curtin, Philip. "The End of the 'White Man's Grave'? Nineteenth Century Mortality." *Journal of Interdisciplinary History* 21, no. 1 (Summer 1990): 63–88.
Curtin, Philip. *The Image of Africa: British Ideas and Action, 1780–1850.* Vol. 1. Madison: University of Wisconsin, 1973.
Curtin, Philip. "'The White Man's Grave': Image and Reality, 1780–1850." *Journal of British Studies* 1, no. 1 (1961): 94–110.
Dalby, David. *Black through White: Patterns of Communication.* Bloomington: Indiana University of African Studies Program, 1970.
Da Silva, Daniel B. Domingues. "The Atlantic Slave Trade from Angola: A Port-by-Port Estimate of Slaves Embarked, 1701–1867." *The International Journal of African Historical Studies* 46, no.1 (2013): 105–122
Da Silva, Daniel B. Domingues, David Eltis, Philip Misevich, and Olatunji Ojo. "The Diaspora of Africans Liberated from Slave Ships in the Nineteenth Century." *Journal of African History* 55, no. 3 (2014): 347–369.
Davey, Arthur. "The Kroomen of Simon's Town." *Simon's Town Historical Bulletin* 16, no. 2 (July 1990): 51–58.
Davey, Arthur. "Tindals, Seedies and Kroomen." *Simon's Town Historical Bulletin* 17, no. 4 (July 1993): 157–158.

Davies, Peter N. *The Trade Makers: Elder Demspter in West Africa, 1852–1872, 1973–1989*. Oxford: Oxford University Press, 2017.
Davies, Peter N., ed. *Trading in West Africa, 1840–1920*. London: Croom Helm, 1976.
Davis, Richard Harding. *The Congo and the Coasts of Africa*. 1907. London: Bexley Publications, 2006.
Davis, Ronald W. *Ethnohistorical Studies on the Kru Coast*. Newark: Liberian Studies Monograph Series 5, 1976.
Davis, Ronald W. "The Liberian Struggle for Authority on the Kru Coast." *International Journal of African Historical Studies* 8, no. 2 (1975): 222–265.
Dawson, Kevin. *Undercurrents of Power: Aquatic Culture in the African Diaspora*. Philadelphia: University of Pennsylvania Press, 2018.
De Barros, Juanita. *Reproducing the British Caribbean: Sex, Gender, and Population Politics after Slavery*. Chapel Hill: University of North Carolina Press, 2014.
Derrick, Jonathan. *Africa, Empire and Fleet Street: Albert Cartwright and the West Africa Magazine*. Oxford: Oxford University Press, 2018.
De Teran, Manuel. *Síntesis Geográfica de Fernando Póo*. Madrid: Institut d'Etudes Africaines, 1962.
Dike, Kenneth. "Origins of the Niger Mission 1841–1891." A paper read at the Centenary of the Mission at Christ Church, Onitsha, on November 13, 1957. Ibadan: Ibadan University Press, 1962.
Dow, George Francis. *Slave Ships and Slaving*. 1927. New York: Dover Publications, 2002.
Drescher, Seymour. *Econocide: British Slavery in the Era of Abolition*. 2nd ed. Chapel Hill: University of North Carolina Press, 2010.
Editorial Committee. "Free and Unfree Labour." *International Review of Social History* 35, no. 1 (1990): 1–2.
Elbl, Ivana. "The Portuguese Trade with West Africa, 1440–1521." Ph.D. thesis, University of Toronto, 1986.
Eltis, David. *Economic Growth and the Ending of the Transatlantic Slave Trade*. New York: Oxford University Press, 1987.
Eltis, David. "The Volume and Structures of the Transatlantic Slave Trade: A Reassessment." *William and Mary Quarterly* (2001): 17–46.
Equiano, Olaudah. *The Interesting Narrative and Other Writings*. 1789. Edited by Vincent Carretta. 2nd ed. London: Penguin Books Ltd, 2003.
Falola, Toyin, and Fallou Ngom. *Facts, Fiction and African Creative Imaginations*. London: Routledge, 2009.
Fay, Peter Ward. *The Opium War, 1840–1842: Barbarians in the Celestial Empire in the Early Part of the Nineteenth Century and the War by Which They Forced Her Gates Ajar*. Chapel Hill: University of North Carolina, 1975.
Featherstone, Donald. *Khartoum, 1885: General Gordon's Last Stand*. Oxford: Osprey Publishing, 1993.
Finkelman, Paul, ed. *Encyclopedia of African-American History, 1619–1895: From the Colonial Period to the Age of Frederick Douglass*. Vol 2. Oxford: Oxford University Press, 2006.
Fisher, Michael H., Shompa Lahiri, and Shinder S. Thandi. *A South-Asian History of Britain: Four Centuries of Peoples from the Indian Sub-Continent*. Westport, CT: Greenwood World Publishers, 2007.

Foster, Charles I. "The Colonization of Free Negroes, in Liberia, 1816–1835." *The Journal of Negro History* 38, no. 1 (1953): 41–66.
Fox, Early Lee. *The American Colonization Society, 1817–1840*. 1919. Reprint, Whitefish, MO: Kessinger Publishers, 2007.
Foy, Charles R. "Britain's Black Tars." In *Britain's Black Past*, edited by Gretchen H. Gerzina, 63–80. Oxford: Oxford University Press, 2020.
Foy, Charles R. "The Royal Navy's Employment of Black Mariners and Maritime Workers, 1754–1783." *The International Journal of Maritime History* 28, no. 1 (2016): 6–35.
Fraenkel, Merran. "Social Change on the Kru Coast of Liberia." *Africa* 36, no. 2 (1966): 154–172.
Fraenkel, Merran. *Tribe and Class in Monrovia*. Oxford: Oxford University Press, 1964.
Franklin, John Hope. *George Washington Williams: A Biography*. Durham: Duke University Press, 1998.
Frost, Diane. "Ethnic Identity, Transience and Settlement: The Kru in Liverpool Since the Late Nineteenth Century." In *Africans in Britain*, edited by D. Killingray, 88–106. London: Frank Cass & Co., 1994.
Frost, Diane. *Work and Community Among West African Migrant Workers Since the Nineteenth Century*. Liverpool: Liverpool University Press, 1999.
Frykman, Niklas. "Seamen on Late Eighteenth-Century European Warships." *International Review of Social History* 54, no. 1 (2009): 67–93.
Fyfe, Christopher. *A History of Sierra Leone*. Oxford: Oxford University Press, 1962.
Fyfe, Christopher. *A Short History of Sierra Leone*. London: Longmans, 1962.
Fyle, Magbaily. *A Nationalist History of Sierra Leone*. Freetown: n.p., 2011.
Fyle, Magbaily. *Historical Dictionary of Sierra Leone*. Lanham: Scarecrow Press, 2006.
Fyle, Magbaily. *The History of Sierra Leone*. Freetown: Sierra Leone Adult Education Association, 1988.
Gann, Lewis H., and Peter Duignan. *Colonialism in Africa, 1870–1960*. London: Cambridge University Press, 1969.
Geary, Sir William M.N. *Nigeria Under British Rule*. London: Routledge, 1927.
Geggus, David. "Sex Ratio, Age and Ethnicity in the Atlantic Slave Trade: Data from French Shipping and Plantation Records." *The Journal of African History* 30, no. 1 (1989): 23–44.
George, Claude. *The Rise of British West Africa*. London: Houlston and Sons, 1903.
Gershoni, Yekutiel. *Black Colonialism. Americo-Liberian Scramble for the Hinterland*. Westview Press Boulder, 1985.
Gershoni, Yekutiel. "The Drawing of Liberian Boundaries in the Nineteenth Century: Treaties with African Chiefs versus Effective Occupation." *The International Journal African Historical Studies* 20, no. 2 (1987): 293–307.
Gilbert, Erik. *Dhows and the Colonial Economy of Zanzibar, 1860–1970*. Athens, OH: Ohio University Press, 2004.
Gilliland, Herbert, ed. *USS Constellation on the Dismal Coast: Willie Leonard's Journal, 1859–1861*. Columbia, SC: University of South Carolina Press, 2013.
Gilroy, Paul. *The Black Atlantic: Modernity and Double Consciousness*. New York: Verso, 1993.
Glissant, Édouard. "Creolization in the Making of the Americas." *Caribbean Quarterly* 54, no. 1–2 (2008): 81–89.

Glissant, Édouard. *Poetics of Relation*. Translated by Betsy Wing. Ann Arbor: The University of Michigan Press, 1997.

Goldenberg, David M. *The Curse of Ham: Race and Slavery in Early Judaism, Christianity, and Islam*. Princeton: Princeton University Press, 2003.

Graham, Gerald S. *Great Britain in the Indian Ocean*. Oxford: Oxford University Press, 1967.

Green, Toby. *The Rise of the Trans-Atlantic Slave Trade in Western Africa, 1300–1589*. Cambridge: Cambridge University Press, 2011.

Greenberg, Joseph H. *The Languages of Africa*. International Journal of American Linguistics 29, no. 1 (Part 2) (Publication of the Indiana University Research Center in Anthropology, Folklore and Linguistics, 25). Bloomington: Indiana University, 1963.

Gunn, Jeffrey. "Homeland, Diasporas and Labour Networks: The Case of Kru Workers, 1792–1900." Ph.D. dissertation, York University, 2019.

Gunn, Jeffrey. "Krutown: A Catalyst for the Kru Diaspora." In *Sierra Leone: Past and Present*, edited by Paul Lovejoy and Suzanne Schwarz. Trenton, NJ: Africa World Press, 2021. In press.

Gutkind, Peter, R. Cohen, and Jean Copans, eds. *African Labour History*. Beverly Hills: Sage Publications, 1978.

Gutkind, Peter. "The Canoemen of the Gold Coast (Ghana)." *Cahiers d'Études Africaines* 29, no. 115–116 (1989): 339–376.

Gutkind, Peter. "Trade and Labor in Early Precolonial African History: The Canoemen of Southern Ghana." In *The Workers of African Trade*, edited by Catherine Coquery-Vidrovitch and Paul E. Lovejoy, 25–50. Beverly Hills: Sage Publications, 1985.

Hair, P.E.H. "Attitudes to Africans in English Primary Sources on Guinea up to 1650." *History in Africa* 26 (1999): 43–68.

Hair, P.E.H. "An Ethnolinguistic Inventory of the Upper Guinea Coast before 1700." *African Language Review* VI (1967): 32–70.

Hair, P.E.H., Adam Jones and Robin Law, eds. *Barbot on Guinea: The Writings of Jean Barbot on West Africa: 1678–1712*. London: Hakluyt Society, 1992.

Hair, P.E.H. "Ethnolinguistic Continuity on the Guinea Coast." *Journal of African History* 8, no. 2 (1967): 247–68.

Hall, Stuart. "Cultural Identity and Diaspora." In *Identity, Community, Culture, Difference*, edited by Jonathan Rutherford, 222–237. London: Lawrence and Wishart, 1996.

Hamilton, Carolyn, ed. *The Mfecane Aftermath: Reconstructive Debates in Southern African History*. Witswatersrand: Wits University Press, 1995.

Hancock, David. *Citizens of the World: London Merchants and the Integration of the British Atlantic Community, 1735–1785*. Cambridge: Cambridge University Press, 1995.

Harms, Robert. *Games Against Nature: A Cultural History of the Nunu of Equatorial Africa*. Cambridge: Cambridge University Press, 1988.

Harrell-Bond, Barbara. *Community Leadership and the Transformation of Freetown, (1801–1976)*. Berlin: De Gruyter Mouton, 1978.

Harris, Lynn. "'A Gulf Between the Mountains': Slavers, Whalers, and Fishers in False Bay, Cape Colony." In *Sea Ports and Sea Power: African Maritime Cultural Landscapes*, edited by Lynn Harris, 27–42. Greenville, NC: Springer, 2016.

Hay, Jonathan. "Primitivism Reconsidered (Part 2): Picasso and the Krumen." *Res: Anthropology and Aesthetics* 69–70 (Spring-Autumn, 2018): 227–250.

Hayden, Thomas E. "A Description of the 1970 Grand Cess Gbo." Unpublished Paper, 1972. n.p.
Hayden, Thomas E. "Kru Religious Concepts." *Liberian Studies Journal* 7, no. 1 (1976–1977): 13–22.
Headrick, Daniel. *Power Over Peoples: Technology, Environments, and Western Imperialism, 1400 to the Present*. Princeton: Princeton University Press, 2012.
Hein, Jeanne. "Portuguese Communication with Africans on the Searoute to India." In *The Globe Encircled and the World Revealed*, edited by Ursula Lamb, 1–11. London: Routledge, 2016.
Helfman, Tara. "The Court of the Vice Admiralty at Sierra Leone and the Abolition of the West African Slave Trade." *The Yale Law Journal* 115, no. 5 (2006): 1124–1159.
Henries, A. Doris Banks. *The Liberian Nation*. New York: Herman Jaffe Publishers, 1954.
Higman, B.W., Carl Campbell, and Patrick Bryan. *Slavery, Freedom and Gender: The Dynamics of Caribbean Society*. Kingston: University of the West Indies Press, 2003.
Hinks, Peter P., and John R. McKivigan. *Encyclopedia of Anti-Slavery and Abolition*. Vol. 2. Westport: Greenwood, 2007.
Hobsbawm, Eric. *Labouring Men: Studies in the History of Labour*. London: Weidenfeld and Nicholson, 1964.
Hollet, David. *Passage from India to El Dorado: Guyana and the Great Migration*. Madison: Associated University Press, 1999.
Holsoe, Svend E. "A Study of Relations between Settlers and Indigenous Peoples in Western Liberia, 1821–1847." *African Historical Studies* 4, no. 2 (1971): 331–362.
Hopper, Matthew. "East Africa and the End of the Indian Ocean Slave Trade." *Journal of African Development* 13, no. 1 (2011): 27–54.
Hopper, Matthew. "Slavery and the Slave Trades in the Indian Ocean and Arab Worlds: Global Connections and Disconnections." Paper presented at conference: "Slaves of One Master:" Globalization and the African Diaspora in Arabia in the Age of Empire. Yale University, New Haven, Connecticut. November 7–8, 2008.
Hopper, Matthew. *Slaves of One Master: Globalization and Slavery in Arabia in the Age of Empire*. New Haven, CT: Yale University Press, 2015.
Hopper, Matthew. "The African Presence in Eastern Arabia." In *The Gulf in Modern Times, People, Ports, and History*. New York: Palgrave-Macmillan, 2014.
Hornell, James. "Kru Canoes of Sierra Leone." *The Mariner's Mirror* 15, issue 3 (1929): 233–237.
Hornell, James. "String Figures from Sierra Leone, Liberia and Zanzibar." *The Journal of the Royal Anthropological Institute of Great Britain and Ireland* 60 (1930): 81–114.
Howell, Raymond C. *The Royal Navy and the Slave Trade*. London: Croom Helm Ltd, 1987.
Hoyt, William D., Jr. "John McDonogh and Maryland Colonization in Liberia, 1834–1835." *The Journal of Negro History* 24, no. 4 (1939): 440–453.
Huberich, Charles Henry. *The Political and Legislative History of Liberia*. Vol. 2. New York: Central Books, 1947.
Ibo, Jonas. "Le phénomène "Krouman" à Sassandra: la marque d'une institution séculaire." *Canadian Journal of African Studies* 32, Issue I (1998): 65–94.
Jalloh, Alusine. "Introduction." In *The African Diaspora*, edited by Alusine Jalloh and Stephen E. Maizlish, 1–6. College Station: Texas A&M University Press, 1996.
Johnston, Harry. *Liberia*. 2 vols. London: Hutchinson & Co., 1906.

Jones, Adam, and Marion Johnson. "Slaves from the Windward Coast." *The Journal of African History* 21, no. 1 (1980): 17–34.

Jones, Hannah Abeodu Bowen. "The Struggle for Political and Cultural Unification in Liberia, 1847–1930." Ph.D. thesis, Northwestern University, 1962.

Keefer, Katrina. "Group Identity, Scarification, and Poro Among Liberated Africans in Sierra Leone, 1808–1819." *Journal of West African History* 3, no.1 (2017): 1–26.

Keefer, Katrina. "Mission Education in Early Sierra Leone, 1793–1820." Ph.D. dissertation, York University, 2015.

Keefer, Katrina. "Scarification and Identity in the Liberated Africans Department Register, 1814–1815." *Canadian Journal of African Studies* 47, no. 3 (2013): 537–553.

Kelly, J. B. *Britain and the Persian Gulf*. Oxford: Oxford University Press, 1968.

Kidd, Colin. *British Identities Before Nationalism: Ethnicity and Nationhood in the Atlantic World, 1600–1800*. Cambridge: Cambridge University Press, 1999.

Korte, Werner, and Andreas Massing. "Institutional Change among the Kru, Liberia-Transformative Response to Change." In *Africana Collecta*. Vol. 2, edited by Dieter Oberndorfer, 119–121. Düsseldorf: Bertelsmann University, 1971.

Kuczynski, Robert R. *Demographic Survey of the British Colonial Empire*. 3 vols. London: Oxford University Press, 1948–1953.

Kuhn, G. "Liberian Contract Labor in Panama, 1887–1897." *Liberian Studies Journal* 6, no. 1 (1975): 43–52.

Kup, Alexander Peter. "Instructions to the Royal African Company's factor at Bunce, 1702." *Sierra Leone Studies*, no. 5 (December 1955): 52.

Kup, Alexander Peter. "John Clarkson and the Sierra Leone Company." *The International Journal of African Historical Studies* 5, no. 2 (1972): 203–220.

Laband, John, and Ian Knight. *The War Correspondents, The Anglo-Zulu War*. KwaZulu-Natal: Jonathan Ball, 1996.

Laurence, K.O. *A Question of Labour: Indentured Immigration into Trinidad and British Guiana, 1875–1917*. New York: St. Martin's Press, 1994.

Law, Robin. "The Politics of Commercial Transition: Factional Conflict in Dahomey in the Context of Ending the Slave Trade." *The Journal of African History* 38, no. 2 (1997): 213–333.

Layton, C.W.T. *Dictionary of Nautical Words and Terms*. Revised by Reverend G. W. Miller. 4th edition. Glasgow: Brown, Son & Ferguson, 1994.

Linebaugh, Peter, and Marcus Rediker. "The Many-Headed Hydra: Sailors, Slaves and the Atlantic Working Class in the Eighteenth Century." *Journal of Historical Sociology* 3, no. 2 (1990): 225–252.

Linebaugh, Peter. *The Many Headed Hydra: Sailors, Slaves, Commoners, and the Hidden History of the Revolutionary Atlantic*. Boston: Beacon Press, 2000.

Lipski, John. "The Spanish of Equatorial Guinea: Research on La Hispanidad's Best-Kept Secret." *Afro-Hispanic Review* 21, no. 1–2 (2002): 70–97.

Lloyd, Christopher. *The Nation and the Navy: A History of Naval Life and Policy*. London: The Cresset Press, 1954.

Look Lai, Walton. *Indentured Labour, Caribbean Sugar: Chinese and Indian Migrants to the British West Indies, 1838–1918*. Baltimore: John Hopkins University Press, 1993.

Lovejoy, Paul, and David Richardson. "Competing Markets for Male and Female Slaves: Prices in the Interior of West Africa, 1780–1850." *The International Journal of African Historical Studies* 28, no. 2 (1995): 261–293.

Lovejoy, Paul. *Transformations in Slavery: A History of Slavery in Africa*. 1983. 3rd ed. Cambridge: Cambridge University Press, 2011.

Lynn, Martin. *Commerce and Economic Change in West Africa: The Palm Oil Trade in the Nineteenth Century*. New York: Cambridge University Press, 1997.

Lynn, Martin. "Commerce, Christianity and The Origins of 'Creoles' of Fernando Po." *The Journal of African History* 25, no. 3 (1984): 257–278.

Lynn, Martin. "From Sail to Steam: The Impact of the Steamship Services on the British Palm Oil Trade with West Africa, 1850–1890." *The Journal of African History* 30, no. 2 (1989): 227–245.

Lynn, Martin. "John Beecroft and West Africa, 1829–54." Ph.D. thesis, University of London, 1979.

Mahmud, Tayyab. "Cheaper than a Slave: Indentured Labor, Colonialism and Capitalism." *Seattle University School of Law Paper Series*, no. 12–34 (2013): 1–31.

Mann, Kristin. "Owners, Slaves and the Struggle for Labour in the Commercial Transition in Lagos." In *From Slave Trade to 'Legitimate' Commerce: The Commercial Transition in Nineteenth Century West Africa*, edited by Robin Law, 195–214. Cambridge: Cambridge University Press, 2002.

Mann, Kristin. *Slavery and the Birth of an African City: Lagos 1760–1900*. Bloomington: Indiana University Press, 2007.

Marchese, Lynell. "City Countryside and Kru Ethnicity." *Africa* 61, no. 2 (1991): 186–201.

Marchese, Lynell. "Kru." In *The Niger-Congo Languages*, edited by Bender Samuel, 113–119. Lanham: University Press of America, 1989.

Marder, Arthur J. *The Anatomy of British Sea Power: A History of British Naval Policy in the Pre Dreadnought Era, 1880–1905*. London: Putnam, 1941.

Marshall, Adam G. *Nemesis: The First Iron Warship and Her World*. Singapore: National University of Singapore, 2016.

Martin, Bernard, and Mark Spurrell, eds. *The Journal of a Slave Trader (John Newton) 1750–1754*. London: Epworth, 1962.

Martin, Jane. "Krumen 'Down the Coast'": Liberian Migrants on the West Africa Coast in the 19th and early 20th century." *The International Journal of Historical Studies* 18, no. 3 (1985): 401–423.

Mason, John Edwin. *Social Death and Resurrection: Slavery and Emancipation in South Africa*. Richmond: University of Virginia Press, 2003.

Massing, Andreas W. *The Economic Anthropology of the Kru*. Wisbaden: Steiner, 1980.

McEvoy, Frederick D. "Understanding Ethnic Realities among the Grebo and Kru Peoples of West Africa." *Africa* 47, no. 1 (1977): 62–80.

McGraw, Mary Tyler. "Free Blacks and African Colonization, 1816–1832." *Journal of American Studies* 21, no. 2 (1987): 207–224.

Meek, Ronald L. *Social Science and The Ignoble Savage*. Cambridge: Cambridge University Press, 1976.

Mendelawitz, Maragret. *Charles Dickens Australia: Selected Essays from Household Words 1850–1859 Book Two*. Sydney: Sydney University Press, 2011.

Mirzai, Behnaz A. "African Presence in Iran: Identity and its Reconstruction." *Outre-Mers revue d'histoire* 89, no. 335–336 (2002): 229–246.

Mirzai, Behnaz A. *A History of Slavery and Emancipation in Iran, 1800–1929.* Austin: University of Texas Press, 2017.

Mirzai, Behnaz A. *The Persian Gulf and Britain: The Suppression of the African Slave Trade.* Austin: University of Texas Press, 2017.

Moore, Brian L. *Cultural Power, Resistance, and Pluralism: Colonial Guyana 1838–1900* Montreal: McGill-Queen's Press, 1998.

Moreno, Nuria Fernández. "Bubi Government at the End of the 19th Century: Resistance to the Colonial Policy of Evangelization on the Island of Bioko, Equitorial Guinea." *Nordic Journal of African Studies* 22, no. 1–2 (2013): 23–48.

Mouser, Bruce. "Iles de Los as Bulking Center in the Slave Trade, 1750–1800." *Outre-Mers Revue d'histoire* 313 (1996): 77–91.

Mouser, Bruce. "Shifting the Littoral Frontiers of EurAfrican and African Trade in the Northern Rivers of Sierra Leone, 1794: Opportunities and Challenges from Changing Conditions." Paper presented at Sierra Leone Studies and Liberian Studies Associations Joint Meeting, Charleston, South Carolina, April 1994.

Mouser, Bruce. "Théophilus Conneau: The Saga of a Tale." *History in Africa* 6 (1979): 97–107.

Mudimbe, V.Y. *The Idea of Africa.* London: James Currey, 1994.

Mudimbe, V.Y. *The Invention of Africa: Gnosis, Philosophy, and the Order of Knowledge.* London: James Currey, 1988.

Murdza, Pete John, Jr. "The Tricolor and the Lone Star: A History of Franco-Liberian Relations 1847–1903." Ph.D. thesis, University of Wisconsin, 1979.

Northrup, David. "African Mortality in the Suppression of the Slave Trade: The Case of the Bight of Biafra." *Journal of Interdisciplinary History* 9 (Summer 1978): 47–64.

Northrup, David. *Indentured Labor in the Age of Imperialism, 1834–1922.* Cambridge: Cambridge University Press, 1985.

Northrup, David. "The Compatibility of the Slave and Palm Oil Trades in the Bight of Biafra." *The Journal of African History* 17, no. 3 (1976): 353–364.

Notholt, Stuart A. "Sailing Against Slavers." *Soldiers of the Queen* Issue 134 (Sept, 2008): 26–30.

Obunbaku, James. "The Use of Tribal Marks in Archaeological and Historical Reconstruction." *Research on Humanities and Social Sciences* 2, no. 6 (2012): 251–260.

Okia, Opolot. "The Windmill of Slavery: The British and Foreign Antislavery Society and Bonded Labor in East Africa." *Middle Ground Journal* 3 (Fall 2011): 1–35.

Opala, Joseph. "Bunce Island: A British Slave Castle in Sierra Leone, Historical Summary." Appendix. In Christopher DeCorse, "Bunce Island Cultural Resource Assessment and Management Plan," Report prepared for the U.S. Embassy in Sierra Leone and Sierra Leone Monuments and Relics Commission. November 2007.

Orie, Olanike. "The Structure and Function of Yoruba Facial Scarification." *Anthropological Linguistics* 53, no. 1 (2011): 15–33.

Paine, Lincoln P. *Warships of the World to 1900.* Boston: Houghton Mifflin Harcourt, 2000.

Pearson, Andrew. *Distant Freedom: St. Helena and the Abolition of the Slave Trade 1840–1872.* Oxford: Oxford University Press, 2016.

Pearson, Andrew. "Waterwitch: A Warship, Its Voyage and its Crew in the Era of Anti-Slavery." *Atlantic Studies* 13, no. 1 (2016): 99–124.

Pentangelo, John. "Sailors and Slaves: USS Constellation and the Transatlantic Slave Trade." In *Navies and Soft Power: Historical Case Studies of Naval Power and the Nonuse of Military Force*, edited by Bruce A. Elleman and S.C.M. Paine, 7–19. Newport: Naval War College Press, 2015.

Pereira, Clifford. "Black Liberators: The Role of Africans & Arabs sailors in the Royal Navy within the Indian Ocean 1841–1941." Paper presented at UNESCO Symposium on 'The Cultural Interactions Resulting from the Slave Trade and Slavery in the Arab-Islamic World.' Rabat, May 18, 2007.

Peterson, John. *Province of Freedom: A History of Sierra Leone 1787–1870*. London: Faber and Faber, 1969.

Philip, Mark, ed. *The French Revolution and British Popular Politics*. Cambridge: Cambridge University Press, 2004.

Poggi, Christine. "Picasso's First Constructed Sculpture: A Tale of Two Guitars." *The Art Bulletin* 94, no. 2 (June 2012): 274–298.

Porter, Arthur Thomas. "The Development of the Creole Society of Freetown, Sierra Leone." Ph.D. dissertation, Boston University, 1960.

Rankin, John. "Nineteenth-Century Royal Navy Sailors from Africa and the African Diaspora: Research Methodology." *African Diasporas* 6, no. 2 (2013): 179–195.

Ratelband, K., ed. *Vijf Dagregisters van Het Kasteel Sao Jorge da Mina (Elmina) aar de Goudkust, 1647–1945*. Gravenhage: Martinus Nijhoff, 1953.

Raugh, Harold E. *Anglo-Zulu War 1879: A Selected Bibliography*. New York: Scarecrow Press, 2011.

Rijpma, Sjoerd. *David Livingstone and the Myth of African Poverty and Disease: A Close Examination of his Writing on the Pre-Colonial Era*. Leiden: Brill, 2015.

Roberts, A.D. "Livingstone, David (1813–1874)." *Oxford Dictionary of National Biography* Oxford: Oxford University Press, 2004. Online, n.p. Accessed August 10, 2018, https://http://www.oxforddnb.com/.

Roberts, George W. *The Population of Jamaica*. Cambridge: Cambridge University Press, 2013.

Rockel, Stephen. *Carriers of Culture: Labor on the Road in Nineteenth-Century East Africa*. Portsmouth, NH: Heinemann, 2006.

Rodney, Walter. *A History of the Guyanese Working People, 1881–1905*. Baltimore: John Hopkins University, 1981.

Rodney, Walter. *How Europe Underdeveloped Africa*. Washington: Howard University Press, 1972.

Rodriguez, Junius P., ed. *Slavery in the Modern World: A History of Political, Social and Economic Oppression*. Vol. 1. Santa Barbara: ABC-CLIO, 2011.

Rodriguez, Junius P. *The Historical Encyclopedia of World Slavery*. Vol. I. Santa Barbara: ABC-CLIO, 1997.

Sabin, James Thomas. "The Making of the Americo-Liberian Community: A Study of Politics and Society in Nineteenth Century Liberia." Ph.D. thesis, Columbia University, 1974.

Said, Edward. *Orientalism*. New York: Vintage, 1978.

Schler, Lynn. *Nation on Board: Becoming Nigerian at Sea*. Athens: Ohio University Press, 2016.

Schmidt, Cynthia. "Kru Mariners and Migrants of the West African Coast." In *The Garland Encyclopedia of World Music: Africa*, edited by Ruth M. Stone, 110–123. London: Routledge, 2017.

Schnapper, Bernand. *La Politique et le commerce Français dans le Golfe de Guinée de 1838 à 1871*. Paris: s.p., 1961.

Scholliers, Peter, and Leonard Schwarz, eds. *Experiencing Wages: Social and Cultural Aspects of Wage Forms in Europe Since 1500*. New York: Berghahn Books, 2003.

Schroeder, Guenter, and Andreas Massing. "A General Outline of Historical Developments within the Kru Cultural Province." Paper presented at the Second Annual Conference on Social Research in Liberia. Indiana University, Indiana. April 30-May 2, 1970.

Schroeder, Guenter. "Letter to Brooks." Unpublished letter. March 31, 1971.

Schuler, Monica. "Kru Emigration to British and French Guiana, 1841–1857." In *Africans in Bondage: Studies in Slavery and the Slave Trade*, edited by Paul E. Lovejoy, 155–202. Madison: University of Wisconsin Press, 1986.

Schuler, Monica. "The Recruitment of African Indentured Labourers for European Colonies in the Nineteenth Century." In *Migration: Indentured Labour Before and After Slavery*, edited by Pieter C. Emmer, 125–161. Dordrecht: Nijhoff, 1986.

Schwarz, Suzanne. "'A Just and Honourable Commerce': Abolitionist Experimentation in Sierra Leone in the Late Eighteenth and Early Nineteenth Centuries." Paper presented at The Hakluyt Society Annual Lecture, 2013.

Schwarz, Suzanne. "Commerce, Civilization and Christianity: The Development of the Sierra Leone." In *Liverpool and Transatlantic Slavery*, edited by David Richardson, Suzanne Schwarz, and Anthony Tibbles, 252–276. Liverpool: Liverpool University Press, 2007.

Schwarz, Suzanne. "Reconstructing the Life Histories of Liberated Africans: Sierra Leone in the Early Nineteenth Century." *History in Africa* 39 (2012): 175–207.

Schwarz, Suzanne. "Zachary Macaulay and the Development of the Sierra Leone Company, 1793–4, Part 1: Journal, June-October 1793." *History and Culture* 4. Leipzig: University of Leipzig, 2000.

Scott, Rebecca. *Slave Emancipation in Cuba: The Transition to Free Labor, 1860–1899*. Pittsburgh: University of Pittsburgh Press, 2000.

Searing, James. *West African Slavery and Atlantic Commerce: The Senegal River Valley, 1700–1860*. Cambridge: Cambridge University Press, 1993.

Shaikh, Farida. "Judicial Diplomacy: British Officials and the Mixed Commission Courts." In *Slavery, Diplomacy and Empire: Britain and the Suppression of the Slave Trade, 1807–1975*, edited by Keith Hamilton and Patrick Salmon, 42–64. Eastbourne: Sussex Academic Press, 2009.

Shank, David A. *Prophet Harris: The 'Black Elijah' of West Africa*. Leiden: Brill, 1994.

Sheriff, Abdul. *Dhow Cultures and the Indian Ocean: Cosmopolitism, Commerce and Islam*. London: C. Hurst, 2010.

Sheriff, Abdul. *Slaves, Spices and Ivory in Zanzibar: Integration of an East African Commercial Empire into the World Economy, 1770–1873*. Columbus: Ohio University Press, 1987.

Sheriff, Abdul. "The Slave Trade and Its Fallout in the Persian Gulf." In *Abolition and Its Aftermath in Indian Ocean Africa and Asia*, edited by Gwyn Campbell, 103–119. New York: Routledge, 2005.

Shick, Tom. "A Quantitative Analysis of Liberian Colonization From 1820 to 1843 with Special Reference to Mortality." *The Journal of African History* 7, no. 1 (1971): 45–59.

Shick, Tom. *Behold the Promised Land*. Baltimore: John Hopkins Press, 1980.

Siegmann, William, and Cynthia E. Schmidt. *Rock of the Ancestors: Namoa Koni*. Suakoko: Cuttington University College, 1977.
Simpson, Donald. *Dark Companions: The African Contribution to the European Exploration of East Africa*. London: Paul Elek Limited, 1975.
Skinner, E.P. "Ethnic Interaction in a British Guiana Rural Community: A Study in Secondary Acculturation and Group Dynamics." Ph.D. diss., Columbia University, 1955.
Smith, Billy G. *Ship of Death: A Voyage that Changed the Atlantic World*. Yale: Yale University Press, 2013.
Smith, Robert. "The Lagos Consulate, 1851–1861." *The Journal of African History* 15, no. 3 (1974): 393–416.
Smith, Robert. "To the Palaver Islands: War and Diplomacy on the Lagos Lagoon in 1852–1854." *Journal of the Historical Society of Nigeria* 5, no. 1 (December, 1969): 3–25.
Spence, Daniel Owen. *A History of the Royal Navy: Empire and Imperialism*. London: I.B. Taurus, 2015.
Stanziani, Alessandro. *Sailors, Slaves and Immigrants: Bondage in the Indian Ocean World, 1750–1914*. New York City: Springer, 2014.
Staudenraus, Philip John. *The History of the American Colonization Society*. Vol. 1. Madison: University of Wisconsin Press, 1958.
Stewart, Henry. *Our Redcoats and Bluejackets: War Pictures, forming a Narrative of the Naval and Military History of England from 1793*. London: Ballantyne Press, 1879.
Sullivan, Jo Mary. "Fishers, Traders and Rebels: The role of the Kabor/Gbeta in the 1915 Kru Coast (Liberia) Revolt." Paper presented to the University of Aberdeen Symposium in Aberdeen, Scotland, 1985.
Sullivan, Jo Mary. "Mississippi in Africa: Settlers Among the Kru, 1835–1847." *Liberian Studies Journal* 8, no. 2 (1978–1979): 79–94.
Sullivan, Jo Mary. "Settlers in Sinoe County, Liberia, and their Relations with the Kru, c. 1835–1920." Ph.D. diss., Boston University, 1978.
Sullivan, Jo Mary. "The Kru of Liberia." Review of *Ethnohistorical Studies on the Kru Coast* by Ronald W. Davis. *The Journal of African History* 19, no. 2 (1978): 280–282.
Sundiata, Ibrahim K. *Brothers and Strangers: Black Zion, Black Slavery, 1914–1940*. Durham: Duke University Press, 2004.
Sundiata, Ibrahim K. *From Slavery to Neo Slavery: The Bight of Biafra and Fernando Po in the Era of Abolition, 1827–1930*. Madison: University of Wisconsin Press, 1996.
Sundiata, Ibrahim K. "Prelude to Scandal: Liberia and Fernando Po, 1880–1930." *The Journal of African History* 15, no. 1 (1974): 97–112.
Sundiata, Ibrahim K. "The Rise and Decline of Kru Power: Fernando Po in the Nineteenth Century." *Liberian Studies* 6, no. 1 (1975): 25–42.
Tabler, Edward C. *Baines on the Zambezi, 1858 to 1859*. Johannesburg, SA: Brenthurst Press, 1982.
Taylor, Alan D. *Mathematics in Politics: Strategy, Voting, Power and Proof*. New York: Springer, 1995.
Teelock, Vijayalakshmi, and Abdul Sheriff. "Slavery and the Slave Trade in the Indian Ocean." In *The Transition from Slavery in Zanzibar and Mauritius* by Abdul Sheriff, Vijayalakshmi Teelock, Saada Omar Wahab, and Satyendra Peerthum, 25–43. Oxford: African Books Collection, 2016.

Thomas, Albert. "'It Changed Everybody's Lives': The Simon's Town Group Areas Removals." In *Lost Communities, Living Memories: Remembering Forced Removals in Cape Town*, edited by Sean Field, 81–99. Cape Town: David Philip, 2001.

Thornton, John. *Africa and Africans in the Making of the Atlantic World, 1400–1800*. 2nd ed. Cambridge: Cambridge University Press, 1998.

Tonkin, Elizabeth. "A Saucy Town? Regional Histories of Conflict, Collusion, and Commerce in the Making of a Southeastern Liberian Polity." In *The Powerful Presence of the Past: Integration and Conflict Along the Upper Guinea Coast*, edited by Jacqueline Knorr and Wilson Trajano Filho, 101–136. Leiden: Brill, 2010.

Tonkin, Elizabeth. "Creating Kroomen: Ethnic Diversity, Economic Specialism and Changing Demand." In *Africa and the Sea*, edited by J. Stone, 27–47. Aberdeen: Aberdeen University African Studies Group, 1985.

Tonkin, Elizabeth. *Narrating Our Pasts: The Social Construction of Oral History*. Cambridge: Cambridge University Press, 1992.

Tonkin, Elizabeth. Review of *The Economic Anthropology of the Kru (West Africa)* by Andreas Massing. *The International Journal of African Historical Studies* 16, no. 1 (1983): 101–103.

Tonkin, Elizabeth. "Sasstown's Transformation: The Jlao Kru 1888–1981." *Liberian Studies Journal* 8 (1978–79): 1–34.

Tonkin, Elizabeth. "The Boundaries of History in Oral Performance." *History in Africa* 9 (1982): 273–284.

Turner, Mary. "Chattel Slaves into Wage Slaves: A Jamaican Case Study." In *Labour in the Caribbean: From Emancipation to Independence*, edited by Malcolm Cross and Gad Heuman, 14–31. London: Macmillan, 1988.

Turner, Michael J. "The Limits of Abolition: Government, Saints and the 'African Question', c. 1780–1820." *The English Historical Review* 112, no. 446 (1997): 319–357.

Ungerer, Gustav. "Recovering a black African's voice in an English lawsuit: Jacques Francis and the salvage operations of the Mary Rose and the Sancta Maria and Sanctus Edwardus, 1545-ca 1550." *Medieval and Renaissance Drama in England* 17 (2005): 255–271.

Veerasawmy, J.A. "The Noitgedacht Murder." *Timehri: The Journal of The Royal Agricultural and Commercial Society of British Guiana* 6, Third Series (1919): 116–127.

Visonà, Monica Blackmun. *Constructing African Art Histories for the Lagoons of Côte d'Ivoire*. London: Routledge, 2017.

Vos, Jelmer. "The Slave Trade from The Windward Coast: The Case of the Dutch, 1740–1805." *African Economic History* 38 (2010): 29–51.

Walker, James W. St. G. *The Black Loyalists: The Search for a Promised Land in Nova Scotia and Sierra Leone, 1783–1870*. Toronto: University of Toronto Press, 1992.

Walker, Sheila S. *The Religious Revolution in the Ivory Coast – The Prophet Harris and the Harrist Church*. Chapel Hill: University of North Carolina Press, 1983.

Wallis, P.R., ed. *The Zambezi Expedition of David Livingstone, 1858–1863*. Vol. 1. London: Chatto & Windus, 1956.

Ward, William Ernst. *The Royal Navy and the Slavers: The Suppression of the Atlantic Slave Trade*. London: Allen & Unwin, 1969.

Webster, J.B., A. A. Boahen, and H.O. Idowu. *The Growth of African Civilisation: the Revolutionary Years. West Africa Since 1800*. London: Longman, 1973.

West, Richard. *Back to Africa: A History of Sierra Leone and Liberia.* London: Cape, 1970.
Westermann, Dietrich, and M.A. Bryan. *Languages of West Africa: Handbook of African Languages.* Vol. 2. London: Oxford University Press, 1952.
Whisson, Michael. *The Fairest Cape? An Account of the Coloured People in Simonstown.* Johannesburg: The South African Institute of Race Relations, 1972.
Whitehouse, Bruce. *Migrants and Strangers in an African City: Exile, Dignity, Belonging.* Bloomington: Indiana University Press, 2012.
Williams, Eric. *Capitalism and Slavery.* Chapel Hill: University of North Carolina Press, 1944.
Wold, Joseph Conrad. *God's Impatience in Liberia.* Grand Rapids, MI: Eerdmans, 1968.
Wolloch, Nathaniel. "The Civilizing Process, Nature, and Stadial Theory." *Eighteenth-Century Studies* 44, no. 2 (2011): 245–259.
Wood, Donald. "Kru Migration to the West Indies." *Journal of Caribbean Studies* 2, no. 2–3 (1981): 266–282.
Worjloh, S. Tugbe. "The Social Structure of the Klao (Kru)." Independent Paper. 2012.
Yarema, Allan. *The American Colonization Society: An Avenue to Freedom?* Lanham: University Press of America, 2006.
Young, Joline. "The West African Kroomen and their Link to Simon's Town." *South African History Online.* Accessed July 17, 2016. http://www.sahistory.org.za/archive/west-african-kroomen-and-their-link-simons-town-joline-young.

Databases

Liberated Africans Database. Accessed February 10, 2017. http://www.liberatedafricans.org.
Naval Database. Accessed March 17, 2017. http://www.pbenyon.plus.com.
Trans-Atlantic Slave Trade Database. Accessed July 7, 2016. http://www.slavevoyages.org.

Films

Voyage au Congo. Directed by Herr Marc Allégret. Based on journal by André Gide. Paris, 1927.

Paintings

Bray, Gabriel. "Three Kroomen of Sierra Leone." c. 1775. Bray album, PAJ2038. National Maritime Museum, Greenwich, London, United Kingdom, accessed on April 21, 2017, http://collections.rmg.co.uk/collections/objects/201002.html.

Maps

Ashmun, Jehudi. "Map of the West Coast of Africa from Sierra Leone to Cape Palmas, Including the Colony of Liberia." 1830.

Bellin, Jacques Nicholas. *Carte de la Coste Occidentale D'Afrique*. Paris, 1739.
Berry, William. *Africa Divided According to the Extent of Its Principall Parts in Which Are Distinguished One from the Other the Empires, Monarchies, Kingdoms, States, and Peoples...* London, 1680.
Mitchell, S. Augustus. *Map of Africa: Map of Liberia*. No. 17. 1839. Engraved by J.H. Young. American Colonization Society, Library of Congress, Washington, D.C., United States.
Moll, Hermann. "New and Exact Map of Guinea." In *New and Accurate Description* by William Bosman. London: J. Knapton, 1705.
Ogilby, John, and Jacob van Meurs, engraver. "Africae Accurata Tabula." London, 1670.
Sanson, Nicolas. *Afrique*. Paris, 1650.

Websites

Ascension Island Government Website. Accessed November 18, 2018. http://www.ascension-island.gov.ac/the-island/history/.
Ascension Island Heritage Society. Accessed June 16, 2016. http://www.ascension-island.gov.ac/heritage-amble/.
British Newspaper Archive. Accessed February 28, 2017. http://www.britishnewspaperarchive.co.uk/.
Equiano's World. Accessed on June 18, 2020. http://equianosworld.org/.
Gary Schulze Collection. Accessed March 27, 2017. http://www.sierra-leone.org/Gspostcards.
Government of Côte d'Ivoire. Demographic survey. 2018. Accessed on May 1, 2017. https://www.indexmundi.com/cote_d_ivoire/demographics_profile.html.
Government of the Republic of Liberia 2008 Population and Housing Census, Preliminary Results. Accessed on May 1, 2017.
Ross Archive of African Images. Accessed May 17, 2017. http://raai.library.yale.edu.
Simon's Town Museum. Accessed May 1, 2017. https://www.simonstown.com/museum/stm_hist_miscellaneous.htm.

Blogs

Expedition South Africa: Cape Town Tavern of the Seas. Accessed April 15, 2017. https://blog.ecu.edu/sites/expeditionsouthafrica/seaforth-cemetery/.

Index

advance 87f., 93, 100, 136, 139, 150, 163f., 166, 219–221
age-sets 41, 92, 216f.
agriculture 6, 8, 25, 42, 110, 113, 138, 175, 177, 200
American Colonization Society (ACS) 6, 18, 179f., 189–191
Americo-Liberians 29, 181, 184–187, 189, 191, 193f., 198, 205
Anglo-Zulu War 31, 129, 152–154, 156, 213
Arabian Peninsula 122, 128
Asante Campaign 150, 153
Ascension Island 6, 30, 82, 104, 107–109, 113, 116–118, 120, 212f.
Ashmun, Jehudi 18, 181, 185, 191, 199
Atlantic Ocean 6, 104, 108, 132, 152

Baikie Expedition 136
Bakwé 3, 19, 23
Bandama River 2f., 17, 19, 24, 50, 53, 55, 62, 71, 188, 203, 209, 216, 224
Bassa 3, 18, 21–23, 30, 36, 53, 58, 68, 95f., 102, 121, 128, 143, 153, 156, 182, 186, 191, 197, 204, 206, 209, 212–214
Bété 3, 18f., 22f., 51, 53, 58, 96, 198, 204, 209
Bight of Biafra 49, 82, 111, 137–139, 152
Bo 21, 42, 93, 120, 152, 224f.
Bombay 31, 103, 120, 123f., 127, 212
Bonny 6, 31, 129, 138f., 213
book 2, 7, 10, 12, 19, 27, 29, 32, 64f., 81, 89, 108f., 113f., 122, 124, 182, 195f., 208, 210, 228
borders 153, 201–203, 216
boycott 88
bride-price 99, 217
British Guiana 5f., 11, 13f., 32, 77, 87, 158, 160–163, 165–171, 174–177, 214
Bunce Island 60–62

Calabar 6, 31, 129, 138–140, 213
Canot, Theophilus 67f.
Canton River 143f.

Cape Coast 6, 30, 66, 104–107, 207, 212f., 215
Cape Palmas 15f., 18, 28, 34, 38, 43, 49–51, 66, 139f., 143, 151, 156, 165, 181, 186f., 189, 193f., 197, 200, 204, 224
Caribbean 1, 9, 11–15, 27, 32, 59, 80, 86, 105, 116f., 136, 152, 158–162, 164, 166, 168, 172–178, 209f., 214
China 43, 116, 123, 129, 143–146, 160, 162, 171
Christianity 9, 26, 29, 32, 109, 112f., 118f., 126f., 130, 134, 155, 157, 179, 187, 199–201, 215
Clapperton, Hugh 31, 40, 45, 57f., 99f., 129–132
Clarkson, John 72f., 75, 79
climate 8, 25, 27, 103, 159
colonial 1, 6, 9, 24, 35, 72, 77f., 89, 93, 97, 115, 130, 134, 138f., 142f., 149f., 152, 154, 157, 165, 167, 171, 174–176, 180f., 187, 189, 194, 197, 207, 210, 214, 216
colony 5f., 18, 32, 73, 75f., 78, 95–98, 106f., 113, 116f., 144f., 149, 153, 164, 177, 179–181, 183–187, 190, 194, 202, 207
Congress of Vienna 13
Constitution 184f., 191
contract 1f., 6, 8, 10, 13–15, 19, 27–30, 32, 37, 44, 47, 72, 74, 76, 79, 82–84, 87f., 91–93, 96f., 99–102, 105, 107, 110f., 114f., 117, 121, 130, 138f., 144, 149f., 156–158, 161f., 164–166, 168, 170f., 175f., 178f., 183f., 190, 195–199, 201, 205, 207–209, 211–217
conversion 32, 112f., 118, 127, 179, 189, 199, 201, 215
Côte d'Ivoire 1f., 16, 19f., 22, 96, 197, 203, 206, 215f., 224
creolization 14, 178, 214
Cugoano, Ottobah 26f., 72–74

dako 3, 17, 19, 21, 23, 40, 50, 53, 91, 95, 175, 182, 193, 209, 212–214, 216, 224
dakwe 2, 17, 23 f., 92, 184, 193, 209, 212–214
dea 21, 224
Dei 182, 184, 190 f.
de Sintra, Pedro 2, 35
dhow 9, 31, 103, 122, 124–127, 212, 217
diaspora 1 f., 5–7, 9–11, 14 f., 20, 23–25, 28–33, 43, 57–59, 63, 70–72, 74, 76, 92 f., 95, 99–104, 107, 111, 113–115, 118 f., 121, 123, 127–129, 138, 140, 143, 148–150, 158 f., 161, 165, 167, 172, 175–179, 185, 196–200, 206 f., 209–217
Dickens, Charles 7, 125
Dida 18, 23, 53, 55, 58, 96, 198, 209
disease 27 f., 73, 87, 103, 108, 131, 136, 142
domestic 1, 42 f., 68, 122, 149, 170, 184

education 73 f., 166, 201
enslaved 4 f., 8–12, 15, 26–28, 44 f., 49, 51–53, 55 f., 58–60, 66–69, 73, 80, 86, 96, 116, 121 f., 125, 127, 138, 180, 210 f., 216
environment 28, 49, 59, 93, 127, 143, 167, 207, 211, 215, 218
Equiano, Olaudah 26 f., 59, 72–74, 85
estate 1, 13 f., 20, 32, 114, 158, 167–174, 177, 199, 210, 214
ethnicity 20 f., 25, 61, 81, 86, 127, 209 f.
exotic 8, 125
expeditions 31, 128–130, 133, 135–137, 140, 143, 157 f., 213
exports 53, 55, 121 f., 146

Fernando Po 6, 17, 30 f., 66, 82, 104, 108–114, 118, 136, 139, 169, 212 f.
First Opium War 31, 129, 143
Freetown 1–6, 8, 16, 20 f., 24, 30, 32, 36, 61, 67 f., 71–79, 81 f., 84, 87–102, 104, 106–113, 115 f., 118, 121, 124, 127 f., 130, 134 f., 137 f., 140–143, 145, 150, 153, 156, 158 f., 161 f., 164 f., 167, 169 f., 173 f., 176 f., 182 f., 198, 206 f., 211–217, 222, 227

free wage labour 1, 9, 10, 15, 25, 27–30, 34, 63, 100–101, 127, 158, 161, 168 f., 186, 206–207, 209–210, 214, 216
French 4, 7, 9, 13, 19 f., 22 f., 30, 32, 35, 50, 63, 67, 81, 86, 96, 157, 159, 179, 181, 190, 192, 195–198, 202–208, 210, 215
French Guiana 50, 160, 197
French Navy 197

Gallinas 25, 65–67, 70, 187, 201, 216
Gbeta 2, 17, 23, 50, 182, 184, 193, 209, 213, 224
German 17, 19 f., 35, 44, 157, 181, 183 f., 206, 208, 210, 215
Godié 18, 22 f., 198, 204, 209
Grand Bassam 179, 197 f., 203, 206 f., 215
Grand Cess 16, 18, 22–24, 30, 41, 50 f., 53, 58, 94 f., 102, 165, 181 f., 188, 191, 193, 195 f., 209, 212–214, 224
gravestones 2, 31, 104, 118 f., 121, 127 f., 210, 213
Grebo, Glebo 7, 18, 20–24, 30, 51, 53, 58, 66, 95 f., 102, 113, 121, 128, 143, 151, 153, 156, 165, 193 f., 198, 200, 202–204, 209, 212–214
grumetta 59–62

headman 2, 14 f., 23, 37, 44, 63–65, 83 f., 86–92, 97–100, 118, 124–126, 131, 135, 139 f., 150, 162, 164, 167, 173, 175, 183, 188, 195 f., 211 f., 214, 222
headmen 15, 23, 30–32, 35, 37, 44, 64 f., 71, 82, 84, 86–91, 97, 99, 102, 104, 115, 118, 135, 139 f., 150, 156, 159, 165, 168 f., 174–176, 178 f., 195 f., 199, 201, 207, 210, 212 f., 215 f., 219
Hong Kong 2, 144–146

indentured 13 f., 116, 158, 160, 167 f.
India 1, 12 f., 17, 25, 32, 43, 45, 52, 60, 72, 116 f., 120, 123 f., 143 f., 151 f., 158–161, 164, 166, 168, 173, 177, 209 f., 217
Indian Ocean 6, 9 f., 12 f., 31, 103, 117, 119, 121–128, 210, 212 f., 217
Islam 9, 26, 155
Ivory Coast 18, 34, 50, 113

Jamaica 9, 14, 25, 32, 48, 69 f., 74, 158, 160–164, 167, 169, 171, 174, 176 f., 214
Jlao, Jloh 17, 23

Kabor 2, 17, 23, 50, 193, 209, 224
Kipling, Rudyard 7, 130, 157
krogba 15, 31 f., 40–42, 44, 47 f., 68, 71, 84, 92, 98, 100–102, 174–176, 179, 196, 199, 201, 207, 212, 214 f., 217, 224
Kroomen 1, 15, 20, 24 f., 28, 30, 38, 41, 61 f., 64, 66, 70, 76, 86, 90, 101 f., 106, 110, 112, 114, 117–119, 128, 132, 141 f., 147, 149, 151, 153, 169, 171, 173, 175, 181, 185, 199, 219–221, 224
Kru Coast 1 f., 10, 16–19, 21, 23 f., 27 f., 30–34, 42 f., 49 f., 52 f., 55, 58, 64, 67, 69 f., 75, 81, 87, 92 f., 95, 98, 100–103, 107, 112–114, 137 f., 140, 143, 152, 154, 159–162, 164–166, 174–177, 179, 181–183, 186–191, 193, 195 f., 198–201, 203–207, 209–217, 224
Kru mark 4 f., 14, 30, 55–58, 66, 71, 89, 96 f., 104, 126, 159, 177 f., 211 f., 214
Kru ring 46
Kru-speaking 1–5, 7, 15, 17, 19 f., 22, 24, 30, 35 f., 51–53, 55, 58, 69, 102, 121, 188, 197 f., 200, 202, 204, 209 f.
Krutown 2 f., 6, 14, 24 f., 28, 30, 36, 93, 95–99, 101–104, 106, 114, 118, 121, 128, 149 f., 159, 172 f., 181–183, 185, 195, 200 f., 211 f., 214 f., 222 f.
Krutown Headman 97–99, 102, 212

Lagos 6, 31, 129, 137 f., 146–151, 207, 213, 215
Laird Expedition 31, 129, 132
Lander Brothers' Expedition 31, 110 f., 129, 132
launch boats 103, 123–125, 128, 147 f., 212, 217
Liberated Africans 5, 12, 20, 68, 82, 127 f., 158, 161, 165, 184 f., 191, 214
Liberia 1–6, 9, 16–23, 29, 32, 38, 40 f., 50, 60, 63, 65, 84, 92, 113 f., 150, 166, 179–207, 210, 215–217, 223 f., 227
Libreville 32, 67, 96, 197

Livingstone, David 31, 123, 129, 133, 140–143

mahdist 155 f.
manilly 46 f.
Maryland Colony 187
medal 12, 25, 125, 153, 210, 213, 217
migration 2, 10, 16, 18, 28, 32, 72, 101, 138, 158–160, 173, 179, 195, 206, 209
mission 5, 32, 73, 76, 78, 103, 113, 121, 126, 130, 132–137, 140, 179, 188 f., 194, 196 f., 199–201, 207, 210
Mississippi Colony 187
monogenetic 25 f.
Monrovia 2, 6, 17, 20, 32, 36, 67, 112, 179, 182–186, 192–195, 200–202, 207, 213, 215, 222 f.

naval brigade 11, 25, 128 f., 143, 152–155, 213
Niger Expedition 38, 133 f., 136, 141
Niger River 31, 129 f., 132, 134, 136
Nile River 90 f., 155–156

Oman 122
oral traditions 2–5, 7, 9, 11, 16, 18, 20, 23, 34, 36, 40, 43, 46, 53, 55, 65, 70, 84, 98, 102, 204, 210, 224
Ottoman 122, 155

Pacific Ocean 1, 13, 25, 32, 129, 143, 209 f., 217
Panama 25, 197
pay list 24 f., 83, 85, 219, 221
Pereira, Duarte Pacheco 2, 4, 35 f., 48, 127, 146
Persian Gulf 122–124, 128
plantation 12 f., 72, 86, 114–116, 122, 158 f., 162–164, 167, 169–172
polygenetic 25 f.
population 1, 10, 16, 22, 30, 77–79, 93, 96, 107–109, 111, 113, 118, 136, 149, 154, 158, 160 f., 163 f., 173, 175, 177, 180–183, 185, 187 f., 191, 194, 196 f., 203, 207, 210–212
porters 12, 25, 31, 105, 143, 153, 167, 172, 213

Port of Entry Laws   32, 179, 186, 194, 196, 199, 205–207, 215
Port of Spain   163 f., 166 f., 169, 173, 214
Proper Kru   2, 4, 16–19, 22–24, 30, 36, 51–53, 58, 94–96, 102, 121, 128, 143, 153, 156, 165, 181 f., 184, 188, 193, 204, 209, 212–214, 224

revolt   50, 193, 203, 206
Rio Pongo   65, 67 f., 70, 216
Royal Navy   2, 6, 9, 11 f., 20, 24 f., 30 f., 47 f., 66–68, 70, 79–82, 84–87, 89, 96, 102–114, 116–129, 131, 134, 142–144, 146 f., 150, 152–154, 158, 161, 170, 180, 208, 211–213, 216 f., 219

Sassandra River   3, 19 f., 53
Sasstown   17, 23, 50, 182, 195, 201, 209, 213, 224
Second Headman   83, 126, 140, 156
secret societies   42
Settra Kru   16, 18, 50 f., 165, 186–189, 192, 195, 200, 206, 213 f.
shoreside labourers   1, 6, 31, 44, 50, 63, 69, 72, 81, 91, 98, 105–107, 129, 134, 141, 149, 169, 172, 179, 211
Sierra Leone   1, 5, 9, 16, 18, 24, 30, 43, 59–63, 66, 68–70, 72–79, 81 f., 87, 91 f., 95–98, 101 f., 110, 114, 134, 140, 158–160, 162 f., 169–171, 174, 180 f., 198, 202, 210 f., 222, 227
Simon's Town   6, 30 f., 103 f., 109, 115–121, 123 f., 128, 145, 153, 212 f.
Singapore   125, 145
slave ships   6 f., 9, 11, 20, 30, 45, 65–70, 79, 81 f., 84, 103 f., 106 f., 109, 123 f., 128, 158, 161, 208, 211 f., 216 f.
slave trade   6, 9–12, 15, 18 f., 26–28, 30 f., 48–50, 52 f., 55, 59 f., 65–70, 72–75, 79, 81 f., 84–86, 88 f., 101, 105, 109 f., 114–117, 120–124, 126–128, 133, 135, 137, 144, 147, 157, 159, 180, 184, 190, 197, 208, 211 f., 216
stadial theory   8, 26

steamship   86, 104, 110, 126, 133, 137, 144, 156
St. Helena   82, 104, 107 f., 110, 116 f., 160
Sudan Campaign   31, 129, 155 f.
surfboats   2, 4, 14 f., 29 f., 34–39, 41, 44, 49 f., 61, 63 f., 66, 71 f., 76, 93, 98, 104, 106, 109 f., 138, 143, 148, 150 f., 158, 168, 172, 179, 199, 209, 211

transformation   10, 17, 27, 29, 32, 43, 50, 78, 98, 121, 127, 138, 175, 191, 199, 211 f., 217
treaty   67, 122, 145 f., 148, 152, 190, 194, 197
Trinidad   6, 13 f., 32, 77, 158–164, 166 f., 169–174, 176 f., 214, 227

United States   9, 69, 114, 146, 180, 189, 191, 201 f., 227

Vai   25, 96, 201, 217

wages   1, 9–12, 15, 24, 28, 32, 45, 47, 61, 72, 76 f., 80, 83–85, 87 f., 100–103, 115, 130, 134, 139, 149, 154, 157, 161, 166, 168–170, 175, 181, 184, 195 f., 199, 211 f., 214 f., 219–221
war   9, 12, 41 f., 53, 80 f., 85, 120 f., 131, 133, 142, 144–146, 150–156, 166, 193, 202, 208, 224 f.
watercraft   35 f., 103 f., 109, 123, 125, 129, 131, 147 f., 158, 168, 211
West Africa Squadron   27, 82 f., 104 f., 107, 149
Windward Coast   2, 4 f., 18 f., 28, 49, 55 f., 60 f., 75
Woermann   183 f.
women   30 f., 42 f., 53, 98, 111, 115, 149, 159, 176–178, 210, 212, 214

Zambezi Expedition   31, 129, 140–142
Zambezi River   130, 141, 143
Zanzibar   5, 9, 12, 31, 63, 103, 120–122, 124, 126–128, 212, 228

www.ingramcontent.com/pod-product-compliance
Lightning Source LLC
Chambersburg PA
CBHW050519170426
43201CB00013B/2010